ELIZABETH
TAYLOR

ELIZABETH TAYLOR

DONALD SPOTO

LITTLE, BROWN AND COMPANY

A *Little, Brown* Book

First published in Great Britain in 1995
by Little, Brown and Company
Published by arrangement with HarperCollins Publishers Inc.,
New York, New York, USA.

Copyright © 1995 by Donald Spoto

The moral right of the author has been asserted.

A CIP catalogue record for this book
is available from the British Library.

ISBN 0 316 91451 7

Printed and bound in Great Britain by
Clays Ltd, St Ives plc

10 9 8 7 6 5 4 3 2 1

Designed by Alma Hochauser Orenstein

Little, Brown and Company (UK)
Brettenham House
Lancaster Place
London WC2E 7EN

Contents

for Greg Dietrich,
dedicated colleague and devoted friend

During an interview for an article that appeared in the June 1991 issue of *Vogue,* Elizabeth Taylor recited the following lines; they were, she said, from her favorite poem.

How to keep—is there any any, is there none such, nowhere

known some, bow or brooch or braid or brace, lace, latch or catch or key to keep

Back beauty, keep it, beauty, beauty, beauty from vanishing away?

> —Gerard Manley Hopkins (1844–1889),
> "The Leaden Echo and the Golden Echo"

Elizabeth Taylor

Chapter One

OCTOBER 6, 1991

T HE INVITATIONS WERE DESIGNED by Cartier in New York, where a team worked for weeks and finally submitted a simple, cream-colored card with black engraving:

Mr. Michael Jackson
requests the pleasure of your company
at the marriage of his beloved friend
Miss Elizabeth Taylor
to Mr. Larry Fortensky
on Sunday, the sixth of October 1991 at 5 p.m.

The location was appropriately fantastic. Even in its glory days, Metro-Goldwyn-Mayer could not have surpassed the sheer scale and prodigality of Neverland, Michael Jackson's secluded ranch nestled in the rolling hills of the Santa Ynez Valley, a hundred miles northwest of Los Angeles.

Neverland rivals Disneyland, for here "the King of Pop, Rock and Soul" (as Elizabeth Taylor called him) has installed an amusement park with a full-size roller coaster, a Ferris wheel, a Zipper that overturns riders in midair—every imaginable kind of carnival ride, as well as swimming pools, playgrounds, trampolines and a swan-shaped ferryboat. There is also a zoo with two hundred creatures: alligators and giraffes, alpacas and wallabies, exotic birds and beasts, a twelve-foot albino python called Madonna, a family of chimpanzees and a four-ton elephant named Gypsy, a gift from Elizabeth Taylor. Michael favors the miniatures of his zoo, like the dwarfed stallion and the tiny pig.

Four dozen gardeners keep 128,000 flowering plants neatly manicured. Oak, maple, sycamore and eucalyptus trees dot the landscape in wild profusion; laced with tiny lights, the place twinkles all night long—like an animated fairyland, sprung magically to life. At the touch of a button, a Disney tune or rock music pours out of speakers camouflaged as boulders or hedges around the estate. Here, Michael Jackson has thrown private parties for groups of youngsters, and two or three child stars, like Macaulay Culkin, have spent vacations at the ranch. Children with cancer have been welcomed, too, and treated to movies, candy stands and all kinds of cheering diversions. In 1991, the year of Elizabeth Taylor's marriage to Larry Fortensky, Jackson turned thirty-three, although some people said that seemed impossible, especially since he usually sounded like a breathless, emotionally wounded teenage girl.

Neverland Valley is not open to the public. The place is really the superstar's secret retreat, where 2,700 emerald green acres surround his opulent, electronically monitored, forty-room mansion. The few guests ever admitted have emerged to describe baronial living and dining rooms, a kiddie playroom like Santa's workshop, a library of children's books—and Michael's bedroom, brimming with antique dolls and a lavishly illustrated, vintage edition of James M. Barrie's classic, *Peter Pan*, about a boy who refused to grow up, fled to Never-Never-Land, and there became the leader of a band of lost children. In fact, Michael Jackson's own favorite toys include, as he has said, "a jack-in-the box, rocking horses and Peter Pan—anything Peter Pan!" Michael and his friend Elizabeth Taylor decided that her wedding would just have to be held at Neverland Valley.

"They're just trying to make it as closed and quiet as possible," said Chen Sam, Elizabeth's Italian-Egyptian publicist, insisting that her client wanted a serene, private service. But the principal players were Jackson and Taylor, so there was no chance that it would be either secret or tranquil. Elizabeth, at fifty-nine, was assuming the role of bride for the eighth time, more than forty-one years after her first trip to the altar. Larry, her new leading man, had not even been born at that time: he was twenty years her junior. Why had she married so often? "I don't know, honey," she had told a reporter after her last divorce, bantering in her best Tennessee Williams, Southern belle accent. "It sure beats the hell out of me."

Outside the ranch, in and around the sleepy town of Los Olivos, newsmen and camera crews from all over the world had pitched camp during that week of October 1991. Waiters and security guards, designers and electricians were paid for information; some of them took home more than a thousand dollars for a few hours of espionage.

At the entrance of Neverland, a large sign with the warning NO CAMERAS greeted the 160 wedding guests—among them family and old friends; agents, lawyers and plastic surgeons; Nancy Reagan, Gregory Peck, Roddy McDowall, Barry Diller, Merv Griffin, David Hockney, Eva Gabor, Quincy Jones, Brooke Shields, Rod McKuen, Franco Zeffirelli, Ray Stark, Diane von Furstenberg and David Geffen. President and Mrs. Bush had been invited, but they sent regrets. Columnist Liz Smith, a loyal and accurate reporter of Taylor lore for decades, was there to tell the world what happened, and photographer Herb Ritts was on hand to document the day in pictures.

At precisely five o'clock, ninety-five-year-old Sara Sothern Taylor, Elizabeth's frail but indomitable widowed mother, was escorted in a wheelchair to the front row, where she joined the groom's parents. A singer was crooning "Ave Maria," but she could only just be heard above the roar of chitchat. The groom then appeared in a white dinner jacket and black trousers, and, ninety minutes later, the star of the show arrived, wearing a yellow, ankle-length gown, a gift from the designer Valentino. Michael Jackson was at her right, wearing a slash of bright red lipstick and carefully applied Cleopatra eyeliner. He was dressed completely in black and sported black gloves, with a huge diamond pin at his throat and his silver boots gleaming in the evening light. Elizabeth's elder son, thirty-eight-year-old Michael Wilding, Jr., was at her left. Bubbles, Michael Jackson's favorite chimp, was perched a few feet away, munching popcorn and enjoying a perfect sight line for the show.

Under a white tent decorated with green swags and vast sprays of gardenias and daisies, the bride and groom took their places for a nondenominational rite conducted by Marianne Williamson. She was Hollywood's cheerfully upbeat guru of the day, making a fortune from books that advised readers to feel good about themselves. "Elizabeth and Larry and all you guests understand," Williamson began, "that so much of the illusion that is happening here right now has nothing to do with the meaning of this ceremony." Anyone paying attention had a lot to think about.

And with that, as if on cue, the illusion altered and the scene changed from merely gaudy to mostly guerrilla. Even Elizabeth, who had a lot of experience as a bride and knew that she could expect a ruckus, was astonished when she glanced up to see a swarm of helicopters jammed with photographers. Then a small biplane zoomed overhead, and an uninvited parachutist floated down, just missing Gregory Peck's head and landing twenty feet from Preacher Williamson, who was so surprised by the jumper's bravado that she almost waved at him. Led by the formidable Moshe Alon, Elizabeth's Israeli-trained security team pounced at once, the deputy sheriff issued a citation, and the intruder was hastily tossed out of Neverland.

"Those sons of bitches!" cried Elizabeth, and then she calmed down. "The hell with them! They can't touch us! This is our day!"

"Do you want me to talk louder, so everyone can hear?" Williamson asked.

"No," said the bride. "Why don't you just speak to Larry and me?"

And so the rite continued, as a dozen enormous yellow and lavender helium balloons were released into the sky, a vain attempt to disperse the flying newsmen. "Larry and I decided to forget all about the helicopters and noise," Elizabeth said later. "We looked into each other's eyes and quietly spoke our vows." They exchanged rings and said in unison, "May we love more deeply than we have ever loved before." Marianne Williamson then announced that the couple certainly seemed to be in love, which was very nice of her, and therefore she said it was all right to pronounce them man and wife. Everyone applauded. The subsequent sound of champagne corks was like a cannonade, and then platters of salmon and chocolate mousse cake were rolled out. Elizabeth kissed everyone and Larry shook so many hands his fingers hurt. He was also so exhausted from stress that he slept through the next day, and when he awoke on his second morning as Elizabeth Taylor's husband, he marveled, "Hey, this isn't so bad!"

In the days following, it became clear that the wedding had been meticulously planned as a magnificent spectacle, carefully orchestrated for the press and the world. Journalists and cameramen had been excluded, but not entirely: after all, there were Liz Smith and Herb Ritts, two of the most influential and respected in their professions. The location was (literally) unreal, the props lavish, the guest list astonishing. The event cost close to $1.5 million dollars, and nothing about it had the marks of a "closed and quiet" ceremony, as Chen Sam proclaimed.

In fact, as Elizabeth said later, many of the details had been supervised by none other than her buddy Michael Jackson, who had a platoon of counselors and caterers to arrange everything. In this regard, she was displaying her typical canny judgment. In 1991, association with Michael Jackson guaranteed that she would have massive free publicity and press coverage on a universal scale. It also made her seem very much of the moment. In fact, several of Jackson's associates believed the relationship was pure business: "pure farce," according to Jackson housekeeper Mark Quindoy—a relationship Elizabeth and Michael exploited "to promote each other." Said another employee, "I never saw them together without the press around. Not once. It was obvious they were feeding off each other's fame. And let's face it, it worked for them both." And according to one biographer, Jackson was in fact "a major investor in Elizabeth's thriving perfume business." In any case, the Fortensky wedding coincided with an advertising campaign for White Diamonds, a new scent marketed under the Taylor banner.

Protestations were to the contrary, of course.

"Michael and I love each other like a brother and sister," she said. In 1990, during her hospitalization for a serious illness, Michael was admitted as a patient. He requested a room very near hers, and when she was able to receive visitors, Elizabeth was wheeled in, bearing a pot of African violets. Earlier in their friendship, she had attended several of his concerts; they had been to horse races together; and she had met privately with him, listening sympathetically as he poured out sad tales of his early life, when he had been physically and psychologically abused by his father and emotionally skewed by an unnatural life of constant adulation as a kiddie star.

"We both started very young and had no childhood to speak of," said Elizabeth. "We both went through the loneliness of that, and we both had the strangeness of trying to grow up as adults." Smokey Robinson called Michael "an old soul in a little body," and for years Elizabeth claimed that she had "the body of a woman and the emotions of a child."

"We had a similar type of childhood, without the opportunities enjoyed by others," according to Michael. "We shared a quest, in search of acceptance from an adoring public who never really knew our inner turmoil. She's someone who knows and understands the loneliness of our business."

"He's a paradox," Elizabeth said of Jackson—and added that he was "the least weird man I've ever known," which was as curious as her next statement: "He has the quality of innocence we'd all like to attain." Yet who could appreciate the trials of stardom better than she, a little actress at nine and a big star at twelve?

Despite so many obvious major differences, Jackson and Taylor had become friends—Michael an increasingly bizarre Peter Pan who had lived with his mother until he was twenty-nine; Elizabeth an astute, sexy, ever-girlish Tinker Bell. Both had lived from childhood in an oddly unrealistic, fairy-tale world of fame, of bright and dangerous glamour, their childhoods protracted, dominated by an ambitious parent, and their adolescences aberrant.

And so it was perhaps no surprise that Elizabeth—for whom each new love meant a fresh role, the first take with a new script—chose Neverland Valley, the fantastic residence of a very peculiar person, for her eighth wedding. To wed Larry, a man so much younger than herself, and so to establish herself in the world of youth and energy, there could be no better setting than this arena of childhood reverie. Elizabeth was giving the impression of eternal youth, mothering her troubled friend Michael as she had mothered the miserable Montgomery Clift, the confused James Dean and others—and perhaps, in a way, nurturing her new husband, also a recovering addict. Marianne Williamson was correct: it was definitely an atmosphere of illusion. But she did not add that the principal players themselves were enfolded in layers of astounding fantasy.

As for Elizabeth, she still yearned for that lost and indefinable "quality of innocence" she believed Michael had in abundance. At the same time, Michael longed for an alliance with a mainstream, maternal movie star. He even cast himself as father of the bride that October day—an odd role, since Elizabeth's much loved brother and sons were available. To Michael's Peter Pan, Elizabeth was Tinker Bell, Wendy, Princess Tiger Lily and warm, maternal Mrs. Darling—all lovingly combined into one hip sister.

The following year, Elizabeth turned sixty, a date she marked with a party at—where else?—Disneyland, that temple to eternal innocence, where she and Larry arrived in a horse-drawn carriage and began the fun by leading a group of friends to the kiddie ride called It's a Small World. There she was, in skin-tight black jeans and a jacket that might have been Michael Jackson's, her hair modishly spiked, rings on her fingers and rhinestones on her shiny boots—a five-foot-four-inch Valley Girl, trying to escape the image of "Elizabeth Taylor."

Like Michael, she had a lifelong fondness for tiny animals—live chipmunks and stuffed beasts, dolls and cute little things in adorable, petite sizes, and her voice often sounded like a little girl's, too. In June 1994, following surgery and a long, self-imposed seclusion, no one who knew her well could have been astonished when Elizabeth reentered society by appearing at the Museum of Miniatures, a shrine to dollhouses and the world of perpetual childhood.

But life was not all cute. Elizabeth was deeply upset, refusing to believe any of the nasty accusations made about Michael Jackson's sexual misconduct with minors. And when he collapsed from drug abuse, she raced to his side and arranged for him to be secretly admitted to a London clinic. But then her value to Jackson (and perhaps her patience with him) seemed to have been exhausted; in any case, he found someone else to stand by his side and attempt to change his image—Lisa Marie Presley.

Lusty, outspoken and mercurial, Elizabeth had clung so passionately to life against frequently appalling odds that she had come to define herself as Mother Courage, with a band of children to save. Generous and compassionate, she could also be completely self-absorbed and astonishingly isolated from anything like daily reality. Elizabeth Taylor became, in other words, the ultimate star—both as achiever and as casualty.

"My toughest role is trying to grow up," she once said. Indeed, that was her life's work.

Chapter Two

1932–1939

S HE WAS NAMED FOR HER FATHER'S
mother, who was also a petite, raven-haired beauty with alabaster
skin.

Born in 1869 in Ohio, of Scottish-Irish ancestry, Elizabeth
Mary Rosemond moved with her family to Springfield, Illinois,
where she married Francis Marion Taylor, a tall, ruggedly handsome
Indiana lad nine years her senior. Not long after the birth of their
son Francis Lenn Taylor, on December 28, 1897, they headed
south—to Arkansas City, a village in southern Kansas that was a
center for both shipping and railroad repairs. There the family pros-
pered in the private, express-mail messenger business, and there the
shy, somewhat passive schoolboy Francis was attracted to Sara Viola
Warmbrodt, a lively extrovert of sturdy German stock. Born in
Arkansas City on August 21, 1896, Sara shared Francis's longing for
something more stimulating than small town midwestern life;
specifically, she was single-minded in her determination to become
an actress on the world's stages. That aspiration was quietly encouraged by her mother, a talented singer and pianist who had more

esthetic interests than her husband, an efficient tinkerer who supervised a local laundry.

As it happened, Francis decamped before Sara, and before finishing high school. His mother's sister, Mabel Rosemond, was married to a wealthy art dealer named Howard Young, who gave the boy
a job as a sales apprentice in St. Louis. By 1919, when Francis was
twenty-one, his keen eye and affable way with clients had much
impressed his uncle, who decided to open a gallery in New York—
just in time to cater to the merry extravagances of the urban-chic
social set during the Roaring Twenties. These two bright and cultivated gentlemen quickly ingratiated themselves in Manhattan society, and the Howard Young Gallery was an instant success, dealing
with special expertise in eighteenth and nineteenth-century European paintings.

Meantime, Sara Warmbrodt, too, fled Arkansas City before
completing high school, and for several years she lost touch with
Francis Taylor. Despite her mother's anxiety about a pretty girl on
her own away from home, Sara was allowed to study acting in
Kansas City. Hell-bent on success, she began by changing her name
to the more euphonious Sara Sothern and managed to meet players
of every touring or repertory company that came to town. By early
1922, she had assumed minor roles with stock companies from
Iowa to Manitoba to Massachusetts, but so far was she from realiz-
ing her dream that she might have abandoned all hope of stardom
had she not landed in Los Angeles in July 1922 and won a small
supporting role in a stock company revival of a melodrama called
The Sign on the Door, by critic and playwright Channing Pollock. (In
1930, Barbara Stanwyck starred in the movie version, *The Locked
Door.*)

As it happened, Pollock was in the audience, looking to cast his
new play *The Fool,* a noble-minded four-act melodrama vaguely
inspired by the life of St. Francis of Assisi. What there was of action
concerned an idealistic young minister (named, none too subtly,
The Reverend Gilchrist) who decries parochial hypocrisies and sets
out to live as did Christ himself. Among twenty-one roles, the most
sympathetic was that of a poor lame girl named Mary Margaret (a

modern Mary Magdalene): she idolizes the preacher and, when he is beset by an angry mob, prays aloud for him—only to find, a moment later, that she has been cured and can now stride quite nimbly without her crutches. Impressed with Sara's artless sincerity and controlled hysteria and captivated by her performance in *The Sign on the Door*, Pollock offered her the part of Mary Margaret.

After three weeks of rehearsals, *The Fool* opened in Los Angeles at the Majestic Theatre. The critics were merciless, but Pollock and producer Arch Selwyn continued on course toward a Broadway premiere. Sara, hoping for a more lucrative movie career, wanted to stay in California, but (as Pollock detailed in his memoirs) no less than the great Russian actress Alla Nazimova was so impressed with the girl from Kansas that she convinced her to go to New York.

After an uncomfortable train journey eastward, the company arrived in New York that October to learn that the sets had just been destroyed in a Manhattan warehouse fire and had to be reconstructed quickly and inexpensively. The Times Square Theatre finally lighted its marquee on October 23, 1922, but *The Fool* did very poor business compared with the likes of Anne Nichols's smash hit, *Abie's Irish Rose*; George Bernard Shaw's *Back to Methusaleh*; Eugene O'Neill's *The Hairy Ape*; George Kelly's *The Torchbearers*; Colton and Randolph's *Rain*; Pirandello's *Six Characters in Search of an Author*; Karel Capek's *R.U.R.*; and successful musicals by Irving Berlin and Victor Herbert, as well as the Ziegfeld *Follies* and George White's *Scandals*.

Amid such an array of better entertainments, Pollock's long and verbose play disappointed the critics, who for the most part deplored it as mawkish and unbearably tedious—although eventually the respected critic Burns Mantle, editor of the annual *Best Plays* series, included it as one of the ten finest of the year 1922. Arch Selwyn, *The Fool*'s producer, was ready to post a closing notice, but Pollock begged for a week's time to launch his own publicity campaign. He took newspaper ads, made speeches before civic groups, provided transportation for church parties and even wrote for pastors sermons containing favorable mention of the play. Thus did Pollock win a reprieve: no less miraculously than Mary Margaret's sudden sprint, the show sold out for almost a year. Before it finally closed, seven nationwide touring companies were playing to more than 85,000 spectators weekly. "I've made a million and a half, and I can tell anybody to go to hell—including the critics," Pollock soon said, perhaps not quite in the spirit of his play.

As it happened, *The New York Times* praised only James Kirkwood, as Reverend Gilchrist, and the young actress from Kansas: "In the final scene of the third act, a little cripple, well played by Sara Sothern, falls on her knees in prayer and rises to find that she can walk." It was, he added, the only truthful moment in more than three hours. *The Theatre* magazine's critic considered that the performances were "creditable but not startling—except for a little girl named Sara Sothern, who is outstandingly fine as a lame girl whose faith brings her to walk."

Sara charmed critics and audiences, but Pollock recalled that she gave him "a good deal of trouble, [because] her father had made me responsible for her, but she had been conspicuously successful everywhere"—indeed, many gentlemen in New York society found the pert actress irresistible. Finding such attention more to her liking than her mediocre salary in *The Fool*, Sara announced to Pollock that she would not travel with the play to London. The playwright's offer of a substantial raise changed her mind, however, and she sailed with the Pollocks on the *Aquitania*.

In London, *The Fool* enjoyed a five-month run at the Apollo Theatre (beginning September 18, 1924), where "Sara more than duplicated her success," according to Pollock. A platoon of policemen rescued her from a first night crowd that (thus Pollock) "clamored for bits of her frock and locks of her hair as souvenirs, and later the Princess Royal went to her dressing room to present her with a diamond brooch the size of a belt buckle." So began Sara Sothern's lifelong passion for precious gems, which she considered proper compensation for a great lady of the theater, which she certainly was not. The fancy for jewelry, of course, was in time inherited by her daughter.

She was also enchanted by the world of the British theater—in fact, by everything English—and after the run of the play she would gladly have settled in London but for the offer of work in New York.

Alas, in her second play, Sara was not so fortunate—*The Dagger*, a silly melodrama of the Paris underworld in which she played a crook's faithful girl. The critics were stupefied that such drivel could be produced. Alexander Woollcott, writing for the majority opinion of the judges, called *The Dagger* "childish rubbish" that could appeal only "to that not inconsiderable minority of the theatergoing public which is not quite bright." After five performances, the play closed in early September 1925. To Sara's great disappointment, Channing Pollock preferred to cast Fay Bainter in the lead of his next play, *The Enemy.* "When I said no [to Sara], she wrote me abusive letters," Pollock recorded with some astonishment.

To pay the rent, therefore, Sara appeared that October in another disappointing endeavor—this time an exotic but hare-brained musical called *Arabesque*, set in the Arabian desert and starring Bela Lugosi as a lecherous sheik. Again enacting a variation on her role as the Sweet Young Thing, Sara all but disappeared amid the show's elephantine production values.

By Christmas, things could not have been less cheerful. Now typecast as the Pollyanna of the piece, she tried to fight her way through the laborious thickets of *Fool's Bells*, a fantasy in which—as a dear lass of the tenements—her character brings spiritual solace to a hunchback. Again after five performances, the play closed before the new year began.

Although the *Times*'s critic praised her for looking "extremely attractive" in *Mama Loves Papa* in February 1926, this matrimonial farce could not draw audiences for more than twenty-five performances. With five supporting roles and four dismal flops behind her, the fair Miss Sothern, now in her thirtieth year, was stymied. She had had no success since *The Fool*, and she thought that perhaps she ought to return to England, or just get married: anything seemed preferable to another Broadway gamble. Although she "had been bitten by the Broadway bug and never got over it" (thus a Hollywood ally, later), Sara found it increasingly hard to maintain her natural optimism and winsome cheer.

As it happened, the opportunities for both marriage and a

return to London very soon came her way—and in none other than the person of her childhood friend Francis Taylor, now a handsome and urbane businessman with a fund of anecdotes gleaned from impressive European travel. They were reunited at a Manhattan nightclub not long after the final curtain fell on *Mama Loves Papa*, and soon Francis was squiring Sara to gallery openings, auctions and dinner parties hosted by those named in the Social Register. Sara liked Francis's courtliness, his quiet sophistication and his romantic gestures—and so, following a few weeks of dating, he sent a bouquet of roses daily to her modest apartment. For his part, he liked her combination of polite humor, irrepressible energy and penchant for high style. When she accepted a part in a pallid comedy called *The Little Spitfire*, in August, he met her almost nightly after the show.

Francis told her that the Howard Young Gallery was about to open a London branch of his business, which he was to manage. Although his uncle was remembered as a wealthy man who was not inclined to share his money, and although Francis's life would always be dependent on this rich, frugal man (whose temper was not improved by living with a wife who had slipped into reclusive alcoholism), it was a good, comfortable and even sometimes a glamorous profession. And so, in the fullness of time, Sara accepted Francis's proposal, and they were married before the end of 1926. When the run of *The Little Spitfire* ended in early 1927, she retired forever from the stage.

For the newlyweds, the next two years were a time of luxury and high excitement. Supported by Young, who remained at the New York gallery, they lived smartly in London, first in an apartment at the Carlton Hotel, whence they traveled to European capitals to find old masters for new clients. Their good manners and refined interests, their elegantly furnished hotel suites and expensive clothes—all underwritten by Uncle Howard—enabled the Taylors to move easily among both aristocrats and the merely rich, and soon they were socializing with the Cazalet family, a wealthy old clan counting among its prominent members Victor Cazalet, a sporty bachelor, art collector and member of Parliament who became an outspoken foe of anti-Semitism in England and championed the cause of Poland after the Nazi invasion in 1939. Cazelet's mother and sister took Sara under their capacious social wing, while Victor introduced Francis to the affluent artists, actors and diplomats of Hampstead Heath. That cultivated, creative district of North London had boulevards of spacious villas, and the neighborhood was the venue for fashionable parties and stylishly bohemian receptions. The innovative Everyman Theatre, also in Hampstead, presented the premiere performances of plays by Shaw, Pirandello, Coward and others for over a quarter century. Visiting such a district, Sara Sothern Taylor was, as she said, in her element, and she forthwith resolved to live there one day.

Her resolutions were realized at the time of her first pregnancy, late in 1928, when the Taylors leased a snugly comfortable two-bedroom residence at 11 Hampstead Way. The nineteenth-century cottage, still in good repair sixty-five years later, featured red brick exterior walls, with picturesque beamed ceilings, fireplaces, leaded windows and a lush garden that gave onto the Heath. From her ground floor sitting room, Sara could spend the final difficult weeks of pregnancy surveying genteel riders on sleek horses as well as ordinary working folk enjoying the vast parklands on Sundays and bank holidays.

By late June 1929, Sara's condition had become complicated, and it was not at all clear that she would survive the delivery of her first child. But almost daily letters of encouragement arrived from her mother in Pasadena, California, where the Warmbrodts were now managing a chicken farm, and Sara willed herself and her baby to endure. "Mother had written me," Sara recalled years later, "that I must keep my mind full of beautiful thoughts to have a beautiful baby. I had worked at it, and no baby in the world could have been more beautiful than Howard"—named, to no one's surprise, for the wealthy uncle. The child, born June 27, was indeed a luminously appealing baby, with China blue eyes and masses of golden ringlets. "From the first, he looked like a Botticelli angel," claimed the proud mother.

In those days of lower wages for servants and lower taxes for the affluent, the Taylors could afford a nurse for the baby and a cook and driver for themselves. For that platoon of help, the cottage was at once too small, and so—again, thanks to Howard Young—Sara and Francis paid cash for a house very nearby, on Wildwood Road, overlooking areas of Hampstead Heath from both front and rear of the house.

For decades afterward, books about Elizabeth Taylor featured photographs of a grand mansion, but these were invariably images of 10 Wildwood Road, just adjacent. The Taylor residence, number 8, had long borne the name Heathwood and was much more modest than the two houses that flanked it. Facing the Heath Extension, Heathwood was not as grand as its neighbors but nonetheless was a desirable family home: a forty-year-old melange of Tudor and Victorian architectures surrounded by flower-filled gardens, it had a large kitchen, a tennis court and rooms for two employees.

By late spring 1931, Sara was again pregnant, and on February 27, 1932 (after a labor not quite as cruel as the first), she bore a healthy daughter at once named Elizabeth, after both grandmothers, and (for a middle name) Rosemond, Granny Taylor's maiden name. The joy of this birth banished Sara's depression over the recent death of her mother in California.

But there was some initial alarm, for the baby girl had residual hypertrichosis, a soft weaving of dark hair all over her body. "Her hair was long and black," Sara recalled, scarcely concealing her memory of this repulsive abnormality. "Her ears were covered with thick black fuzz and inlaid into the sides of her head; her nose looked like a tip-tilted button, and her tiny face [was] so tightly closed it looked as if it would never unfold." Whereas Howard resembled a Renaissance angel, Elizabeth had the frank appearance of a demonic little freak. "Poor little girl," said visitors, sighing sympathetically. "Isn't it too bad she isn't the boy and Howard the girl?"

But after several weeks, everyone relaxed. The unsightly hair vanished, the child's lavender-blue eyes gazed serenely up at her parents, and tiny Elizabeth Taylor—at first unnaturally quiet but soon playfully curious about everything inside and outside the house—was enchanting everyone. Usually indifferent to childish antics, Victor Cazalet was smitten by the girl, and although Sara was vaguely Christian Scientist and therefore eschewed sacramental baptism, Cazalet became Elizabeth's unofficial godfather.

In the 1930s, very many English families, like their American counterparts, were suffering the ravages of the worldwide Depression; the Taylors, however, were untouched by economic strife. Servants attended them, and the children had an abundance of toys, frequent holidays by the sea in Norfolk and picnics in the lush fields of Kent and Sussex; they were, in other words, both privileged and spoiled. In addition, Sara routinely bundled her children into a hired caravan or trailer; packed tents and provisions; engaged the cook Hilda and the nursemaid Daisy for extra time; put a leash on Monty, the golden retriever; and whisked Howard and Elizabeth away for an excursion to Suffolk or Devon.

At Sara's insistence, Elizabeth and Howard were also introduced quite early to the pleasures and rigors of foreign travel. Her first two Christmases and her first and second birthdays were celebrated in America, where the four Taylors escaped the long, dark English winter days. They first visited the Taylor grandparents in Kansas and then proceeded to the warmth of Pasadena to see widowed Grandfather Warmbrodt. From there, they doubled back to Star Island, Florida, the sunny winter retreat of Howard and Mabel Young. Everywhere, as Sara and Francis recalled, Elizabeth was regarded with adoration by adults, who remarked on her astonishingly luminous eyes, her thick eyelashes, her dark hair framing unblemished skin—and a tiny, plain birthmark on her right cheek, which even in childhood Sara often highlighted with a cosmetic pencil. Endlessly curious but given to childish tantrums, Elizabeth was subjected to the doting blandishments of virtually every adult who met her. Embraced by a loving family, alert servants and a steady stream of admiring visitors, she learned in childhood to take attention and esteem for granted.

This situation, combined with her mother's irrepressible optimism, bred in the child a certain fearlessness. Everything would

tion delivered by her mother and her mother's friends; medicines were a court of last resort, and then only prescribed after some insistence from Francis.

"Never talk about [her] parents," said a man who knew the family well a decade later. "Talk about Sara." There was, of course, good reason for this: "My dad and I didn't really become close until after I'd left home," as Elizabeth said later—and in fact they were not particularly close, even then.

And so Victor Cazalet continued to be a prime mover in Elizabeth's life, especially in the increasing professional absence and emotional distance of Francis Taylor. Weeks after Elizabeth's fourth birthday, in early spring 1936, Cazalet moved into a new country house, Great Swifts, in Kent. "My brother lent [the Taylors] a small house on his estate," recalled Thelma Cazalet-Keir, who later also became a member of Parliament. "It was there that Elizabeth passed some of her childhood and learned to ride, among other accomplishments useful to a film career."

Electricity and water were installed at Cazalet's expense, and the sixteenth-century residence—scarcely a "small house" with its fourteen rooms—was quickly dubbed Little Swallows, the logical designation for an offspring of Great Swifts. Here Sara Sothern Taylor and her family repaired for weekends, and here the privileges of English country life were firmly established.

One of these prerogatives was the cult of the horse. Cazalet arrived one day with a gift for Elizabeth, a mare named Betty that "bucked me into a patch of stinging needles. But they made me get right back on, and I hardly got off again till we left England . . . I soon became an accomplished horsewoman. I rode bareback for hours all over the property."

As it happened, this was a privilege Betty permitted no one except four-year-old Elizabeth. So contemptuous was the beast toward everyone else in the human race that she threw off no less an august rider than Foreign Minister (and later Prime Minister) Anthony Eden, who limped away from the hedgerows, cursing. In no time, Elizabeth was virtually the mistress of the estate: "The Cazalets thought such a lot of her, she was more or less spoiled," according to Frederick Hougham, Elizabeth's groom and Betty's trainer.

The gifts of the carriage trade were not limited to trotting with Betty, however. One day that autumn of 1936, the Taylors visited one of Francis's clients, who was presenting a dance recital featuring some children who had taken their first ballet steps under the tutelage of a woman named Mrs. Rankin. With an eye to tutoring the children of society doyennes, she had assumed the more exotic monicker Madame Vacani and opened a school of ballet atop an old building in Knightsbridge, not far from Harrod's. After watching the little girls dressed in crinoline and trying to flutter like butterflies, Sara swung into action: her children, too, would study dance with Madame Vacani.

And so they did, although Howard soon put his foot firmly down and ran instead onto the playing field. As for Elizabeth, she "was so shy she couldn't move a foot," Sara remembered. This awkwardness prevailed until the first group recital in which the child was to appear. Elizabeth was at last persuaded to glide onto the makeshift stage with the other little butterflies, but when the number was complete and the children moved offstage, she held her ground. The curtain was lowered and raised again and lowered yet again. Still, there was the four-year-old starlet, "reveling in her solo performance," according to her mother. "She circled around to the center of the stage and curtsied . . . The house went wild! . . . She took several curtain calls alone, and loved it!"

This, too, would be simply a moment of ordinary maternal pride had Sara not again given it a portentous complexion:

> I gave up my career when I married . . . But I knew from that benefit recital that . . . there would come a time when she would want to follow in my footsteps. I could still hear the applause of that wonderful night ten years before when *The Fool* had opened in London at the Apollo Theatre and I, playing the part of the little crippled girl, had stood alone in the middle of the stage and had taken a dozen curtain calls, while a reputedly staid British audience called, "Bravo, bravo, bravo!"

The theatrical die, as it were, was cast, and while the rosy glow of retrospect (and Elizabeth's ultimate fame) doubtless affected Sara in her comments years later, subsequent developments during her daughter's childhood indicated that from about this time Sara saw her daughter as ordained to fulfill her own aborted dreams of stardom. To this destiny Sara dedicated herself with something like religious fervor. As for the recital at Madame Vacani's, it virtually took on the hue of a religious moment and became much exaggerated: at the peak of her stardom years later, Elizabeth was hailed by the press as one who had danced before the king in a command performance at London's Hippodrome—an event, of course, that never occurred. But newspapers, after all, receive their cues from publicists, and publicists from their clients.

With future fame for Elizabeth now shining in Sara's eyes, she took the children to Arkansas City to visit the ailing Grandmother Taylor in early 1937. Six weeks into the visit, just as Howard and his sister were settling into the local school, Granny died, at the age of sixty-one. The family returned to London, where Elizabeth was enrolled at the Byron House School, Highgate, and where she remained for the next two years. "She wasn't an outstanding pupil, but she had such charm," recalled Mary Mason, one of her teachers.

Life at Heathwood and Little Swallows finally came to an end in early 1939, with the threat of war. Victor Cazalet, who was concerned for the safety of his adopted family, prevailed on Francis to quit England as soon as possible. There was, however, the matter of the Howard Young Gallery in Bond Street, and that would take months to vacate. Well, then, replied Cazalet, Taylor ought to send Sara and the children to America and follow later. Thus, shortly after Easter, Sara, Howard and Elizabeth left Southampton aboard the S.S. *Manhattan,* which was in fact its destination. From New York they boarded a train for Pasadena and Grandpa Warmbrodt, where Francis finally joined them in early December. Alas, he was able to export with him only a few drawings by the contemporary artist Augustus John, and one valuable painting by Frans Hals that became the cornerstone of his (and later his daughter's) private and valuable collection. The rest of the Young Gallery's acquisitions had to remain in London. "He had to start his life all over again," his daughter said years later. "It must have been hard on him, pulling up roots from England."

Precisely why the Taylors chose to live in Southern California is unclear, although it must have been inspired by Sara's happy memories of her first success, in *The Fool*. She was not, after all, particularly roused to fervor at the thought of living on her father's chicken ranch. Quite the contrary: she had always loved the excitement of what was later termed "the industry," even though in 1922 she had never been closer to the world of film than a front row seat at a movie palace.

Now, with two handsome offspring and a culture that, in 1939, placed a very high priority on adorable child actors, she may have been hatching a plot. Shirley Temple was now eleven, Judy Garland seventeen. Who, her mother wondered aloud, would replace them as the new child star? In no time, the Taylors' own Kansas background faded like a watercolor exposed to the sun. "Sara Taylor did bring Elizabeth to Arkansas City for several summers when she was a little girl," remembered a Kansas neighbor, "but then she went to Hollywood and dropped everyone she ever knew." As for Elizabeth, she had seen only one movie in her life—*Snow White*, aboard the *Manhattan*: of real live movie stars she knew nothing.

It was, to be sure, a new life. To exhibit his collection of Augustus John and a few other items he had brought from Young's New York gallery, Francis rented a suite of rooms at the Chateau Elysée Hotel on Franklin Avenue. This was rather a long drive from the house Sara wanted to lease, and into which they moved in early 1940, a rambling bungalow near the ocean in Pacific Palisades. There, Elizabeth attended school with the children of Darryl F. Zanuck, chief of production at Twentieth Century-Fox Studios, and with the children of actress Norma Shearer. "I don't think [Howard and Elizabeth] learned much at the Pacific Palisades school," Sara said airily, "but they had a lot of fun." Thanks to Sara, the children also made important social connections there.

Sara's intention was becoming clearer and clearer. "Agents came up to us on the street and wanted to take us to see David Selznick—and have a screen test," Sara reported, doubtless somewhat hyperbolically. "Wherever I took the children, people would stop and stare at Elizabeth, rave about her eyes and tell me she should be in pictures . . . Everywhere we went, people would say, 'That child is the image of Vivien Leigh!'"

Her remarks, it has become clear, were a case of *post hoc, ergo propter hoc*: much later, Sara saw Elizabeth's subsequent stardom, not firmly established until she was twelve in 1944, as if it were predestined. Even allowing for maternal pride, photographs of Elizabeth in early 1940 show a thin child with rather too much unkempt hair framing a pretty face but not one over which audiences would swoon. Eight-year-old girls, to be sure, may present a sweetly docile expression, but unless there is extraordinary talent—à la the young Shirley Temple—one cannot expect the heavens to stop in their course. At eight, Elizabeth Taylor showed no special aptitude for singing or dancing or acting. And as for her appearance, she needed more help from Mother Nature than from Mother Taylor.

Chapter Three

1940-1948

*T*O ATTRACT A MORE AFFLUENT clientele, Francis Taylor (with Howard Young's approval) moved the art gallery westward, from the Chateau Elysée apartment building to the Beverly Hills Hotel, a far more desirable venue on Sunset Boulevard. At about the same time—in late 1940—he moved his family from Pacific Palisades to a house not far from the hotel. A small but attractive place at 703 North Elm Drive, built in the popular style of a Meditteranean villa, this would be Elizabeth's residence until she left home to marry.

A mostly residential community completely surrounded by the city of Los Angeles, Beverly Hills has been known, since its incorporation in 1914, for its luxurious homes and its concentration of people working in film (and later television). The city had relatively easy access, via the wider boulevards and the canyons, to film studios in Culver City to the south (MGM), Hollywood to the east (Columbia, Goldwyn and Fox) and the San Fernando Valley to the north (Warner, Universal and Disney). In 1940, its population was 26,823, and for the most part people knew who lived where and which children went to what school. (Fifty years later, the census recorded only five thousand more citizens. Few seem to relish an entire lifetime in Beverly Hills, which, like those who work in the movies themselves, has always counted a considerable number of transients.)

For Howard and Elizabeth, their education resumed at the Hawthorne Elementary School, at 624 North Rexford Drive, a short distance from home. Initially, their tincture of British accents annoyed classmates, who imitated them with wacky mockery: "I cawn't take a bawth on the grawss with the banawnas." Elizabeth, according to one reporter who knew her that year, "promptly altered her *a*'s to an almost Texas extreme," and sounded—as she often would throughout her life—like a native of the South, where she never lived.

But for Sara, Elizabeth's elementary school classes had to be supplemented, just as Madame Vacani had supplemented the spelling drills of Byron House. So that she could entertain guests at Elm Drive, she was sent to singing and dancing lessons after school. Her riding lessons continued in Pacific Palisades, so that she would not compare unfavorably when invited—as indeed she must be—to join the activities of wealthier children. "My mother," she said later, "was my best girl friend, my guide, my mentor, my constant companion."

In that remarkable fusion of functions, Sara proceeded with single-minded intent in the autumn of 1940. Somehow, Victor Cazalet had known the stage and screen matinee idol William DeWolf Hopper, and was now on friendly terms with Hopper's ex-wife, Hedda, and their young son. In response to a letter from Sara, Victor provided a letter of introduction to Mrs. Hopper.

Born Elda Furry, Hedda Hopper was a fifty-year-old actress who had appeared in scores of silent and sound films. After her divorce in 1922, she also became something of a Hollywood socialite, and in 1938—after hosting a radio talk show for two years—she began a long career as a Hollywood columnist. This made her more famous than her acting, as did her lavish hats and melodramatic feuds with the rival gossip Louella Parsons.

Advice from Hedda Hopper, or a mention in her syndicated newspaper column, or an invitation to her home, would be of enormous help in determining just how Sara ought to proceed with the presentation of her adorable Elizabeth. And so, armed with Cazalet's letter as if it were Letters Patent from the king of England expressing the royal will and favor, she took her daughter to meet Hopper, who found the child

> innocent and lovely as a day in spring. I liked and pitied her from the start, when her mother, bursting with ambition, brought her to my house one day to have her sing for me. Sara Taylor had never gotten over Broadway. She wanted to have a glamorous life again through her child. She had the idea, at first, that Elizabeth could be turned into another Deanna Durbin, who had a glittering name in those days.

The reason for Hopper's pity was at once clear: she found it "a terrifying thing" when Sara commanded that Elizabeth sing for her hostess—which the poor child did, in a quivering, fearful voice, her expressive violet eyes brimming with tears. "It was," Hopper remembered forever after, "one of the most painful ordeals I've ever witnessed."

Obviously, at this stage, the child did not share her mother's ambitions for her, and of this time, Elizabeth later said, "I never wanted a career—it was forced on me." Eleanor Harris, a journalist who knew Elizabeth at the time, put it plainly: "She had never really been interested in acting: it was part of her life only because she had been propelled into it at the age of eight by her mother." Eventually, Elizabeth Taylor's indifference would alter—but only when she came to believe that she had no alternative. For the present, "Elizabeth's mother was the dominating force in the Taylor household, the strong one who told everyone else what was good for them," as Hedda Hopper said; of Francis, she knew nothing. "Elizabeth always swore she would never be [like her mother] when she grew up." Sensing trouble, or at least unwilling to contribute to the youngster's evident anxiety, Hopper refrained from taking up Elizabeth's cause.

But Sara was not easily put off. Erin Considine was Elizabeth's playmate on Elm Drive, and her father, John W. Considine, Jr., was a successful producer for Metro-Goldwyn-Mayer Studios. *Boys Town* had recently been one of his major hits. The amiable Considine gladly escorted Sara, Francis and Elizabeth on a tour of the Metro facilities. More than two dozen films were in production during late 1940, and the 117 acres, as Elizabeth recalled, were "teeming with life—people dressed up in Greek clothes, people dressed up as cowboys, people dressed up as apes, and real live movie stars." In more than 140 buildings and thirty sound stages, 4,000 employees toiled six days each week. Cosmetics were applied to 1,200 players an hour, wardrobe supervisors clothed 5,000 a day, and ten million feet of film were printed each month. After that tour, Elizabeth's cool indifference to the world of fantasy warmed appreciably.

In fact, Considine managed a meeting that same day with the formidable Louis B. Mayer, the studio's general manager, who gazed at the child and said, "I want to hear this little girl sing"—which she did, without musical accompaniment. "Sign her," he said almost absentmindedly—perhaps thinking of Margaret O'Brien, age three, whom he had also just put under contract. Mayer then rushed off for an appointment.

Somehow, the contract never arrived. For one thing, Elizabeth had no agent or attorney to plead her case. Perhaps, too, the busy, mercurial Mayer was simply disinclined to offend Considine, one of his money-making producers, and so the necessary sequence of business details never reached the legal department. Sara was undeterred.

The lounges and dining room of the Beverly Hills Hotel were a regular meeting place for producers, stars and agents for business meetings, and soon the Taylor gallery attracted not only casual strollers and curious shoppers but also the movie trade. One visitor was the wife of J. Cheever Cowdin, chairman of Universal Pictures since 1936: by sheer coincidence, Mrs. Cowdin happened to be at the gallery late one afternoon when Sara and Elizabeth were also visiting. Sara seized the moment, and a week later she welcomed the

Cowdins to her home—officially to inspect some additional paintings, but there was of course a hidden agenda.

The afternoon tea party, around the time of Elizabeth's ninth
birthday in February 1941, was successful, most of all because
Cowdin was as much an Anglophile as Sara. As it happened, he had
come to Hollywood by accident (although his wife was an aspiring
actress). As director of a Wall Street firm called Standard Capital
Corporation, he was a specialist in bailing out beleaguered companies and turning that to Standard Capital's ultimate advantage. In
1935, he had arranged for a loan of $750,000 to Universal, then
beset almost to bankruptcy with financial troubles. The deal was a
simple and successful one: if the studio was unable to repay the loan
after ninety days, Cowdin had an option to purchase five-and-a-half
million dollars of stock. This he did, installing a new president and
board and running the studio as chairman.

Still, despite the successful Deanna Durbin musicals, Universal
was considered a grade-B studio, specializing in Abbott and Costello
farces, Flash Gordon serials, a discount newsreel service, Gothic
horror melodramas and a few low-budget W. C. Fields comedies.

Cowdin and his wife liked the Taylors' refinement and shared
their affinity for Britain. He was also on the lookout for young talent, and very young talent came cheap. The Universal Pictures
Company offered Elizabeth Taylor a six-month contract, renewable
for an identical term, dated April 21, 1941; it would take effect
three days later. The deal, negotiated with the help of agent Myron
Selznick, provided a guaranteed weekly salary of $100 for twenty
weeks, the money to be paid to Mrs. Sara Sothern Taylor—not, it
should be noted, to Mr. Francis Taylor; scrupulously, Sara held the
accumulation of monies in trust until her daughter's maturity. But
Mother, in fact, benefitted, too: she and Selznick saw to it that 10
percent of Elizabeth's salary would be paid directly to Sara, who was
to come to the studio daily with her daughter "to assist in the performance of such services as shall be required by the Studio." Sara
crowed with delight to her old friend Victor Cazalet, who had telephoned from New York: "Imagine excitement of Taylors," he wrote
in his diary. "Elizabeth has a contract for 7 years with a big Cinema

group." (The six-month, renewable contract had, it seemed, been extended to seven years in her report to Cazalet.) It was the family's last contact with Cazalet, who died in an airplane crash during the war.

The subject of all this excitement was not so pleased as her elders. Informed of the contract with Universal and told to prepare for her first day on the lot, Elizabeth surprised her parents by bursting into tears: "*I* wanted to be at MGM!" She dried her eyes and waited—until late summer, as it happened—to go to work.

Waiting meant traveling to the studio daily, in case a role considered suitable should suddenly arise. As the law required, Universal had its schoolroom for kiddie actors. This Elizabeth liked much less than Hawthorne, where she had just begun to make friends and whence she was suddenly plucked. "She was painfully shy," remembered Universal aspirant Gloria Jean. "Occasionally, some of the executives would come into the schoolroom to see how we were doing. The minute she heard them coming, Elizabeth hid under the table. One day, I fished her out and explained that she shouldn't be afraid. And she just looked at me and said, 'But Gloria, I don't like people!'" This opinion betokened no misanthropy: "I was constricted by shyness," Elizabeth said later, which was precisely the impression everyone had—and not only during her youth.

Finally, she was ushered onto a set, in the late summer of 1941. But the result of her first assignment as a little movie star may well have set her again crying for MGM. For less than a week, she worked on a feeble sixty-minute formula comedy called *Man or Mouse,* which was rechristened *There's One Born Every Minute* just before its release and quick box-office death. Miscast as one of two obstreperous brats, she had nothing to do but pretend bad manners "and shoot rubber bands at ladies' bottoms," as she later said. Nothing could have been more foreign to her upbringing.

Like the sparse audiences that saw the film in its brief release at the bottom of double bills in August 1942, the men at Universal were not thrilled with what they saw in Elizabeth Taylor. "The kid has nothing," reported the studio's casting director, Dan Kelly. "Her eyes are too old. She doesn't have the face of a kid." The problem, however—soon evident—was that Elizabeth Taylor simply was not a movie brat. Nor was she, at nine, enough of an actress to fake it. And since casting directors are not paid to be prophets, but rather to do what they can with what they have, no harsh judgment ought to be retrospectively laid at the feet of Mr. Kelly, who was reminded of his judgment for years after.

Cheever Cowdin had weightier matters on his mind than defending the cause of an inexpensive and unpromising investment. On September 29, 1941, two weeks after finishing her few scenes, Elizabeth was dismissed indefinitely. When her contract was due for renewal, Myron Selznick heard nothing from the studio. She had $1,800 in the bank, Sara $200.

As for her mother—unlike Elizabeth, who seemed to be profoundly indifferent—Sara was beside herself with chagrin and knew not what to do. The next year passed pleasantly enough for her daughter, but anxiously for Mother: she simply refused to believe her daughter's inchoate career would founder so quickly, but she had no evidence to the contrary.

After a year—by the summer of 1942—Elizabeth's confidence had gained considerably. Returning without fuss or detail to the Hawthorne School, she studied and played easily with other local children. Asked what she dreamed of for the future, she replied, "A ballerina . . . a nurse . . . a veterinarian . . . the first female fire-engine driver. My father [is] very much against my being an actress." But such normalcy as she then enjoyed, during her tenth year, would never be resumed in her lifetime.

Precisely how her fortunes altered has been a matter of considerable Hollywood fantasy, much of it cast in the form of a romantic tale from the pen of Sara Sothern Taylor. According to the received tradition, Francis Taylor was doing air raid warden duty in Beverly Hills one night with a neighbor, the Metro producer Samuel Marx. He was having some difficulty, Marx said, in finding the right little girl with an English accent for a small role in *Lassie Come Home,* the first in that canine series, which was scheduled to begin production that autumn of 1942. Neighbor Taylor came to the rescue and, suppressing his disdain for the movies, suggested that his own little girl might fill the bill just perfectly.

The tale thus told was as heartwarming as a scene from a Lassie movie, but the actual event owed less to chance than to raw parental determination. When Sara heard that producer Marx attended Civil Defense classes with her husband, she pressured Francis to act as agent. "At every one [of the air raid warden meetings]," said Marx years later, "Francis Taylor took me aside and told me about his beautiful daughter." It was, he added quietly, as if Taylor's wife had told him not to come home without a deal. In fact, *Lassie Come Home* was already in production, but the girl contracted for a small supporting role was too tall to play opposite fourteen-year-old Roddy McDowall, the leading player with whom she would have several scenes. In 1942, such a disparity in height was an untenable cinematic situation. Sara proposed her daughter as a substitute and the rest was history.

But it was history only in retrospect, and a repetition of the fiasco at Universal was certainly possible. Every evening for a week, Sara sat down, brandishing a weather-beaten copy of *The Fool* as if it were a talisman, while Elizabeth stood in the living room at Elm Drive and listened to her mother's instructions: "Now, honey, here is the big scene. You read the part of the crippled girl. I will be Mr. Gilchrist, who has been beaten up by the mob."

"Here was my daughter," Sara told a reporter some time later, "playing the part I had played! She gave a great performance! When the scene ended, Elizabeth was weeping, I cried, and Mr. Taylor had tears in his eyes. If Mr. Marx wanted her, we wouldn't object." Object, indeed. As it happened, Marx had five other girls lined up for readings when mother and daughter arrived at the studio.

After a quick reading of a few lines by Elizabeth—who was completely serene and had a perfectly clipped English accent in the bargain—Lassie had a new playmate and Elizabeth a new friend for life, Roddy McDowall. An appealing child actor in his native London, he had become the leading juvenile at Twentieth Century-Fox, who loaned him to Metro for *Lassie Come Home.* "My initial impression of her? She was Little Miss Gorgeous, and she had extremely thick, long eyelashes. The cameraman thought they were fake and asked her to take them off!"

Such a reaction from a member of the company would not have been unexpected. For one thing, Elizabeth's behavior and appearance during filming was almost unnaturally grown-up. Drilled by Sara, she was obedient, attentive, and always word-perfect. "She often told me that she hoped she would become as beautiful as her mother," recalled Donald Crisp, who played McDowall's father. In addition, because her skin was so white and her hair so dark, rather too much lipstick had been applied for the Technicolor film stock: thus the cameraman's remark about her eyelashes was not off the mark.

But it would be inaccurate to describe her as anything like the costar of the picture: on-screen in four brief sequences for less than ten minutes, she cut a pretty but passive presence. The film, of course, placed every human in a role supporting the radiant collie, who was so carefully lighted and edited as to intimate the complex feelings of a Method actor. Nor did the studio foresee any dramatic change in Elizabeth's circumstances. She was neither seen nor mentioned in the theatrical trailers, and when *Lassie Come Home* was released and reviewed in October 1943, she received no special mention from the critics. But she was now established as a contract player at Metro, with a guarantee of $100 a week (10 percent for Sara) for a year—nothing more, for there was no telling how adolescence might alter her appearance, or what talent might (or might not) emerge. At the same time, Mayer and company considered changing her name to Virginia Taylor, but Francis forbade it. Then they said her hair was too dark and would photograph blue-black: her locks would have to be dyed chestnut or red or blond. Again, Francis was adamant—as he was against eyebrow plucking. "They wanted to remove the mole from my face, too," Elizabeth recalled. "That became my trademark! They wanted to change the shape of my mouth, my eyebrows—and I said no."

By the time *Lassie Come Home* was complete, at the end of 1942, Elizabeth's poise and charm had been duly noted by the casting department at Metro, but there was no forthcoming production suitable for her. She was, therefore, loaned out to Twentieth Century-Fox, which needed a large detachment of girls age ten to eighteen for the early sequences of *Jane Eyre*. Without credit (or subsequent notice from the press), Elizabeth appeared for less than three minutes in five early sequences, as pious Helen Burns, a friend of young Jane at a dismal, Dickensian school. Photographed in black and white during the early summer of 1943, she appeared far more mature than in *Lassie Come Home,* despite her high, thin voice and still diminutive figure. Full face to the camera, she exudes confidence, telling Peggy Ann Garner (as Jane), "It's wrong to hate people" with the conviction of a medieval mystic. Then, in luminous profile, Elizabeth had her first crack at dying prettily in the movies. She seems scarcely to breathe, and her features and gaze are tranquil, unclouded by fear as her character peers into the face of ultimacy.

It would be easy to make too much of what is little more than a cameo appearance (her scenes are regularly excised from prints circulated and televised). But it would also be foolish to ignore the difference between Elizabeth, acting in *Jane Eyre* at the age of eleven, and almost every other young player in the history of American film. Judy Garland was exuberant, Margaret O'Brien winsome, Peggy Ann Garner charmingly unpredictable. But Elizabeth Taylor was from the start something different. She seemed to be pitching herself into the future; she seemed to know, by some mysterious inner light, things hidden even from adults. Unsurprised by the evil Mr. Brocklehurst, unastonished at her imminent death, Elizabeth as Helen has no parallel among the dozens of other girls in the picture, just as she had no other acting trainer besides Sara as coach. When the film rolled, she seemed to turn some kind of inner switch: this instinct, of course, is demanded by the craft of screen acting, which is achieved in small, brief bits and pieces of performance, a moment at a time between the cry of "Action!" and "Cut!" As Helen Burns in *Jane Eyre,* Elizabeth Taylor exuded for the first time the sort of quiet intelligence that would characterize every performance—no matter how sultry or sexy—for the rest of her career.

* * *

Part of this derived from a talent being shaped by Sara without reference to a child's life, and part derived from the fact that Elizabeth was increasingly being denied the normal life of a child. Back in Culver City by early autumn 1943, the commencement of the school year meant reentering the one-room schoolhouse at Metro, where her companions were other little aspiring movie stars. She was living in a hermetically sealed world of illusion that made no reference to the normal components of a youngster's life: "Being in films then was like the most magical extension of make-believe."

But in the process, she was left unprepared for anything other than making movies and growing up to be a glamorous star like Greta Garbo or Ava Gardner. "How come I missed so much? When was I ever a child?" she later asked wistfully. Too much in her life was made subject to a strange and studied artifice, not enough according to the ordinary rhythms of growth and maturity. "Of course the child stars did not have normal childhoods!" said Emily Torchia, a Metro publicist. "They weren't normal because they were working." Many years later, Elizabeth recognized this herself: "It was not a normal life course. I had no childhood. I was brought up around adults, but I had no real childhood."

The studio school, most egregiously, "wasn't school," as she herself admitted. "I hated it!" Ten minutes of arithmetic for Elizabeth and a dozen classmates were inserted between costume fittings and still photography sessions; a quarter hour of spelling or geography interrupted film takes on a set; makeup was applied while a tutor rattled off the names of state capitals. "Poor Elizabeth," said Richard Burton years later. "She was educated at MGM." And this, as anyone could see, was hardly an education at all—which her parents, who never graduated high school, never seemed to consider. But for a clever and sensitive girl like Elizabeth, it was inevitable that she would soon become acutely conscious of her pathetic lack of instruction, which only exacerbated her lifelong shyness.

From her earliest years, then, her perceptions were defined by the studio, its method of storytelling and its approach to relationships. Her life, her way of approaching ordinary reality, were formed within the cocoon of an extraordinary (and extraordinarily self-centered) belief in playacting, in pretending to be various other people who struggled through to a happy ending. Henceforth, movies told her what she was.

Everything was subordinate to fantasy, everything was, as she later said, "overscheduled and overdisciplined." Even at home on Elm Drive, there were strict codes of deportment. Forbidden to run and romp with other children because she might sustain an injury, she felt strange and apart. "The fact is that I stopped being a child the moment I started working in pictures," and the result was a poignant lack of peer companionship. The closest to her age was her brother, Howard, who was now well into his teens and whose life had nothing to do with movies. (When his mother insisted he take a screen test, he arrived at the studio with his head shaved completely bald, thus effectively aborting a career.)

And so perhaps it was inevitable that Elizabeth lavished her free time and affection on animals—three dogs, a cat, horses, eventually a team of chipmunks. But even this little menagerie was exploited by the studio publicists: what more darling images could be presented for public delight than this adorable child with her adorable pets?

What little there was of schooling, that autumn of 1943, was interrupted by preproduction for her role in *The White Cliffs of Dover*, Louis B. Mayer's paean to British pluck in wartime. Anyone who blinks might easily fail to find Elizabeth in her two fleeting scenes as a shy little country lass who says no more than "Hello" and "Goodbye" to the local little squire (again, Roddy McDowall). Except for her parents, no one noted her appearance when this epic film was released in May 1944, and (like her contribution to *Jane Eyre*) it is often snipped out of surviving prints. By 1944, however, her fortunes had changed dramatically.

The cause was her first leading role, as Velvet Brown, the girl in love with horses in *National Velvet*. Based on Enid Bagnold's novel, the property had been rattling around Hollywood for years, variously planned for Katharine Hepburn, Margaret Sullavan, Vivien Leigh and Shirley Temple before producer Pandro Berman decided to look outside Hollywood for a new starlet. In late autumn 1943, Lucille Ryman Carroll, head of the studio talent department, was preparing to traverse the country in search of a young actress.

"I don't know why you're wasting your time," announced eleven-year-old Elizabeth, bursting into Mrs. Carroll's office. "I am going to play Velvet!" She loved horses, she said, she had been riding since the age of four, she could affect a credible English accent, and she was energetic and a quick study. Why look elsewhere?

Elizabeth's name had in fact been mentioned at casting sessions, but everyone from Berman to director Clarence Brown to Louis B. Mayer himself felt she was too small, too short, too young—too everything but what the robust part required. She was "not quite ready," as Lucille Ryman Carroll said.

"What do you mean, I'm 'not quite ready'?"

"Well, dear, the part calls for a girl who is just beginning to blossom and she needs little bosoms, and you are—well, like a little boy."

A look of steely determination came into the damson-soft eyes. "I am going to play that part, and I will have bosoms for you."

At Christmastime, Carroll returned to the studio, with no serious contenders to suggest for the role. "One of the first people to walk in was Elizabeth," she recalled years later. "'Look!'" she announced. "'I have boobs!'" Well, almost.

Part of the great myth of Elizabeth Taylor is that between October and December she embarked on a regime of diet (high in protein and carbohydrates) and exercise (much riding, some swimming), with the result that she had grown three inches. "She ate and slept so much that in three months she grew three inches: she literally grew herself into this coveted job." So read MGM's publicity bulletin, which the Los Angeles Times trumpeted on Sunday morning, February 27, 1944. This, of course, is not exactly the truth. Photographs of Elizabeth Taylor that season indicate that she had gained some weight, but also that she thinned out her hair, experimented with makeup, tried to lower her voice: in other words, she put on a convincing performance of a maturing preteen—and won the role. Of no small importance was the fact that she was also developing into a refreshingly natural young actress, free of cloying cuteness and tricky mannerisms. She had also become a first-rate rider and, having discovered which was to be the horse in the film, had managed to feed and lead him. Sara, who still knew a good scene for herself, cried for joy at the news that her daughter had landed a leading role in a color film.

Elizabeth acted her first scenes in *National Velvet* on February 4, 1944, and the first rushes showed that she had not been foolhardy in crashing the talent department. As the spirited little Sussex girl who wins a horse in a raffle, disguises herself as a boy and rides him to victory in the Grand National Steeplechase, she appeared in almost every scene in the picture, regarding the adult actors without hesitation or childish seduction. She was lovable, but not saccharine; she was strong, but not (as she could be in the studio schoolroom) abrasive; she was on the cusp of womanhood, but nothing like a coquette.

To broaden its audience base, Metro had already produced several pictures in the category of "family fare," movies featuring Mickey Rooney, Judy Garland, Margaret O'Brien and Jackie Jenkins. But here was someone with a difference: Elizabeth Taylor, twelve years old, shone with an unusual combination of warmth and intelligence. Working with players like Anne Revere and Donald Crisp, she was as prompt and efficient as those seasoned professionals, and as confident as Angela Lansbury (then eighteen and fresh from her performance as a tarty maid in *Gaslight*).

For one emotional scene, in which Velvet learns her sick horse may not survive, tears were called for. Mickey Rooney (with more than sixty films and one wife, Ava Gardner, behind him), took Elizabeth aside to offer an acting lesson. She should, Rooney said tutorially, imagine that her father was dying of drink, that her mother was an exhausted laundress, that her brother had no shoes and that her puppy had just been killed by a car. Hearing this advice, Elizabeth began to snicker, then to laugh aloud. This was ridiculous, she thought. "When I did the scene, instead of imagining my father drunk and dying and my mother doing laundry in the snow, all I thought about was this horse being very sick, and that I was the little girl who owned him. And the tears came." Her faintly acidulous coda: "How generous of Mickey to try to help me."

"As natural and excellent a little actress as you would ever hope to see.". . . "Elizabeth Taylor emerges as one of the most outstanding discoveries of the year.". . . "She and the picture are wonderful."

It would be ludicrous to suppose that the rave reviews did not turn Elizabeth's head, or that she remained humble and unaffected by the leap to stardom after the release of *National Velvet* at Christmas 1944. Fame is a seductive and difficult mantle to bear at any age, and for a child it is often disastrous. Photographs, interviews, absurd lionization, applause, requests for autographs, constant praise and sappy compliments, avalanches of love letters and presents from strangers—these unavoidably made Elizabeth aware of her attraction and her power, which could be used to her benefit.

For one thing, she desperately wanted to keep the horse she rode in the picture, and so the studio circulated the agreeable fiction that as a reward for her performance the gift was their idea and a great surprise to her on her thirteenth birthday in February 1945. The circumstances, however, were somewhat different. Throughout filming, as producer Pandro Berman recalled, she so badgered him to let her keep the horse that Louis B. Mayer himself had to be petitioned to authorize the gift. In addition, Metro, aware of its young treasure, wrote her a bonus of $7,500 and a new seven-year contract starting at $300 a week—which was more shrewd than generous, since it bound her to them for an additional year should they choose to exercise their annual options.

The Taylor family was instantly changed by the hurricane of publicity, and at once the household was quietly divided. Sara and Elizabeth met reporters from fan magazines and fielded questions from the trade press. "There were from six to twelve photographs of Elizabeth in each room of the house on Elm Drive," recalled a visitor, "with Elizabeth sometimes posed alone, sometimes posed beside her mother. You'd never have known there was a Taylor male around!"

Metro now became her family, and hair stylist Sydney Guilaroff "my surrogate father." Even more of a surrogate, and the man on whom she was most dependent (and therefore resented), was Louis B. Mayer, who was the object of her youthful scorn not long after *National Velvet*, when the studio rushed her into another adorable animal picture, *The Courage of Lassie.*

Hearing that her daughter was being considered for a musical to follow the *Lassie* sequel, Sara took Elizabeth to Mayer's office. Should Elizabeth begin dancing lessons? Ought they to hire a voice coach? At the moment, Mayer was in no mood to deal directly with the ambitious mother and her eager offspring, and no decision had been made about the musical—and so he brusquely dismissed them with some common vulgarism. "Don't you dare speak to my mother like that!" piped up Elizabeth. "You and your studio can both go to hell!" Ordered to apologize, she refused. Mayer's reaction to this display of forbidden independence was undocumented, but Elizabeth's position at Metro did not suffer.

The Courage of Lassie, which Elizabeth began in late 1944, is an odd title for a story about a collie named Bill, impersonated by a male dog named Pal who was passed off on the public as a female star, Lassie. In fact, the picture was called *Hold High the Torch* and then *Blue Sierra* during production, but just before its release in the summer of 1946, someone at Metro realized that Miss Taylor had better be directly linked to the famous animal of her early career. Audiences, it was hoped, would forget the title once the film rolled. And so they did, although the picture (Elizabeth's last with a quadruped costar) is unendurably tedious. Shell-shocked Bill, after being dragooned into fighting with the troops in World War II, finds life in peacetime difficult, and the story's chain of unlikely disasters and unreal heroics gave Elizabeth little to do but stand by her collie, crying, "Oh, Bill!" every few minutes. Well might she have hankered for her horse.

The production was not facilitated by Sara, who was as usual present, off in a corner of the set but visible to her daughter, whom she coached with an elaborate series of hand signals. If Elizabeth's voice was too high, Sara put her hand on her stomach.

If Elizabeth's reading of a line lacked sufficient feeling, she saw her mother put a hand to her heart. If Elizabeth seemed distracted or was not heeding a director's instruction, Sara touched her head with a forefinger. Directors, cameramen and producers were at a loss. According to the contract, Mother was to accompany Daughter to each day's work and was paid to "assist her in the performances." Sara knew better than to collide with executives, but there she was, a smiling, affable but somewhat marmoreally imposing figure. And in this capacity she remained for several more years.

For over a year, from spring 1945 to summer 1946, Metro could find no script suitable for her, and so their newest star was unexpectedly idle. She attended school three hours each day, drew her weekly salary and wrote—to whom it cannot be known, although some have suggested it was King Charles, her horse—morbidly romantic poetry apt for a fourteen-year-old:

> *Loving you,*
> *Loving you,*
> *Could be such heavenly bliss,*
> *And, as our hearts would tenderly kiss,*
> *I would know how happy I could be—*
> *Happier still, if only you'd love me.*
> *If only you'd love me.*

At the same time, Elizabeth had the idea that if she looked older she might leapfrog over teen roles to play adults. She had affected everything she could to land the part of young Velvet, so now she hectored her mother until she bought her a strapless black evening gown and let her bring lipstick and face powder home from the makeup department. Elizabeth "was becoming more conscious of clothes and of her appearance," her mother said years later, "and she began collecting perfume." She also apparently developed a jewelry fetish almost as intense as her love for animals ("the bigger bangles the better," according to one reporter) and began to worry about her weight ("I like everything that's fattening—I can eat a whole pie"). Sara coached her to lower the pitch of her voice, which was the least successful effort.

"She tried everything to look older," according to Sara. "She painted her fingernails and toenails scarlet. She wore earrings the size of curtain rings, and peasant skirts and blouses that made her look like a fortune teller. She belted her waist in until she had a perfect hourglass figure—but all to no avail. No one asked her for a date." The reason for that was simple: the overscheduling and exaggerated discipline of which Elizabeth later complained removed almost every opportunity of normal socializing on her own time. But in this enterprise Sara was not alone: Metro insisted on preserving her reputation, and so warnings were issued about the contractual clause proscribing "moral turpitude." It was, in other words, a life of constant supervision and restraint. If she was to be a child star, there would be no precipitous rush to adulthood. Only when Sara and the studio decided she should be an adult—by playing an adult on-screen and in public—could Elizabeth move forward. Until then,

> My life was not my own. The studio and my parents formed a conspiracy to protect my innocence. I couldn't go to the ladies' room on the lot without my mother or the teacher accompanying me. They were convinced I'd be attacked. They meant well, but it was such an invasion of my sense of self [that] I felt as if I were living under a microscope.

"Her life," according to Darryl Hickman, another MGM juvenile star, "belonged to the studio and the public."

Metro, meanwhile, had to keep her name and face in the press; the alternative was instant oblivion. Chief publicist Howard Strickling and his staff were charged, therefore, with supplying a flow of suitably edifying stories to magazines and newspapers.

"Elizabeth Taylor Loves Animals and Out-of-doors," ran a headline story in *Life* on February 26, 1945. There she was, with her pet chipmunk Nibbles; her cat Jill; Twinkle, a cocker spaniel; Monty, a golden retriever; and Spot, a springer spaniel. Her quiet, affectionate personality, said the story, had a "hypnotic effect on dogs and horses." The *Los Angeles Times* caught the bait, too, with a story titled "Horses or Chipmunks—They All Love Elizabeth Taylor." And *Look* magazine, which began a lifetime love affair, took Strickling's lead and hailed her as the "junior screen find" whose "British-born father" had rescued her from "bomb-rocked England" after she "danced for the King and Queen." And so continued the media mythicizing of Elizabeth Taylor, created and disseminated according to the post–World War II ethos of charm and innocence of which the American girl was to be the epitome.

The publicity department at Metro also invented a literary phenomenon for Elizabeth. She was encouraged to chronicle her adventures with animals in a notebook, which the studio then turned over to a New York publisher. Thus it happened that, in 1946, the firm of Duell, Sloan and Pearce published *Nibbles and Me*, Elizabeth's tale of her friendship with a chipmunk. The book was of course intended as free publicity before the release of *The Courage of Lassie* during the summer of 1946, and, chock full of production photographs for more advertising, so it was (although the text refers only to *Blue Sierra*, which must have confused moviegoers).

After more than a year of idleness, there was still no script for Elizabeth. In the spring of 1946, however, Jack Warner negotiated with Metro to borrow her for his screen version of *Life With Father*, the Broadway hit that tallied a run of 3,224 performances. This comedy, set in New York, 1883, was essentially a series of family vignettes, but there was a minor role for a visiting ingenue who falls in love with Father's oldest son. Elizabeth stood for fittings for her period costumes in early April and played her first scene before the cameras in Burbank at the end of that month. (Despite her small role, Metro insisted that "no other member of the cast can be billed in as large-sized type, which is 75% of the size for [Irene] Dunne and [William] Powell.")

Elizabeth's appearances in the film show her a radiantly beautiful fourteen-year-old, of whom is required nothing more than the stereotypical romantic swoons and feigned haughtiness of a petulant teenager. The critics, when they noticed her at all, simply mentioned her evident physical charm. After completing *Life With Father*, she could list seven films on her résumé, but only one leading role, the preteen Velvet. Nothing suggested that the swiftly maturing Elizabeth Taylor would be an exception on the list of those eventually described as "former child stars" and dismissed into history.

From her first day at work with Elizabeth at Warner Bros., Sara's supervision caused problems—most of all, because she treated her daughter like a fragile, precious porcelain and expected similar consideration from the men at the studio. At her insistence, for example, the Warner studio teacher came for private sessions in Elizabeth's dressing room, "so that she would not be subjected to any draft and can rest easily" (thus production manager Eric Stacey, in a note filed on April 29). This, of course, further isolated the girl from normal socializing.

Furthermore, on May 25, Stacey wrote that Elizabeth arrived cheerfully on the set but "Mrs. Taylor claimed her daughter was not able to work due to [a] sore throat." Because Elizabeth's sudden withdrawal would upset the schedule of *Life With Father*, she was first sent to the studio nurse. But the girl felt quite well, her temperature was normal, and (Stacey continued) "First Aid says she is not sick— but her mother insisted on her not working. Accordingly, Miss Taylor was permitted to go home."

Sara's action is not easy to fathom—until it is understood that Irene Dunne, not alone among Hollywood actresses, was permitted by terms of her contract to be absent from filming during the days of her menstrual period. When Sara learned of this privilege, she forthwith demanded a similar privilege for her daughter on every subsequent picture. Meantime, she took Elizabeth home on precisely those days each month, pleading either a sinus infection or a bad cold. No one at Warner was deceived, and there was considerable resentment when her absences caused a series of costly interruptions to *Life With Father.*

In this regard, there is an important memorandum in the *Life*

With Father files of the Warner Bros. Collection at the University of Southern California. Written by Warner executive Phil Friedman to colleague Irving Kumin on May 29, 1946, the item reports a conversation between Friedman and Billy Grady, a member of the Metro talent department. Grady warned Friedman that "Elizabeth Taylor is a nervous, highstrung youngster whose condition has caused her to absent herself fairly frequently from the pictures which she worked on for them." The crews of Elizabeth's films learned that Sara's presence on the set, coaching and encouraging her daughter, was not an unmixed blessing.

But most difficult of all for Elizabeth was her parents' separation, beginning in the autumn of 1946. At least two biographers have claimed that this was caused by Sara Taylor's romantic involvement with Michael Curtiz, the director of *Life With Father.* In the absence of supporting evidence or statements from those involved, it is impossible to assess the rumor. What is clear is that a rupture occurred in the Taylor household, lasting almost a year, until the summer of 1947. Elizabeth and Sara moved to a beach house in Malibu, while Francis and Howard Taylor stayed at Elm Drive and spent several long holidays with the Youngs at their country home in Wisconsin. Of this time, Elizabeth later said significantly, "I looked on Benny Thau [an MGM executive] and Jules Goldstone [her attorney] as my two fathers, and I went to them for help and for advice." With Sydney Guilaroff also in attendance, she did not lack for paternal surrogates, which, given her father's stated indifference to her career, she much needed.

Elizabeth's first dates were with older men, too. An escort named Bill Lyon, from Metro's publicity department, accompanied her to Roddy McDowall's eighteenth birthday party, in September 1946. He recalled that Elizabeth "danced continually, but with older men." And so, as she said later, Elizabeth "didn't date. I had no friends my age except for other child actors at MGM. I rode horses and acted." Indeed, boys her own age were mostly awed by her. "They didn't dare approach her," according to Lyon, "because they felt they didn't have a chance with her." Her glamorous appearance, her quickly blossoming figure, her constant publicity—all these conspired to widen the separation from other young people, and to deny her the chance for any normal socializing.

This cycle of isolation, the first great disadvantage she was to feel from fame and looks, aggravated the anxiety Elizabeth must have felt about her parents' troubled relationship. She was glad, that autumn of 1946, to begin work as the title character of a little gem called *Cynthia*, based on Viña Delmar's play *The Rich Full Life*. But as rehearsals began, she saw how clearly the girl's situation mirrored her own. The script told of Cynthia's sheltered life, and of her anxious parents. Her first date, and her release from an imposed social isolation, occurs when she is courted by an ex-marine at the high school dance. The role was ideally suited for Elizabeth, whose performance was poignantly affecting.

To it, she brought much of her recent experience. During a week of rehearsals, writers Harold Buchman and Charles Kaufman—at Elizabeth's suggestion, it must be noted—added an adorable puppy Cynthia wishes to keep but has to turn out because of her allergies. She was, in other words, still the same gentle friend of animals, the heroine of *National Velvet* and the Lassie movies, but carefully presented by Metro: a girl whose charm is still Hollywood-innocent, unseductive, uncompromised by sexual adventure and unchallenged by the responsibilities of adulthood. In addition, the element of sickness as excuse was more sharply focused as the shooting progressed. And just as Elizabeth's minor physical complaints were exploited by Sara during *Life With Father*—the better to present her daughter as a delicate star who deserved special attention—so *Cynthia* confirmed Elizabeth in her only frame of reference, her movie role. "I think she might have carried her ill and ailing on-camera role into real life," said a crew member.

Playing to the hilt a girl who is disallowed a life of her own, an ingenue smothered by benevolent overprotection, Elizabeth further closed the gap between her on-screen role and her offscreen self. "I've never heard anything but 'You can't' and 'No,' Mother!" Cynthia cries to Mary Astor in a line straight from her own life. Longing to rebel, to move out into the world as an adult woman, Elizabeth the actress helped director Robert Z. Leonard find the telling touches to illuminate the feelings of a young woman trapped by circumstances. "If I could only have one dress without such a high neck!" Elizabeth/Cynthia laments before slicing off a prim covering so she can wear an off-the-shoulder prom gown. The drafts of the script and the production files of *Cynthia* are unambiguous: the star of the film was no passive pawn. Summoned by the writers and director to help shape the role, she did so with pithy suggestions that made Cynthia honest, generous and compassionate—precisely the qualities Elizabeth most admired in others. "Miss Taylor breathes plenty of life into the title role," wrote the critic for *Variety*, and Howard Barnes, writing in the New York *Herald Tribune*, rightly noted her "grave charm and subtle authority."

More to the point, the first day the creators of *Cynthia* encouraged her participation in refining the wardrobe, dialogue and action of her character, Elizabeth Taylor began to see each Hollywood story as containing the only resolutions to life's problems. School was the Metro school, wardrobe the Metro wardrobe. Knowing little of life except what the studio provided, she pitched herself into her teenage years knowing only the discipline and the forms of movie stories. With "no real life of my own," as she said, she was only the Elizabeth Taylor who was coiffed, dressed, given dialogue—only the person she was in the movies. Cossetted at school and overprotected at home, Cynthia and Elizabeth both longed to be independent women. With fathers submerged in their businesses and mothers absorbed in the lives of their daughters, Cynthia and Elizabeth seemed to have no chance. But Cynthia met Ricky—by design, the same lanky, likable James Lydon who had courted her in *Life With Father*—and so Elizabeth, too, believed a boy would rescue her. "If my celebrity status didn't keep friends away," she said later,

> then my protected upbringing did. My parents wouldn't let me enjoy any of the normal activities I played on screen, [and] the result was that I never relied much on relationships outside my family . . . Without the usual crowd of peers most teens use to define themselves, I knew I would have to grow up even faster . . . to find a place away from both my parents' house and the studio.

And so by a slow process of immersion into those stories—and because she was a naturally gifted actress—she grafted small elements of her own life onto her characters. The movies became first for her, as the studio hoped they would become for audiences, a kind of sympathetic magic, talismen of illusions. But for audiences departing theaters, there was a sudden reconnection to reality. Not so for Elizabeth Taylor. After a day's work or a film's production, she took away the structure and neatness of the movie as if it were her guide to life. This, of course, was courting disaster. In time, with her growing power over entire projects, the roles and the woman would often fuse ever more closely, and audiences would, equally often, see only the Elizabeth she wanted them to see—the only Elizabeth of whom she could be confident.

By the summer of 1947, however, fifteen-year-old Elizabeth was confident of very little. On July 13, she was interviewed on the radio show of gossip columnist Louella Parsons, where she dismissed any conversation about her father and brother, from whom she was still temporarily separated. "Daddy is busy with the art gallery and my brother is all concentrated on his own concerns. But Mother looks after my career and doles out my allowance." As for her future: "I want to become a great actress. But most of all I really want to snare a husband." The desire for freedom, from the restrictions imposed by Sara and the studio, had never been more clearly felt or implied.

The Taylor domestic crisis placed Metro in a potentially embarrassing situation: adverse publicity about an ingenue's family was to be avoided at all cost. Therefore, with a hint and a helpful check (delivered as a bonus), Sara and Elizabeth were sent off to England for a holiday. They closed the house at Malibu the last week of July, and as Francis and Howard departed for a fishing trip with the Youngs in Wisconsin, mother and daughter departed on the *Queen Mary* for Southampton. Food or water contamination sent a number of passengers to bed with intestinal distress and high fever, the Taylors among them, and at her sickest Elizabeth comforted herself with the thought that, like the frail Cynthia, she would like to have a house pet. "Please, mother, may I have a dog?" she begged again and again, bringing to life an early scene from her most recent picture. "As soon as she was able," Sara recalled, "we went to a pet shop and bought not one but two dogs." Once recovered, Elizabeth's two months in London were spent mostly shopping for clothes and revisiting scenes of her childhood.

A cable brought them back to Hollywood in September, where a supporting role had been assigned to her in a silly Metro picture about teenage romantic anxieties, based on a popular radio program of the time. In *A Date With Judy*, Elizabeth was the dark-haired, vaguely sultry schoolmate and friendly rival of blond Jane Powell. In luscious Technicolor, she again looked splendid in sumptuous outfits by Helen Rose, and she acted appropriately haughty at one moment and lovestruck the next. But this pallid comedy provided her with wooden dialogue and a one-dimensional character, and once again Hollywood—like the critics—saw little more to require of her than a pleasing appearance.

Unfortunately, her real acting talent, which was becoming more natural, more delicate and suggestive with each characterization, went ignored by both the studio and the critics, and because the scripts were inferior, the public saw little more than a hauntingly lovely face and an alluring figure. At precisely the same time, Marilyn Monroe (to name only one other apprentice whose beauty was a burden) was coming up through the Hollywood ranks. She, too, would develop an impressive ability based on intuition rather than intellection, and, like Elizabeth, her gifts would be generally ignored; she was put in picture after picture simply as a pretty presence.

Robert Stack, a costar in *A Date With Judy*, felt that Elizabeth's life was unnatural and unhappy—that instead of being a movie star, always enveloped in a life that was "all tinsel and moonlight," she should have been allowed a more normal life in the world. "She wanted to know what it was like to go to a basketball game, or to go on a date to a drive-in—simple things that would never happen in her life," recalled Debbie Reynolds, who met Elizabeth that year and was exactly her age.

When she was not filming, she was posing for still photographers; when she was not on the set, she was in the studio school-room. Her life so far had been a dutiful acquiescence whose financial assets were obvious but whose liabilities were not yet entirely clear to her. And so, preoccupied with finding a means of escape, she naturally dreamed of romance as the answer to her problems, just as it was for the characters she portrayed. "I know exactly the man I want to marry," she told Jane Powell in words worthy of Velvet Brown on the make. "I want someone who can keep me in horses."

In early 1948, Elizabeth completed *A Date With Judy*, and when it was released that summer she was hailed as "a young woman as exciting to the eye as Vivien Leigh once was" and "a 14-carat, 100-proof siren with a whole new career opening in front of her," for she was "rapidly developing into one of the real beauties of the screen." Thus a representative sampling of the reviews.

But the rapid development had short-circuited the natural process of maturation. Denied the ordinary experiences of the adolescent girl and rushed into glamorous roles, she remained in some ways younger than her age. "I had the body of a woman and the mind of a child," she said accurately of this time, when she reached her full adult height of five foot four and her ideal weight of 120 pounds. Impatient with her life and her career, lonely for friends outside and constricted at home, she was pitched into a fierce depression for several weeks that winter.

Her sixteenth birthday, in February 1948, was celebrated during the production of *Julia Misbehaves*, which was the lowest point of her early film work. A party was thrown on the film set, and a buffet was served with the cast still in costume. Metro gave her a new wardrobe, fans sent cards and presents. Where did illusion end and life begin? Certainly there was nothing realistic about the gift from her parents, a new Cadillac convertible (with gold keys) which she was forbidden to drive. It was fitted with a miniature steering wheel on the passenger side for Elizabeth's year of lessons with her mother.

Julia Misbehaves, alas, was a tedious, damp and unfunny project. Elizabeth was cast as Susan Packett, a wealthy girl who invites her estranged actress mother to her wedding. In so doing, she not only rediscovers this lost relationship but also orchestrates the reconciliation of her divorced parents (Greer Garson and Walter Pidgeon, in their sixth film together) and—longing for a life of her own—shifts her romantic allegiance from one (unseen) beau to a handsome new one (Peter Lawford).

Elizabeth and Sara found that *Julia Misbehaves* paralleled events in their own family life: like Susan Packett, Elizabeth had, quietly but successfully, arranged for her parents to meet and begged them to patch up their differences. And there was a further blurring of the distinction between on-screen roles and offscreen reality: not long after completing the picture, Elizabeth was convinced that, also like Susan, she had found true love, and that therefore she would soon have a new life. "When other teenage girls were reading romantic stories and imagining themselves as the heroine," said Sara, "Elizabeth was *living* her dream world, by acting the role of the heroine— that is, at the studio."

Precisely how should Sara Taylor's odd remark be understood?

She believed that playing a role *was* living a life, and Elizabeth certainly took each role as an ordained, almost prophetic guide to finding her way. But this is at the least a slippery illusion and at the worst a dangerous self-deception. Her daughter could not indeed "live a dream world by acting the role of the heroine at the studio." To believe in the illusion and attempt to make reality coincide with it made that illusion no longer innocent: it became more fantastic than any ordinary adolescent's daydreams, easily punctured by a mother's call to household chores, or a reminder of algebra homework, or a classmate's invitation to a game. But these, after all, were realities completely foreign to Elizabeth Taylor, who was now considered, far and wide, one of the real beauties of the screen.

Chapter Four

1948–1951

M Y TEENAGE VISION OF THE world," said Elizabeth Taylor at fifty-five, "was distorted by the fact that I never had many girlfriends my own age." In fact she seems to have had none, and this was a singularly poignant deficiency when her first feelings of romantic love blossomed. A peer would have asked questions, raised doubts and challenged her—or at least given Elizabeth the chance to talk out her feelings. As it was, there was only Sara, and this meant problems from the start. To her mother, nothing should stand in the way of the sixteen-year-old's ongoing career.

The object of her affections was a tall, russet-haired, twenty-three-year-old athlete named Glenn Davis, a 1947 West Point graduate with (thus the United States Military Academy yearbook) "a prize-winning smile and a good-natured personality." Winner of the Heisman Trophy and numerous football awards, he was also a star center fielder with a .350 batting average. Doris Kearns, who was handling Elizabeth's publicity at Metro, brought Davis along to the Taylors' summer bungalow at Malibu for a Sunday brunch. "I took one look at him," said Elizabeth, "and thought, 'O ye gods, no!' He was so wonderful!"

Davis was equally captivated by Elizabeth and flattered by her attention and hero worship. But there was an additional element in the setup. After graduating West Point, Glenn Davis had come on leave to Hollywood, where he appeared as himself in a low-budget movie called *The Spirit of West Point*. To this there were favorable reactions and, it was hoped, perhaps a future career in movies (if not one in professional sport). That summer of 1948, he had just completed twenty-two weeks of infantry training at Fort Benning; now he was spending the summer in Los Angeles, playing football and preparing for a two-year tour of duty in Korea, scheduled to begin in September.

Doris Kearns immediately saw some potentially favorable publicity, in the spirit of "All-American Hero Dates MGM's Teenage Star." Kearns also knew she need not worry about Davis's conduct or Elizabeth's virginity, for Sara supervised her daughter, and Glenn was a sensible man not inclined to ruin his life—which at that time would have been the immediate result of anything other than virtuous, chaperoned dating with a famous sixteen-year-old. "From then on," recalled Sara, remembering her concern, "Glenn was down at our beach house every minute that Elizabeth was there."

The romance proceeded innocently that summer. Because she was filming *Little Women* at Metro from late June to mid-September, her meeting times with Davis were restricted to weekends. One Sunday afternoon, they window-shopped in Beverly Hills, and Elizabeth admired a piece of jewelry on display in a window. Next day, Davis bought it for her: a necklace of sixty-nine graduated pearls. It was, he said sweetly, only what a movie star deserved. And with that, Elizabeth Taylor received the first in a lifelong series of additions to a collection she, too, always considered "only what she deserved" as a movie star.

Also on weekends, Elizabeth watched Davis playing on the football field with the Los Angeles Rams, in their exhibition games. With the fans, she shouted, "We want Davis! We want Davis!" and then her voice topped them all: "I want Davis—I want Davis!"

Whereupon, she turned to her shocked mother and added, "And don't think I don't mean it!" The press—encouraged by Doris Kearns and company—headlined the matter out of all proportion to reality: a teenage crush became a romance of major international importance. For the first time, journalists could offer the public something other than news of her film career.

From this time and for the rest of her life, Elizabeth Taylor would always live within the unnatural world of publicity. *Little Women* was, by contrast, an unexceptional event. Fitted with a strawberry blond wig, Elizabeth played the nervous, haughty Amy with sharp, restrained comic timing, but hers was very much a supporting role to June Allyson as Jo. Episodic and drenched in bogus sentimentality, *Little Women* sank under the weight of its own bloated production values.

On September 8, the eve of his departure from Los Angeles for Korea, Glenn Davis added to his gifts for Elizabeth his all-America sweater and a gold football, sentimental trophies much in the spirit of the time. "Letters came in bunches from Korea," according to Sara, "and she spent half her time hanging over her desk writing in return. All of which proves that my daughter's movie career has given her no degree of sophistication." This odd comment can be explained by the fact that Sara did not quite approve of Davis and hoped that Elizabeth would meet another young man with more favorable credentials. Her daughter's contract for the coming year, after all, had just been renegotiated for $1,000 weekly: she should, in Sara's judgment, select a better (which meant a wealthier) beau than a professional athlete—a career that did not, at the time, provide a princely salary. Besides, her daughter was only sixteen.

"Elizabeth and I are so close we practically think as one person," Sara told a reporter. "When she makes a decision, I find it's always the same thing I would have done. We always seem to agree on everything." Which was an oblique way of saying that Elizabeth, like it or not, would do what she was told.

Metro had the right to give orders, too, and in fact the studio had plans for her to travel—with her mother, of course—to England, where Metro would star Elizabeth in her first adult leading role. Beginning November 9, 1948, she appeared as the twenty-one-year-old wife of Robert Taylor in *Conspirator*, the story of a British officer who is a spy for Russia. The result, a pallid thriller, owed its best moments more to Elizabeth's mature acting than to her costar's somewhat languid, unctuous glamour and the cliché-peppered script. She plays a loving wife without arch coyness, and, when she learns her husband is a traitor, her face registers more than shock: one senses the haze of happier memories flashing across the screen of her mind. In love scenes, she is composed without being remote or wooden; in tense sequences, she is anguished but controlled. One singularly fine moment occurs when a friend asks if she is still in love with her husband after learning the truth: "No," she replies in a choked whisper, her lips trembling, "I'm only afraid of him."

"She has acquired complete repose in her work," said director Victor Saville, and so she had. *Conspirator*, another mediocre picture with yet another redeeming performance by Elizabeth Taylor, showed ever more clearly that this was an actress routinely assigned to projects beneath her talent. But Elizabeth was characteristically unaware of her own achievement: "I hope not many people have seen [it.]" Nor did she, in the matter of the source or basis of her gifts, make any grand esthetic pretensions.

> I never had an acting lesson, and I don't know how to act per se.
> I just developed as an actress. Acting is instinctive with me. It's
> mostly concentration . . . Usually it isn't at all hard to get a char-
> acter. Mostly, I just read my lines through three times at night
> and then I go to sleep like a log and don't think about anything. I
> don't sit down and figure should I do this gesture or should I do
> that. I know it sounds funny for me to say, but it just seems easy,
> that's all.

Which, in fact, is one of the reasons why her performances always seem so unforced, natural and inevitable. They were achieved without self-consciousness, without analysis, without any attempt to vitiate spontaneity by intellection. "I went from childhood to

ingenue to leading lady at sixteen," she said years later. And as leading lady, she believed that she was a mature woman; as she soon
learned, that was another matter entirely.

During that autumn at the MGM studios outside London, she
lunched with Victor Cazalet's niece, an old friend from her childhood, who asked if Elizabeth might arrange an introduction to
Michael Wilding, who was also at work on a film there. A producer
easily did so the next day.

Twenty years Elizabeth's senior, the handsome English actor was
an elegant, polished gentleman, indulgent toward the cute, naive
sayings of teenage girls. He spoke of art, for he had been an artist
before turning to acting, and he still painted often and brilliantly.
He talked of European travel, making it sound somehow more
exotic and alluring than Elizabeth had imagined. He fascinated the
girls with accounts of British bravery on the home front during the
war. A few days earlier, Elizabeth and her mother had been presented to the Queen at a command performance in London, and a
week later she met Prince Philip, husband of Princess Elizabeth. But
in the eyes of Sara Sothern's daughter, Michael Wilding eclipsed
even the royal family. But for the moment, that was that: Wilding
returned to work on his movie, Elizabeth on hers.

After a shopping expedition to Paris, where Elizabeth temporarily
slaked her thirst for new clothes, she and her mother returned to
America in February 1949. Francis met them in New York, whence
they proceeded to Howard Young's winter retreat at Star Island,
Florida, for Elizabeth's seventeenth birthday. And there, at a dinner
party on March 3, she proved that she was, as she said, "wildly
infatuated with love." This time the man was William D. Pawley, Jr.,
the twenty-eight-year-old son of a former ambassador to Brazil who
was then president of the Miami Transit Company.

Dark-haired, with a rakish mustache and the good looks of a
movie star, Pawley had been a pilot during the war and was a successful businessman. He was also profoundly conservative in his
views on just about everything. At once he smothered Elizabeth

with attention: driving lessons, golf lessons, luncheon parties, dances. Sara Taylor was enchanted by the wealthy bachelor with *Social Register* status. And Elizabeth, on vacation, forgot her career and fell precipitously in love as only an isolated seventeen-year-old can—as much with the good life as with the smooth and confident Mr. Pawley. As for Sara, she, too, was caught in a dilemma. She had never resolved the collision between her own love of career and her choice of marriage, and now she was spurring her daughter in the same two opposing directions. She might be willing to allow Elizabeth to be sprung free from her job, but only into the arms of a desirable husband.

And then things became more complicated still. When Glenn Davis returned from Korea on leave in March, he rang the Taylors from California: could he travel to see Elizabeth in Florida? Of course, she replied, and she brought her parents with her to meet him at the airport. Flashbulbs popped, and photographs of the army's football hero and the movie star were wired round the world. "He is expected to give Elizabeth Taylor her engagement ring," ran the accompanying stories, breathless with presumptuous prophetic insight.

But, in fact, as Sara acknowledged, "Elizabeth had outgrown her first love." After two days of polite meetings, Glenn Davis (who never proposed marriage) returned to California on March 21. "Maybe I should have fallen for a busboy or something," she told reporter Bob Thomas at the time. "Then the whole thing wouldn't cause so much attention." And to Louella Parsons (and thus the nation) she confided, "I was never in love with Glenn." Later, she elaborated: "Neither of us had come anywhere near the point where the public believed we had arrived. Even though I had thought myself so worldly and mature, I simply didn't know how to handle it all."

As it happened, Bill Pawley was soon talking of an imminent engagement. But he expressed his resentment of Elizabeth's career (which he saw as distracting her from him); he decried the constant publicity; he denounced her deep décolletage; he hated her interviews and her meetings with visiting Metro producers; he berated her plans to make just one more film before settling down. Pawley was intractable: if Elizabeth Taylor was to become Mrs. Pawley, she would have to change her name and give up this silly business of movie stardom. For the time being, she found this strong, controlling man an exciting presence in her life. Her own father was by now a shadowy presence, cordial but emotionally distant, while the Metro executives were impersonal bosses. Bill Pawley took charge, and Bill Pawley meant freedom from both home and work.

However one judges Pawley's exacting attitude, he was on the mark in assessing Elizabeth's life as fantastic. Not yet eighteen, she had become a national ideal of beauty, and nothing about her was made to appear typical. Part of the fiction, of course, was the bromide that she was just a normal, everyday teenager—a recurring cliché that was too absurd for comment. Surrounded by people telling her she was gorgeous, important, gifted, charming and irresistible, Elizabeth was simultaneously warned not to wear the wrong clothes, not to appear without makeup or with her hair undone, not to eat too many potatoes or too much ice cream. She was irreplaceable, she was magical, she was stunning—but she must take care to stand still for the cameras, to smile for the press, to sit demurely and say the right things in public, and to please lower her voice, for although her diction was fine, she tended to a certain shrillness. She was, in other words, the American equivalent of a royal person— but she had better be careful, or she would be rejected by her people and replaced by some pretty parvenue.

On March 23, two days after Glenn Davis left Florida for California, Metro summoned Elizabeth back to Hollywood, where Davis gallantly escorted her to the town's rites of spring and she presented the Oscar for costume design. Wearing a low-cut white taffeta gown, she walked onstage to the tune of "Did You Ever See a Dream Walking?"

Pawley followed soon after, pressing his intentions, urging her to leave Hollywood and move permanently to Florida. Elizabeth was confused, for (thus Sara) "I think she knew even then she couldn't give up acting"—perhaps because it was all she knew and represented her only security; perhaps, too, because she had become dependent on the attention, the privileges, the adoration. She was queen of the Miss Junior America Pageant, and the Jewelry Council named her Princess of the Industry's 1949 Jubilee. Wearing a $22,000 diamond tiara, she asked, "May I keep it?" She could not, but she was allowed to wear it around town for a week.

"She has the temperament to become a great star," said Billy Grady of Metro's talent department, "and when she begins to show it—oh, brother!" And show it she did. She needed more clothes, she told her bosses at Metro. She wanted a mink stole. She had overdrawn her account during her Paris shopping spree: would Metro cover the deficit? They did. "That's when I knew I was important to them—otherwise they would have sacked me!"

On June 2, Elizabeth and her mother were back in Florida as houseguests of Pawley's parents, and four days later Bill slipped an emerald-cut diamond on her finger and Sara formally announced her daughter's engagement. The wedding, she said, would be the following spring, after Elizabeth's eighteenth birthday, and then the Pawleys would live permanently in Florida. "In Hollywood, I could never be anything but Elizabeth Taylor," the actress said, "but in Miami I'll be Elizabeth Pawley—and I'll like that!"

But it was only the idea of independence that she really liked, and as the summer of 1949 continued, the condition of being engaged to the somewhat autocratic Pawley lost its charm. And Elizabeth missed Hollywood. "The big diamond on her finger began to look less glamorous," wrote hostess Elsa Maxwell, who was on the scene. "She began to be irked by the restrictions of being engaged. She had asked for it, yes, but she became less and less sure she wanted it when she watched a young group pair off without her." By the end of July, Elizabeth was more uncertain than ever: she had acted a wife only once—in *Conspirator*, and that had a tragic finale. Of actual marriage she knew nothing other than her parents' strained and detached situation. Happy endings occurred only in the movies.

As if on cue, Metro provided the necessary breathing space. On August 1, she was summoned back to Culver City to appear in a comedy called *The Big Hangover*, in which Van Johnson played a veteran whose allergy to alcohol threatens his future as a lawyer. Elizabeth was cast as the wealthy boss's daughter, an amateur psychologist who falls in love with him precisely because of his problem. "She's maternal, that's all!" her on-screen mother tells her on-screen father in *The Big Hangover.* "She was that way as a child, even with her pets."

Her performance, as usual, was notable for her blithe charm and casual confidence; the role, designed for the girl who had tended sick horses and dogs in movies, intrigued her. To the production, she gave herself energetically, asking for textbooks on alcoholism and on psychiatric therapy. And as filming progressed that August, Elizabeth came to believe—this was the subtheme of the picture, after all—that a woman ought to provide care, that she ought to be a healer for her man.

Bill Pawley, meantime, flew to Hollywood and continually urged her to fix the date of their wedding and to inform Metro that her contract would forthwith be dissolved. His pressure, however, was counterproductive. On September 17, they attended Jane Powell's wedding. Elizabeth caught the bridal bouquet, but the cheers must have rung hollow for her. That night, after a long, private conversation with his fiancée, Pawley returned to Florida, and next day the end of their engagement was released to the press. The immediate reason for the breakup was Elizabeth's announcement to Bill that she was about to begin work on a major movie that would take her out of town and keep her occupied for the next several months.

"I love her very much and I believe she loves me," said Pawley, "but due to the distance and her constant work, which all her energy should go into, I feel the only fair thing is to release her from her engagement. So we are calling it off, you might say, because of circumstances beyond our control." Elizabeth, years later, was more trenchant: "We went well together under the palm trees; we looked nice on the dance floor; we loved to go boating; we had nothing in common in our lives."

Whatever may have been the admixture of disappointment and relief, Elizabeth seemed not to grieve. The night Pawley departed, she and the Powell wedding party hopped off to the Mocambo nightclub to hear Vic Damone, who subsequently dated Elizabeth once or twice—with the expected result, for some journalists wrongly announced that love was again in the Taylor air. But by this time, Metro had concluded negotiations to loan her out to Paramount Studios for a starring role, opposite Montgomery Clift, in George Stevens's production of *A Place in the Sun*. For ten weeks of work on the film, she received her contracted Metro salary of $1,000 weekly, and so Metro, charging Paramount $35,000, made a handy $25,000 profit. On October 2, she and Sara left Los Angeles for location shooting at Lake Tahoe.

The film became something like a signature work in the life and career of Elizabeth Taylor, for her darkly sensuous appeal, high-lighted by strapless gowns and lush, filtered lighting, is an emblem of everything Clift's character desires.

The story is straightforward: Clift portrays a poor young man who longs for a higher place on the corporate and social ladder. His dreams of marrying the wealthy Taylor are threatened when his girl-friend, played by Winters, becomes pregnant. She drowns in a boat-ing accident and he is (wrongly) convicted of murder and executed.

As Angela Vickers, Elizabeth herself is a living portrait of the place in the sun, the beautiful, unwittingly seductive doll set oppo-site the whining, mousy character played by blond Shelley Winters. Theodore Dreiser's naturalistic, moralizing novel *An American Tragedy* had indicted America's mechanized society, which (he believed) seduces men with dreams of extravagant luxury. George Stevens's film of Michael Wilson and Harry Brown's script, on the other hand, is something both more and less. The best job, the right car, entrance into an aristocratic society, the longing for everything that is The Good Life—all of it is linked to a man's disordered sexual desires. Yet *A Place in the Sun* has it both ways: the viewer likes Clift (despite his character's almost complete lack of volition) and wants him to be with Taylor rather than Winters.

Elizabeth gave her most finely modulated performance thus far, thanks to Stevens's insistence that she go deeper with each repeated take he demanded. "He didn't make me feel like a puppet," she said. "He was an insinuating director. He gave indications of what

he wanted but didn't tell you specifically what to do or how to
move. He would just say, 'No, stop—that's not quite right,' and
make you get it from your insides and do it again until it was the
way he wanted it." As for Stevens:

> If she thought I was more severe [with her] than needed, she'd
> spit fire. But the following morning she had forgotten it com-
> pletely. [She] simply couldn't bear a grudge. What a lovely child
> she was . . . She had enormous beauty but she wasn't charmed by
> it. It was there. It was a handicap and she discouraged people
> being overimpressed with it. She was seventeen, and she had
> been an actress all her life. The only thing was to prod her a bit
> into realizing her dramatic potential.

Stevens also appreciated how much the movie studio was like a
surrogate father to Elizabeth: "like a domineering parent," he called
it. "All day long, some official was telling her what to do and what
not to do."

Although she would work in two later films under Stevens's
direction and two with Montgomery Clift, the most significant relationship Elizabeth took away from *A Place in the Sun* was with the
gravely self-destructive and almost psychotically guilt-ridden Clift,
twelve years her senior. Certainly one of the most beautiful couples
to costar since Greta Garbo and John Gilbert or Ingrid Bergman
and Cary Grant, Taylor and Clift supplemented their work with a
deepening friendship offscreen, and with a growing interdependence that was somehow eerily reflected in an astonishingly similar
appearance. Both were dark-haired, with radiant, almost translucent
eyes, and both had a kind of painful shyness, a lack of conviction
about their talents; each, too, implied that within there were passionate fires just barely banked. Regarding them in profile years
later, it takes only a little imagination to see them as halves of a single person—anima and animus, neatly conjoined.

To no one's surprise, Elizabeth quickly fell in love with the
angular, brooding, hard-drinking Clift, and she committed herself
to encouraging him in his tenuous self-esteem just as he coached

her in a more serious approach to acting. Although he had romantic feelings for women, Clift's sexual passion was reserved for men, and he was simply unavailable to Elizabeth on any level except warm, platonic affection; the full acceptance of this fact required some time for her, especially because Clift was not immediately honest with her. To be sure, Elizabeth was acquainted with many gay actors, directors, executives and producers in Hollywood, and some were among her few friends. But homosexuality was not a matter for conversation in 1949, and until Montgomery Clift, it did not seem to occur to her that a serious, attractive, established stage and screen actor could be unenthusiastic about a physical attachment to a woman.

Years later, she admitted that in some way she recognized "that Monty was torn between what he thought he should be and what he actually was." Until his death, she accepted what he actually was and discouraged his attempts to be anything other. That year, however—both on location and back at the studio in November and December—there was little time to spend quietly with Clift, mostly because of Sara's vigilance. "She's a large pain in the ass," said Elizabeth. Indeed, all during production, elaborated Stevens, the girl was "kept in a cocoon by her mother."

The picture was, as Elizabeth said later, "my first real chance to probe myself, and Monty helped me . . . At first, I was absolutely terrified because Monty was the New York stage actor and I felt very much the inadequate teenage Hollywood sort of puppet that had just worn pretty clothes and hadn't really acted except with horses and dogs." From Clift, she learned the importance of introspection, the value of joining intuition and spontaneity with a certain interior quiet, so that whatever there was in herself of Angela Vickers could surface immediately from concentration. This sense of focus, she said modestly, became "the key to my kind of acting, if you can call it acting." Critics and audiences certainly did when *A Place in the Sun* was finally released in August 1951, after more than a year and a half of editorial tinkering by Stevens. Her performance was (thus *Variety*) "far beyond anything she has done previously"; *Box Office* touted her for an Academy Award; and *The New York Times* praised her "shaded, tender performance."

Her work on it was completed at the end of December 1949, and by this time Elizabeth was being rushed into a very heady courtship indeed. Conrad Nicholas Hilton—always called Nicky— was the twenty-three-year-old son of the international hotelier. Tall and handsome, with brown hair, fair skin and a quick smile, he was one of the country's most eligible bachelors. After navy service, Nicky had studied hotel management in Switzerland, whence he returned to Los Angeles and assumed managerial duties at the luxurious Bel-Air Hotel, in which his father's company had a major interest. A spoiled playboy with little to recommend him apart from material advantages, Nicky had numerous social connections with the beautiful people of the era. "The trouble with me is that I have a millionaire dad," he once said, defending his irresponsible carousing. Indeed, Conrad Hilton, Sr., who liked to cavort with movie stars, had been romantically linked with more than one of them after his divorce from the children's mother, and he had subsequently been married to the most incandescent of the pack, Zsa Zsa Gabor.

Nicky, it was said, first saw Elizabeth in person the previous September evening at the Mocambo; next day, he sought an introduction through a friend whose father was a Paramount executive. This was arranged between takes for a scene of *A Place in the Sun,* and within a week Nicky was escorting Elizabeth on dates—but only after winning the approval of Sara, who proudly said that her daughter "never accepted invitations or made dates until the young men had been at our house and met with our approval." By early in the new year 1950, the Taylors had been guests at the Hilton mansion in Bel-Air, at the lavish Hilton hotel at Arrowhead Springs and the Hilton family retreat on Lake Arrowhead. With Elizabeth, Nicky—all charm—gave the impression of being more settled, less restive than his reputation suggested. But the charm masked a suave guile: if he did not drink heavily in front of the Taylors, he continued to do so secretly—most of all, when he gambled away the night hours with cronies.

Meantime, the increasingly starry-eyed Elizabeth was in the curious position of being wooed by a dashing man-about-town while she tried to complete what passed for a high school education at the Metro schoolhouse. Further complicating that issue was Nicky's request, during the third week of January, that Francis agree to their engagement. This he did, on condition that they await her eighteenth birthday and her earning a high school diploma, which would at least give some patina of maturity to his daughter. With that reply, Nicky prevailed on Elizabeth to expedite the matter of graduation. But the State Board of Education, they learned, required a formal graduation ceremony at a certified school. And would that not mean a delay until at least June?

Not necessarily so, with Metro pulling the academic strings. Elizabeth rushed to complete pro forma examinations in civics, English literature, ceramics and Social Problems, for which her studio tutor gave her a B+ average, rating her "a good student, very good in art, with a flair for writing." As it happened, University High School, in West Los Angeles, scheduled its usual midyear commencement on January 26, and so, with a cadre of reporters and photographers duly alerted by the studio, Elizabeth walked demurely in cap and gown to receive her diploma. But before the ceremony, recalled her classmate Debbie Reynolds, Elizabeth was in tears: she had no friends her own age, she said. She had always been a star and nothing else, and she found life strange and frightening and unfair. "She made my heart hurt," Debbie Reynolds recalled. "Elizabeth went to graduation at University High, but she wasn't one of the class, really. It was more like making a personal appearance. Everybody wanted her autograph. There was no teenage girl's life for Elizabeth."

On February 21, the Taylors hosted a formal tea at their home to announce Elizabeth's engagement. But once again, Nicky was the advance man, as the previous evening he prevailed on his father to tell Louella Parsons that the handsome couple would be married on May 6 in Good Shepherd Catholic Church, Beverly Hills; the Hiltons, after all, were nominally Catholic. The newlyweds would then depart on a three-month honeymoon to Europe, a gift from the Hilton clan. Sara was ecstatic, for the Hilton empire comprised sixteen hotels and was valued at $80,000,000. Marriage into the family, as she saw it, would give the Taylors entrance to a higher life (as the Cazalets had done for them years before)—in effect, they now had a crack at being linked to a real social aristocracy.

As for Elizabeth, marriage meant freedom, independence and the opportunity to live like a grown-up at last, which is what she had been in the movies but not realized in life. In *Life With Father*, *A Date With Judy*, *Julia Misbehaves*, *Conspirator*, *The Big Hangover* and *A Place in the Sun* she had played wealthy young women aspiring to the right marriage: now she would actualize the roles in her life. "I liked playing the role of a young woman in love," she said later, "and when I met Nicky Hilton I was ripe to get married." She would be married, she would soon be a mother. "I don't think I even analyzed whether it was maturity I wanted," she said later. It was, she added, "probably just the glamour of being a [married] woman . . . and the reason I did it so early was to get away from all the supervision, and to begin to live life for myself." Did she think the marriage would last? "Yes, because we both adore oversize sweaters, hamburgers with onions and Ezio Pinza." In so reasoning, said several reporters, she was absolutely serious.

There was also no doubt that sheer physical desire was a major element in her decision to marry, too. She was, Elizabeth said, "driven by feelings that could not be indulged outside of marriage"; at the same time, she was "inexperienced and naive and knew nothing about sex . . . I was married a virgin." Forced to simulate love scenes for the camera, she had no experience of the real thing. It was perhaps not surprising, therefore, when this willowy young beauty sprinkled her speech with obscenities of the most vulgar sort: denied an outlet, her fantasies spilled out into common conversation, as many friends and acquaintances could not forget. Blaine Waller, a nineteen-year-old friend of Montgomery Clift, recalled that "she used more four-letter words than [all] of us put together"; and Harvey Zim, a Paramount press representative, recalled riding with Elizabeth and Clift to the premiere of Clift's film *The Heiress*. Everyone was terrifically nervous for Clift—until

Elizabeth joined the party in the limousine. "She looked ravishing, and she was so foul-mouthed and unconcerned . . . that everybody else relaxed, too."

Once again, the distinction between her roles and herself was blurred by her next studio assignment, in which she played a girl startlingly like herself. On January 16, 1950, she had begun the role of the girl about to be married to a society boy in Vincente Minnelli's film of *Father of the Bride.* Shot in twenty-eight days and completed just hours before the formal announcement of her own engagement, this was a warmly amusing if deeply conventional comedy of manners that elaborated not on the character of the bride but on the social foibles of her parents. Metro, who first announced the details of Elizabeth's forthcoming marriage, saw a potential gold mine: Elizabeth the young bride in a major film, Elizabeth the young bride in reality.

The coincidence of art and life was uncanny. Making movies, she said, had been "like the most magical extension of make-believe," and much that she did was an attempt to make life coincide with that pretense. As she rehearsed a wedding scene in the film, for example, she had only her own imminent ceremony in mind: "Every time we did the shot of me walking up the aisle to the altar, I was living it!" So much, in fact, that the performance remains among her finest, gently comic and deeply affecting. In scenes with Spencer Tracy and Joan Bennett (as her devoted but nervous parents), Elizabeth performed a minor miracle: she conveyed love not with the cliché of the usual breathless, glazed demeanor, but with an occasional catch in her throat, her voice shaking almost to tears as she praises her fiancé's virtues.

Producer Pandro Berman and director Vincente Minnelli everywhere used the props of Elizabeth's own life and instructed the art directors to use her childhood pictures for those of her character, Kay Banks. Her own marriage, she decided as the shooting progressed, would surely be as happy as the final scenes of *Father of the Bride,* notwithstanding forebodings and apprehensions to the contrary. "I closed my eyes to any problems and walked radiantly down the aisle," she said of her real-life marriage, "[but] I was too romantic and unrealistic." Elsewhere, those who knew her and Nicky were fearful: "He'll make a very nice first husband," muttered one savvy studio executive.

As the day approached, Elizabeth's own misgivings began to surface, and, filled with sudden fear and depression, she pleaded a severe cold and was absent from small dinner parties and receptions for three days before the ceremony. There was nothing to do, however, but go ahead with the event.

In many ways, she did this because it was like a call to the set, and this marriage was her new role. After all, Metro had taken over the supervision and planning of every material element of the wedding—their gift, she was told—and they had assigned Helen Rose, who dressed Elizabeth at the studio, to create her wedding gown, which was of course virtually a copy of what she wore in *Father of the Bride*. Delighted with the turn of events in the life of their young contract star, Metro at once planned to release *Father of the Bride* within two weeks of the Hilton wedding, after the first nationwide press frenzy. Studio designers, therefore, were dispatched to the church, to the Taylor home, to the bridesmaids' houses. The flowers, the design of the church sanctuary, the music, the attendants' outfits, the reception at the Bel-Air Hotel: everything was modeled after the wedding in *Father of the Bride*, everything was studio ordered, was made to serve the upcoming product, to show that the movies, after all, are just like life.

On May 6, more than 2,500 people gathered outside the Church of the Good Shepherd and spilled onto the lanes of Santa Monica Boulevard. A squadron from the Beverly Hills Police Department was augmented by a platoon of studio guards from Metro-Goldwyn-Mayer, but they could do little to control the public chaos. By contrast, the five o'clock ceremony was brief and quiet; roars and applause erupted only when the Hiltons emerged from the church and made their way into a limousine. Among the seven hundred guests invited to the reception at the Bel-Air Hotel were Governor Earl Warren, most of the Hollywood A-list of celebrities, and every available person who had been associated with Elizabeth's films. Late that evening, the Hiltons slipped away to their suite, and next day they departed for Pebble Beach, on the Monterey Peninsula. Four days later, they left for a three-month European honeymoon.

"I didn't have one clue how to cope with it."

Fourteen years later, Elizabeth Taylor used those carefully chosen words to describe her misery from the first day of her first marriage. The immediate cause was not difficult to fathom: "She told me," said Raymond Vignale, who later worked several years for her, "that Nicky Hilton had not consummated their marriage until the third night." The reason for this unusual delay—if, as seems unlikely, it had not to do with her maidenly modesty—must be sought in other than simple exhaustion or wedding jitters. The truth is that Nicky drank, Nicky gambled, Nicky drank some more, Nicky became angry, Nicky slept alone. And perhaps, as his later life suggested, Nicky was, in the final analysis, happier with his cronies at the gambling table than in the bridal chamber.

There was, alas, more for her to sustain during the European summer. Reporters waiting in Paris found the Hiltons barely talking, he glum and gum chewing, she impassive, pale, chain-smoking. In three months, she lost twenty pounds. She was traveling with a poodle and seventeen steamer trunks full of new clothes: nothing diverted her from evident unhappiness. She asked him to dance; he declined. In London, Paris and Monte Carlo, she suggested a quiet dinner in their hotel suite; he left her alone. "My first husband was a gambler," she said years later, "and my first honeymoon was one long session at the card and roulette tables. Five months around the casinos. Even the croupiers felt sorry for me." Journalists then found her alone at breakfast, alone on the deck of the *Queen Mary,* always alone unless she accompanied Nicky to the games. The Hiltons quarreled their way across Europe, and it was for her a time of "disillusionment—rude and brutal," as she later said quietly. "I fell off my pink cloud with a thud."

By the time they reached Rome, late that torrid summer, Elizabeth was near collapse after one particularly violent fight. Fleeing their hotel suite and knowing only role-playing as her real life, she learned that Mervyn LeRoy (who had directed her in *Little Women*) was nearby filming the epic *Quo Vadis*. "Can you hide me, Mervyn?" she cried on the telephone. "I don't want him to find me." LeRoy gave her directions to the production site, and, when she arrived, Elizabeth was hurriedly dressed in historic garb and maneuvered into a crowd scene as an unbilled (and unseen) extra. But at the end of the day, she had no choice: after dining with the director, she returned to the hotel. There was a temporary cease-fire in the domestic war.

For years after—until and even after the death of the physically and mentally ravaged Nicky Hilton in 1969, at the age of forty-two—Elizabeth Taylor kept a discreet silence as to the precise cause of the instantaneous breakdown of what was touted as the fairy-tale wedding of postwar America. The sad fact is that there occurred something she could in no way have anticipated: from whatever dark confusion of urges and motives, Nicky Hilton beat his wife.

"He became sullen, angry and abusive, physically and mentally," she said many years later, adding that the marriage collapsed as soon as it had begun. "Bad things were going on—worse than unpleasant . . . really horrendous things." Very soon, a few people knew the shocking truth, when she returned to Los Angeles in September, ill and shaking and easily pitched to tears. One friend remembered Elizabeth wearing a white blouse buttoned to the neck and wrists, but "the marks all the way up her arms" were visible through the sheer fabric. Debbie Reynolds learned, too, that Nicky treated Elizabeth "so terribly" that all her old friends and colleagues were much dismayed. Seventeen years later, the third Mrs. Hilton likewise sued Nicky for divorce, accusing him of "repeated acts and threats of physical violence." The marriage, said Elizabeth, "scarred me and left me with horrible memories."

But in the autumn of 1950, Elizabeth Taylor Hilton suffered in silence. "She no longer confided in us about anything," wailed Sara, who was not easily yielding control of her daughter's life. Also, Elizabeth's shame at the failure of her marriage was too great for protest, her fear of public humiliation too deep, her ignorance of the means of recourse too pervasive. All her life, she had been ordered, arranged and directed, had been constantly told what to do, had made not a single important decision on her own. Now, when she needed to do so, she had to find the emotional and psychological mechanisms to take an immediate, serious step on behalf of her own health and maturity.

When she was not working that autumn, Elizabeth took some of the unctions traditionally applied to a wounded ego: she shopped obsessively, buying things she did not need, purchasing for others lavish gifts in wild profusion and filling their suite at the Bel-Air Hotel to overflowing with items destined, she said, for their future house; few people were fooled. But if she was unloved, she would surround herself with pretty things; if she felt lost and betrayed, she would win the love of others the only way a child knew—things would beam her love and her lovelessness to friends and strangers.

As anyone might have guessed, Metro was busily planning to use the beautiful bride just as soon as she returned, and on October 9 she began a new picture, again playing Kay, the dewy ingenue now a young mother in *Father's Little Dividend*. But the offscreen marriage would have neither issue (as her on-screen marriage did in this sequel) nor happy ending. Twenty-three days later, the film was complete, and Elizabeth was in a state of near collapse, suffering from spastic colitis and constant headaches. Still, she denied the pervasive rumors that her marriage was in ruins.

Whatever his accountability, it must be said that Hilton could not have found life with Elizabeth easy. From the day of their marriage, they had been hounded by an ever more ravenous press. Wherever they went, photographers and reporters leaped out at them. Hotel foyers were mobbed with fans eager for a glimpse of the beautiful, rich and famous couple, and everywhere the merely curious stopped to stare. "I didn't marry a girl," he said later. "I married an institution . . . Some couples have the privilege of working out their problems in privacy. We don't. The whole world knows every time we quarrel, and [the whole world] gets in the ring as referee—just like at a prizefight."

By early December, life with Nicky was intolerable for Elizabeth, and—just as it had stage-managed the glamorous wedding—so Metro would produce the unhappy real-life sequel. "Nicky and I have come to a final parting of the ways," she said in a Metro-Goldwyn-Mayer publicity release. "There is no possibility of a reconciliation." He went to Mexico on business, and on his return went to visit his mother; Elizabeth, after a holiday in Palm Springs with her mother, returned to the relative security of Elm Drive, where Sara offered privacy and the comfort of soothing foods.

At the same time, Elizabeth was about to start work on her new assignment, a movie with the savagely ironic title *Love Is Better Than Ever,* in which the lowest ebb of her personal life thus far was paralleled by the nadir of her career. In this remarkably uninspired story, Elizabeth played a children's dance teacher from Connecticut who falls in love with a New York agent (Larry Parks), whom she pursues until he can withstand no more. Flat, humorless dialogue; a complete lack of chemistry with her leading man; and, again, a series of scenes in which she was surrounded by more than a dozen photographs of herself as a child—these ingredients made her work dull and the final product joyless, although as usual she was lovely to behold. That season, love was not better than ever, on-screen or off.

At the same time, a garrulous Metro-Goldwyn-Mayer spokesman answered press queries: "It's doubtful whether they'll get together again. They always fight about the same thing—his gambling and playing around and ignoring her as a wife. They both have a temper." Francis Taylor, too, made a contribution to the avalanche of articles on the marital discord: "Nicky does like to gamble. And people who get started keep playing and don't want to go home. Nick's used to having his own way. I guess a lot of boys who inherit money are that way." But there were also family conferences about the inadvisability of divorce. The first year was always the hardest, she was told: could not she and Nicky somehow resolve their problems? There were, after all, so many potential benefits to this union.

Elizabeth gave her reply to Hedda Hopper: "I will file suit for divorce when I complete my present picture." And so she did, on December 22, on grounds of "extreme mental cruelty." In court the following month, she said her husband had become very violent, had used abusive language and had insulted her mother and herself in the presence of friends—"which was absolutely the smallest, weakest grounds possible, and the only ones I would allow my lawyers to go into." She waived alimony but asked for the return of her maiden name. Hilton, who was not present before the judge, offered no contest. Elizabeth Taylor was not yet nineteen years old and abruptly—in less than two years—she had experienced one crushed romance, one broken engagement and one shattered marriage. A sheltered, childlike life had been rushed precipitously into the arena of painful adult experiences. "When I married him, I was too young to know my own mind," she said eight years later. "As for Nicky, he was just too young."

Elizabeth's was not a unique problem in Hollywood, where the lives of juvenile stars were often riddled with problems. The first marriages of Shirley Temple, Deanna Durbin and Judy Garland, who went to the altar in their teens, soon collapsed. In 1943, twenty-two-year-old Mickey Rooney separated from twenty-year-old Ava Gardner. Carl ("Alfalfa") Switzer, one of "Our Gang" and Elizabeth's kiddie costar in *There's One Born Every Minute,* fell on bad times and was shot to death in a drinking brawl in 1959. Young Billy Gray, who charmed the country as Robert Young's clean-cut television son in "Father Knows Best," served time for drug possession. And Bobby Driscoll, a major star for Disney at the age of eight, won a special Oscar as the outstanding juvenile actor of 1949. But he had no job offers after the age of twenty, and—forlorn and directionless—he became a vagrant drug addict. At thirty, he was found dead in the rubble of an abandoned Manhattan tenement, and his worn and wasted body, unidentified for over a year, was buried in a pauper's grave. There are many such stories, even in the 1990s.

One need not be a licensed therapist to locate the source of their problems. Corralled into a life of bogus glamour, pampered and cossetted in artificial surroundings, these youngsters could not distinguish reality from illusion. All decisions were made for them, and they were denied normal peer relationships. Whenever they appeared in public, someone would note their presence: people would stare, gasp, ask for autographs. Observed, applauded, praised, photographed, lionized, overwhelmed with gifts and care, they in fact were subject to a kind of exploitive abuse that many parents, mistaking fame for significance, have sometimes gladly negotiated for their children. Often (as in the case of Elizabeth) they married too soon—not for love but for escape—and because they were accustomed to something like reverence, they could not comprehend the requirements, the normal give-and-take of friendship, much less the demands of marriage. Physically mature but emotionally undeveloped, they were aliens in anything like an ordinary human situation.

Whatever Elizabeth's regret at the start of the new year 1951, she did not long nurse her grievances. Even before the divorce hearing, in fact, she was much consoled by the director of *Love Is Better Than Ever*. Stanley Donen, twenty-six, had been a Broadway dancer and choreographer before coming to Hollywood as a director (notably, of *On the Town* and *Royal Wedding*). A final divorce from his first wife was still pending when he began courting Elizabeth, whose "recovery," as Louella Parsons wrote, "was hastened by the attentions paid her by Stanley Donen." In February, they were photographed dancing together in a nightclub; he sent "a mountain of flowers" on her nineteenth birthday; and (to hell with the gossips) Donen squired her to the Oscar ceremony in March and to the premiere of *Father's Little Dividend* in April, by which time he was (thus the Hollywood *Citizen-News* on April 6) "her constant escort." Week after week throughout that winter and spring they were seen together, daily and nightly. "She clung to him more and more," wrote one journalist who was on the scene.

The romance must not be dismissed as a facile dalliance. During the shooting of *Love Is Better Than Ever*, Elizabeth was often ill with nerves over the breakdown of her marriage and the possible repercussions from the public, and Donen's patience was crucial to her recovery in ways that Louella Parsons's acid-dipped pen did not describe. Elizabeth still suffered from colitis, unpopularly known as the irritable bowel syndrome and often exacerbated by nervous tension; she frequently broke down weeping on the set of the picture; and she moved like a refugee from one place to another. In all these circumstances, Donen was a supporting ally as much as an ardent suitor. Solitude was intolerable to her; a man was a necessity.

Elizabeth's worst anxiety, it became evident, was indeed the prospect of being alone, a condition she had never known in her life. Until she found a small place of her own, she stayed occasionally with her stand-in, actress Marjorie Dillon; other nights she moved into the guest room at the home of her lawyer, Jules Goldstone. She would not, she insisted, return to Elm Drive, ever. Finally, Elizabeth engaged a secretary-companion and confirmed spinster named Peggy Rutledge, and in March 1951 the two young women moved a few items into a snug apartment on Wilshire Boulevard in Westwood, not far from UCLA and a quick drive south to Metro.

To make matters more inconvenient, that moving day coincided with the time of her assigned cameo in a satire called *Callaway Went Thataway*. Three Metro stars—the other two were Clark Gable and Esther Williams—were dropped into a scene in a nightclub. Playing herself, Elizabeth greets Howard Keel: "Good evening, Mr. Callaway," and that was that. Less than five seconds on-screen, which took the usual half-day at the studio.

That spring, Elizabeth's gastric distress worsened, and a physician prescribed a strict diet of pureed baby food, an apt regime in light of what her mother termed infantile behavior. Why could her daughter not simply act the grown-up? Why must she flout convention and incite rumors? By late spring, Elizabeth was pale, smoking more than ever and alarmingly thin. Since her appearance in *Love Is Better Than Ever*, she had seemed uncharacteristically flat-chested, a difference noted by Hedda Hopper, who dropped into the Wilshire Boulevard apartment for a visit and asked if Elizabeth was happy. "I am happy," she replied poignantly, "but not nineteen happy."

The publicity surrounding her divorce had not hurt Elizabeth's popularity, thanks largely to Metro's management of a sympathetic local press, which documented her ailments, and to the bulletins from Louella Parsons and Hedda Hopper, who tempered their pious moralism with comforting admonitions. But by June 1951 the studio was increasingly nervous about the Taylor-Donen rendezvous, which were cited in the press to an extent that far exceeded the Hilton engagement period. The public might forgive an injudicious marriage, but the temper of the country would not countenance her blithe, precipitous entrance into a new romance: it was just not seemly.

In a monarchy, such requirements are traditionally exacted of a royal family; democratic America, however, has only its celebrities—movie stars, especially—to regard as the anointed, those who represent the assumption that glamour means grandeur. In England that year, George VI was king, his consort Queen Elizabeth; in America, Clark Gable was the king, John Wayne the duke and Elizabeth Taylor the reigning movie queen. In them and a few others, human nature seemed to wear a little majesty.

Thus it was that Metro, although uneasy about the conduct of a very young and popular star, nevertheless prepared to renew the seven-year contract that had run from 1945 through 1951: she would begin the 1952-through-1958 term with an escalating salary of $5,000 weekly guaranteed for forty weeks—her mother still receiving 10 percent of that amount. At that time, such salaries were taxed in the 90 percent bracket, which left Elizabeth's income (before fees for lawyers, publicists and accountants, among others) at about $20,000. Still, if she had not such an increasingly lavish style of life, that might have been a very comfortable income indeed in the early 1950s.

At the same time, Metro had to act strongly and quickly, to avert a publicity catastrophe in the matter of Stanley Donen, especially when Elizabeth began to speak freely to the press: "I think it is instinct for a woman to like marriage," she said, as if prophesying a career. "I think I shall marry again, but I don't know when." The studio could take no chances with so frank a woman as this, and so Elizabeth Taylor was suddenly announced for the supporting role of Rebecca in the medieval epic *Ivanhoe*, based on Sir Walter Scott's sweeping romantic novel—to be filmed the summer of 1951 in England, far from Los Angeles and Stanley Donen. With Peggy Rutledge in tow (but not, at last, Sara Taylor), and with crates of baby food and steamer trunks for her wardrobe, Elizabeth departed for London after mutually promised troths of eternal devotion with Donen.

The director of *Ivanhoe* met her when she arrived that June. "I expected her to break down any minute," said Richard Thorpe, who had known a very different person when he had directed her in *A Date With Judy* four years earlier; he now found her anxious and worn out. "She was extremely thin," added Pandro Berman, producing his fourth Taylor film, "in fact so thin that she was afraid to come to England to make the picture, for health reasons. But her doctor finally allowed her to come on condition that we guard her health and didn't work her too hard."

The company need not have worried, for Elizabeth—for the first time in her career—seemed to float almost without affect through *Ivanhoe*. So indifferent was she, in fact, that after two weeks Thorpe had bad news for Berman: not only was she giving nothing to the role, she was driving the sound editor mad with her mostly incomprehensible line readings. Just proceed with the filming, Berman said: audio corrections could be made later. Thus, when Taylor returned to Hollywood, her entire performance was looped—carefully rerecorded to synchronize the dubbed dialogue with her lip movements on-screen. All this was unknown to 1952 audiences, of course, who flocked to see the colorful swashbuckler in record numbers: *Ivanhoe* took in more than $6 million dollars in its first release. But to Elizabeth (and to reviewers, who appreciated her appearance and little else) it was just "a big medieval western."

Her performance in England was completed in October 1951. And by this time, Nicky Hilton and Stanley Donen were like characters in earlier films, consigned to a bank of mixed memories. As Elizabeth prepared to return to America, she was in far cheerier spirits, and again the reason was a great new romance.

Chapter Five

1951–1955

A T THE SIGHT OF HIM, I decided to forget all my baby food," said Elizabeth Taylor after her reunion with Michael Wilding in London during the summer of 1951.

The circumstances of their reunion were not at all glamorous, nor did Wilding, who considered her a child star, initiate the pursuit. He met her by coincidence at the studio canteen, they exchanged pleasantries, and soon after she invited him to dinner. With twenty years separating them, he was wary of anything like romance, but Elizabeth was not to be denied. By August they were dining almost every night. "I ate anything I liked," she said, "and in a month I was cured of all my ailments." Except, perhaps, that of a chronic disposition to fall easily in love.

Often voted the most popular male actor in England, Michael Wilding turned thirty-nine on July 23, 1951, an event he celebrated with Elizabeth and two friends. During the evening, she sent a cable to her parents: "We are all thinking of you and wishing you were here. We are having a wonderful reunion together. All very happy.

Can't wait to see you in Beverly Hills. All our love, Elizabeth, Melvina and Kenny McEldowney and Michael Wilding." And with that, Elizabeth was swinging into action.

From the age of twenty-one, Wilding had been offered stage and screen roles because of his patrician good looks, appealing voice and refined bearing. The money (and, as he admitted, the access to lovely young ladies) was too good to reject: thus his embryonic career as a portraitist and commercial artist dwindled into an avocation.

Typical of his early reviews was one he received while touring in Australia: "The most finished performance of the evening was given by Michael Wilding in the relatively small role of Prince Ernst [in *Victoria Regina*]. His presence lights up the whole stage." Back in London, he fell in love with Kay Young, a costar at the Gate Theatre, who after several weeks of a torrid affair proposed marriage. "Like all women who have figured in my life, before or since, Kay was the dominant partner," he said later. But while ardent ladies—and a number of men friends—sensed that Wilding was a passive personality who dreaded commitment, not everyone was aware that his lack of assertion derived at least in part from a physical ailment. From young adulthood, he suffered from epilepsy, a condition at the time poorly understood, unevenly treated and, by many sufferers and their families, wrongly regarded with embarrassment or contempt. This made him sometimes cautious in public and fearful in private—notwithstanding his consummate charm. There was something quietly needy about Michael Wilding, and to many women this was perhaps the most salient point of the attraction.

When Kay left London for the safety of the country during the 1940 Blitz, Wilding stayed in town, sometimes pursuing his career, always hunting paramours. By 1941, the marriage was irretrievably shattered: "I was nobody's idea of an ideal mate and, although I was too ashamed to do so at the time, in retrospect I take all the blame for the failure of a marriage to a very wonderful person who deserved a better husband." Neither of them mentioned divorce, which in England at that time was not in any case advantageous for public careers. Wilding's, as it happened, flourished, especially after he was engaged by producer Herbert Wilcox for several popular films starring one of the most beloved British stars, Wilcox's wife, Anna Neagle.

When reunited with Elizabeth that summer of 1951, Wilding was still talking about *Stage Fright*, his second picture for Alfred Hitchcock, which earned him splendid reviews and the blandishments of his fifty-year-old costar, Marlene Dietrich. That affair (initiated and sustained by her ardent insistence) ended when Elizabeth Taylor came to town. "What's she got that I haven't got?" complained Dietrich, who might have guessed.

In fact, Wilding seemed just as diffident with Elizabeth as with other women. But apparent coolness is very often the most potent aphrodisiac, and so it was for her. That summer, she set her cap for a man she imagined to be, in the words of his recent film's title, an ideal husband. "He was everything I admired in a man, and I thought him remarkable," she said, perhaps noting most of all how different he was from Nicky Hilton. Nothing was more foreign to Wilding's character than quarreling, much less any kind of violence: indeed, he was the soul of gentility and equanimity. He was endlessly polite, always elegant, invariably unpretentious, impressively cultured—and he was English, the kind of man she would have married had she not gone to California at all. "He represented tranquillity, security, maturity—all the things I needed in myself." He was, in other words, everything that was unlike the ordinary Hollywood stud. Just as appealing may have been the fact that—also unlike the dominating, abusive Hilton—Wilding seemed to need her. In this regard, she may have regarded him as something of a wounded, frightened creature, rather like a pet that required gentle, tender attention. "But he said I was too young for him, that I'd change my mind," she recalled. "When I objected, he said we should wait." How long he did not say.

But Elizabeth inherited her mother's persistence. She pleaded; she wept; she would do anything to please; she was irresistible. Her final divorce decree would be effective in January 1952, she said: was it not time for Wilding to seek a divorce from Kay, whom he had not seen in more than five years? But the more she cajoled, the more he temporized. After the final shots of *Ivanhoe* in October, he had still not acted. Furious, Elizabeth then took another approach. Quitting England, she flew to New York, where she was met by her parents. She took a lavish suite at the Plaza Hotel, which she used as her base of operations that autumn.

With Wilding in mind, Elizabeth knew how to exploit the press without seeming to do so. Thus she did not politely cooperate with newsmen who wanted photo stories about her nightclubbing with Montgomery Clift and, more tantalizing still, about her meetings in New York and Connecticut with none other than Nicky Hilton. In fact, she and her ex-husband were discussing only final points of the divorce settlement such as the Hilton Hotel stock she had received as a wedding present from the family. But the wire services, as any-one might have expected, trilled with reports that she was "emo-tionally upset" over Nicky's apparently serious romance with the twenty-year-old German baroness and Broadway actress Betsy von Furstenberg.

At the time, the Plaza was a Hilton hotel, and so Elizabeth, accustomed to privileges and perquisites, presumed she would stay there without charge. But to her horror, she was presented, after three weeks, with a bill for $2,500: as it turned out, normal fees had been routinely levied against her after a five-day free period. Outraged, she rang Montgomery Clift, who was at home a few blocks away, and at once he sprang to her aid, helping her to move into a single room and joining in her childish mischief. This occurred with the aid of a pitcher of dry martinis, which gave them the false courage to wreak vengeance. When she left the suite, its pictures had been turned upside down, the bathroom fixtures had been unscrewed, tissue had been torn into scraps and littered the room, and, after a hilarious flower fight, petals and stems were strewn on the carpet. Finally, Clift stole away with the hotel towels, which forever after he set out for Elizabeth when she visited his house on East Sixty-first Street.

Nothing succeeds like excess, and when the British press picked up stories of a glamorously timorous Elizabeth meeting with Nicky

Hilton, taking him to her Uncle Howard Young's Connecticut home and driving with him in New England, Wilding took note. He tracked her to the Plaza, where he telephoned his concern; thereafter, they spoke at length daily for a month.

Then, shortly after her return to Metro for the dubbing of her lines in *Ivanhoe* that November, Elizabeth prevailed on Wilding to come for a visit, and because he had close friends there and was between assignments, he agreed. In December, he and Elizabeth were off for a Las Vegas holiday with Stewart Granger and his wife, Jean Simmons—and with that the press was buzzing again. "Liz, Wilding in Las Vegas," ran Louella Parson's provocative, double entendre headline on December 12. A week later, behaving impeccably, Kay Young agreed to an uncontested London divorce, charging, as Wilding asked, years of desertion.

That night, Elizabeth asked Michael Wilding to be her husband. They were dining in Los Angeles at Romanoff's, and he took from his pocket a sapphire and diamond ring, which he intended as a token of devotion but not a formal proposal of marriage. "I reached for her right hand," he recalled,

> but she snatched it away, putting out her left hand and waggling her third finger. "That's where it belongs," she said. Then, admiring the ring, she kissed me and said, "That makes it official, doesn't it? Or shall I spell it out for you? Dear Mr. Shilly-shally, will you marry me?"

He would. Still, they could not announce wedding plans until her divorce was final. Elizabeth wished to marry in London, and Wilding returned there in mid-January 1952; at Metro's request, she remained in Los Angeles, awaiting the final divorce decree, which became effective February 1. She then met with Helen Rose, who was designing the costumes for her next film, and after the fitting sessions revealed she had regained the weight lost the previous year, she sped away to Palm Springs for diet and exercise. On February 17, Metro announced the news of her forthcoming marriage to Michael Wilding, although there was no mention of a date or place. That evening, Elizabeth flew alone to London and checked into a room at the Berkeley Hotel.

Shortly before noon on February 21, she and Michael slipped through a rear door into the Caxton Registry Hall, Westminster, emerging ten minutes later as man and wife. His parents and brother, and Herbert and Anna Neagle Wilcox, accompanied them. The traditional trappings of public mourning had enveloped London since the death of King George VI two weeks earlier, but over a thousand curious onlookers stampeded the newlyweds, cheering wildly and disrupting traffic throughout the district. "I am glad to be British again," Elizabeth cried out, referring to the dual citizenship English law had just bestowed on her. For the cameras, she waved and smiled more warmly and enthusiastically than a member of the royal family at Ascot. A reporter then asked if the twenty-year age difference bothered them. "Michael is just a child at heart," she replied, perhaps to her husband's astonishment. They then slowly made their way through the mob to a waiting car; the scene, sniffed the London *Evening News*, "would not have disgraced a Hollywood premiere." After a reception at Claridge's, the couple spent the night in her suite at the Berkeley and departed next morning for Paris, and the day after for a holiday in the Swiss Alps.

They returned to London two weeks later, and Michael completed his last picture for Herbert Wilcox, who then graciously released him from their contract so that he could move to America and accept a Metro contract Elizabeth had negotiated for him. Before they departed England in June, Inland Revenue presented Michael with a tax bill of £40,000, then about $100,000—virtually every penny he owned. Suddenly, the adored English actor was cash poor and entirely dependent on his wife, a situation which, for the time being, was not disagreeable to her.

As summer 1952 approached, Metro announced a start date for her next assignment, *The Girl Who Had Everything*—which the American press and pollsters considered a definition of Elizabeth herself. In this case, the girl may have had very much indeed, but she certainly lacked a good script. The picture was a remake of a 1931 movie that had starred Norma Shearer, Clark Gable and Lionel Barrymore, but then it had fared somewhat better; now, it creaked with phony sentiment and a plot that defied belief. Again, as in *A Date With Judy*, *Julia Misbehaves*, *The Big Hangover* and *A Place in the Sun*, Elizabeth was cast as the daughter of a rich and successful man—in this case, a criminal lawyer (William Powell). She falls in love with a handsome Latin lover (Fernando Lamas), only to learn that he is a notorious crook. From this unfortunate situation she is rescued when he is killed by mobsters. The moral of the story was clear: the girl who had everything needs to be tested by life. "I learned my lesson . . . I won't make the same mistake again . . . Let's go home," she tells her father. The same dialogue runs like an antiphon through the Poor Little Rich Girl cycle of Elizabeth Taylor's early career.

Yet *The Girl Who Had Everything*, written by a man named Art Cohn, who had an unrequited crush on her and would later become a good friend, is laced with references to the star. Her character is an animal lover and horse fancier (Elizabeth as a child) who falls for a man who slaps her around (Nicky Hilton). She was glad to have finished the production.

During filming, the director was challenged by more than this dreary scenario: by late August, Elizabeth was almost five months pregnant, and some fancy camera work was required to avoid completely altering the story. The Wildings were happy to be prospective parents, but at once there were practical problems. The small, cramped house they had rented would have to be exchanged for larger quarters, but this would be difficult in light of the fact that the studio at once placed her on suspension: as specified in her contract, she would not be paid for her pregnancy leave. Then, Michael Wilding refused to accept an assignment in Metro's *Latin Lovers* (which eventually starred none other than Fernando Lamas, which was far better casting)—and so Michael, too, was placed on punitive suspension. For many months, the Wildings were living on her dwindling savings. The girl who supposedly had everything was, in fact, in straitened circumstances.

But with her usual irrepressible optimism and a much longed-for baby on the way, the Wildings seemed to expect pennies from heaven, and in a way they were not disappointed. That November, Elizabeth received $47,100 worth of bonds, held in trust for her maturity since the time of her childhood movies, and Metro-Goldwyn-Mayer (not from a rush of sentimental generosity but because it suited their business purposes) loaned the Wildings the balance needed to buy their first home, high up in Beverly Hills, priced at $75,000. The loan was to be repaid from their joint salaries when they returned to work.

These financial details might be considered unremarkable except for the fact that Elizabeth could have approached her wealthy Uncle Howard Young for a loan. But she did not relish reviving a state of family dependency; much preferable to this, which would have imposed an added burden of psychological debt, was the rather less personal indebtedness to the studio.

From late summer 1952 to early spring 1953, then, Elizabeth was without income. Despite months of unpleasant morning sickness, she thrived on being pregnant. She and Michael planned the redecoration of the snug, two-bedroom house with its spacious yard for their four cats, six dogs, and, eventually, assorted birds, various rabbits, some wandering deer and a few ducks.

With Elizabeth the animal lover as mistress, this menagerie (absent the deer) was not confined to a yard but had free run of the house, to disastrously messy effect: friends routinely pitched in to clean up after this untrained dog or that duck had soiled the carpet or chair or bedspread.

In this regard, Michael quickly learned to his dismay that his wife's impeccable manners and ambient glamour were entirely a creation of the movie set. "When she takes off a dress," he said without an amorous glint in his eye, "she simply steps out of it. This would be fine in a large house, but in a smallish place like this it is a terrible nuisance." But Elizabeth was accustomed to studio dressers who were always present to take care of such things, and the ordinary details of housewifery did not come naturally to her. "Her worst fault has always been untidiness," agreed Sara.

On January 6, 1953, Michael Howard Wilding was born after his mother, with admirable composure, underwent an emergency cesarean section. Until winter's end, Elizabeth remained on suspension, a doting mother who constantly supervised the part-time nanny but blithely ignored the chaos of a domestic life she could not manage. As expenses increased, it became clear that eventually she would have to accept whatever assignments Metro imposed.

At first, Michael seemed content, too. Essentially, he did not really like acting and was glad of any excuse to avoid its obligations. Because he was a desirable import to the Hollywood social circuit and easily made friends, the Wildings welcomed the likes of Gene Kelly, Spencer Tracy, Judy Garland and Errol Flynn for casual suppers, usually set out after frantic, last-minute calls to delicatessens, for Elizabeth could barely fry an egg.

As for Michael's professional life, Metro did not really know what to do with Michael's brand of quiet, understated charm, nor was there an abundance of roles for a cultivated English gentleman. They did not really understand his type—and he returned the sentiment, loathing the studio's high-handed, unilateral assignment of roles for which he was badly suited. He was miserable, for example, playing a blind pianist to the formidable Joan Crawford in *Torch Song*, and he hated every day's work on *The Egyptian*, which was virtually comic in its bloated, epic pretensions.

Nor was life made easier by Hedda Hopper's unfounded imputations, in her syndicated column, that Michael and his old friend Stewart Granger were lovers—insinuations that evoked laughter from their past and present wives, as well as from the many mistresses of their earlier years. In this matter, Wilding won a judgment for libel against Hopper.

There were, however, pleasanter diversions. At one Sunday afternoon pool party at the home of Stewart Granger and Jean Simmons, the Wildings met a Welsh actor making his debut in Hollywood films. He was twenty-six, married, brilliant, a gifted actor with a voice of grave authority and a devastating charm. His name was Richard Burton.

Born in 1925 as Richard Jenkins, he was the twelfth of thirteen children born to an alcoholic miner and a woman who died when he was two. Richard was then raised by an older sister and by a teacher named Philip Burton, who recognized his talent, supported him and trained him for a career on the stage. When he could do so, Richard took the man's surname in grateful tribute.

From childhood, he seemed destined for stardom. He memorized quickly and often gave impromptu recitals of verse and prose for his family and whomever would listen; he made up "sermons" he delivered in spellbinding oratorical fashion; and, during a six-month term at Oxford, he impressed no less a master than Nevill Coghill with an expert performance in a student production of Shakespeare's *Measure for Measure.* An important career was predicted for Richard Burton—if he could develop the discipline and avoid a habit of excessive drinking, for which he inherited a perilous predilection.

Related to his alcohol consumption and perhaps linked to a profound inferiority complex about his poor origins and his severely pockmarked face, Richard had an inordinate desire to be praised, to be reassured that yes, he was important to others. And like many with that yearning, he tried to win favor by proving himself irresistible to women and by giving extravagant gifts he could scarce afford.

At twenty-three, he married the actress Sybil Williams, who eventually bore him two daughters. Although he loved Sybil and was a devoted father, Richard was in every way cast in the romantic-heroic mold, or so he believed: marriage and a family did not curtail his capacity for wild nights of prodigal drinking and rampant wenching. "I'll never divorce Sybil," he said, "and she will never divorce me, because she loves me, she understands me, and [she] thinks I'm a genius." For the time being, so much was true. Sybil waited, and after Richard amused himself (with almost every one of his leading ladies and scores of others), he always returned home to her.

Although he expressed frank contempt for the specious glamour of Hollywood, Richard was too enamored of the good life to reject movie offers, which of course paid hundreds of times more for a few weeks of easy work than he could earn after a year in the theater. Awarded the Foreign Press Association's Golden Globe Award for his first American picture, *My Cousin Rachel*, he was at once beguiled by easy money and the trappings of fame. *Desert Rats* and *The Robe* followed, as did instant stardom. Despite these lucrative performances, Richard always had the highest regard for the theater: he had made a splendid impression as Prince Hal at Stratford in 1951, when Kenneth Tynan hailed him as "awesome":

> Fluent and sparing of gesture, compact and spruce of build, Burton smiles where other Hals have guffawed, relaxes where they have strained, and Falstaff must work hard to divert him. In battle, Burton's voice cuts urgent and keen—always likeable, always amiable.

From that time, he always had one eye on the great roles—among them Hamlet, the role he would assume in London the following year. Forever after, he would be torn to the point of painful rage, drawn simultaneously to a life of sybaritic luxury and to that of a serious artist: "All I wanted," he said, summarizing the conflict, "was to live, to pick up a new Jaguar, and to act at the Old Vic."

Richard Burton also had aspirations as a writer, as attested by a brilliantly articulated diary that surfaced years later, and by his published account of meeting Elizabeth Taylor on that summer day at the Granger poolside. "She was, I decided, the most astonishingly self-contained, pulchritudinous, remote, removed, inaccessible woman I had ever seen. She spoke to no one. She looked at no one. She steadily kept on reading her book. Was she merely sullen? I thought not. There was no trace of sulkiness in the divine face." His fantasies, he admitted, went further, and he expressed them with humorous awe: "Her breasts were apocalyptic, they would topple empires down before they withered. Indeed, her body was a miracle of construction and the work of an engineer of genius."

Finally, he approached Elizabeth that afternoon, only to hear this creature of unearthly beauty utter a string of profanities as she described her opinion of a certain Metro producer. "You have a remarkable command of Old English," Burton said.

"Don't you use words like that at the Old Vic?" Elizabeth asked, as if her diction were unexceptional.

"They do, but I don't," said Burton, absurdly, testing the waters. "I come from a family and an attitude that believe such words are an indication of weakness in vocabulary and emptiness of mind." And for a few moments he babbled on about the nature of language.

"Well, well, well," said Elizabeth, unimpressed and without expression as Richard stopped for breath and a sip of Scotch. Then she turned away, and that, until many years passed, was that. "I didn't fancy him then," she said years later. "I thought he talked too much."

But while Richard Burton was the toast of Hollywood in 1952 and 1953, Michael Wilding was most egregiously not. "We sat on a hilltop in Hollywood," he said years later, "watching my career turn to ashes."

As they did so, the temperamental differences between husband and wife became clearer, one of them being that Elizabeth was a loving and demonstrative parent, unlike Michael. As early as spring 1953, they were fighting over small things, which is often the first sign of deeper problems. One morning, for example, Elizabeth decided that she had had enough of Michael's habit of trying to solve the daily newspaper crossword at breakfast. "She snatched the paper from my hand, tore it in half and threw it into the fire. 'So much for you and your stupid games,' she screamed, adding, 'Go on, hit me! Why don't you?'"

"I've never gone in for hitting hysterical females," Michael replied calmly.

"Oh, God!" she moaned, "if only you would! At least that would prove you are flesh and blood instead of a stuffed dummy!"

The moment was emblematic of very much in Elizabeth's character. For one thing, she obviously knew that her act had been childish, and perhaps longed to be treated like a naughty child. The only experience she had of correction, however, had been the extreme reactions of Nicky Hilton. And so she picked a fight with Michael, creating a little drama to see if she might rouse him to action. "You must not rub her the wrong way," said Michael Wilding. "She upsets very easily." In a sense, this was her way of turning ordinary living into a series of minor scenarios she could act out: thus uncertain life would have the movement and, at last, the structure and desirable resolution of a movie script. Once again, movies were all she knew of life; when stymied, life would be given the elements of an Elizabeth Taylor picture.

After Hilton, she had turned to the security of Wilding—a corrective to her violent first husband and to her unenthusiastic father. But in the final analysis she did not wish to be quite so dominant the personality as she believed. For his part, Michael struggled to survive, to correct or at least sustain her chronic untidiness and tardiness. He was not jealous of her stardom, but he felt like a displaced person. And he could not seem to avoid being merely Elizabeth Taylor's husband.

His wife's friendship with Montgomery Clift, contrary to the gossips' innuendo of a love affair, was an important stabilizing influence. "We were best friends," she said years later. "We had a language between us. We could read each other even over the phone." As for Clift, he was at first a willing but eventually a weary go-between for the Wildings. "She would cry on his shoulder during the day," according to Michael, "while I would pour out my grievances far into the night after she had gone to bed. He acted as interpreter for two people who no longer spoke the same language, and [he] must have got a clearer picture of the reasons for the breakdown of our marriage than anyone else in Hollywood."

For Elizabeth, then, work was both a financial and a psychological necessity. When an acute nervous breakdown forced Vivien Leigh to withdraw, after months of filming, from a picture called *Elephant Walk*, an actress had to be found who had her size, coloring, beauty and popular appeal. On March 18, 1953, therefore, Paramount announced that the studio had concluded swift negotiations to borrow Elizabeth from Metro, and the following Monday, March 23, she reported for work. (Metro charged Paramount $150,000 for her services; Elizabeth, of course, was paid her contracted salary, which amounted to $42,500.) "Vivien Leigh was my heroine," she said, replying to those who noted a striking similarity between the two brunette beauties. "She was innocence on the verge of decadence, always there to be saved."

Like a ghost, Vivien hovered over the production she had been forced to quit: for budgetary reasons, producer Irving Asher had to retain the sequences filmed in what was then called Ceylon. And so viewers of the finished picture saw an actress who was obviously Vivien Leigh in the long shots filmed on location, and even in several medium close shots; Elizabeth then appeared in the interiors, and in several hastily revised sequences. But—for neither the first nor last time—Elizabeth made a virtue of necessity, turning her underwritten character into a small miracle of slightly subdued sexual hysteria and shining, in glorious Technicolor, against the most unlikely projected backgrounds.

She was, in fact, the most interesting thing about this rather damp fable of men and pachyderms. Elizabeth played a young bride who goes to the subtropical jungle with husband, Peter Finch, a man with an ancestral plantation built in the traditional ancient path of the elephants' walk. Alcoholic and tyrannical, Finch unaccountably ignores his wife's ardent pleas for love and effectively forces her into the arms of Dana Andrews, but (it was 1953, after all) she remains true to her caddish spouse. The highlight of the film remains the violent climax in which the beasts, claiming their right of way, upset all the traffic patterns and reduce Finch's estate to rubble.

The havoc of the story was accompanied, at the end of production, with an accident that might have been tragic. Posing for publicity photos, Elizabeth, Finch and Andrews sat in a studio Jeep as a huge fan blew "wind" in their hair. But a tiny splinter of steel flew into her eye. This was removed by a surgeon, who instructed her to remain quiet over the weekend to insure recovery. But Sunday was Mother's Day, and Elizabeth could not resist a frolic with her son, who accidentally smacked her, sending her off to the hospital, where, for several days, doctors feared blindness in the twice-injured eye. With her extraordinary sangfroid in the face of such a frightening possibility, Elizabeth cheered Michael and embraced her baby.

Within two weeks, her eyesight had been fully restored and she was back at work on what she called another of the "films that never should have gone before the camera." This was *Rhapsody*, which occupied her from the end of May until late July 1953. Critics, more than ever accustomed to singling out her performance as the sole virtue in unworthy projects, again praised her as an "adult and honest actress" who could make an outlandish story credible.

Rhapsody is a soggy, verbose affair, a woeful tale of (again!) a rich girl who flees her stifling home and father for (again!) a pair of unsympathetic men, a pianist (John Ericson) and a violinist (Vittorio Gassman) who prefer music to love. Tangled and lush, this is 99 percent soap opera and one percent high-toned MGM antialcoholism tract, but it is finally successful as neither. Yet there was Elizabeth, in constantly changing moods and gowns, as phrases of Rachmaninoff, Liszt and Tchaikovsky floated on the soundtrack.

Her performance, as usual, was affecting, even though her character was one of the most incoherently maddening she ever had to play: first, she is in love with the selfish violinist, then she is in love with the brilliant, undisciplined, passionate pianist, whom she marries. But he turns to alcohol—shades of Peter Finch in *Elephant Walk*, although just why these men turn away from Elizabeth to whiskey is hard to fathom, nor is it anywhere clarified in the script. Then she decides to leave the pianist and run away with the violinist. But duty (and perhaps the Motion Picture Production Code and the Legion of Decency) bring her back to the pianist at the fadeout. The music is lovely, Elizabeth is stunning in Technicolor, and the story is hilariously inept. Metro, incapable of finding something better, was by this time presenting her in stories better suited to Joan Crawford at fifty than Elizabeth Taylor at twenty-one. But the project was so disappointing that critics limited themselves to commenting on her beauty.

Rhapsody was followed by something even worse, a talky and arid remake of the period piece *Beau Brummell*, to be produced at

Metro's London studio in late 1953 and early 1954. Before that, Metro allowed her a few days holiday in Europe with Michael, but in Copenhagen she came down with influenza. The world's press swung into action, pitching camp outside the Hotel d'Angleterre and elaborating, from every minor statement, a dramatically over-wrought bulletin: Elizabeth had had a nervous collapse; she broke her back and could not walk; she had pneumonia; she was dying, after a heart attack.

"Elizabeth Taylor is ailing," began an ominous story from the Associated Press dated September 25, continuing with wild asser-tions of "a nervous ailment that worsened heart trouble." She was still in bed a few days later, and it was learned that the Wildings had sent for their baby, who had been left in London with the nanny. The press was now certain that death was stalking the corridor of the Hotel d'Angleterre.

Finally, Michael Wilding summoned a few British newsmen he trusted. "It's all been a fantastic mistake," he said. "Elizabeth has a cold and a backache. That's all." And so it was, as he elaborated: "She's had a touch of flu, and all she needs is a week's rest." But Elizabeth was not free of the press, which maintained the world's interest with provocatively tear-jerking and downright misleading stories: "Baby Restores Liz Taylor's Smile" (*Los Angeles Examiner*, September 27); "Elizabeth Taylor Rests in Denmark" (United Press International wire story, October 3); "Liz Taylor Flies to London" (Associated Press wire story, October 10, hinting that only a British physician could save her life).

The fact is that Elizabeth herself had something to do with these flights of fancy. "We are amazed at these rumors," she said on the telephone to a British journalist—but she then proceeded to have it both ways, appearing to dismiss the rumors but actually throwing herself on the sympathy of her public by implying that she was after all a cause for concern:

> I admit I felt dreadful last night. I had a flush, my pulse was slow, and it's true my heart sometimes flutters through nerves. But I only have to rest for a while. Now Michael is coming to rub my back.

Ever since the time of *Life With Father*, when her mother obtained star treatment and attention for her daughter by exaggerating ordinary complaints, Elizabeth knew the benefits of sympathy. Her baby would not have been placed serenely in his mother's arms had she a perilous communicable disease, nor would she have scurried off for a few days in the Danish countryside, which she subsequently enjoyed, if her life were at stake. But the event was instructive to whatever journalist took note: Elizabeth knew she had to maintain sympathetic support. To do this, she would never fabricate. But she knew from Sara how to use certain versions of the truth for her own best ends. "She has a nervous heart," said her husband at the time, perhaps with double intention.

Later, Michael clarified his thoughts on Elizabeth and her hypersensitivity to illness. "If she gets a cold, she reacts so violently she's almost dead from pneumonia. During the first year of our marriage, I had been lolling by our pool and a bee stung me. I pulled the stinger out, and that was the end of it. Elizabeth was stung, too, and though I pulled that stinger out, the swelling lasted for a week and a half." In 1954, extraction of an abscessed tooth was delayed so that she could complete *The Last Time I Saw Paris*; after a visit to her dentist, she was ill for two weeks. "If she opens a beer can, she cuts herself," said Richard Brooks, the director of that film. "If there is a chair in the middle of the set, she falls over it."

These were certainly not self-inflicted injuries, nor can her ailments be dismissed as psychosomatic in origin; there were, after all, several serious matters later in her life that required medical and surgical intervention. But there are people whose craving for attention leads to a general exploitation of minor complaints and a tendency to accidents. Elizabeth, a canny little actress, found that she could win emotional support, sympathetic endorsement and practical, medical aid, the better to be delivered of all aspects of pain.

Remarkably brave—as doubtless she had to be in those dark moments of childhood confusion— she naturally took advantage of every opportunity to gain sympathy for her pain. Sympathy, after all, was her only refuge from treatment she neither deserved nor comprehended, and she knew her mother would provide comfort and escape. In adulthood, Elizabeth repeatedly sought relief from discomfort by seeking the compassion of husbands, the succor of caring physicians and even the sympathy of the general public. In this regard, when she spoke in 1994 to entertainment reporter Liz Smith, she discussed details of her hip replacement surgery. Elizabeth attempted to justify for the entire nation her increasingly reclusive life, insisting that she was ordered to spend months in bed—a doubtful prescription for her kind of joint surgery.

Her exhaustion while recovering from the bout of influenza that autumn of 1953 was certainly exacerbated after the return journey to England, where she began filming *Beau Brummell* in late November. On landing at London Airport, Elizabeth discovered that her jewel case had been stolen from her during the flight. Just how this occurred was never explained, but she reported the loss of jade-and-gold earrings, a braided gold bracelet and a pearl, ruby and emerald pin. Insurance provided some reimbursement; in the years to come, she did not, however, abandon her habit of publicly wearing and traveling with such precious items. They gave her pleasure, and she rightly sensed that appearing with them pleased many spectators, too.

As for the movie she made that winter, Elizabeth had no illusions, then or later, about her affectless performance as Lady Patricia, who falls in love with the dandy Beau Brummell, advisor to the Prince of Wales who became King George IV (Peter Ustinov, doing his usual turn as movie sybarite). She rightly remembered it as one of her (few) bad performances:

God, when I think of some of the movies, like *Beau Brummell!* I never saw that film until after Richard [Burton] and I were married. It was on television and Richard turned it on. I had to change stations after about five minutes—I mean I was so embarrassing in it!

"Metro wanted her in my film," recalled director Curtis Bern-hardt. "I didn't particularly want her, and she didn't want to be in it. She was not essential to the plot. But the studio said, 'For five thousand bucks a week, you can do it!'" In fact, this was very likely the only time Elizabeth was downright rude to her director, as her friend and costar Stewart Granger recalled: she yawned widely in Bernhardt's face "when he was giving her minute instructions as to how to play a certain scene. She was bored with the whole thing." As, indeed, were audiences.

By early March 1954, the Wildings were at home in Beverly Hills, where they received an invitation to present the Academy Award for Best Documentary. This they did, Elizabeth appearing fashionably chic with an ultrashort haircut. By early summer, she was pregnant again, and the Wildings found a larger house perched even higher up in Beverly Hills—a $150,000 glass and adobe showplace designed for her by architect George MacLean. One wall of the liv-ing room was made of bark from which grew ferns. On a wide indoor-outdoor deck was a driftwood tree that supported part of the ceiling, and another forty-five-foot-long fieldstone wall enclosed a chimneyless fireplace that curved round into a bar. It was all very 1954 California contemporary.

The swimming pool, the splendid panoramas and the expanse of rooms did not betoken any formality, however. Visitors found the mistress of the house invariably barefooted, and guests ate buffet-style from mismatched plates and hastily retrieved flatware; if guests were spending the night, they found the bedsheets threadbare or torn and the bedroom wallpaper shredded by cat claws. "Why not be comfortable at home?" Elizabeth asked airily. Why not, indeed.

Michael, at first exasperated by such sloppy informality, capitulated. "You'd better watch out or you'll be known as Mr. Elizabeth Taylor," fellow actor John Garfield had warned him, and in 1954 this grim admonition seemed a self-fulfilling prophecy, made all the more poignant by the fact that Michael was in many ways a surrogate father to Elizabeth and so doomed to outlive his usefulness, his benevolent function of compensating for what Francis Taylor had failed to supply. In some way, it seemed to her close friends, Elizabeth was growing weary of a marriage based on her gratitude and filial devotion and his mentorship. "I thought I'd influence this trembling little creature," Wilding told an interviewer. "I thought I'd guide her along life's stony path. Not at all. Lately, I'm simply told to shut up."

To no one's surprise, his wife required excitement, diversion, passionate fulfillment, and Michael—sweet, patient, always slightly timorous and now completely disillusioned with Hollywood—neither shared her desires nor understood her need for expensive luxuries and clothes, appetites she would not curb even when financial counselors urged otherwise. The Wildings, after all, had a lavish lifestyle, a debt to the studio, a flurry of current and future doctor bills, fees for secretaries, a cook and a nanny. The prospect of a loss of income from pregnancy suspension briefly panicked her, and she negotiated with Metro: if they would pay her during her time off, she would give them another year on her contract and an additional picture.

That stipulation duly settled, Elizabeth dispatched her next Metro assignment, one that provided her best role since Angela in *A Place in the Sun*, and a director (Richard Brooks) whose guidance she much respected. Based on F. Scott Fitzgerald's tragic love story "Babylon Revisited," *The Last Time I Saw Paris* told of an American expatriate writer (Van Johnson) whose creative disappointments lead to alcoholism, the destruction of his marriage and the death of his wife. Elizabeth's performance was a study in earnest devotion and muted anxiety, but the film was so turgid and unmoving that it was difficult to take her seriously. Her character's disillusionment, unfortunately, infected her characterization.

Christopher Edward Wilding, like his brother, was born by cesarean section; the date chosen was his mother's twenty-third birthday, February 27, 1955. Stewart Granger remembered that during her last four months of pregnancy "she was always complaining of pains in her stomach, her back, her legs," and in fact Elizabeth was forced into a lengthy recuperation, during which Metro kept her on suspension.

She was glad, therefore, when her old friend George Stevens, the director of *A Place in the Sun*, invited her to play the female lead in *Giant*, a three-hour-twenty-minute saga of two generations of Texans, based on Edna Ferber's popular novel; for this, Elizabeth would be loaned out to Warner Bros. Like many Hollywood films of the time (*The Greatest Show on Earth*, *The Ten Commandments*, *The Big Country*, *War and Peace* and *Around the World in 80 Days*), *Giant* was planned as an extravagant, sprawling, long, colorful, highly dramatic epic—everything, in other words, that an audience could not find on its television screens at home.

Elizabeth knew that Grace Kelly had been Stevens's first choice, and that only Kelly's unavailability encouraged him to offer the role to Elizabeth; she was aware, too, that the role of Leslie Linton Benedict would be the greatest challenge of her career thus far. "Strong-willed, independent, graceful and romantic," she read of the character in the production notes, "Leslie is Virginia-bred and has a taste for good clothes and lost causes. She reads liberally and is something of a crusader. As such, she will take the war, if necessary, to the enemy's camp, even if that happens to be her husband's bedroom. She is attractive, stubborn, tender and consoling. Her age starts at about 21, goes through 45." Elizabeth would have to create a complex portrait of a woman tested by an often hostile family, by time, chance and the ethos of modern Texas ranch-estate values. By the end of filming that autumn, she had done this beyond even Stevens's expectations. Spirited yet sensitive, her Leslie Benedict ranks as one of her half-dozen great roles.

As it happened, this was the longest project of Elizabeth's career: she worked from May 19 to October 12, on location in Virginia and Texas and, for the most part, on soundstages in Burbank.

After wardrobe, makeup and camera tests in late April, Elizabeth arrived for her first day of work at the Warner studio on May 19. "I was no longer a teenager and I no longer had anybody on the set to protect me," she said years later, alluding to the director's habit of requiring multiple takes of almost every shot on *Giant*. In fact, the easy relationship Elizabeth had enjoyed with Stevens during the filming of *A Place in the Sun* was not to be repeated. "He could really be quite cold," she added, and her costar, Rock Hudson, remembered that "George Stevens and Elizabeth fought a lot" over the repeated takes, usually demanded without explanation of the reason, and thus without criticism or suggestion.

These conflicts were made more difficult in the excruciating heat of the Texas summer, where the company moved from June 6 to July 9, working in the sleepy town of Marfa, population 2,000. There, daytime temperatures routinely hit 120 degrees in the shade, and there, despite the rugged life and rustic discomforts, Elizabeth sealed her friendships with Rock Hudson and with James Dean, two very different personalities who shared the common terror that disclosure of their homosexuality would alienate potential friends and ultimately destroy their careers. It was, after all, America in 1955: being gay was worse than being Communist. Death was held to be preferable.

Hudson was otherwise an easygoing soul, accustomed (like Elizabeth) to being considered merely an attractive presence, with no fair assessment of his desire to be a good actor. Dean, on the other hand, was a tangle of conflicts, ornery, difficult and enormously vain. He was, to be sure, committed to the art of acting, but at twenty-four he was caught in a vise of personal anxiety. To both men, Elizabeth was a warm friend, encouraging and completely accepting of their sexual orientation, which she regarded as unremarkable. Life was a chain of mysteries and nothing was more mysterious than sex, for which rules and regulations and norms of conduct (so she always believed) were absurd. In this regard, she was certainly a woman ahead of her time. It would have been unthinkable for her to reject a friend or colleague on the basis of sexual orientation. Shy, she identified with homosexuals' fears of disclosure; compassionate by nature, she was moved to condole what she considered needless human suffering caused by smug moralism—just as she appreciated consolation in the sufferings of her own love life.

"The creativity of homosexuals has made so much possible in

this town, in all the arts!" she said. "Take out the homosexuals and there's no Hollywood!" Even in 1992, when she spoke those words on Whoopi Goldberg's television show, Elizabeth was not uttering a common creed; she had long worked in a town and industry noted for a fierce homophobia and a profound moral hypocrisy. When Goldberg suggested that Elizabeth's words were sending shock waves all across town, she replied, "I certainly hope so!"

Nor was Elizabeth's spirit a case of mere liberal lip service. She had at least one lesbian secretary, always a good and loyal friend to her, and later many of her male secretaries were gay. Years later, when her interior decorator, Waldo Fernandez, and Trip Haenisch, his companion of fourteen years, adopted a child, Elizabeth asked to be the godmother, and saw to it that her new husband ("who probably never met a homosexual until he moved into this house," as she cheerfully said) became the godfather.

Such an unprejudiced attitude, it must be recalled, was neither widespread nor particularly prudent in Hollywood, where (thus the conventional wisdom) everything must conform to middle-class American values. But from her teenage years, she had accepted gays as friends—Hudson, Dean, Clift, among the many. This she did because such relationships were free of sexual tension or pressure, and because she sympathized with the beleaguered and benighted gays of her time, those forced to hide (and, like Hudson, even forced to marry), those who were constrained by absurd standards of what supposedly comprised "normal" human conduct. Elizabeth Taylor's open, accepting, nonjudgmental attitude explains why, with the outbreak of the AIDS pandemic in the 1980s, she was the first celebrity to fight against prejudice as well as a disease, against ignorance as much as a virus.

With Rock Hudson, she had an uncomplicated friendship.

Rock and I hit it off right away and acted like a pair of kids. The heat, humidity and dust [in Marfa] were so thoroughly oppressive we had to bolster our spirits any way we could. So we stayed out drinking all night and luckily were young enough and resilient

enough to go straight to the set in the morning with fresh com-
plexions and never even bags under our eyes. During our toots,
we concocted the best drink I ever tasted—a chocolate martini,
made with vodka, Hershey's syrup and Kahlua. How we survived
I'll never know.

Hudson made no secret of his dislike for Dean, who recipro-
cated. "Jimmy was always late, really very unprofessional," Hudson
complained later. "You know the type: the Broadway actor who
comes to California and deigns to make a motion picture—that
attitude." But again to her credit, Elizabeth befriended Dean
despite Hudson.

After four bit parts, James Dean had landed three leading roles
in succession (in *East of Eden* and *Rebel Without a Cause*, just before
Giant) and had very quickly achieved stardom as the prototype of
the disaffected, sensitive postwar American youth. Disconnected
from his feelings and full of neurotic self-loathing, he found a sympathetic listener in Elizabeth, who was (as with Montgomery Clift)
both nurturing and respectful.

> Sometimes Jimmy and I would sit up until three in the morning
> talking, and he would tell me about his past life, his conflicts and
> some of his loves and tragedies. And the next day it was almost as
> if he didn't want to recognize me, or to remember that he had
> revealed so much of himself the night before. And so he would
> pass me and ignore me, or just give me a cursory nod of the
> head. And then it took him a day or two to become my friend
> again. I found all that hard to understand.

Back at the studio, Elizabeth began to endure a series of ailments and illnesses; none of them was grave, and each won her a
temporary reprieve from what she considered George Stevens's
inordinate demands. From July 16 to August 11, she complained
variously of sciatica, a throat infection and abdominal pains, and Dr.
Robert Buckley ordered her to bed. An examination on August 2
revealed a simple bruise under her knee, but Dr. Buckley told the

unit managers (Tom Andrew and Eric Stacey) that crutches were needed. She worked from August 12 to September 26, but on that day she was coming down with a head cold and was again out for four days.

Early in the evening of September 30, she was sitting in a Warner screening room with Stevens, nursing her sniffles and reviewing rough cuts of her last day's work. A telephone rang, and the director answered. A moment later he announced to the group that James Dean, who had been driving his new Porsche at almost a hundred miles per hour while heading north to an auto race, had been killed in a head-on collision near Paso Robles. He had completed his work in *Giant* on September 22, had just signed a contract for nine films in the next six years and had celebrated by buying a new roadster he raced to his death.

Elizabeth was devastated, and although Stevens had to continue with filming next day, she could not work. She arrived three hours late to the set and, almost catatonic with grief, had to be sent home. By October 4, she had been admitted to UCLA General Hospital (as the Medical Center was then called), "but they have been unable to reach a diagnosis of her condition," as the production manager wrote to Jack Warner. She then ran a fever and lost her voice. Finally, Elizabeth returned on October 11 and 12 to complete her final shots.

The last quarter of *Giant* slips dangerously in the suds of soap opera—rather like "Dallas" with a social conscience and a richer cast of characters—yet despite its lack of focus and its languid, often overwritten sequences, *Giant* remains a rich and fascinating movie, strong on character, full of mood and allusion. Vast panoramas fill the screen, vistas against which people with big ideas seem comparatively vacuous, important only according to their own narrow standards. *Giant* also tackles the racism of the Texas rich, who pay Mexicans slave wages, will not allow Texas doctors to aid them, bar "wetbacks" from Texas diners and condemn mixed marriages.

Its greatest asset remains the performance of Elizabeth Taylor. "She's a seething mass of feminine wiles," said Michael Wilding of his wife about this time, and the same can be said of her portrait of

Leslie Linton Benedict. Challenged by the rugged life of the Texas plains and by a Texas culture inimical to her intelligence and liberalism, the character could have been simply a cipher, a mouthpiece for the film's liberal philosophy. Instead, Elizabeth gave her the perfect combination of confidence and coyness. From the early breakfast scene, she is both arrogant and reserved, and as the sequences progress there emerges a coherent character whose common sense is admirable but not unrealistic. Unfortunately, Metro indicated the passing of a quarter century only by fitting her with a gray-streaked hairpiece; she would gladly have applied aging makeup and padding, and thus appeared matronly. As it is, Leslie as a grandmother was slightly incredible—although twenty years later the same would be said of Elizabeth. But her scenes with Rock Hudson, particularly in the last half-hour, have the ring of emotional truth, of obstacles overcome and rapprochement achieved.

Ironically, there was in Elizabeth's life no such happy ending to the current problem-ridden arrangement. Although it would be unknown in Hollywood for many months, her marriage to Michael Wilding was in irredeemable disarray, and that autumn of 1955 they no longer shared the same bedroom. "We had a brother-sister kind of relationship," she said, "which is not my idea of a marriage."

Chapter Six

1956

WEARY OF PROFESSIONAL INACTIVITY but afraid to pursue success, Michael Wilding had become, as John Garfield had ominously predicted, Mr. Elizabeth Taylor. "I follow you around," he said during the Christmas 1955 holiday. "And I'm left alone in a corner." The clinging child he married had grown into an independent (if not yet really mature) young woman. Restless and eager for distraction after the death of James Dean, she had concluded *Giant*, her twenty-fifth film, in a state of acute depression.

Thus on her twenty-fourth birthday, in February 1956, she was not at all a contented young wife and mother, nor was she the mythic movie star of popular American imagination, happy in love, content in riches and basking in the perquisites of fame. Eager for diversion, hungry for activity and excitement, she confided more and more in the darkly meditative, tortured Montgomery Clift. He was always sympathetic, but at the same time he was battling his own demon, a kind of self-hatred he tried to drown with alcohol and suffocate with narcotics. Since the age of nineteen, Elizabeth enjoyed social drinking—a glass or two of champagne at a party, the occasional whiskey or wine—but seeing the effects of drugs on Clift, she was discouraged from such experimentation. His problems did not, however, obscure for Elizabeth the value of his intelligence, the sensitivity of his feelings or the rightness of his understanding of her.

If drugs were unappealing and alcohol not a problem, food, at least, seemed an innocent indulgence, and in the early months of 1956, she ate with alarming abandon: she had already gained weight during her second pregnancy, and now the pounds quickly accumulated. "My taste buds get in an uproar," she said, "and I get a lusty, sensual thing out of eating." Montgomery Clift was concerned about the effect on her health: "She really became terribly overweight," he said, "and when she came out in an evening dress, I said, 'Honey, you're the broadest broad I ever saw!'" Her reaction was wild laughter.

Elizabeth's binge overeating, as so often in such cases, was the direct result of emotional problems she was not quite ready to face, issues that had to do with her failed marriage. "I know of only a few marriages that are happy when a wife is the star," she told a reporter knowingly. Hers was not one of those happy marriages. At forty-three, Michael seemed too settled, too calm and unambitious for Elizabeth. She no longer saw him as the suave gentleman whose presence spelled dignity and maturity; now, Michael merely represented the past. "He had offered her a stable relationship after the nightmare of her first marriage," said Elizabeth's friend Debbie Reynolds. "But Michael was a sweet, sensitive, gentle man and did not offer the passion and excitement that Elizabeth needed."

Michael was not oblivious. By spring 1956, he and his wife had separate social lives, and were together only with the children. "I was still in love with her," he said later, "but a barrier of silence and rejection had grown between us." He could suffer her chronic tardiness, her habitual sloppiness, her apparent need for two hours at the dressing table before an engagement. But there was nothing for them to discuss any longer.

"I'm afraid in those last years I gave him rather a rough time,"

Elizabeth admitted later. "[I] sort of henpecked him and probably wasn't mature enough for him." For one thing, she was anxious about money. Over 80 percent of her $190,000 annual income was withheld for taxes; 10 percent went to her lawyer Jules Goldstone and 5 percent more to her business manager; and the mortgage on the new home was almost $2,000 monthly. Add to that the expenses of nannies and secretaries and a lavish general lifestyle, and the Wildings were never out of debt.

Financial concerns in fact caused a fatal rift when Michael turned down a lucrative offer that spring to play the role of Henry Higgins in the first American tour of the hit musical *My Fair Lady*. This decision was not made from laziness or indifference, however: he felt he had not the stamina for a tour, and he was embarrassed and worried over the seizures not yet completely controlled by epilepsy medication. But Elizabeth, whose attitude toward illness was that one coped by overcoming, was furious when her husband rejected the role that brought Rex Harrison his greatest fame and fortune. "You're nothing but a coward," she cried, bursting into his room, her face flushed with rage. "To think that the man I once loved turns out to be nothing but a coward!" The Wilding marriage was history from that afternoon, and although neither he nor Elizabeth took steps toward a formal separation, Michael packed a suitcase and spent several days with Joseph Cotten and his wife, Lenore. Wilding and Cotten had acted together in Hitchcock's *Under Capricorn* in 1948 and after that were constant friends.

Elizabeth, meantime, had her distractions from marital strife: a script to study for the film she was to begin that April, and a crash diet before the start of production. By restricting herself to coffee for breakfast, two scrambled eggs for lunch and steak for dinner (a diet soon to be pronounced dangerously unhealthy), she lost fifteen pounds in just over two weeks.

The immediate motivation for such discipline was her forthcoming role in *Raintree County*. With Montgomery Clift as her costar, a provocative (if overwritten) script by Millard Kaufman and the sensitive and evocative guidance of director Edward Dmytryk, Elizabeth began this picture with a new earnestness about her career. She had enjoyed making only four of her previous films (*National Velvet*, *A Place in the Sun*, *The Last Time I Saw Paris* and *Giant*), but in *Raintree County* she had a mature and complex role in a film with credible adult relationships, an important antiwar and antiracist theme, and a pointed exploration of the nature of true parenthood. With this project and Montgomery Clift as her unofficial mentor, she began to take her craft and her gifts far more seriously than ever before.

"I got tired of all the garbage," she said frankly that spring, "tired of acting year after year in movies with no story content." And then, with the refreshing lack of egotism that marked her self-assessment throughout her life, she added:

> Don't ask me about acting. Some day, I hope to be really good. I'm now learning and developing. I'm trying. I've always been an intuitive actress as opposed to an instructed one. I have no technique, I just try to become the other person. Some people act by charts or by the Stanislavski method. I can only do it by forgetting myself completely, even moving or picking up things by impulse. I've been good so few times, but I'd like to be good always.

Yet the truth is that she had been consistently good and often downright excellent.

To review the early films of Elizabeth Taylor is to discover how superlative she was in mediocre or shallow pictures (*Conspirator* and *The Big Hangover*, for example) as in better vehicles (*Cynthia* and *A Place in the Sun*). From the age of eleven, in *National Velvet*, she had been completely natural and credible in her delineation of a character, investing each with subtle emotions and integrating herself within each dramatic situation rather than extracting herself from it by histrionic devices that called attention to her exceptional presence. In addition, she had learned to extend the range of her voice, which tended to be high, sometimes pinched and shrill; and her diction was invariably like crystal. This lack of pretense—a quality of character that marked her life as it did her art—was not, it must be emphasized, simply the result of directorial authoritarianism.

Her modest remarks about herself that season were, therefore, not uttered in a spirit of deliberately endearing false humility. For herself as for many critics, she believed she was at her best in roles requiring little more than competent photography: unwittingly, she endorsed the absurd American idea that a woman of great beauty cannot possibly be a great talent. That same year, 1956, Marilyn Monroe was judged according to the same specious standard: even her first-rate performances in *The Prince and the Showgirl* and *Bus Stop* (which Monroe also produced) were underestimated by most critics. She was alluringly beautiful, she was opulent, she was desirable; she could not, therefore, be any good. Just so for Elizabeth Taylor, who also came to believe that she was at her best when carefully dressed, made up and lighted. That she was one of the finest screen actresses of her generation never occurred to critics (much less to studio executives or producers), and because her performances seemed so artless, unforced and inevitable, even the public did not think her much of an actress—precisely because she never seemed to be acting.

For anyone doubting her impressive palette of talents, *Raintree County* (for which she received a flat fee of $100,000, $50,000 less than Clift's) remains an unassailable corrective. Based on the 1948 novel by Ross Lockridge, Jr., the six-million-dollar movie has often been glibly called a Yankee version of *Gone With the Wind*. Filmed on the Metro back lot in Culver City; in New Orleans; in Natchez, Mississippi; and in Danville, Kentucky, *Raintree County* is rich in character and theme. In brief résumé, it is a story, set against the background of the Civil War and racial prejudice, of an idealistic Indiana man (Clift) whose Southern wife (Elizabeth) becomes progressively insane.

Filming began in early April 1956, after Elizabeth had submitted to complicated costume fittings for her 1859 wardrobe, and after she had studied with dialect coach Marguerite Littman, who trained her in the fine points of Southern speech. According to Edward Dmytryk, during the long shooting schedule Elizabeth displayed not a drop of star temperament; quite the contrary, she was the consummate professional—word-perfect, on time to the set, both unassuming and genial with everyone from costars to technicians. "She really was the compassionate person I had heard about," Dmytryk recalled. "She's the kind of woman who made everyone else's problems her own." Her major problem on this film was the worrisome Montgomery Clift, whose drinking and drug abuse were now clearly dangerous. Dore Schary, now in charge of production at Metro, took a half-million-dollar insurance policy in case the production should be halted by anyone's illness. As it happened, this was a prudent gesture.

Elizabeth's sympathetic nature was certainly evident on the night of May 12, when a dreadful accident occurred.

After a day at the studio, she invited a few friends to Beverly Estate Drive for an impromptu supper; the guests included Edward and Jean Dmytryk, Rock Hudson, Kevin McCarthy and, later in the evening, Montgomery Clift. He seemed tired but he drank nothing, as Edward Dmytryk clearly remembered. Monty and Elizabeth told the director how amused (and doubtless pleased) they were that Robert Surtees, the cinematographer of Raintree County, was photographing them to appear so young and beautiful, but this was not such a difficult assignment.

The party dispersed early, led by a weary Monty Clift. Because he disliked the tortuous curves descending from the Wilding home to the flats of Beverly Hills, he asked McCarthy to lead the way. But not far down the road, McCarthy heard a terrific crash and returned to find Clift almost dead in his car, which had crashed into a telephone pole. "I had one blink too many," he said before slipping into unconsciousness.

McCarthy ran back to the Wilding house for help, and Elizabeth raced to the scene. Cradling Clift's bloodied head in her lap, she comforted him until an ambulance arrived. Miraculously, although Clift's nose and jaw were broken, he healed brilliantly and without any need for plastic surgery. This took nine weeks, and so *Raintree County* was shut down until July. But by the time Clift returned to work, the pain of his recovery had aggravated his drug addiction. Throughout his ordeal, "Bessie Mae," as he called her (as in a punning conjunction of her name and *Besame mucho*), was his loyal ally, and she supported his desire to return to work as soon as possible. "Elizabeth was afraid he would kill himself if he wasn't allowed to go back to work," said Dore Schary. With Elizabeth's patience and encouragement, he did so, returning to work in July, when the film went forward toward a successful completion.

One of the most remarkable aspects of Elizabeth's performance in *Raintree County* was her superb Southern accent. "She really was miraculous," said Dmytryk, "and some of the credit for her training has to go to Monty Clift, who helped her in little private rehearsals, just the two of them. While she was trying to encourage him in his private life, he was a constant source of strength for her in her acting. It was really a very loving, very devoted, nonsexual friendship."

The addition of a convincing drawl to her acting repertoire would be useful again later in, for example, *Cat on a Hot Tin Roof*. But in that case, too, Elizabeth's regional diction was so natural and unforced that it went largely unremarked by critics; ironically, then, her achievement was underrated precisely because it seemed less like acting than real life. Added to this was her unusual combination of vulnerability and strength as Susanna, her girlish dependence and the intimation of a heroic struggle against madness. Particularly haunting are her monologues describing scenes of her childhood memories, and her terrifying scene in a lunatic asylum, when for just a moment the awful curtain of madness parts to reveal the contours of a character once full of sweetness, courage and hope. As Susanna in *Raintree County*, Elizabeth very much deserved her Academy Award nomination as best actress of the year, a prize that eventually went to Joanne Woodward.

During the early spring of 1956, it was clear to Elizabeth and Michael—and to many friends—that their marriage was over. Just as she began work on the picture, Elizabeth was, to no one's surprise, in love again, this time with the handsome young Kevin McClory, once a production assistant on several John Huston films and now a second unit director on Mike Todd's spectacle *Around the World in 80 Days*. She had met McClory at the Malibu home of

Shirley MacLaine and her husband, Steve Parker. "Elizabeth's marriage with Michael Wilding was on the rocks by then," McClory said years later,

> and she and I were seeing quite a lot of each other—very, very quietly. The only people who really knew about us were Shirley and Steve, because we used to go out to their place in Malibu. I was in love with Elizabeth, and I think she was in love with me. Anyway, we were planning to get married. But I told her I couldn't afford to keep her in a big house with a pool in the Beverly Hills area, and she said she'd be happy to live with me in a small place like Shirley and Steve had at Malibu. At that time, I was having a real struggle visualizing myself getting married to a star like Elizabeth on my meager finances.

In June, while Elizabeth and the *Raintree County* production company awaited Montgomery Clift's recovery, she had little to do but visit him daily and accept more social invitations than usual. Kevin McClory was naturally more attentive than ever during this time, and soon the columns were buzzing. "The Mocambo [nightclub] tried to shush up her appearance one recent evening with Kevin McClory," wrote columnist Dick Williams in the Los Angeles *Mirror-News*. Finally, word reached Mike Todd, McClory's boss.

"Everybody knows who you're seeing," Todd said, adding that he would like to meet the Wildings. "This took me completely by surprise," recalled McClory, "but I thought, 'Sure, why not,' and I said that I would fix it up when the next suitable occasion arose."

That happened on June 30, when Mike Todd hired a yacht called *The Hyding* and asked McClory to invite some people for a weekend cruise. Todd would steer them all north to Santa Barbara, where they would watch the filming of a Japanese schooner being used for a Far Eastern sequence of *Around the World in 80 Days*. The guest list finally included the actress Evelyn Keyes; Todd's secretary Richard Hanley; the agent Kurt Frings and his wife, playwright Ketti

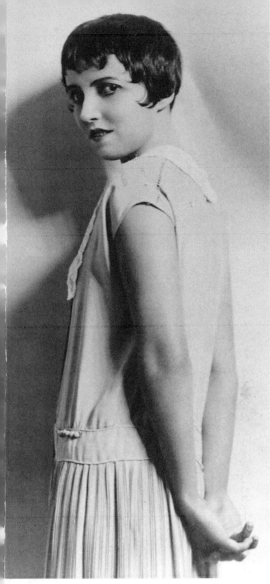

Sara Sothern, on Broadway in *The Little Spitfire*: 1926. (Culver Pictures)

ABOVE RIGHT: Elizabeth Taylor, age four, with her brother, Howard, six: 1936. (Courtesy of the Academy of Motion Picture Arts and Sciences)

Age five, with Sara and Howard: 1937. (Courtesy of the Academy of Motion Picture Arts and Sciences)

OPPOSITE, TOP:
Age twelve, with
Mickey Rooney in
National Velvet: 1944.
(Culver Pictures)

OPPOSITE, BOTTOM:
MGM studio chief
Louis B. Mayer offers a
memento on the last day
of filming *National Velvet*:
1944. (Courtesy of
the Academy of Motion
Picture Arts and
Sciences)

Age eleven, at Metro-
Goldwyn-Mayer: 1943.
(Culver Pictures)

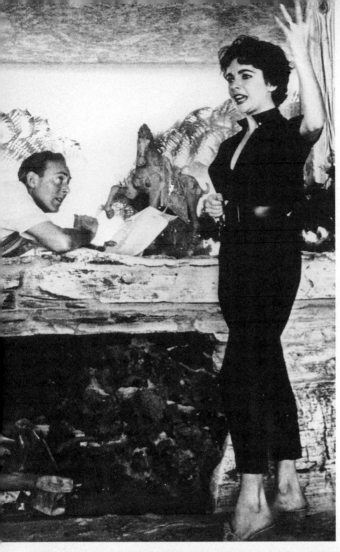

Rehearsing at home, with Michael Wilding giving cues: 1953. (Sanford Roth/Culver Pictures)

OPPOSITE: With James Dean, during filming of *Giant*: 1955. (Culver Pictures)

Mr. and Mrs. Michael Wilding at the Coconut Grove, Hollywood: 1954. (Culver Pictures)

OPPOSITE: Mr. and Mrs. Conrad Nicholas Hilton, on honeymoon at Pebble Beach: May 9, 1950. (Courtesy of the Academy of Motion Picture Arts and Sciences)

Paramount's lead publicity photo for the release of *A Place in the Sun*: 1951. (Courtesy of the Academy of Motion Picture Arts and Sciences)

BELOW: Age nineteen, with director Stanley Donen, at the 1951 Academy Awards. (Courtesy of the Academy of Motion Picture Arts and Sciences)

With UCLA athlete Bob Precht, assigned by MGM to escort Elizabeth
to her school prom: December 1949. (Courtesy of the Academy of
Motion Picture Arts and Sciences)

OPPOSITE: Age eighteen, as Kay Banks, in *Father of the Bride*: 1950.
(Courtesy of the Academy of Motion Picture Arts and Sciences)

With costar Montgomery Clift, on location at Lake Tahoe for *A Place in the Sun*:
autumn 1949. (Courtesy of the Academy of Motion Picture Arts and Sciences)

With actor and occasional
escort Marshall Thompson:
1949. (Courtesy of the
Academy of Motion Picture
Arts and Sciences)

Back to the MGM school-
room, age seventeen: 1949.
(Courtesy of the Academy
of Motion Picture Arts
and Sciences)

Wearing Glenn Davis's football sweater: 1948. (Movie Star News)

In her new Cadillac with Sara: 1948. (Culver Pictures)

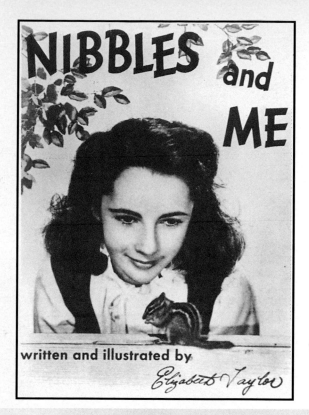

NIBBLES and ME

written and illustrated by

Elizabeth Taylor

Her first book: 1946.
(Courtesy of the Academy
of Motion Picture Arts
and Sciences)

On the beach at Malibu,
age fourteen: 1946.
(Courtesy of the Academy
of Motion Picture Arts
and Sciences)

Traveling with Rock Hudson and George Stevens for the location shooting on *Giant*: 1955. (Culver Pictures)

With Montgomery Clift, in *Raintree County*: 1956. (Culver Pictures)

Mr. and Mrs. Mike Todd, at the premiere of *Giant*: 1956.
(Culver Pictures)

With sons Michael and Christopher Wilding: 1957. (Culver Pictures)

Frings; Art Cohn, who had written *The Girl Who Had Everything* and who was then writing Todd's biography; and Elizabeth and Michael Wilding.

Mike Todd, who had just marked his forty-ninth birthday, was a flamboyant producer in the tradition of Diamond Jim Brady and P. T. Barnum; indeed, he combined the spirit of a carnival pitchman with the ambition of Napoleon. Born Avrom Goldbogen in Minneapolis on June 22, 1907, he was the son of an Orthodox rabbi who had immigrated from Poland. Called "Toddy" in childhood, he had no education after the sixth grade in Chicago, where he began his career as an entrepreneur, peddling newspapers, selling shoes and playing the shill for sidewalk hawkers. At fifteen he changed his name, lied convincingly about his age and married a girl named Bertha Freshman, who bore him a son who was several years older than Elizabeth. Todd lost small fortunes in the lumber, paving and steamship businesses, and during the 1930s gathered gags for Olsen and Johnson, the vaudeville comics. "Dames and comedy," he said, was his theatrical menu: "High dames and low comedy—that's my message." This recipe has rarely been unsuccessful.

By 1940, Todd was a Broadway producer with at least one success—*The Hot Mikado,* a jazzy version of the Gilbert and Sullivan operetta. Not long after, he was dating Joan Blondell, the actress who was still married to film star Dick Powell. Bertha, however, would not grant Mike's request for divorce. Concurrent with the Blondell affair, Todd was romancing the humorous and intelligent ecdysiast Gypsy Rose Lee, who led the cast of his immensely successful musical burlesque *Star and Garter*, one of nine shows (among them *Mexican Hayride* and *Up in Central Park*) he produced between 1942 and 1946. During that time, Dick Powell met June Allyson, Joan Blondell filed for divorce, and Bertha died under tragic and mysterious circumstances. During a fight with Todd, a kitchen knife was brandished. The tendons of Bertha's hand were severed and she was rushed to an emergency room. While surgeons labored to repair the damage, she suddenly died—of shock, it was finally reported, resulting from an adverse reaction to the anesthetic.

There were more Broadway successes and a few flops, and in 1947 he married Joan Blondell. But when he squandered her money and filed for bankruptcy, she, too, became disenchanted, and by the end of 1950 they were separated. Perhaps Blondell's broken arm, sustained during an argument with Todd, contributed to her decision, too.

His sense of spectacle grew with his ego. During the summers of 1952 and 1953, he produced "A Night in Venice" at the Jones Beach Marine Stadium in New York, where he filled the stage with three hundred performers, among them Metropolitan Opera singers. The show, set to waltz music by Johann Strauss, was a curious (but successful) cross between a Viennese rhapsody and a Coney Island hot dog. It was, in other words, a Mike Todd production.

In 1952, with the threat of television, Hollywood studios frantically sought anything that would lure audiences from their living rooms. Among the ploys were a wider use of color; three-dimensional gimmicks; great spectacles; a gradual increase in insinuated sex and simulated violence; and (in a mercifully brief experiment) Smell-O-Vision, which was exactly what its name implied. One of the first of these gimmicks, in 1952, was a curved-screen, three-projector technique known as Cinerama, a clumsy but provocative system that (unlike 3-D) required no special glasses and seemed to pitch viewers right into the action.

Todd invested in Cinerama, and this good judgment prepared for his deal with the American Optical Company, which developed a new wide-screen process remarkable for crisp color definition. Their joint venture was called Todd-AO, and the first film made with it, *Oklahoma!*, was hugely successful when it opened in autumn 1955. By this time, he had sold his stock in Todd-AO to finance *Around the World in 80 Days*, which took him around the world for over a year. By delaying payment to his stars (David Niven and Cantinflas) and his writer (S. J. Perelman) and by cajoling the likes of Frank Sinatra, Marlene Dietrich, Noël Coward, Shirley MacLaine, Charles Boyer, Ronald Colman, John Gielgud, Cedric Hardwicke, Buster Keaton, Ava Gardner and dozens more, he assembled the most impressive cast in American movie history.

* * *

Neither tall nor conventionally handsome in the movie star way, Todd in no way resembled Nicky Hilton or Michael Wilding. He had black hair, a strong face with a prominent, aggressive jaw and a magnetic presence that made him seem like an ex-prize fighter who had become a savvy accountant. He peppered his speech with the fiercest obscenities, smoked malodorous cigars, waved away any objections to his ideas and—even when he was cash poor, which was very often—lavished wildly extravagant gifts on his women and his friends. "Money," he once said, "is only important to people who haven't got it. I've never been poor, only broke. Being poor is a frame of mind. Being broke is a temporary situation." Had he so chosen, and had he survived into the brave new world of two decades later, such a homespun, uplifting philosophy might well have earned him political popularity.

For all his apparent vulgarity, Mike Todd had a certain raw charm and a keen theatrical imagination. He also had many friends, and not because he was occasionally wealthy: he was, in the complex nature of many such men, a compassionate man inclined to acts of astonishing kindness even to those who could in no way reciprocate. Whatever his faults, no one ever accused him of being dull. "When he entered a room, he took over," said Debbie Reynolds. "He was rugged and sensuous-looking and utterly charming." Her husband, Eddie Fisher, was an adoring acolyte in Todd's retinue, and Fisher's career as a television crooner and recording star was much aided by Todd's advice and backing.

"He was certainly a character right out of Damon Runyon," said the actress Evelyn Keyes, who had been living with Todd for three years by the summer of 1956, and who was a great help to him in many aspects of filming *Around the World*. An energetic, bright and comely blond star since 1938 (in, among others, *Gone With the Wind, Here Comes Mr. Jordan* and *The Jolson Story*), she had been married to directors Charles Vidor and John Huston before she met Todd. (Later, she was also the author of several books, among them a witty, frank and informative memoir.)

"He won millions one week and lost them the next," according to Evelyn Keyes. "But when he lost, he didn't stop being generous. When Mike liked someone, he gave not only gifts, he gave of himself. He cared, he was a mensch, and that person's life meant something to him. There was much more to him than mere braggadocio." That opinion was echoed by many who knew him, in and out of the Hollywood popularity contest.

That last day of June, at sea, no one suspected that very soon the lives of Mike Todd and Elizabeth Taylor would forever change. Evelyn, for one, noticed nothing unusual. Elizabeth sipped champagne—rather too liberally that day, Evelyn thought—she read, she took the sun. To Mike, who made no attempt to ingratiate himself with his guest, Elizabeth represented everything he seemed to reject. "Besides actresses, Mike didn't like women who drank a great deal," Evelyn recalled. "And she had a husband." There was, to put the matter succinctly, nothing in Mike's or Elizabeth's manner to suggest the sudden, loud ringing of romantic sirens.

Soon after the weekend cruise, Todd invited the Wildings to a dinner party for Edward R. Murrow, and then to a barbecue. He also asked Evelyn to fly to Caracas, Venezuela, to see if that city's largest movie theater would accommodate the specifics of the Todd-AO projection system; she was then to proceed to London and Paris, to meet with actors in *Around the World*. These duties Evelyn was delighted to undertake: to her this signaled—in addition to the fifteen-carat diamond ring he had offered her—that Todd was inviting her to full participation in his life and career.

Weeks later, she learned that something else was in the works.

"I was in Paris when the telephone call came from Mike," Evelyn recalled. "I've fallen in love with Elizabeth," he said.

He was teasing, she thought. He wanted to make her jealous. And so she went along with the game. "Elizabeth who?"

But he was not joking, he explained. She listened. "Well, sure," she said with admirable calm. "I understand. Listen. Good luck to you."

And then, in her solitude, Evelyn realized why she had been shipped out of town. And why, when the ring was too big for her finger, he had taken it back. It was, she felt, a tawdry setup—"his script, from beginning to end." The scenario called for Evelyn to exit; she did so, with consummate grace and without rancor.

"To tell the truth," she said years later, "Mike and I had run our course. I never wanted to marry him and Elizabeth did. He couldn't do much better, could he? For a while, he thought he could have both Elizabeth and me, and when I moved to Paris he was very upset. He loved all the attention he got from his affair and marriage to Elizabeth. And he was furious when I went off with Artie [Shaw, whom she married in 1957]."

Falling in love, of course, was a Hollywood thing to do. Actors did it constantly on-screen and were expected to do it offscreen, too. Their job is pretense, acting roles in little bits and pieces all day long. Elizabeth, among the most instinctive actors, read scripts that guided her life, then went to work with directors who guided the performance. With each script, there was a new story for her to play out, a new chance to endure and to enact something that would have a final resolution—a plot that would provide her with the logic and the closure so often denied by the apparently crazy rhythms of life experience.

Elizabeth remembered some things about that summer quite differently. Mike Todd's eyes followed her everywhere that June day on the boat, she wrote years later. He called her a "latent intellectual." He refilled her champagne glass, saying, "Drink as much as you want. It's your head." She liked his lack of awe for her stardom. She liked his brash, go-all-the-way attitude on first meetings. She liked his fascinating mixture of connoisseur and con man, his Broadway jargon and casual vulgarities. She liked everything about him, in fact, and he seemed more at ease with himself than Michael Wilding did.

In the years to come, Elizabeth said repeatedly that the day after the studio announced her separation from Michael Wilding (on July 19), Mike Todd asked her to meet him at Metro.

I had a feeling it might be for a picture . . . Mike came over and picked me up by the arm and without a word just dragged me

> out of the office and took me down the corridor, shoved me in
> an elevator and down another corridor—still not speaking, just
> marching along breaking my arm [shades of Joan Blondell]—and
> [he] went into a deserted office. He spoke very softly for about
> forty-five minutes. He told me that he loved me, that he had
> been thinking about me constantly, and he said he was going to
> marry me. I sat like a mongoose mesmerized by a cobra. He
> didn't ask me, he told me. He was irresistible . . . I left that
> office knowing I soon would be Mrs. Michael Todd.

According to Hedda Hopper, in whom Elizabeth later confided,
the conversation was somewhat spicier. "Elizabeth," he said, "I love
you and I'm going to marry you, and from now on you'll know
nobody but me." But "he didn't say 'know,'" added Hopper coyly:
another four-letter word sliced through the air that summer morning.

Such blunt forcefulness, foreign to Michael Wilding, was
instantly attractive to Elizabeth. It was, indeed, her latest role,
which might be called that of the young actress, yearning for the
excitement of love, who is swept away by the passion of a flamboyant producer. "I went from a weak man to a strong man," she said
years later. "I've done that a couple of times in my life."

In her attraction to Mike Todd, Elizabeth may also have sought
to cancel out the unhappy past with her remote father. By attentive
devotion and willing obedience, she would attempt to reverse the
hurt and undo the perceived rejection of her youth. "At last, I've got
a real man," she said, implying that Michael Wilding was not a real
man. This "real man" perhaps made her think of a nice Jewish
father who adored her.

The meeting with Todd, she said, occurred the day after her
separation from Michael Wilding was publicly announced. That
press release, distributed on July 19, 1956, was unequivocal:

> Much careful thought has been given to the step we are taking. It
> is being done so that we will have an opportunity to thoroughly
> work out our personal situation. We are in complete accord in
> making this amicable decision.

But the meeting with Todd occurred before her separation and was the direct cause of it.

On July 19, when the announcement was made, Elizabeth was on location in the South, resuming her role in *Raintree County*. The meeting with Todd actually took place on July 8—less than a week after they were introduced, when Elizabeth was at the studio for final costume fittings. And by July 8, she believed with all her heart that she had fallen so deeply in love that an immediate end to a failed marriage was justified. As it happened, she was not quite overwhelmed by Todd, as she later insisted: she was a willing participant in a remarkably precipitous romance.

In fact, within hours of her meeting with Todd at Metro that July 8, Wilding received "an ominous phone call from [Elizabeth]," as he detailed not long before his death. "I knew from her tone that she had something more on her mind than an exchange of small talk about the boys. 'You sound sad,' I remarked. 'Anything I can do to help?'

"'Yes,' came her prompt reply. 'Can you be your usual darling, understanding self and bear with me and listen to a statement I've just written? It's for the press, making our separation official, but I'd like you to hear it before it's published.'

"'Thanks,' I said, 'but I'd rather just read it in the papers, then I can believe it's about two other people.'

"'Oh, Mike,' she cried, on the edge of tears. 'I still love you. I'll always love you. But it isn't ring-a-ding-ding anymore. Do you understand?'"

He did—just as he understood that Metro had advised Elizabeth that they would in fact not release the news until after Eleanor Harris's three-part story on Elizabeth had run in *Look* magazine: the final installment, dated July 24, would be available to the public on July 18. And so the press release was issued on July 19 and ran in Los Angeles papers the next day.

As for Kevin McClory, he was just as confused as Michael Wilding. The same day as her meeting with Todd, she telephoned McClory, asking him to come to her at once. When he arrived,

McClory recalled, Elizabeth told him of her meeting with Todd, who had informed her "that she was going to marry [Todd]—he had made up his mind and that was it. She said, 'I told him about us and that I was going to marry you, and Mike went absolutely berserk.'"

Indeed, he had made up his mind. He would virtually intimidate Elizabeth by lavish displays of affection, alternating these with a strength of purpose she found impossible to resist. Michael Wilding was history, as he had known without doubt when he realized the seriousness of the McClory affair. "It isn't the Todd romance that hurt Wilding," several friends commented. "It's the one before it."

And then things happened more quickly than ever.

To visit Elizabeth on location, Mike Todd flew in his private plane from business appointments in Los Angeles and Manhattan. He brought gifts that Wilding could never afford, movie star presents that bedazzled her—furs and flowers and fabulously expensive jewels, for a start: bracelets, rings, lavalieres. He lunched with her and the company, he took her to dinner, and next morning he flew back to California or New York. A few days later, he arrived unannounced, awaited her completion of the day's shooting, then whisked her off to dinner in Chicago or St. Louis and returned her to the set on time next morning. Money was spent with wild prodigality, the champagne flowed like champagne. Todd's ostentation was Corinthian, her astonishment obvious. And so began a fierce love affair that would soon become a passionate whirlwind of a marriage. But there also began a slow, distinct diminution of the public's favorable view of beautiful Elizabeth Taylor, actress, wife and mother of two. Keeping only her own counsel, she ignored public opinion.

The pursuit continued throughout the summer. Dozens of roses arrived each morning at her dressing room, wherever she was. They spoke on the telephone for two, three, four hours each evening. A pearl ring was shipped, diamond earrings were presented in person. She was seen in New York with Todd, where she told a *Time* reporter, "I love Mike. I love him passionately."

At twenty-four, Elizabeth was being rushed into romance like a high school prom queen courted by the captain of the football team. On the Labor Day weekend, they sped off to Atlantic City, and there she received another pricey bauble. Returning late to work, she excused herself by flashing a twenty-carat diamond at the waiting Edward Dmytryk: "I'm engaged to Mike Todd," she said. "I always thought Elizabeth was a woman who needed a man more than almost anybody I know," said Dmytryk years later, "and it's interesting that she was a lot stronger than the men in her life, except for Mike Todd—he was the strongest."

Location work in Louisiana, Mississippi and Kentucky presented several problems—not the least, Clift's inexorable descent into a drug addiction from which he would never recover, and which would effectively cause his death at the age of forty-five a decade later. Elizabeth had lesser problems, but she suffered during production that summer, too, collapsing under the weight of her costumes, which were heavy with the authentic period fabrics demanded by the studio. "She was literally gasping for breath with hyperventilation," recalled Dmytryk, "and we had to put her to bed with sedation. But the local doctor assigned to us was unavailable to prescribe something. Monty leaped to the rescue, producing a drug and a syringe."

By September 26, the *Raintree County* company had returned to Los Angeles. The following evening, Elizabeth, George Stevens and Rock Hudson impressed their hand-and-footprints in cement in the forecourt of Grauman's Chinese Theatre, where *Giant* would have its Hollywood premiere on October 17. By this time, the Taylor-Todd romance was common knowledge: in his column, Sidney Skolsky reported that Elizabeth's sister-in-law, Mara (wife of her brother, Howard) was pregnant: this, Skolsky added, would make Elizabeth and Mike the aunt and uncle. Eddie Fisher and Debbie Reynolds frequently joined them to make a foursome, and according to Debbie the affair was oddly advertised: more than once while the Fishers were dining with them there was an awkward moment. "It wasn't unlike [Todd] to look across the dinner table and say to Elizabeth, 'I'd like to fuck you as soon as I finish this [dinner].'"

Elizabeth giggled; she found his bluntness refreshingly passionate. "It was not until she met Mike Todd that [Elizabeth and I] became friends," added Eddie. "I was his best audience, and he was my favorite performer."

In late October, Elizabeth and Mike flew to New York for the East Coast premieres of *Giant* and *Around the World in 80 Days*; at the same time, it was announced that she would establish Nevada residence in order to obtain a swift divorce. Wilding made no objections.

"I have already had quite a lengthy career in pictures," Elizabeth told a reporter. "I know what it is to be a star, but to me it is far more important now to be a woman rather than an actress. The blending of a career with marriage does not seem to work out satisfactorily. So retirement from maximum activity is the most desirable thing."

Her remarks were significant, revealing the extent to which Elizabeth was a woman of her time who regarded career and marriage as discordant, rival commitments. For many men and women, this was a false opposition. But in her case, it was real on a subtler level: she could not be a working actress and a married woman— not only because thus far she had not been able to manage both, but because she saw them as roles, and she could not play them simultaneously. True to her word, after *Raintree County* she did not work again for over a year, and during this time she was in a way living according to the demands of a new role: that of the globe-trotting, romantic young bride of that powerful personality Mike Todd.

Elizabeth Taylor filed for divorce from Michael Wilding on November 14—charging, in the absurdly contradictory terms of the day, "mental cruelty" in a suit her attorney described as "a friendly one." She waived alimony, asked $250 monthly for child support and agreed to divide common property; two weeks later, their Beverly Hills house was listed for sale at $200,000. That night, she and Todd departed for a brief holiday in Miami. Asked when they would marry, he winked at reporters and said, "She hasn't asked me yet." Michael Wilding, like Evelyn Keyes, withdrew gracefully from the story.

The Christmas holidays were Elizabeth's merriest—until, aboard a yacht in the Bahamas with Mike, she slipped and injured her back. Within two days, her legs were alarmingly numb and walking was all but impossible. She was rushed to the Harkness Pavilion of Columbia-Presbyterian Hospital in New York, where doctors discovered two things. Elizabeth had sustained serious damage to disks in her spine, and she was pregnant.

Chapter Seven

1957–1958

ON JANUARY 20, 1957, ELIZABETH Taylor, wearing a cumbersome back brace, was discharged from Columbia-Presbyterian Medical Center, New York City. To replace three crushed disks, her spine was fused with bone grafted from her hip, and the subsequent recuperation was acutely painful. Mike Todd paid for a room adjacent to hers, and there he spent almost every night so that he could attend her without interruption. He purchased four major artworks—by Utrillo, Cézanne, Monet and Cassatt (with a total worth of $315,000)—and hung them in her room; he also fastened round her neck a gold necklace. "I love being surrounded by beautiful things and I love being looked after," she said. Like no one else in her life before or after, Mike Todd responded to those cravings.

As for news of the pregnancy, this was, according to the prevailing morality, duly guarded until Metro-Goldwyn-Mayer, like a corporate midwife, announced almost two months after their marriage that Elizabeth was expecting a child at year's end. Columnists and Hollywood watchers began a scrupulous countdown.

Three days later, on January 23, Elizabeth and Mike left New York for Acapulco, where Michael Wilding had agreed to meet them and accelerate divorce proceedings. "It seems to me," said Wilding, "that it is high time we got the divorce and got it over with. I don't know anything about Mexican divorce procedure, but I am told my presence will simplify matters."

So it did, and on Saturday, February 2, the Todd wedding was held at the Mexican villa of Cantinflas, star of *Around the World in 80 Days*. Indeed, the event, produced and directed by Mike Todd, resembled nothing so much as an extravagant sequence from that movie. His wedding present to Elizabeth was a $90,000 diamond bracelet. Eddie Fisher was best man and his wife, Debbie Reynolds, joined Elizabeth's sister-in-law, Mara Taylor, attending the bride. Fifteen thousand white gladioli decorated the villa. Hundreds of guests were treated to twenty-five cases of vintage champagne and tons of caviar, crab, lobsters and smoked turkeys. For three days before the ceremony, Todd raced about town and around the villa, supervising every detail, commanding the troops of servants. When his son, Mike, put red-and-white carnations on the tables, Todd was shocked: only white blooms, he insisted. "Mike's the kind of guy Elizabeth needs—he'll lay down the law to her," said Francis Taylor, who knew whereof he spoke.

The Jewish ceremony was held at nine that evening, on a terrace illuminated by torches, and as the bride and groom kissed, a volley of fireworks was detonated and two orchestras struck up melodies. The festival lasted until dawn, when Elizabeth (dressed again for her wedding by Metro's Helen Rose) had to retire from sheer exhaustion.

The honeymoon at seaside was interrupted when Elizabeth's pain forced them back to New York on February 11, but she was released from Columbia-Presbyterian Hospital the same day with the news that she had only normal postoperative discomfort. The Todds made the rounds of New York nightclubs, restaurants and jewelry shops, where Mike learned that his wife certainly appreciated the little things of life—little rubies, little emeralds and little diamonds. Then they flew to Palm Springs, where they settled into a period of pleasant indolence, leasing Marion Davies's desert estate until mid-April.

Except for a few final pickup shots for *Raintree County* that spring, Elizabeth had been comfortably idle since the previous summer and would remain so for almost another year. For one thing, she was pregnant and looked forward to leisure time as wife and mother; for another—to put the matter in Todd's succinct tone— "She doesn't want to work and wants to be bossed." With this assessment, Elizabeth apparently agreed: "I knew I wanted more than anything else in the world a man who could control me," she said. "Mike was strong, which was very good for me, [and] I loved it when he would lose his temper and dominate me." And the more he did just that, the more lost she was in love. She had found her father, and he loved her.

The marriage of Elizabeth Taylor and Mike Todd—very like that she had contracted with Nicky Hilton, but this one long hailed as the great love match of the decade—must be assessed without reference to romantic exaggerations. It was Elizabeth's most clearly dependent relationship, that in which she was most obviously the daughter of a dominant father figure. But she was a woman who could not be passionately in love unless there was a thread of danger and domination to sustain mutual desire.

To describe the marriage in these terms is neither to condemn nor belittle it, but to understand the couple's deepest emotional needs, which prompted a vulgarity of lavishness and the superabundance of material things with which they surrounded themselves. In some way, both parties were wounded by their past: in Mike, Elizabeth found a new, generous father who still conformed in some ways to the old pattern with which she was familiar. He could be tyrannical, like Hilton; and exuberant in his love, like Wilding. And in Elizabeth, Mike found a more glamorous variation on Bertha (whom he controlled) and Joan (whom he did not). Familiar with severe discipline, accustomed to following orders at home and at work, Elizabeth longed to please—and nothing could accomplish that as much as rank subservience. This was all she knew of relations with men except for Michael Wilding, who was so different that she considered him weak and, at the end, no man at all.

The hostility that bound them together and defined their love was often witnessed. "Sure, we had a hell of a fight," Todd told a reporter who had heard tales of a melée at a London hotel that summer. "This gal's been looking for a fight all her life. Trouble is, everybody was too nice to fight back. Not me. When she flies into a tantrum, I fly into a bigger one. She's been on a milktoast diet all her life with men—but me, I'm red meat!" Yes, he admitted, they fought hard—"because we love it, and because it's so damn much fun to make up again."

"We really were the most raucous fighters, no holds barred in public or otherwise," Elizabeth said a few years after Todd's death, as if hostilities were the stuff of every love affair. She gave as an example the day they missed a flight because of Todd's tardiness. She teased him, he broke into a torrent of obscenities at the airport, and she responded with equal volume and extravagantly offensive hand gestures. A photograph of this altercation was wired round the world and remained one of the most famous documents of the Todds.

With some astonishment, Debbie Reynolds recorded an incident that seemed more perilous. One evening at the Todds' rented home in Beverly Hills, Debbie recalled, Mike

clobbered [Elizabeth], knocking her to the floor! He really hit her! Elizabeth screamed, walloped him right back and from there they went right into a huge fight. He dragged her by her hair—while she was screaming and kicking at him—across the room into the foyer. I went running after him, jumping on his back to help Elizabeth. The two of them were slapping each other around, [and] I was trying to pull Mike off, shouting at him to stop, and the next thing I knew they were wrestling on the floor, kissing and making up . . . They both got mad at me for interfering . . . They were like that during their entire relationship. They loved having a massive fight and then they would make up and make love.

Similarly, writer Leonard Mosley, who knew the Todds well in 1957, claimed he had "never once come across such a brawling, quarrelsome, argumentative and successful marriage" as theirs. Hollywood columnists knew that the marriage was indeed "full of fireworks, explosions, rockets," as Louella Parsons wrote.

"I'm red meat," Todd insisted. But whether hamburger or filet, he was not to be casually weighed. In return for her willing self-abasement, and as a perpetual part of the game, she accepted ever more lavish gifts of jewelry, fur coats, wardrobes and paintings by Old Masters. To the March Oscar ceremony, at which she gave the award for costume design, she wore a little something Mike had just presented—a $25,000 diamond tiara that gave her the look of a royal princess. "Doesn't every girl have one?" he asked Hedda Hopper, who inquired about its significance. Besides, that night he won, as producer, the Best Picture Oscar for *Around the World in 80 Days,* and he was not to be challenged.

The tiara, the art, the chokers and rings and bracelets and sables and ermines were presents that meant that she had been good, that she had played the perfect consort for her man, that she was worthy of him. They were also presents given by him in a kind of sacrificial homage—and to show her off, to parade the great star as his most prized achievement. Like the stereotypical older man with a young mistress—a Peter Arno cartoon sprung not altogether amusingly to life from the pages of *The New Yorker*—Todd overwhelmed Elizabeth with treasures and trinkets, borrowing against the income as yet unrealized from his epic picture. And so the cycle continued, with its own brand of interdependence and doubtless of love, too.

Socially, the Todds spent more time with the Fishers than any other friends or colleagues. Eddie became ever more emotionally dependent on Mike and, everyone noticed, ever more an imitator of Mike's manners and style. "I idolized Mike," he admitted. "I wanted to be like him and he became the most important and influential man in my life." Eddie learned to use extravagant language; he tipped lavishly; he smoked large, expensive cigars; he spoke of producing vast spectacles on stage and screen; he affected the swagger of a wealthy and powerful mogul. He was, in other words, becoming quite impossible.

Debbie and Elizabeth, on the other hand, were cordial but not as connected to each other as their husbands. "Elizabeth has no girl friends," said Debbie sympathetically. "She's not a woman's woman. Women don't seem to give her the strength she gets from a male relationship. We were friendly, but never deep, close friends."

Elizabeth's pregnancy was as much an item for the gossips as her chance to be nominated for *Giant* that year. "Congratulations—we all know you have it in you!" wired one bold critic to Elizabeth when the front-runners were announced and she was not on the list. The baby was due in late October, said the studio publicists; but as Elizabeth continued to grow larger that spring, it was clear that an earlier delivery was to be anticipated.

But pregnancy did not prevent her from traveling round the world with her husband to promote his film. In May, they were at Cannes for the annual film festival, and afterward they rented a villa at Cap Ferrat, where they welcomed the Fishers for a holiday. From there they all proceeded to London, remaining until July and hawking *Around the World.*

At this point, an odd element gradually crept into the cordiality of the foursome, however. More and more frequently, Eddie Fisher unfavorably compared his wife to Elizabeth: "Why don't you dress up, the way she does?" he asked Debbie. Nor was Reynolds happy when Elizabeth rang Fisher in the middle of the night and asked him to come to her aid: Mike had stormed out after a particularly violent fight, and she feared she had lost him forever.

For the London premiere of *Around the World,* Todd threw a lavish party in the Festival Gardens, Battersea, complete with amusement booths, games, rides and food for thousands. Princess Marina, the widowed Duchess of Kent, and her twenty-year-old daughter, Princess Alexandra—cousins to Queen Elizabeth II—were presented to the Todds. The movie star Elizabeth's fabulous necklace of diamonds and rubies with matching earrings, a birthday gift from Mike the previous February, outglittered all other jewelry that evening. Regarding the film, she was more subdued: "It will be the twenty-fifth time I've seen it," she said wearily.

All the while, the education of Elizabeth Taylor under the tutelage of Mike Todd was continuing apace. Her language became saltier, her enjoyment of luxury more constant. Like Sara Taylor, Mike both encouraged and indulged her; like Francis Taylor, he disciplined her. And like a modern mogul, he treated her like the ultimate movie queen, smothering her with the props of opulence. "Being Mike's wife took fifty hours a day," said Elizabeth after his death. "He was twenty-five years my senior and eternally young [and] a bit of a madman, [but] I can be content only with a man who's a bit crazy."

By mid-July, the Todds were at their rented home in Westport, Connecticut, and the Fishers had returned to California. Now well into her seventh month of pregnancy and in constant discomfort from chronic back pain, she went into labor on July 26 and was rushed to Columbia-Presbyterian. On August 6, she was delivered by cesarean section of a tiny premature girl who weighed under five pounds. The Todds named her Elizabeth Frances, and she was always called Liza. With the two Wilding boys living in the household as well, things were, for the time being, happily chaotic.

After two months at home, life as led by Elizabeth and Mike resumed its madcap stride. Convinced that *Around the World in 80 Days* would remain a major box-office draw only with a continual bombardment of publicity, Todd hit on the idea of a one-year anniversary party for the movie's premiere. Only Madison Square Garden would do, of course, and so, on October 17, he and Elizabeth were hosts for the most outrageous, tasteless and futile example of hoopla in the history of entertainment.

"A Little Party Celebrating the First Birthday of *Around the World*," as it was called, was televised live on the CBS-TV program "Playhouse 90," which usually provided live drama and which paid the cost of the party ($250,000). But Todd produced something else. For 18,000 "intimate friends," he engaged entertainment worthy of the circus: the clown Emmet Kelly, Scottish Highland Pipers, juggler Deeter Tasso, marching bands, menageries, Texas baton twirlers, Thai dancers, Harlem Elks, Minnesota Senator Hubert H. Humphrey (then chairman of the Senate Foreign Relations Committee) and, atop a woozy and uncertain elephant, actor Sir Cedric Hardwicke, looking alternately nauseated and foolish.

A forty-foot floral replica of the Oscar was stationed at one end of the Garden, and fifty Jeeps careened round the arena, first handing out and then throwing to the crowd cartons of frankfurters, pizza pies, apples, cookies, doughnuts and bottles of champagne. Festooned in ropes of pearls, diamonds and rubies, Elizabeth climbed a ladder to cut a thirty-foot-wide, fourteen-foot-high cake, pieces of which were then unceremoniously tossed to spectators as the evening devolved into a raucous melée worthy of a Roman orgy. The event joined café society, international party crashers, Hollywood exhibitors, Broadway producers, stars of every medium and the usual mix of jaded New Yorkers. And confusion and bedlam reigned; fights for food and drink broke out everywhere; waiters sold glasses of champagne (and pocketed the cash) instead of serving it free; no one could hear the voice of Todd introducing the French comedian Fernandel, whom the producer was announcing as the star of his forthcoming epic, *Don Quixote.*

The party was monumental in size and historic in coarseness, and it achieved absolutely nothing worthwhile for anyone. With all the dignity of a fraternity house panty raid, it was symptomatic of very much in American style of the 1950s, an era of consummate vulgarity: big cars and wide movie screens, broad hemlines, deep pleats, heavy makeup and ever more lavish parties. "Bigness is excellence" was the American ethos during the 1950s, a time when conspicuous consumption became almost a virtue, the scramble for wealth and social position a national obsession.

At precisely this time, everything about Elizabeth Taylor during her marriage to Mike Todd seemed to stand for the country's aspirations. Everything about her conduct epitomized young America, the people who idolized extravagance, were fascinated by rebellion and yet longed for acceptance. Marlon Brando as *The Wild One* rode into town on his motorcycle in 1953, epitomizing the fringe element of dangerous delinquents and calling attention to the rift between the exuberance of youth and the staid, overconfident middle class. In 1955, James Dean twitched with histrionic anxiety in *Rebel Without a Cause,* a character resenting the fact that his on-screen parents had given him everything material, but that he was, spiritually, very much a pauper. Marilyn Monroe, in *The Prince and the Showgirl* and *Bus Stop,* blithely challenged everything that was morally smug and, while reveling in her frank sexuality, seemed at the same time as innocent as a cherub.

Elizabeth, on the other hand, represented the grand scale of American achievement. "I think it would be nice for everybody to have a Rolls-Royce," she said, dead serious. When asked if he really had a private plane, Mike Todd replied, "Of course, doesn't everyone? We live a simple life. My wife pours her own champagne and I make my own caviar sandwiches."

But of course there was nothing simple about her tastes or expectations, nothing disciplined (except in her work), nothing dark, cryptic or ominous, nothing marginal or threatening. She was right there, at the center of America's blithe, frank materialism, and she loved it. There were her collections of husbands and jewels, her opulent figure, her luxuriant life. She was apparently supreme in her self-confidence, leading the rest of the world toward adoration of everything sensually appealing. Her public function, in other words, might be called something like that of Miss Libertine, holding the torch of absolute autonomy and lighting the way to pleasure—but she was also a flesh-and-blood woman, on perpetual holiday, and this role she played to perfection. The Todds thus continued on their indulgent way at year's end, when they traveled to Australia and Hong Kong, continuing to promote a film that had by then been in general release over a year.

Early in the new year 1958, the Todds signed a lease on a twelve-room white stucco house on Schuyler Road, high up in Coldwater Canyon, Beverly Hills. They then departed for London, where Todd had the idea that Elizabeth could be more than just a glamorous publicist: why not present her to the world as a goodwill ambassador? She could warm the Cold War and charm the Russians right out of their belligerence, he reasoned with punchy patriotism. And so Mike Todd called a press conference, and with no thought of what Washington's reaction might be, he announced that "because she's the best secret weapon we've got," he would soon escort his wife to Moscow, where "she would undermine their whole structure."

With this, his impresario skills were taking him over the top, and soon gentle pleadings arrived from Secretary of State John Foster Dulles and a team of pleading congressmen. The United States did not see Elizabeth Taylor as ambassador, consul or cultural attaché to the Union of Soviet Socialist Republics. Todd backed off, but Elizabeth was seduced by the idea and would not. Well, Todd told the press, they would go to Moscow to talk about a Russian-American coproduction—a film of *War and Peace*, with Elizabeth starring, of course. That too was stymied: Culture Minister Mikhailov and his deputy were ill with influenza and could not confirm a meeting.

Elizabeth, however, would not be stopped. "I am finding it difficult to convince her," Todd told the press from London, "that there is no point in going to Moscow now that no one is available there." But on she fared, and Todd was powerless to stop the insistent tornado of her newly created role. She was acting, it seemed, like a combination of Eleanor Roosevelt and Shirley Temple, embarking on a mission to establish amity between hostile powers. By January 24, they were in Prague, en route to Moscow. "I want to have tea with Khrushchev," Elizabeth told newsmen.

And so she did, leaving the State Department speechless.

On January 27, the Todds managed an invitation to an international diplomatic reception hosted by the Indian ambassador, where they met Khrushchev, Bulganin, Mikoyan and Gromyko. "He has a fascinating face which gives the impression of massive strength but also has a touch of wry humor," Elizabeth said of Khrushchev, adding that for a while she was afraid her husband was going to try to sign him up for a personal appearance tour of America. She then happily signed an autograph for a young woman who thought Elizabeth was Deanna Durbin, so long had it been since American films were screened in Russia.

As if that were not enough, Elizabeth thought that Chinese-American relations required some warming, too. And so she and Mike moved over to the Peking Hotel, where she made a grand staircase descent in a gown of skintight black Oriental silk embroidered with yellow and green. Next day, she visited the Kremlin, where another young Russian approached her for her signature. She was not Deanna Durbin, cautioned Elizabeth. The girl nodded, smiled and then thanked "Miss Monroe" for the autograph.

By this time, the Todds were convinced they had new roles as cultural ambassadors, and on February 10 they flew to Belgrade, "to promote [he said] cultural relations between Yugoslavia and the United States." But those relations began badly at the airport lounge, when Elizabeth ordered a Scotch and soda and had to accept slivovitz, a fiery plum brandy that caused a choking fit. Poor food and filthy weather drove them, three days later, to the French Riviera, where Elizabeth was hailed at the annual flower festival. As soon as her next film role was completed—that of Dulcinea in her husband's production of *Don Quixote*, she said—she would retire forever from the screen.

> I don't want to be a movie star anymore. I just want to be a wife and mother . . . I've been an actress for fifteen years: now I want to be a woman . . . I think the man in the family should drive the car, order the food in restaurants and wear the pants . . . I never liked acting that much. It's really been more or less a hobby with me.

And then she repeated her curious creed: "You can't be an actress and a woman."

Under the circumstances, this was one of the strangest conjunctions of statements ever to come from Elizabeth Taylor.

In the first place, she was ignoring the many actresses with strong and substantial personal lives. Her own had been lived in public, and in that life the actress and the woman had fused with remarkable, sometimes troubling cohesion. Therein lay the source of much of her anxiety, from this point in her life forward: feeling in some profound way unachieved, ungrown-up, she could only blame her feelings of insufficiency on having been an actress from the time of her childhood. In a way, she was right, for she had been allowed little time for anything like a normal maturation process, and the constant glare of public observation and adulation had made all of life a movie set on which she felt constantly observed and assessed. To further complicate matters, her youth and beauty—combined with the worship of stereotype in Hollywood— had mostly limited her roles to that of a woman who is tested or somehow taught a lesson about life, men and marriage.

A second remarkable point was her belief in male primacy, that a husband should "wear the pants"—a cultural shibboleth patently false in relationships of parity and in those of wifely dominance. It seemed, to be sure, that much of the appeal of Todd was that he "wore the pants," that because he was father as much as lover, he dominated—and to some extent, indeed he did. But this relationship was complex, for Elizabeth had a strong and independent streak, not to say a stubborn one (as her recent foray into international diplomacy had demonstrated). In her marriage to Todd, she was, in fact, the substantially greater wage earner: just as Wilding had been mostly on suspension or in debt, Todd's wealth, as she was soon to learn, was a mammoth illusion.

This illusion, too—that she was committed *tout court* to manly supremacy—created a profoundly disturbing contradiction: beginning with her decision to terminate the Hilton and Wilding marriages, and relying greatly on her charm and wiles, she was in many ways an astonishingly self-defined woman, shy but not weak. "It's nice to be married to someone who thinks I have a brain," she said at the same time, implying that this was a new matrimonial experience. That affirmative sense Todd provided was in critical contrast to whatever subservient position the other side of Elizabeth Taylor felt was divinely or at least culturally ordained for her as a woman.

One of her fondest delusions in early 1958, therefore, was that she could indeed be happy without her career, but that was as much an impossible dream as Mike's plan for a film of *Don Quixote*.

Thus it was that Elizabeth, at Mike's insistence because they needed the cash, accepted Metro's next assignment without prevarication—and this she did in high excitement, with not another word about retiring. In March, she began work as Maggie Pollitt in a film of Tennessee Williams's Pulitzer Prize–winning play *Cat on a Hot Tin Roof*, certainly the most challenging role of her career so far, as much for the coincidence of tragedy in her personal life as for the grave beauty of the film.

The play developed from "Three Players of a Summer Game," a 1951 short story by Williams about an alcoholic ex-athlete named Brick Pollitt, whose disastrous affair with his doctor's widow ends with his abandonment by the widow and his pathetic dependence on his embittered wife. By 1955, *Cat on a Hot Tin Roof* had become a full-length play in which the same Brick is now guilt-ridden over the suicide of his friend Skipper, with whom, it is implied, he had a perhaps unrealized erotic attachment. His remorse and the intimations of his sexual insecurity have led Brick to alcoholic impotence and concomitant indifference to his sultry, sex-starved and ambitious wife, Maggie, who is as uneasy and agitated as a cat on a hot tin roof. Brick is also apathetic toward the machinations of his venal brother and sister-in-law, who covet the enormous estate owned by their "Big Daddy" Pollitt, who is dying of cancer.

Structured as a series of confrontations between members of the family, the play—essentially a meditation on the nature of moral responsibility—ends with the distinct possibility that Maggie's love will overcome Brick's self-destructive insensibility and save the Pollitt fortune from Brick's greedy brother. In this regard, Maggie herself was one of Williams's favorite characters, a woman not defined solely by sensual need but also by a passion for the truth. "Maggie was the only aristocrat," said Williams. "She was the only one free of greed. I sympathized with her and liked her, and [she] had become steadily more charming to me as I worked on her characterization." His efforts were successful with critics and audiences, who supported it for twenty months and 694 performances.

As director Richard Brooks adapted the play for his screen version, he had more to do than erase any veiled references to homosexuality, which Hollywood forbade in 1958. But that is, in any case, not the central issue of the play. Whereas "Three Players of a Summer Game" much recalled Edith Wharton's *Ethan Frome*, *Cat on a Hot Tin Roof* showed how clearly a debt Williams had to August Strindberg. The precipitating action of the film occurred before the story begins, and very little happens in the running time: it is, to the contrary, a work of mood and reaction.

In its final version, the screenplay explores the convoluted, often cruel machinery of family strife. A dying man's birthday becomes the catalyst for an insistence on moral truth and self-confrontation, and the issue of a great inheritance becomes a powerful symbol of a legacy of greed and lovelessness. Much to the credit of Richard Brooks and a splendid cast, the film of *Cat* became (the playwright's reservations notwithstanding) a kind of impressionistic reflection on truth and mendacity, on self-knowledge against self-rejection. Not merely a film about greed, guilt and the refusal to acknowledge homosexual impulses, *Cat on a Hot Tin Roof* has the tragic sense of the ultimately mysterious nature of personality. Brick's paralyzing guilt—externalized by his broken, cast-bound leg—owes to a refusal to be true to a friendship for which he had claimed total devotion.

Dependent on the stronger Maggie, Brick's hope of salvation lies in his ability at last to trust one who can lead him with love. In this regard, it is frivolous to belittle the screen version of *Cat* because it bent to the constraints of the time and suppressed the subtext of homosexual self-awareness. In fact, necessity became a virtue, and the film became something deeper, more problematic than a tract on sexual identity and in some ways even more successful than the play. It remains a wrenching, often almost unbearable statement about heedless cruelty and needless suffering, and a dramatic testimony to the redemptive power of forgiving love. With an array of exquisitely wrought performances from Elizabeth Taylor, Paul Newman, Burl Ives, Judith Anderson, Madeleine Sherwood and Jack Carson, *Cat on a Hot Tin Roof* deserved the vast audiences it attracted and the half-dozen Academy nominations it received.

* * *

The script "really intrigued me," said Elizabeth, and Mike, who appreciated her talent (not to say her salary of $125,000, which would provide seed money for his *Don Quixote*) was on the mark in considering Maggie the best role she had ever been offered.

But as soon as rehearsals with Brooks began that March—a year and a half since her last work on a movie set—there were problems. Paul Newman, trained at the Yale Drama School and the Actors Studio, had a specific kind of stage technique behind his movie acting, whereas Elizabeth admitted that she had "no technique" at all. "I'm laid back during run-throughs and unleash real emotion only when the camera is actually rolling." Her lack of fire during rehearsals alarmed Newman, who was astonished when the scene was subsequently filmed. "You have to understand," said the director. "Elizabeth doesn't rehearse the way you do. She goes through all the business and learns to hit her marks, but she can't give a full performance until she knows it's for real." She was, he added, perfect for the role because she was not only "a beauty [but also] a combination of child and bitch who wants to love and be loved"—uncannily, in fact, like Maggie-the-cat Pollitt.

After the initial tension of rehearsals, things proceeded smoothly on the sets of *Cat on a Hot Tin Roof*. And then, in one dreadful moment, everything changed.

On Friday, March 21, the Todds planned to fly in his small private plane, *The Liz*, to New York, where he was to be honored by the entertainment fraternity known as the Friars Club. But Elizabeth came down with a nasty cold, and Los Angeles was enveloped in a chilly drizzle: it was wiser, everyone agreed, for her to rest over the weekend in preparation for Monday's work call. Mike departed, accompanied by two pilots and his friend Art Cohn. The men were traveling to refuel in Tulsa, Oklahoma, when a patch of bad weather worsened in the skies over New Mexico. About twenty miles southwest of Grants, the plane, enveloped in thick fog, crashed in the Zuni Mountains. All four men died. Mike Todd was fifty years old, and he had been married to Elizabeth Taylor for 414 days.

His secretary, Richard Hanley, and her physician, Rexford Kennamer, sped to the house on Schuyler Road early Saturday morning.

Hoping to reach her before a telephone call or radio report, they went to her bedroom, where she was still sleeping. There was a moment of silence when she stirred and saw them, and then, when the news was broken to her, she leaped from her bed and ran round the house weeping hysterically. Kennamer administered the first of massive injections of sedation. Elizabeth Taylor, one of the most famous women in the world, had appeared in twenty-seven movies, had been married three times, was twice divorced, had three children by two husbands and was now a widow. She had just marked her twenty-sixth birthday.

Three days later, what remained of Mike Todd's charred corpse (identified only by his money clip) was buried near Chicago, where he was raised. At the Jewish cemetery in Lake Zurich, a platoon of the press and the merely curious awaited in the cold, sipping coffee, gulping whiskey from flasks and littering the grounds with candy wrappers and sandwich bags. To the last, Mike Todd was playing to a sold-out crowd.

Elizabeth, ashen and veiled, was supported by her doctor, her brother and her secretary, whose task was to shield her from the crush: the event seemed much like a grim publicity stunt orchestrated by Todd himself.

His gold wedding band had somehow been salvaged from the wreck, and at the graveside Elizabeth removed her gloves, as if deliberately to signal to the cameramen and thus to the world that she was still married to Mike Todd. "I'll wear it always," she said, and in fact she wore it throughout her next marriage. Her reason: "I remained totally dependent on Mike's memory for many years after his death." This is, of course, not an uncommon reaction to the sudden death of an adored spouse. But in her case, the dependence immediately took a singular drift. Elizabeth turned for comfort to Eddie Fisher, who had been virtually her husband's shadow, was best man at the wedding, had traveled and socialized constantly with the Todds, and now became the surrogate Mike. "Elizabeth was in shock and pain," according to Debbie Reynolds Fisher, who cared for Elizabeth's children during this time. "She needed him."

This turned out to be one of the titanic understatements of history: from the time of Mike Todd's burial, Eddie Fisher was constantly at the side of the grieving widow. The beautiful Elizabeth, young and weeping at the graveside, was, to be sure, a touching sight. As her photograph was for days reproduced across the pages of the world's newspapers and magazines, however, she seemed not just a bereft young mother but also a national figure of tragic stature. From there, it was a short route to her transformation into a soap opera heroine: "NO! NO! NO!" SCREAMS LIZ AT GRAVE-SIDE ran the headlines—adding, with extravagant exaggeration, SHE THROWS HERSELF ONTO COFFIN. In fact, she threw herself only on the attention of Eddie Fisher, who assumed the duties of full-time comforter and counselor. "You're with her more than me," Debbie was soon complaining.

But like the most joyful moments of life, those defined by grief also, in the fullness of time, lose their first sharpness. For a month, she remained in dazed, anorexic isolation at home, where she admitted only a few: her doctor and family; Eddie; and, from Metro, hairstylist Sydney Guilaroff and costume designer Helen Rose. But then Elizabeth felt the fundamental instinct to get on with life, which meant going back to work on *Cat on a Hot Tin Roof*. "The only reason I want to do it is because of Mike," she said. "Mike liked me in this picture and I want to finish it for him."

She did not add the harsh, practical matter that she needed cash: the lavish and generous Mike Todd, whom all the world considered a very rich man indeed, left his widow a tangled estate that took years to settle. He had a vast tax debt that increased with the income from *Around the World in 80 Days,* and fully half of any forthcoming profit was left to Mike Jr. With him, she filed a $5 million lawsuit, charging negligence against the owners and operators of the doomed airplane. Five years later, she received a settlement of $27,000, which was assigned by the court to their daughter, Liza.

Facing the responsibility for three children, two dependent parents, a staff of retainers, a lavish lifestyle and a pile of bills from recent world travels, Elizabeth knew she had to recover. And so, eight pounds thinner than before March 21, Elizabeth returned to

Culver City on Monday morning, April 14, promptly at seven-thirty. The cast and crew had filled her dressing room with violets, her favorite flowers, and everyone welcomed her with a quiet shyness that bordered on reverence. "She was so weak from lack of food," said producer Lawrence Weingarten, "that she couldn't lift [an empty gift box] off a bed in the first scene she played. But she was remarkable. You can't see a flaw in her performance."

Weingarten was on the mark, for Elizabeth was the ultimate professional. Everyone in the cast remembered, forever after, her insistence on getting things right, her undemanding attitude at work, and her consideration—especially for the child actors, who were often required to rehearse and repeat the most annoying sort of nasty antics. Hugh Corcoran, playing one of the "No-Neck-Monster" Pollitt brats, recalled years later that Elizabeth was "wonderfully kind to all of us, without any condescension. She was never the Grande Dame, but instead worked hard along with everyone else and made a difficult task seem easy for us. The truth was, everyone adored her."

Elizabeth's Maggie was triumphantly realized: *Cat* won her a second Oscar nomination and was Metro's biggest hit of 1958. Her Maggie was "well-accented and perceptive," as one influential critic noted; Elizabeth was simply "terrific," according to another; and a third hailed the "surprising sureness" of her acting. The praise was certainly earned. Elizabeth brought a riveting combination of nervy intensity and hopeful seductiveness to the role of Maggie. In scenes that required her to express erotic yearning for the aloof Brick, her desire is almost unbearable and becomes more subtly acute the more he repulses her. Controlled, nuanced, laced with pain yet driven by hope, Elizabeth's Maggie certainly derived from the reservoirs of her own tragedy that season.

When the picture was released that September, polls, audience ratings and movie magazine ballots universally acclaimed her to be the biggest star in America. She was also the most controversial. Some columnists, like the public whose appetite they whetted, considered her a brave and brilliant actress at the top of her craft, while others rated her a dangerous, amoral influence on American womanhood. And linked to sex (in the movie) and death (in real life), she tapped into everything disturbing in art and life. This complex of reactions drew crowds at the theaters, especially after the appearances of print advertisements and billboards of Elizabeth clad only in a slip and, like Baby Doll, curled seductively on a brass bed—and in light of a dramatic shift in her public life that coincided with the film's New York premiere in September.

Before the camera, Elizabeth was coming back to life; privately, there were insidious omens. During her entire life, Elizabeth had never lived alone: she went from her parents on Elm Drive to her honeymoon with Nicky Hilton and then to a shared apartment with a companion-secretary. Abroad on filmmaking assignments, there was always her mother or an assistant—until the day she married Wilding—and then there was Todd. The possibility of having to live on her own was devastating, and although she certainly tried to be a loving mother, her career required that her children were mostly attended by nannies. In any case, she was accustomed to (and needed) as much care and attention.

"I could not sleep," Elizabeth recalled years later. "As a result, I began to take sleeping pills." And soon these were being washed down at the end of long evenings with Eddie: "We sat and drank and talked about Mike for hours, [and] at the time I thought he needed me and I needed him." The situation was not difficult to understand; with mutual grief compounded by raw sex, it was a situation that was savagely difficult to negotiate.

Edwin Jack Fisher was only four years older than Elizabeth Taylor, but his background and breeding could not have been more different. The fourth of seven children born to a Russian tailor in Philadelphia, he got attention amid his large family by singing loud and clear, at home, in synagogue and on children's radio shows. Eddie was then engaged, at seventeen, to sing with hotel and nightclub bands in New York, and in 1950 and 1951, he was at the top of the record charts four times. Back in civilian life after two years of military service in Korea, he accumulated legions of fans on the Borscht circuit, and, eventually, on his own television show.

Each stage of Eddie's rise to popularity had been very much aided by Mike Todd, who first auditioned him for a New York show and then took him under his influential wing. In 1955, at Mike's encouragement and with Metro's hearty approval, Eddie married that studio's pert, vivacious musical and comedy star, Debbie Reynolds, whom he had met in Los Angeles the previous year. Their daughter, Carrie, was born in October 1956, and then, in February 1958, their son, Todd, whose given name surprised no one who knew them. Eddie and Debbie, America's sweetheart couple, were even pitchforked into a film together—*Bundle of Joy,* whose title told the story. Their marriage was very satisfying for Hollywood press agents, fan clubs and the general public. It was less so for themselves.

"Debbie and I were unhappy from the start," said Eddie. "We were cast as America's sweethearts, and nobody wanted to believe otherwise." Countered Elizabeth, "I never had that problem, since I was never America's sweetheart."

In fact, the Fishers needed no time to find that they were virtually incompatible. Eddie was an East Coast Jewish boy, while Debbie had been raised in California, in a strict, fundamentalist Christian sect. She was a thrifty, even penny-pinching homemaker; he made lavish gestures worthy of Mike Todd. She was exactly Elizabeth's age and had been to bed with one man in her life; Eddie had a roving eye and openly spoke to his wife of the likelihood of straying. She rarely took alcohol; he had a taste for it that would become an addiction.

"We had lots of problems the first year and a half we were married," according to Debbie, recalling Eddie's fierce ambition, his almost pathognomonic imitation of Mike Todd, and his restlessness—not only for fame, but for its obvious advantages, for Eddie wanted a reputation not only as a romantic singer but as a great lover. They tried counseling several times, and at least once they consulted a divorce lawyer. The Fishers remained, however, the movie marriage of the decade, great for the public but a shabby reality at home.

A major cause of their problems was in Eddie's reliance on the ministrations of Max Jacobson, the notorious "Dr. Feelgood" of the 1950s, who from 1953 had been providing him with regular injections of mysterious "vitamin" concoctions that were nothing less than dangerous and habit-forming drugs. Jacobson's roster of patients was long and impressive (among them were Tennessee Williams, Cecil B. De Mille, Zero Mostel and Margaret Leighton), and the physical and psychological dependencies he created in them with his drugs brought the rich and famous constantly to his door.

Medical science, much less government agencies, knew very little about the perils of drug abuse in the 1950s, and many of the most common drugs were neither strictly controlled nor difficult to obtain. Pills, shots, amphetamines, barbiturates—it was the arsenal of the good life, a sign of a busy and glamorous schedule, a regimen almost as popular as frequent visits to therapists and psychiatrists. Nembutal, Doriden, Luminal, Seconal and phenobarbital were among the most popular, but for many celebrities, Max Jacobson's "speed" shot was the best of them all. This was an intravenous dose of amphetamines—which Jacobson soon taught Fisher to self-inject—that provided an instant sense of enhanced mental capacity, diminished the need for sleep and brought an unnatural state of euphoria. Controversial but not yet illegal, it was prized by many until the horrors of addiction were evident.

"My mind was racing," Eddie recalled after his first injection. "My whole body was charged with energy. I couldn't sit still, and I couldn't stop talking." But when the effect wore off and the aftermath was exhaustion and depression the next day, another injection was necessary, and so the cycle continued. "Dr. Jacobson came to my dressing room at the Paramount at least once a day," according to Fisher. "I needed the energy and self-confidence I got from the shots. Max and his magic elixir were made for me." Mike Todd saw the quackery and the danger and so warned Eddie, but his counsel was in vain: "I not only ignored him, I became Max's most devoted disciple." In Hollywood as in New York, there were others besides Jacobson to cater to Eddie and hundreds like him.

As for Debbie and Elizabeth, they were, along with the general population, woefully ignorant of the dangers of drugs: a doctor was attending Eddie, so what could be bad? Eddie seemed to work well, he kept to a demanding schedule, he was full of energy. When his moods altered dramatically, his sleep patterns became erratic and his nutrition was madly unregulated—well, these things happened to a "performing artist," as the new terminology described anyone in show business. It was a brave new world, and the brave new people in it were considered to require and deserve special treatment.

The last week of August 1958, Eddie left Los Angeles for New York—for only five days of business meetings, he told his wife, and with his busy schedule it would be better if she stayed home with the children. "He kissed me good-bye," said Debbie later. "I thought we were happy. I thought we were trying to make our marriage work." So she may have thought, and so she told the press. But since March there had been only trouble between the Fishers over his growing attachment to Elizabeth—who, Debbie and the rest of the country believed, was in New York only to promote *Cat on a Hot Tin Roof.* Elizabeth even told the press that she was en route to a European vacation, but she never got farther than the Hudson Valley of New York State.

As it turned out, Eddie's business was Elizabeth herself: "I fabricated a meeting with my sponsors in New York to be with her." From the end of August, things happened quickly and all too publicly. Elizabeth, until now still esteemed as a grieving young widow, was blithely ignoring the tradition of a year's decent mourning, a period of bereavement during which no dignified spouse would consider remarriage, much less a romantic affair. According to the social liturgies of postwar America, this was especially required of public figures, politicians and celebrities, and as she flouted the convention so she risked public disapproval, which did not bother her one whit.

In fact, Elizabeth seemed quite recovered from her tragedy and not at all mired in Gothic gloom, as columnist Earl Wilson gleefully reported on August 29:

> Elizabeth Taylor and Eddie Fisher were dancing it up at the Har-
> wyn [nightclub] this morning, Eddie having been Mike Todd's
> close friend and now sort of an escort service for Liz. They saw
> [the play] *Two for the Seesaw* the night before.

With that, all journalistic hell broke loose nationwide, and the
condoled widow was now perceived as something like the mythic
figure *la belle dame sans merci* (from Chartier via Keats)—a woman
with uncanny powers to cause romantic chaos and destruction by
the sheer force of her passion, a femme fatale who went about
destroying and devouring whom she would. In 1958, the postwar
birth rate in America peaked, and divorce was widely considered a
matter for public censure. Such was the force of an established
moral climate that Elizabeth Taylor fell from grace in September as
quickly as Todd's death had elevated her in March.

"They thought they could live their lives loving Mike and consoling each other," Sara Taylor wrote of her and Eddie Fisher,
adding that their relationship was an unhealthy "living in the past,
keeping Mike's memory alive, and it was doomed to fail from the
start." This was an assessment expressed years later, but privately
she confided it to Elizabeth at the time, and this again created a rift
between mother and daughter.

While Elizabeth and Eddie provided the columns with daily
news bulletins that September, Debbie awaited her husband's
return to California. On September 4, Earl Wilson reported that
the lovers were at the Quo Vadis restaurant and then at The Embers
nightclub. This followed the nationwide bulletin that Debbie's husband and the widow Todd had spent the Labor Day weekend
together at Grossinger's Resort in the Catskill Mountains of New
York. The visit, said Eddie's agent Danny Welks, was simply so that
the singer could dedicate the new hotel pool; Miss Taylor was simply a friend, along for the ride. Agents have been dismissed for con-
cocting much better stories than this.

Debbie could no longer affect passive indifference. At two
o'clock New York time on the morning of September 6, she rang
Eddie's suite at the Essex House Hotel in Manhattan, but there was

no reply. She then telephoned the Plaza Hotel, where Metro's contract players were housed, and she announced to the switchboard operator that she had Dean Martin on the line for Eddie Fisher. Debbie was immediately connected to Elizabeth Taylor's suite, where Eddie took the call and greeted, as he thought, his old friend Dean Martin.

"It's not Dean, Eddie. It's Debbie."

"Oh, shit! What the hell do you think you're doing, calling me here at this time of night? Goddammit, you had no goddamn business calling me here!"

Debbie asked to speak with Elizabeth, but Eddie refused: "Look, this is ridiculous. We're talking. I just stopped by."

"Eddie, it's getting close to three in the morning. You didn't just stop by. I woke you up." Or something. But Eddie, who certainly underestimated his wife's intelligence, insisted that he was not in bed with Elizabeth, that he and she were just talking.

Debbie was not put off, however, and finally Eddie interrupted her to admit, "Elizabeth and I are here, and we are very much in love. I'll fly back to California tomorrow."

"Well, you don't have to bother!" cried Debbie, slamming down the receiver.

Such was her memory, in 1987, of a sad telephone call twenty-nine years before. But at the time, Debbie was not entirely surprised: the marriage had indeed been a troubled one, foundering on the shoals of conflicting desires—Eddie's for the high life and Debbie's for home and family. In 1957, when the Fishers were considering divorce, Eddie had agreed to pay his wife a million-dollar settlement. Debbie's pregnancy temporarily scuttled their plans. "I knew it would be someone," she said in 1959, speaking of a hypothetical third party she believed would one day divert Eddie from his family, "but I didn't think it would be Elizabeth."

By the following morning, Debbie's telephone was ringing nonstop, and a team of reporters and photographers had camped on her front lawn. Prudently, she appeared in her doorway, holding one baby or the other, her hair tied in a bandana, her face radiant with her usual smile. "I played dumb. I wasn't going to talk to my husband through the press."

On September 9, Eddie returned to his home in West Los Angeles; Elizabeth, traveling in another plane, proceeded to Bel-Air, the expensive enclave west of Beverly Hills where she had just rented a house from Tyrone Power. Fisher was nothing if not direct with his wife: "I love her," he told Debbie, "and I never loved you, and I want a divorce." His manner was worthy of a Pollitt.

But Debbie was not an easy target, nor did she collapse in hysteria. "You go off and be with her," she said calmly. "She'll throw you out within a year and a half. And then we'll see if we can work it out, because I'll never give you a divorce. We have two children." But then she made a tactical error: "She doesn't love you, Eddie. She'll never love you. You're not her type."

Like Sara, Debbie was on the mark, but her timing was not. Her husband, meantime, was becoming his dead idol, Mike Todd: he saw the bright lights and the brightest star and the most beautiful woman in the world, and he would have it all. As for Debbie Reynolds, she suffered enormously but maintained an admirable equanimity in public, and when it became clear by that December that Eddie and Elizabeth were not soon to be separated, she acceded to his demand for divorce. "Eddie is a very lucky man," said Debbie. "How many men ever have two women who love them?"

So went the real-life soap opera of the decade, with the traditional cast of Wronged Wife, Errant Husband and Wicked Widow. The script could not have been improved by any team of writers, but the story could have come from the files of any Hollywood studio. "The storybook marriage of Eddie Fisher and Debbie Reynolds," commented the New York *Daily Mirror*, "skidded on a series of curves yesterday—Liz Taylor's." According to the *Daily News,* the blissful Fisher union hit "a snag—in the graceful shape of sultry Liz Taylor."

Elizabeth, meanwhile, saw in Eddie the man she thought she wanted, and the elements would not withstand her determination. Furthermore, she refused to hide her love: quintessential romantic that she was, Elizabeth in some way saw herself as the dusky hero-ine, rejected by a hostile world, true to the motions of her heart, a cause of pain to blond Debbie only by fate, not by intent. For his part, Eddie had now become the man he idolized. Just as in the Todd marriage, Eddie and Elizabeth exchanged lavish gifts—Cartier and Piaget jewelry and watches in absurd and vulgar profusion. "I felt she needed me, desperately," he reflected later. "I was a father, a brother, a friend, a lover. She was a baby I held and rocked in my arms."

The drama had developed precipitously—from the employment of "misunderstanding" on September 9 (Eddie to the press, regard-ing his relations with Debbie) to the use of "separation" on September 10 (Eddie's attorney to the press, regarding Eddie and Debbie) to a firm prediction of "divorce" on September 11 (Eddie to the world, after a news report). Modern life was certainly moving at a rapid pace.

On the advice of her agent, Kurt Frings, Elizabeth gave a tele-phone interview on September 10 to the importunate Hedda Hop-per, who at once asked about the Fisher affair—because, she said truthfully, she was receiving hundreds of letters daily from outraged women across America, condemning Elizabeth for destroying a per-fect Hollywood marriage. The story ran on September 11, one day after the Fishers' separation was announced.

"Her reply was unprintable," according to Hopper's story, which ran at once. Years later, Hopper relented and shared the unprintable with her readers: "What do you expect me to do?" Elizabeth asked without sarcasm. "Sleep alone?"

"You know," continued Elizabeth, "I don't go around breaking up marriages. Besides, you can't break up a happy marriage." And then it was her turn for the tactical error that lost her an enormous cadre of supporters: "Debbie's and Eddie's marriage has never been a happy one." She was correct, but as she later admitted, this remark was not the most sensible one of her life.

What about her and Fisher? "I've felt happier and more like a human being for the past two weeks than I have since Mike's death."

Hopper pressed on. "What do you suppose Mike would say to this?"

"He and Eddie loved each other," replied Elizabeth.

"No, you're wrong," countered Hopper. "Mike loved Eddie. In my opinion, Eddie never loved anybody but himself."

"Well, Mike is dead and I'm alive."

That comment was actually the only one Hopper concocted, as she wrote years later. What Elizabeth said plaintively was "What do you expect me to do—sleep alone?" Hopper deemed this statement "unprintable," and all America would have agreed. Such a remark, in 1958, was virtually full-scale pornography.

What about Debbie? asked Hopper.

"He's not in love with her and never has been," Elizabeth replied, as if she and Eddie had prepared the same script. "Only a year ago they were about to get a divorce but stopped it when they found out she was going to have another baby. I'm not taking anything away from Debbie Reynolds because she never really had it."

The Hopper interview was published in hundreds of American newspapers and translated for readers round the world. Unfortunately, the worst comment Elizabeth was judged to have made was not her statement on the history of the Fishers' affections: ironically, it was Hopper's bowdlerizing paraphrase of "What do you expect me to do—sleep alone?" to "Mike's dead and I'm alive," which Hopper had, knowingly or not, lifted right from the anguished cry of Maggie to Brick: "Skipper's dead and I'm alive!" The sanitized version was interpreted to mean: "Mike's dead and I love Eddie," which is something very different.

"I was terribly naive," said Elizabeth not long after the Hopper interview. "It was my fault." Perhaps not entirely. But everyone was hurt by it—in the short term, Debbie Reynolds, who not long after was actually grateful to Elizabeth for being the unwitting agitator who ended an unhappy marriage; and in the long term, Elizabeth, who endured much more pain from her forthcoming marriage than ignominy from the press and public. Hate mail arrived by the ton, and Hollywood, which has always raised hypocrisy to the level of a fine art, smugly turned its collective back on both Eddie and Elizabeth.

As for Elizabeth's career, Richard Brooks summed up the feelings of many who felt she would certainly have won the Oscar the following spring for *Cat on a Hot Tin Roof* but for the scandal. "People in her own studio turned against her," recalled Brooks. "There's no question they changed their minds on the voting. It's the phony morality of the bull artists all over this town." Brooks had his finger on Hollywood's erratic pulse. After Mike Todd's death, Metro executives shook their heads, clucked their sympathy and observed that it would be so good if Elizabeth had some male companionship. When it was Eddie Fisher, they wrung their hands in horror—perhaps, after all, because it was Eddie Fisher and not one of themselves.

For all that Eddie found himself in the luxuriant spotlight turned on him by an adoring Elizabeth, he, too, was in for a professional reprisal. On September 30, she threw a supper party in Bel-Air for Eddie as he began his new television season; Elizabeth, reported one columnist, called it her "You-Can-All-Go-to-Hell Party." The press at once opened the throttle: LIZ FROLICS ON LAWN WITH EDDIE AT PARTY, trumpeted the Los Angeles *Evening Mirror,* as if the rather modest *déjeuner sur l'herbe* had deteriorated into a full-blown orgy of licentious wood nymphs and satyrs. Soon after, his show was canceled by NBC and Coca-Cola, the sponsor. Not to worry, said Elizabeth comfortingly. She had just been approached by the producer Walter Wanger, who for years had been planning a movie about Cleopatra. Perhaps when she was free of her Metro contract, something would come of that.

At year's end, the influential poll conducted by *Motion Picture* magazine placed Elizabeth first in readers' interest and Debbie second. It would never have occurred to Elizabeth, but there she was in a kind of mock epic with Debbie as her counterpart. Elizabeth, the contemporary Isolde-the-dark, set against the modern Isolde-the-fair, and Eddie Fisher was the unlikely Tristan who had drunk the fatal love potion. "We were fighting the world," she said soon after this first great scandal of her life. Crowded by newsmen, surrounded by protectors, the observed of all observers (as Ophelia said of Hamlet), she was on the pages of every magazine and newspaper in the country and most in the Western Hemisphere. She had been a tragic icon when Mike died. Now she was a figure of tragic-heroic-romantic proportions: there was no other medley of roles by which she could consider herself. Meantime, the Greek chorus—Louella Parsons, Hedda Hopper, Earl Wilson—was in full chant, moving round the principals in a stately pace, lamenting, questioning, chiding, prophesying weal for none and woe for all.

Chapter Eight

1959–1960

O n January 8, 1959, the story buzzed around Hollywood that Elizabeth Taylor suffered a severe mental collapse and was rushed to the Menninger Clinic in Topeka, Kansas. This was nonsense, and she proved it by dining out the next evening with Eddie Fisher at Chasen's, the popular celebrity restaurant on Beverly Boulevard. "I'm going out with Eddie where everybody can see me," she said, inviting the entire Hollywood press corps to join them. She was relaxed, she joked, she made four-letter words sound almost elegant, she drank champagne. In fact, she was every inch the star, and she looked more than fit: Elizabeth was opulent to the point of a plumpness not seen since her pregnancies. She was not expecting a baby—that was the next canard to be denied—but already she looked like a Merry Wife of Westwood. "Liz Taylor is putting on too much weight," chided *Photoplay* in April, creating a tradition of reportorial comments on her appearance that would endure for the rest of her life.

By mid-March, the press everywhere followed "Liz and Eddie," as they were now familiarly dubbed—a designation particularly galling to Elizabeth, whose preference, then as always, was for the use of her full given name.

"We wouldn't really be news if we were married," she said, announcing that she had leased quarters at the luxurious Hidden Well, a hideaway in Las Vegas, beginning April 1, the date when Eddie was to commence a four-week engagement at the Tropicana Hotel. "I want to be near him, and I thought it would be a good place for my two boys and the girl." Such frankness about cohabitation was not commonplace in 1959, but as usual Elizabeth lived by her own code and refused to pretend: life was much simpler, she insisted, if one did not try to deny the truth. As it was, Debbie Reynolds had divorced Eddie Fisher in February, but that was only an interlocutory decree, and the final dissolution of the marriage would require a year's wait.

Just before her departure for Las Vegas, Elizabeth was driven to Temple Israel in Hollywood, where she was formally accepted into the Jewish faith, the heritage of both Mike Todd and Eddie Fisher. (Many might have recalled a similar step taken by Marilyn Monroe, when she married playwright Arthur Miller in 1956.) When Elizabeth further expressed her solidarity by purchasing Israeli bonds, her movies were forthwith banned in Egypt; by year's end, the Arab League had gone further and issued an injunction against the screening of all her pictures in every Arab country of the Middle East and Africa. This was particularly ironic, since negotiations for her to play the Queen of the Nile were proceeding apace, and auspicious cables and letters were exchanged weekly among her agent Kurt Frings, the producer Walter Wanger and the executives at Fox. As for honors at home, Richard Brooks's intuition served him well and her badly: she did not win the Academy Award for *Cat*—a prize, observed columnist Sidney Skolsky slyly, that she had really lost at Grossinger's the previous September.

On April 2, the day after her twenty-seventh birthday and Eddie's Las Vegas opening, Debbie Reynolds returned from filming in Spain. The press gathered to greet her, shouting questions about the possibility of her consenting to a swifter divorce decree than the

California statute provided. "Elizabeth said that you were holding them back from happiness," shouted one reporter—an assertion confirmed to her by a call from her husband. The role of spoiler was not to be relished, and Debbie immediately consented to Eddie's request that after his six-week Nevada residency he would, with his wife's consent, have the right to a swift and universally recognized divorce.

"I don't think Eddie ever knew who he was," Debbie wrote sadly years later.

> Perhaps the drugs totally put him away. He wanted to be a movie star. So he married one. Then [he] left me for someone even bigger. I was not a woman of the world, or a passionate woman like Elizabeth. He was [not well matched] with her, but he didn't know that, and she didn't realize it at the time, probably because she was in despair.

Debbie did not see Eddie again until 1973, when their daughter, Carrie, brought him to visit backstage in London. "I didn't even recognize him," she recalled. "I felt sorry for him. He looked like an old, beaten man."

But on receiving the news that he could marry Elizabeth six weeks later that spring, Eddie was nothing like an old man. The night of Debbie's agreement, he sang "Makin' Whoopee" at the Tropicana, crooning about "another bride, another June, another sunny honeymoon" and then introduced "my favorite actress," Elizabeth Taylor. After the show, Eddie answered questions about the obstacles to his forthcoming marriage—civil laws, Nevada residency and the necessity for Elizabeth to have a tonsillectomy within the next two weeks.

"They're putting a lot of stumbling blocks in our way, but we'll hurdle every one of them," said Eddie. He then turned to Elizabeth: "Won't we, baby?"

Baby said they would. She then added her usual pledge that, after just one more movie (or maybe two) she would quit movies and be a housewife and mother forever. "How many Hollywood marriages do you know of where the wife is an actress and the marriage still works?" she asked reporters. But before any of them could give her the substantial list of just such marriages, she ordered a round of champagne and changed the subject.

It was all very Las Vegas.

The soap opera saga of the Fishers and the Widow Todd finally ended during the morning of May 12, when Eddie's divorce was granted in Las Vegas and, moments later, he married Elizabeth in a civil ceremony followed by a Jewish blessing that afternoon. Their parents were present, and their agents, attorneys, hairdressers, physicians and publicists; the children were kenneled elsewhere. That night, Mr. and Mrs. Eddie Fisher flew to New York, changed planes and headed for Spain before proceeding to London and Elizabeth's next assignment.

The reason for the Spanish interlude was strictly financial, for it allowed the Fishers to deduct the holiday as a business expense. Briefly, Elizabeth was a partner in a company with Mike Todd, Jr., whose choice for a premiere production was *Scent of Mystery* (also called *Holiday in Spain*). In the tradition of his father's eccentric extravaganzas, Mike planned it as the first picture with the gimmick known as Smell-O-Vision. As the rambling, colorful but unexciting thriller unspooled, devices pumped into the air of a few movie theaters (in New York, Chicago and Los Angeles) the aromas of fruits and flowers, tobacco, wine, fresh bread, coffee, peppermint—whatever bouquet was apt for the scene.

When the picture was released the following year, the few who saw it could spot Elizabeth, unbilled and unadvertised—and aromatically identified by the scent of expensive perfume—in a brief cameo at the story's conclusion. Also in Spain, Elizabeth stepped before the cameras for the exterior location sequences of the film whose interiors she was about to shoot in England. By chance, Evelyn Keyes was also on the Costa Brava. Since she and Elizabeth had last met, Evelyn had married the musician Artie Shaw; now they were all guests aboard the yacht of Sam

Spiegel, producer of Elizabeth's forthcoming picture. "Elizabeth and Eddie came on to Sam's yacht with her two sons," recalled Evelyn,

> but Eddie was furious that reporters were all over the place. Artie took him aside and set him straight about all that, reminding Eddie that Elizabeth needed the press, even when she complained about it. While they were talking, Elizabeth said to me, "You know, Evelyn, you had the best years with Mike." And only years later did I realize that she was right. There had been something frantic and manic about the year she had with him—the two of them always buying things and running here and there and desperately trying to find their importance and their supremacy amid such professional competition.

Elizabeth, Evelyn remembered, was still wearing Mike's wedding band on her right hand, and Eddie's on her left.

On May 24, the Fishers finally arrived in London, so she could join the rest of the cast and director of *Suddenly, Last Summer.* This was her second consecutive picture based on a play by Tennessee Williams, and her first (except for the loan-outs for *Elephant Walk* and *Giant*) outside her contract for MGM, which would forever expire after one picture to follow *Suddenly, Last Summer.**

At Shepperton Studios, director Joseph L. Mankiewicz had already begun filming with her costars, Katharine Hepburn and Montgomery Clift. By this time, a year of creative indolence and culinary indulgence had taken a greater toll than ever on Elizabeth, and Mankiewicz was alarmed at the sight of her. "Are you planning on losing any weight?" he asked bluntly on first meeting, lifting up her arm, shaking the flab and adding, "I think maybe you should do a little toning up." She did—and lost twenty pounds.

Suddenly, Last Summer, a one-act play much expanded for the screen by Tennessee Williams and Gore Vidal, was "a scandal to the

*The title of the play bears no comma, which for some odd reason was added for the movie.

jaybirds," as Catherine Holly (Elizabeth) says in the script. On its release later that year, critics and audiences were (as usual with something of Williams) divisible into two vocal and violently opposed factions, those who considered it tawdry smut and those who saw its merit as a moral fable.

The disclosure of a painful truth by unmasking a guilty secret is an important dramatic device in a number of plays by Williams—among them *A Streetcar Named Desire*, *Cat on a Hot Tin Roof*, *Sweet Bird of Youth*, *The Night of the Iguana* and, perhaps most obviously, *Suddenly Last Summer*, which is simultaneously one of his most nakedly auto-biographical and most universal works. In its film version espe-cially—a work that much improves on the static, elliptical brevity of the play—all the dialogue prepares for Catherine's final speech.

The story alone, with two monologues about devouring flesh, two about seduction, one about lobotomy and a detailed description of the sexual exploitation of poverty-stricken children, contained enough issues to alienate many puritans in 1959. Set in 1937 and based on the real-life lobotomy of Williams's sister Rose that same year, *Suddenly, Last Summer* tells a complex and horrifying tale. Violet Venable (Hepburn, as the most malignant example of the Terrible Mother archetype in the Williams canon), is the mother of Cather-ine's dead cousin Sebastian. Mrs. Venable attempts to bribe doctors to perform on Catherine a prefrontal lobotomy, an experimental operation on the brain that would rob her of memory and personal-ity, thus silencing forever the girl's "hallucinations," half-remem-bered dreams and "ravings" about her travels with Sebastian and what happened suddenly last summer. The truth is learned only at the end, when Catherine is led by a compassionate doctor (Clift) to recall fully what happened: Sebastian, with Catherine as his unwit-ting procurer, was devoured by poor, hungry Spanish urchins whom he had (it is implied) bribed for sex.

Tennessee Williams knew precisely what he was doing in this very personal work, and he and Vidal chose each word of the script meticulously. *Venable*, an old form of the word *venal*, describes one who both bribes and corrupts, which is exactly the vice of both Sebastian and his mother. Preying on people is in fact the theme of the story, for in *Suddenly, Last Summer*, the playwright indicts the habit of "devouring" others by exploiting human weakness, by "treating people as if they were items on a menu," as Catherine says.

Aptly, the central setting of the play and film is Sebastian's fantastic garden, a frightening, tropical jungle wrenched as if from "the dawn of creation" (thus Mrs. Venable), with (in Williams's own stage directions) "massive tree-flowers that suggest organs of a body, torn out." The reference is to what Sebastian saw on the Galapagos Islands: newly hatched sea turtles, torn open and devoured, in their futile race from the beach to sea, by the swooping birds of prey. The sterile, effete poet Sebastian, negater and denier of life, sees this apparently cruel moment in nature as "the face of God"—and so he perceives others and eventually himself as sacrificial victims, pawns at the mercy of a malevolent deity. At the finale, Sebastian becomes what he believed in—a broken, demonically inverted "sacrament," slaughtered and devoured in a frenzied Dionysian ritual by the people he had gathered as devout adherents, slaves to his own "venable" pleasure.

The effect of the garden setting and Catherine's dream-remembrance is linked to the beach at Cabeza de Lobo: "Wolf's Head," which points by association to the deadly, depersonalizing hospital named "Lion's Head" and to the surgical suite where personality will be "cut out of the brain." Thus the promontory above the beach where Sebastian is torn apart and devoured is the dreadful term of his self-created destiny: here he, as bird of prey, becomes the victim of those upon whom he preyed.

In *Suddenly, Last Summer,* just beneath the surface of the genteel artifice of an apparently advanced civilization lies the tendency for reversion to savagery. In this regard, there is a thematic connection to works like William Golding's *Lord of the Flies.* We live, says Williams, the serious moral cynic, in a garden of our own tending, far from paradise, a place where we feed living things to living things, fruit flies to Venus's-flytraps and one another to one another. Doctors can be bought, relatives bribed, attorneys compromised— and innocent children corrupted by the unfeeling lusts of detached adults. Sebastian Venable's exploitation of others, his empty, decreative life and his abuse of his cousin Catherine were for Williams the ultimate examples of corruption. Sebastian lived and died with reference to no one but himself, and such deliberate isolation is the essence of real contempt.

In *Giant*, *Raintree County*, and *Cat on a Hot Tin Roof*, Elizabeth's performances were remarkable for their quicksilver changes of moods within sequences, for her unpredictable and wide range of emotions, for her unerring sense of a character's inner odyssey. But her portrait of Catherine Holly in *Suddenly, Last Summer* goes deeper: it is memorable for a sense of sustained anxiety that never becomes tiresome or pretentious. In her long monologues—doubtless made easier by playing them with her good friend Monty Clift—she slowly built a character from blank despair to the terrified agitation in the face of half-concealed memories too awful to confront all at once. Her last monologue, in which the awfulness of Sebastian's death is gruesomely described even as we see it fade in and out of the frame, is very like an aria from a tragic opera of lunacy and death; such an "operatic" direction was precisely Mankiewicz's intent on the set with Elizabeth. The speech, twelve pages long, was shot in two days, with repeated takes for variant camera angles, and after its completion she went to bed for two days.

Preparing for this scene, she extended the range of her voice, breathing and conveying emotions to a pitch very close to mania itself. At the end of her monologue, she collapsed on the set: the weeping was very real, Elizabeth's own response to the character's grief and the dreadful memories at last disclosed. Never had she so understood another's pain, never so identified with what the playwright called the awfulness of life. *Suddenly, Last Summer* explores not what all life is like, but what some life is like—and what all life is in constant danger of becoming. And by this point in her life, Elizabeth at twenty-seven had known enough of brutality, of infidelity, of confusion and loss and death—and the "trails of debris" (thus the script)—that she could, with all the powerful instincts available to her talent, deliver a performance that would justly earn her a third consecutive Academy Award nomination. It was, she maintained, her favorite film, "the greatest, the most emotionally draining, the most emotionally stimulating professional experience of my life."

Whereas Elizabeth achieved a stunning performance through artful pretense, her friend Clift was, alas, not far from the real frontiers of lunacy and despair. Since his accident in 1956, Clift's drug addiction and alcoholism had worsened, and his performance here was strangulated and neurasthenic. In the best of circumstances, Dr. Cukrowicz is a difficult role: he does little more than repeat the statements of others in question form. Depending on one's viewpoint, therefore, Clift's flatness of affect in this film sounds either brilliantly appropriate—the man of logic stunned by appalling cruelty—or, on the other hand, his performance is pathetically unrealized. In fact, when producer Sam Spiegel saw the first few days of film, he decided to dismiss Clift—over their dead bodies, replied Elizabeth Taylor and Katharine Hepburn, whose compassion saved the day. Of Hepburn herself, it can only be noted that she gave the role of Violet Venable an icy malignity, tinted with terrifying humor and the deceptive grace of a deadly nightshade.

The chilling, disturbing intensity of acting in *Suddenly, Last Summer* did nothing to alleviate Elizabeth's growing conviction that her marriage to Eddie Fisher had been "clearly a terrible mistake," as she confided to Joe Mankiewicz. "I thought I could keep Mike's memory alive [through Eddie]. But I have only his ghost." Later, she was even more frank: "I didn't love Eddie, and it wasn't I who needed him. I married him because he needed me." Yet the decision to ally herself with her late husband's "ghost" was certainly more complicated than that. Her marriage to both Nicky Hilton and Mike Todd had been defined by various kinds of subjugation and submission; those that followed each (to Wilding and Fisher), on the other hand, were much under her control. But this was not what she wanted, either, and she admitted that she inflicted on Eddie considerable "indignities."

For his part, Eddie claimed that he was fascinated, even

obsessed with Elizabeth. But by early autumn 1959, he began to chafe under the double situation of inactivity and the occasional cool indifference of his wife. For one thing, he must have found it difficult to face her ubiquitous photographs of Mike Todd and to see his wedding ring on her right hand. "I never took it off," she said of the twisted, charred band that had been recovered from the wreckage. "If I couldn't wear it in a film, I'd pin it to my underwear. It was like I was still married to Mike."

Since the marriage, Eddie's popularity had declined precipitously, and because he had little talent for anything other than singing, he found himself in the curious position of being an assistant to Elizabeth, an unofficial manager. He transported her to the studio and often waited during shooting; he delivered her back home. Occasional meetings for imminent deals were a sad pretense: he was, like Michael Wilding in Hollywood six years earlier, Mr. Elizabeth Taylor.

For the present, only unprecedented luxury in their lives and the distracting presence of Elizabeth's children, shipped to London for a visit, forestalled confrontations more serious than arguments between her and Eddie. There was also some excitement surrounding the arrival in London, late that August, of her agent Kurt Frings, who was—supposedly secretly—bearing the film script for *Cleopatra*. She read it and was very interested, but did not really commit to the idea. But Elizabeth was canny. When Wanger telephoned her on September 1, she said she would play Cleopatra if a few script changes were made, if she could be guaranteed a salary of a million, and if the picture could be shot in England or Europe (she wished to avoid Hollywood for tax and publicity reasons).

"I said that a million dollars was an unheard-of price for an actress," wrote Wanger in a diary. "She said that this was going to be a long, hard picture, [and that she would] take the money on a spread payment, so much per year, since she really wants it to put in trust for her children."

Six days later, the Fishers returned to Los Angeles and a rented suite at the Beverly Hills Hotel, there to await the outcome of increasingly thorny negotiations over *Cleopatra*. On October 9,

Wanger rang Elizabeth to tell her that executives at Fox had decided on Susan Hayward for the Queen of the Nile.

"I want to do it," she said, weeping over the phone. "Why don't they want me?"

"They won't pay your price," Wanger replied.

And then, acting without her agent (as she had from London and as Wanger doubtless hoped she would again), Elizabeth said, "I'll do it for a guarantee of $750,000 plus 10 percent of the gross."

On October 16, newspapers featured a photo story of Elizabeth Taylor signing a contract to play Cleopatra, to be produced the following year in London. But this was a ruse, arranged as Fox's first publicity stunt: Elizabeth signed only blank pages—the actual papers were not ready for almost a year. Five days later, Rouben Mamoulian signed a real contract to direct, and Dale Wasserman was engaged as the third or fourth writer on an already tangled and difficult scenario.*

There was, Elizabeth believed, good reason for her to hold out for her original price: Eddie, inactive, bored and more than ever given over to numerous addictions, was losing huge wads of cash each week in card games with friends—much to the anger of his wife. When a reporter asked about her marriage, she smiled and said the usual sweet clichés; regarding her career, she was frank: "My ambition is to win an Oscar before I retire."

As it happened, that award would be handed to her for a role then being rewritten for production early in the new year: this would be the picture she most hated, with the role of the prosperous Gloria Wandrous, high-fashion model by day, low-life call girl by night, in a film of John O'Hara's squalid little novel *Butterfield 8*.

"I've been here for seventeen years," Elizabeth wrote to Sol

---

*Mamoulian had directed Garbo and Dietrich, among others, on screen; for Broadway, he had directed *Porgy and Bess*, *Oklahoma!* and *Carousel*. Dale Wasserman had enormous success with *Man of La Mancha*, his adaptation of the Don Quixote epic.

Siegel, MGM's vice president in charge of production, "and I was never asked to play such a horrible role as Gloria Wandrous. She's a sick nymphomaniac. I won't do it for anything." Of course, she had no choice: she needed the salary of $125,000, not a lawsuit that would have kept her unemployable for years and thus deprived her of *Cleopatra*. Besides, as producer Pandro Berman observed, Elizabeth's objection was not that her character was a lady of the evening, but that she had to do one final picture for Metro before she began *Cleopatra* at many times the salary. "We simply told her," Berman recalled, "that we would never allow her to make *Cleopatra* until she made this picture." Very well, then, Elizabeth said: the script would have to include a part for Eddie. And so it did: with alarming awkwardness, he played Gloria's platonic friend, a composer who tries in vain to help her change her messy life.

Then, as if it were a ploy to avoid making the film altogether, Elizabeth came down with influenza during a shopping trip to New York, and on November 26, diagnosed with viral pneumonia, she was admitted to the Harkness Pavilion of Columbia-Presbyterian. "She looked well but was weak and complained bitterly about the climate in New York," wrote Wanger in his diary after visiting her on December 7. "If she is miserable and sick *here*, how will she be in *England*?" Well might he have asked.

The title *Butterfield 8* refers to a telephone exchange in the so-called silk stocking district of Manhattan's Upper East Side, an expensive residential neighborhood; it is also the name of the switchboard answering service Gloria uses (and, by unsubtle implication, the designation for the prostitution service). For almost two hours of screen time, Elizabeth smirked and smoked her way through a bitter and sordid little story whose characters have no dimension and whose theme is merely depressing, never tragic. Gloria, whose anxious mother (lovingly played by the fine actress Mildred Dunnock) ignores the nasty truth about her daughter's night life, finally falls in love with married Mr. Wrong, a suburban cad (Laurence Harvey) who is as cold and conniving as herself. Gloria, sick of her life and herself, decides to go respectable and heads for Boston, where presumably even she might absorb good old Puritan values. But her lover, convinced they can be happy together, pursues her, and everything ends miserably when she dies in an auto crash. This gives the surviving antihero just the epiphany he needs, and he returns, chastened, to his unrealistically patient wife (Dina Merrill).

On January 4, 1960, because of an industry strike in Hollywood, *Butterfield 8* began filming in a chilly, dusty old studio on New York's West Side. "It was very clear that she hated it and didn't want to do this picture," recalled playwright and producer Mart Crowley, who worked briefly on it as a production assistant. "But Elizabeth was such a professional that she couldn't help herself. When [the director Daniel] Mann was satisfied with a scene but she was not, she said, 'Wait, I think I can do it better.'" In fact, her performance was entirely right for the role and the picture: disaffected and detached, she gave Gloria a guilty edginess, a kind of awful apathy that suggested this girl might just, long before, have had the stamina to become a more traditional businesswoman. Her marriage to Todd, his sudden death, the scandal over Eddie: the pattern of Elizabeth's life from 1957 had evoked something dark, sensual and angry in her as in her performances. She had forever graduated from playing only sweet, innocent or troubled young ladies.

But whereas professionalism conquered reluctance about her own part, Elizabeth was powerless to alter Eddie's: his colorless, negligible role was more and more truncated during production and editing, and this further exacerbated his ill humor and lack of confidence. He drank and gambled more, and Elizabeth spent many Manhattan nights alone, telephoning friends in Los Angeles and finally falling asleep with the help of a few sleeping pills and a hefty shot of bourbon. "I was very self-destructive," she said of that time. "All [Eddie and I] had in common was Mike, and that was sick. Boy, did I realize how sick it was." So, she contended again and again, was the script for *Butterfield 8*. "This picture stinks!" she cried, quarreling with anyone who would sustain her unusual outbursts of temper.

After *Butterfield 8* was completed in late March, the Fishers flew to Los Angeles, where they attended the Academy Awards ceremony, and Elizabeth again watched another nominee (Simone Signoret) walk off with the statuette she hoped to have for *Suddenly, Last Summer.* Yes, she told reporters, she was now officially an alumna of Metro-Goldwyn-Mayer, en route to Twentieth Century-Fox. That week, MGM changed the name of its commissary's "Elizabeth Taylor Salad" to the "Lana Turner Salad," which may have been lighter, although it was probably not less spicy. The Fishers also took a brief holiday in Jamaica, and visited Eddie's mother, who was ill in Philadelphia. There, Elizabeth took a tumble on an icy sidewalk and was taken to New York with bruised but unbroken limbs.

Meetings on the much delayed *Cleopatra* continued in Manhattan, where Fox's East Coast executives were almost maniacal over the escalating budget and where yet another writer, Lawrence Durrell, flew in to do battle with the script. Dining with Wanger, Elizabeth insisted that she would have her old friend from Metro, Sydney Guilaroff, as hairstylist for the film, and that both penthouse suites at the Dorchester Hotel would be reserved for her—the second for her children and a nanny when they visited, and for her ever-growing entourage (secretary and chauffeur, for example). At these demands, Wanger winced and Spyros Skouras, president of Fox, abraded his worry beads. But they had to capitulate, especially when she almost withdrew from the project when informed that the film would be made entirely in England, with not a single exterior in Italy or Egypt, where the winter weather would not be so perilous. She was ready, she told Wanger, to jump ship—to proceed with plans to star in, and to coproduce with Eddie, a remake of *Anna Karenina*, earlier a starring role for both Greta Garbo and Vivien Leigh. Besides, Wanger and Fox had no signed contract for her.

Thus Wanger ran interference with the studio, finally winning the concession for some exterior work in Egypt. "The weather is terrible," wrote Wanger in his diary in London on June 4. "It is cold, rainy and cloudy," and he told Skouras this would be troublesome for Elizabeth: "There's no sun. It's cold now and it's going to get colder in the fall. Elizabeth may get pneumonia again!"

"The weather is going to be fine," said Skouras, who was a

movie tycoon but no meteorologist. "No one will get sick. England is the best place to make this picture. Go ahead. Shoot it."

To do that, Elizabeth of course had to sign a contract, which she finally did in her New York hotel suite on July 28. The document, to no one's surprise, secured for her some of the most astonishing clauses in movie history up to 1960:

- salary of $125,000 per week for sixteen weeks;
- $50,000 weekly after sixteen weeks;
- 10 percent of the film's gross box-office receipts;
- $3,000 per week living expenses, plus food and lodging;
- first-class, roundtrip airfare to the film's locations for herself, three additional adults and three children.

"She stands to make two or three million dollars from this!" noted Wanger in his diary. He was far off the mark: Elizabeth's total income from *Cleopatra* (which was not completed until the summer of 1962) eventually surpassed $7,000,000, most of it conveniently sheltered in a corporation she formed with Eddie. This they registered as MCL, Inc., the initials of her three children, Michael, Christopher and Liza. In 1963, the highest paid American business executive earned $650,000, and President Kennedy, $150,000. Elizabeth received at least $2.4 million.

To rest before the rigors of an autumn and winter shooting of *Cleopatra,* Elizabeth treated herself (and her husband and children) to a summer Mediterranean cruise. When the Fishers arrived in London on August 31, the press met them in full force at the airport. Wanger negotiated a swift exit through a customs door, but they had to face a squad of cameramen and reporters an hour later at the Dorchester. Elizabeth, still smarting from what she considered the intrusive manner of the London press the previous year, refused to give an interview, nor would she pose for a single photo. Wanger conveyed to her their comments that they would boycott *Cleopatra.* "She shrugged," he wrote in his diary. "I must say she has a lot of courage."

On September 28, filming began at Pinewood, with Elizabeth's first scene scheduled. But she awoke with a cold, and so the company shot around her, managing a few takes with Peter Finch (as Caesar) and Stephen Boyd (as Mark Antony)—and thousands of extras as citizens of Alexandria. Mamoulian was having trouble handling the crowd scenes, the script was being changed from hour to hour, the weather was distressingly unstable—and Wanger feared that his tribulations were only beginning. He could not have been more correct.

On October 10, a respiratory specialist was called to Elizabeth's suite to see about her lingering fever, headaches and congestion. Eddie, weary of idleness, packed for a trip to New York (ostensibly to discuss a recording contract), and his departure threw Elizabeth into panic. Fearing a repetition of the earlier tragedy, she wept, begged her husband not to leave, and when he finally extricated himself from her embrace, she ran to the telephone and paged him in the lobby, begging him to return quickly and saying she would not sleep until he had landed safely.

A week later, he was back, but she had not recovered. Finally, none other than Queen Elizabeth II's personal physician was summoned, and he diagnosed the cause of the patient's lingering fever and headaches: an abscessed tooth (neither emotional breakdown nor a miscarriage, as the hostile press implied), and this required immediate extraction, a debilitating course of antibiotics and a week in the London Clinic. Skouras and his colleagues, meantime, were arguing with insurance carriers that the star's illness should be compensated. At the same time, he did not like the ten minutes of film Mamoulian had managed and ordered Wanger to look for a new director.

The press leapt on all these developments, claiming that Elizabeth was the cause of all the problems. When she returned to her hotel, a reporter from the Associated Press sent out the fiction that she was hiding out there because she was too fat for the film's costumes. This was nonsense: the costumes were no more ready than the script, which now had writer Nunnally Johnson trying to surmount its thorny dilemmas.

By late November, the London weather was, it seemed, permanently filthy. Even under the best circumstances, the vast studio space at Pinewood was a drafty and hazardous place: for a woman recovering from infection, it was downright perilous. Her doctors, accordingly, ordered another week of rest, and with that Fox's insurance company ordered the production closed and the role of Cleopatra recast: more than $2,000,000 had gone to waste thus far. "You've ruined us by having that girl in the picture," Skouras muttered to Wanger. "I wish to hell we'd done it with Joanne Woodward or Susan Hayward—we'd be making money now." That was an interesting (and unverifiable) fantasy, although it is not easy to imagine the admirable Misses Woodward and Hayward in the role of the wily and seductive Egyptian minx (or the two other names highest on Skouras's list: Audrey Hepburn and Marilyn Monroe).

Wanger again went to the mat for his star, and remarkably, the insurance executives recanted and said that they would reinsure both Elizabeth and the production—but only after the script was complete, every costume and wig ready, and physicians had unanimously agreed to allow Elizabeth to return. On Friday, December 2, the Fishers flew to Palm Springs for a sunny winter holiday. A new starting date of January 3, 1961, was set, and *Cleopatra* would begin once again. Mamoulian, under pressure, withdrew; after three months, he had managed less than ten minutes of *Cleopatra* on film and suspected, quite rightly, that none of it would be used. In January, Wanger replaced him with Joseph L. Mankiewicz, who immediately set to work as director and final screenwriter. Mankiewicz had not only Elizabeth's trust and Wanger's respect: he also had a sharp sense of classical history, having adapted and directed a film of Shakespeare's *Julius Caesar* in 1953. At last, Elizabeth began to believe that *Cleopatra* might, indeed, be produced.

Chapter Nine

1961-1962

*T*HE MOTION PICTURE HERALD, AN influential trade journal that polled the public about such things as audience favorites, reported early in 1961 that Elizabeth Taylor was the country's top box-office star; next in popularity were Rock Hudson, Doris Day, John Wayne, Cary Grant, Sandra Dee, Jerry Lewis, William Holden, Tony Curtis and Elvis Presley. News of this favorable national standing broke as she prepared to depart the bright warmth of the Palm Springs desert for the inclement grayness of London in January.

Elizabeth was not, however, cheered by the *Herald*'s report. She had spent the month's holiday in a state of quiet but real anxiety, lounging in bed, poring listlessly over magazines, playing card games, eating, smoking and drinking imprudently, and, inevitably, gaining weight. Contrary to her pretense that acting was unimportant and that retirement was always just around the corner, Elizabeth's reputation as an actress was the primary care of her life. The reason for her apparent loss of affect that winter was concern over *Cleopatra*, a project that, in Eddie's words, made her "terrified that she was trapped in the biggest turkey of her career," and that not even the trusted Joe Mankiewicz could rescue her or the picture.

By mid-January, the Fishers and their retinue were reinstalled at the Dorchester. "They live like royalty," noted Walter Wanger,

> with children, dogs, cats, retainers and supplicants for favor all over the place. Famous people are always dropping in. The phone rings continuously with friends or agents calling from Hollywood or Switzerland or Rome. The order of the day is deals. [She] is enthusiastically interested in everything, especially films and the theater. She knows enough about show business to edit Variety.

The comparison to royalty was not fanciful. Secretaries dashed in and out, the chauffeur arrived with packages, servants came to walk the dogs or amuse the children, and telephones rang ceaselessly with requests for interviews, for autographs, for appointments, for endorsements. And Elizabeth acted like a royal, too, which is how she had been treated for most of her life. She ordered chili flown over from Chasen's in Los Angeles, stone crabs from the coast of Florida, smoked salmon from Barney Greengrass in New York, sirloin steaks from Chicago, shrimp creole from New Orleans, spare ribs from St. Louis, white asparagus from the French countryside, fresh linguini from Genoa.

When dinner was served in their suite, however, the Fishers always had company, even if that meant a secretary or a nanny at the table. "Elizabeth did not want to be alone with Eddie," reported Shelley Winters, who also resided at the Dorchester that season (and, nearby, was filming Stanley Kubrick's Lolita). After dining often with the Fishers that season, Winters added, with uncharacteristic understatement, that they "were beginning to be rather testy with each other."

Opulent meals and expensive champagnes were a kind of refuge for Elizabeth; so was shopping, which she sometimes did with the same wacky prodigality of her food orders: the same style of handmade negligée, for example, she purchased in eight colors. Thus distracted, her mood temporarily improved—especially when Mankiewicz, in late January, sat down with his star and the producer to outline an entirely new concept of *Cleopatra*. He had in mind more than a stereotypical epic with the traditional dashes of De Millian sex and violence. Mankiewicz understood Antony as a desperate follower in Caesar's capacious footsteps, but insecure in battle, politics and love and eventually destroyed by his fatal love for Cleopatra. As for the queen, the writer-director saw her as the first woman to rule in a man's world and in a man's way. With such ideas, Mankiewicz fired Elizabeth's imagination. She would be the seventh Cleopatra in film history, and the greatest.*

But as the time passed in January and February, with Mankiewicz churning out pages of script during the long, raw winter days of London, Elizabeth had little to do but entertain friends, fight with Eddie, and drink rather too much champagne or bourbon in an attempt to calm her marital and professional anxieties. She turned twenty-nine that February and little of her beauty was lost, but her energy declined with her spirits.

Thus it happened that she was particularly susceptible to colds throughout February, and by month's end she had spiked a fever. On the night of March 3, her breathing was severely compromised, doctors were summoned to her suite, and by the morning of March 4 she had developed a fulminant viral pneumonia, complicated by a rampant staphylococcus infection. That night at the London Clinic, surgeons performed an emergency tracheotomy, opening a direct air passage into her windpipe. "She had almost stopped breathing completely," recalled Dr. Middleton Price. "She might have survived fifteen minutes longer, but no more." Her fever rose, her lungs could not be cleared, and she slipped in and out of deep coma. There was no exaggeration in the news bulletins flashed around the world that

*In 1906, an unknown Parisian actress played Cleopatra in a short Pathé film. Subsequently, the role was assumed in silent films by Helen Gardner (US, 1912), Gianna Terribili Gonzalez (Italy, 1913) and Theda Bara (US, 1916), and in talkies by Claudette Colbert (US, 1934) and Vivien Leigh (England, 1945).

weekend: Elizabeth Taylor was dying, and so the physicians told Eddie Fisher.

For two days and nights, obituaries were prepared and headline space cleared; her parents, informed of the grave situation, arrived from America; thousands gathered in the streets near the London Clinic; cameramen set up tripods for the death announcement; Mankiewicz and Fisher scurried in and out of the intensive care unit where she lay, shrunken, pale and unresponsive; gifts and "miracle cures" arrived from all over the world. "I'm going to lose my girl," sobbed Eddie to a newsman outside the Clinic—which, as it happened, would soon enough be true, though in another sense.

It is no hyperbole to say that Elizabeth's morbid condition bumped all other international news from the world's headlines for several days that March. Vast cartons of mail and truckloads of flowers arrived at the Dorchester and at the Clinic. "Six thousand of us are praying for you here at the Boeing plant!" read a letter from America. "Don't give up, Liz!" ran the message from a submarine crew somewhere deep in the Indian Ocean. Everywhere, people were photographed at prayer services. The final hours in the life of Pope Pius XII, in 1958, were scarcely more fervently and elaborately documented.

At one point, a wire service actually reported that she had died—an announcement that at once threw more panic than grief into the East and West Coast offices of Twentieth Century-Fox. "My God, how did it happen?" cried Spyros Skouras over a crackling phone line to Wanger in London before Wanger set him right. But Wanger could not easily give many correcting details: his own physician, who had been told by colleagues at the Clinic that Elizabeth would not survive, had administered sedatives to the producer, and he was not at his clearest when a frantic Skouras needed something to report to stockholders.

Thus began, that winter, the second long hiatus on the production of the ill-fated *Cleopatra*. The slow stages of her recuperation were documented universally, too: the removal of her breathing tube, the eventual subsiding of fever, the gradual clearing of her lungs. On March 12, she was sitting up in her hospital bed, sipping champagne and joking with visitors. Two days later, after doctors advised a long recovery, Wanger and Mankiewicz finally got their wish: Skouras and company agreed to demolish $600,000 worth of sets at Pinewood and resume Cleopatra in the balmier climate of Rome later that summer. Peter Finch, who had been cast as Caesar, was paid the balance of his $150,000 and sent off with a handshake; the same treatment was accorded Stephen Boyd, the first Mark Antony.

Eventually, Mankiewicz and Wanger came up with inspired replacements: Rex Harrison as Caesar and, as Antony, Richard Burton. Harrison had enjoyed a long run in the musical *My Fair Lady* and then moved easily and enjoyably from stage to screen and back again. Not so Burton. After the release of *The Robe* in 1953, he had returned briefly to England for several Shakespearean roles, but "the lure of the zeroes was simply too great," as he said. Thus he returned to movies exclusively from 1954 to 1960, except for a run of *Time Remembered* on Broadway in 1957, which he most recalled for his passionate affair with his lovely and gifted nineteen-year-old costar, Susan Strasberg. This relationship his wife, Sybil, endured patiently, for it passed and Richard returned to his family—as he did after the liaisons with other leading ladies and an array of other available women.

Sybil Burton's love for her husband, it must be said, had nothing to do with a kind of pathetic masochism: the sober Richard Burton was one of the wittiest, best-read, famous actors of his time—an autodidact with a lively intelligence, a bright gift for words, a sense of irony and a Chekhovian wistfulness for his own lost innocence. Self-indulgent and undisciplined, hedonistic and indolent, stubborn and devoted to the life of the senses, he was very clear about his frailties and never exacted from others what he could not achieve himself. A legion of women offered themselves to him, perhaps because he was a skillful and flattering lover. But Richard Burton's essential kindness and generosity attracted both men and women to him as platonic friends, too. His inner anguish, his alcoholism, therefore, evoked from those who loved him more sorrow than anger. "I couldn't be unfaithful to my wife without feeling a profound sense of guilt," he once said honestly in a long, revealing interview; his life, accordingly, was wreathed in remorse. This would in time be exacerbated by his absence from his daughters Kate and Jessica—the latter a singularly poignant situation, for the child was diagnosed as an autistic schizophrenic and was placed in an institution from the age of six.

In 1961, Burton opened in the Broadway hit musical *Camelot* (which won him a Tony Award), and its producers had to be paid handsomely to release him for *Cleopatra*. This he agreed to with alacrity, although he had only contempt for movie work and secretly longed to be what many believed he could be—a new Olivier and Gielgud in one. "My decision to do *Cleopatra*," he said, "was prompted by laziness and cupidity." Burton and Harrison, among hundreds of others, were told to report to Rome in September.

Twentieth Century-Fox, meantime, had lost $40 million through fiscal mismanagement in general and the expenses of *Cleopatra* in particular, originally budgeted at $2 million and quickly skyrocketing to over $35 million. In this regard, the epic changed the map of Los Angeles: that year, the studio was forced to sell most of its back lot to a real estate developer. The result was Century City, one of the most attractive commercial and residential lots to rise on the city's West Side.

When Elizabeth departed the London Clinic at the end of March, there was, at the sight of her, a tumult of hysterical, congratulatory rejoicing in the surrounding streets not seen in London since the end of World War II or the coronation of King George VI. "The door was almost torn off her Rolls-Royce," according to Wanger, "and she had to be moved to another car." At any time, there are only a few celebrities in the world who, by the mere force of their presence, could claim to bring everyday life to a halt; for much of her life, that can certainly be said of Elizabeth Taylor.

The besieged car's destination was not the Dorchester Hotel: the Fishers departed immediately for California—for a long rest and for the industry's rites of spring. For the fourth consecutive year, Elizabeth had been nominated for an Academy Award as best actress; at last, on April 17, she won—for the hated *Butterfield 8*. To thunderous applause, she made her way to the stage and accepted the statuette from Yul Brynner. Then, shaky of voice and body, she told the world, "I don't really know how to express my gratitude for this and for everything. All I can say is thank you, thank you with all my heart."

To her credit, she had not changed her mind about the film or the role: "I still think it's a piece of shit," she said backstage to anyone who would listen; she had written exactly that critique, in lipstick, on the screen after she saw a rough cut. Elizabeth was also savvy enough to know that this was a sympathy vote, given in recognition of her survival as much as her previous achievements. "I should've won for *Suddenly, Last Summer,* but I was a bad girl then," she said later. ("I lost to a tracheotomy!" cried Shirley MacLaine, who had been nominated for *The Apartment*). Elizabeth's judgment was that "the Academy wanted to make sure they honored me before anything else happened." Would she raise her price now, beyond a million dollars a picture? "No," she said. "After all, I don't want to be greedy."

In 1949, Ingrid Bergman had been condemned from the floor of Congress and was a social and professional pariah when she quit Hollywood for Italy and director Roberto Rossellini, by whom she had become pregnant before their marriage. By 1957, all was forgiven, and she was welcomed back with an Oscar for her performance in *Anastasia*. Now, it was Elizabeth's turn for Hollywood's absolution: "When the Academy forgives and presents a wayward actress with one of its Oscars," noted veteran columnist Sidney Skolsky, "she is considered forgiven by the public." And so Elizabeth was. In favor as the tragic Widow Todd, then out during *l'affaire Fisher,* she was now restored to the state of public grace—a mythic figure like the heroine Alcestis of Greek mythology, brought back from the jaws of death.

Apart from the Oscar evening, Elizabeth spent the spring of 1961 in a bungalow at the Beverly Hills Hotel, her recovery retarded by phlebitis and the danger of blood clotting in her right leg. The seclusion made her cranky: "All those antibiotics ruin your appetite," she told a visiting reporter. "Food tastes like balsa wood to me." But for that, she was eventually glad: by late summer, after a depressed appetite not sharpened by indolence and Russian cuisine, she had lost something like sixteen pounds.

Her next public appearance, smiling radiantly, was even more like the return of Alcestis, for she too was a person once "dead," she claimed. At a July 8 fund-raising dinner for Cedars of Lebanon–Mt. Sinai Hospital (renamed later the less clumsy Cedars-Sinai), Elizabeth was seated next to Attorney General Robert Kennedy, among more than a thousand guests who paid $2,500 each to praise Elizabeth, rather extravagantly, as "the most dramatic example of the miracle of modern medicine" for having overcome pneumonia; she was not, of course, the only person in history to have survived that illness, but what the hell.

The evening was perhaps the single most crucial event that elevated Elizabeth to the status of actress-as-goddess. Reading from a text drafted by Joe Mankiewicz, Elizabeth described her experience of death and resurrection itself—an account that left her audience gasping and provided her with a dramatic incident to which she returned in interviews for decades to come.

Dying is many things, but most of all, it is wanting to live. Throughout many critical hours in the operating theater, it was as if every nerve, every muscle were being strained to the last ounce of my strength. Gradually and inevitably, that last ounce was drawn, and there was no more breath. I remember I had focused desperately on the hospital light hanging directly above me. It had become something I needed almost fanatically to continue to see, the vision of life itself. Slowly it faded and dimmed, like a well-done theatrical effect to blackness. . . . I died. Shall I tell you what it was like? Being down a long, dark tunnel, and there was a small light at the end. I had to keep looking at that light . . . and I heard the voices, urging me to come back, come back . . . The experience I had was painful, but beautiful, too. It was like childbirth—painful but so beautiful.

She concluded with almost idolatrous praise of hospital workers, which seemed anticlimactic but was marvelously effective. The Fishers contributed $100,000 to the hospital; dinner guests pledged an additional $7,000,000 that night.

During her sojourn at the Desert Inn, Las Vegas, while Eddie fulfilled a nightclub engagement contract, Elizabeth regained her appetite with a vengeance. "I'm lazy, I'm unpunctual, I'm sloppy," she said of herself that May.

> Food is one of my major vices. I like anything fattening. But having double pneumonia is a great way to lose weight. I'm still terribly weak, so I indulge in very big breakfasts and dinners. For breakfast, I have a choice of dollar pancakes, a batch of hashed brown potatoes, eggs Benedict, sausages, waffles and sometimes kippers. Sometimes I have all of these! For dinner, I like anything from steaks Diane to pizza, and I also like to eat before I go to bed.

But all was not lazy self-indulgence. Elizabeth also studied the accumulating pages of *Cleopatra*, now arriving almost daily from Mankiewicz, who was rewriting drafts submitted by Lawrence Durrell, Sidney Buchman and Ranald MacDougall. Her Cleopatra, the new Cleopatra, was to be not merely a crafty exploiter of sexual power, the first woman to meet men on their own terms: she was also becoming a character dedicated to a goal of world peace, not unilateral domination, and this streak of nobility appealed to Elizabeth's best instincts.

"Rome and Alexandria will bring the world together in peace," ran a new line for Cleopatra to urge Caesar, her eyes aglow with a complex of ardors. Then, in a hallucinatory sequence of passion, ritual and political revolution, she bears Caesar his longed-for son. Elizabeth, always on the side of the angels regarding international relations, recalled her earlier visit to Russia in 1958; now, as she prepared to incarnate Cleopatra, she saw herself as the revolutionary harbinger of peace, a messenger of warm harmony in a world of cold discord. This time, the publicity department at Fox, who recognized a good thing when they saw it, handily obtained for Elizabeth the blessing of the State Department.

And so, three days after delivering her resurrection narrative at the benefit dinner, the Fishers were off on an official goodwill tour to the Moscow Film Festival. Each time they exited and reentered the Sovietskaya Hotel in Moscow, Elizabeth—protected by Eddie, her physician Rex Kennamer and her hairdresser Alexandre of Paris—was besieged almost to the point of fainting. All this excitement was wired to the international press, who wrote extensively about the forthcoming star of *Cleopatra* (it was invariably highlighted in the press release) and everything about her journey behind the Iron Curtain and her return stopover in Paris, where Elizabeth announced that "to further Soviet-American cultural relations," she hoped to make a movie in Russia. There she was, the modern Cleopatra indeed, assimilating the contours of her new character.

This approach to life was, after all, the *eidos,* the shape and shadow of her only reality, the plan of action through which she beheld the world ever since her earliest days as a child actress. Having started at nine, whatever other method could she adopt as an onslaught to and against a chaotic life? She had come to perceive the world and her place in it through the only prism she knew, that of a movie script; relationships and interactions with society had as their only analogues the structure of movies.

She tried even to think of a relevant coproduction but could come upon only the *Anna Karenina* she and Eddie once planned, "which would give a new boost to exchanges between my country and Russia." On July 18, the Fishers returned to Los Angeles, where reporters and photographers remained camped around a hospital next day. Inside, Dr. Michael Gurdin, that gifted sculptor to the stars, applied his trusty scalpel and trustworthy skills to erase the remnants of her tracheotomy scar.

The gap between herself and Cleopatra was closing even further. Just as the queen gave Caesar a child to win his confidence and collaboration, so Elizabeth suggested that she and Eddie adopt a child. Her three earlier pregnancies had been difficult and dangerous, her doctor advised against a fourth, and in any case her career would not admit a pregnancy now. And so just as the Fishers arrived in Rome as autumn began, they asked their friend actress Maria Schell to act as intermediary in the adoption of a Swiss, Viennese or German baby. Again, Fox's publicists cheered: earlier, Bette Davis, Joan Crawford and other stars had been highly rated for their humanitarian adoption of poor, sickly or unwanted children. Now, just months before the Fishers separated, Elizabeth was encouraged by Fox in her stated desire to adopt, and to do so quickly.

The consensus of friends and colleagues is that Elizabeth certainly wanted a child, and all evidence points to good motives, especially in light of her enormous kindness and generosity to the one she eventually chose. But as Thomas More rightly observed, only God is love straight through, and although an admixture of motives was certainly not reprehensible, the move to adopt could only enhance Elizabeth's public image—as, she hoped, it might be a balm for her troubled marriage. "The new child was intended to cement [the Fishers'] shaky union," according to a reporter close to that child in later life. Another admitted that yes, the effort to adopt occurred precisely when an enduring marriage seemed no longer realistic—"just a little more than six months before they separated."

And so Maria Schell placed an ad in a German magazine, stating that a wealthy, childless foreign couple wished to adopt a baby. At once, a poor family responded, offering their ailing eight-month-old girl. Maria Schell sent her secretary, Frau Königsbauer, to Augsburg late on September 1 to see the weak and ailing infant—the same day Elizabeth arrived in Rome to resume *Cleopatra*.

But there was a problem. The baby, named Petra Heisig, had a congenitally deformed hip; malnourished and covered with bedsores, she was, to say the least, unresponsive and unattractive. When she finally came to see the baby, Elizabeth Taylor's finest instincts rose to the occasion. At once, she set in motion the necessary legal steps to adopt the child and contacted the best clinics in Germany and Switzerland to arrange for the first corrective surgeries. The girl was forthwith named Maria, after Schell; she arrived at the Fishers' villa in Rome that Christmas of 1961, although final approval of adoption took longer.

To those who knew Elizabeth, the adoption of the girl was not at all out of character. On intimate terms with loss, childhood confusion and pain and, since her earliest days, a regimen of constant manipulation, she had grown up with a keen sensitivity to the sufferings of others. At first, the objects of her attention and compassion were birds with broken wings or scrawny chipmunks or horses. Then she developed the lifelong habit of befriending the frightened, the lonely, the social outcasts, the psychologically disturbed, the addicted, those of shattered spirit or broken heart. However unhelpful she was to herself at critical times of her life, however unwisely she may have chosen what she thought was her heart's desire, Elizabeth's sensibility was always for those in pain, for the disaffected, those at the margin of polite life. Throughout her life, even when ill and self-destructive, she never lost her compassion for others who were ill or self-destructive. She could have said, with the heartbroken Dido in Vergil's *Aeneid*, *Non ignara mali, miseris succurrere disco*—"No stranger to unhappiness, I have learned how to help others in pain."

During the first weeks of September, the production company of *Cleopatra* might have been mistaken for a traveling circus. Rex Harrison and Richard Burton and more costars arrived with their spouses and retinues. One area of the film studio, Cinecittà, housed a company of Italians in training for "land battles." At Anzio, an hour from Rome, vast schooners were being constructed to simulate the naval battle of Actium. Cleopatra's barge was outfitted with royal sails for the trip to the isle of Ischia, where her scenes on board would eventually be filmed. A fake Forum nearly twice the size of the original was built, and hundreds of exotic dancers were in rehearsal—all for the huge procession when Cleopatra enters Rome. Six thousand extras were outfitted for the same sequence, and more than 20,000 costumes were being sewn for the picture. Athletes were pole-vaulting, actors were at swordplay, marksmen shot arrows, stuntmen fell from horses and buildings. A fortune had been spent on *Cleopatra* so far—and there was not a second of footage to be used. And everywhere were the relentless, aggressive paparazzi—freelance photographers in search of candid celebrity shots, men with the manners and morals of ravenous jackals.

But the atmosphere for the remainder of production, which lasted from September 1961 through July 1962, had, indeed, very little of circus amusement.

For one thing, as the cameras rolled on September 25, only one of the sixty sets needed was fully built and ready. Worse, Mankiewicz's script was only half complete, which placed him, his designers, his cast and his crew in the curious position of telling a story blindly, with no sure sense of where they were going. This threw Mankiewicz, otherwise a man of great intelligence and a clear idea of movie narrative, into a round-the-clock schedule, shooting by day and writing at night. "I awoke at five-thirty or six and gulped down a Dexedrine," he said, describing his habit of living that year on amphetamines for energy and barbiturates for sleep. "I was then given a shot after lunch to keep me going through the afternoon. Then I was given a shot after dinner so I could write till two in the morning, and then I got a final shot at two so I could go to sleep."

Amid this early chaos, however, Elizabeth—for the time being, at least—stood unhysterical, in good spirits for her first scenes and (having lost the weight she had gained that spring) looking radiant. "She looks gorgeous and in general is behaving quite nicely," Jack Brodsky, Fox's assistant publicity manager, wrote to his colleague Nathan Weiss in New York. "Elizabeth is truly queen of Rome," noted Wanger with satisfaction in his diary on September 28. And so she was treated that evening, when she received the Italian equivalent of an Oscar for her performance in *Suddenly, Last Summer.* Forty policemen had to restrain hundreds of paparazzi at the theater, and thousands of people nearly tore her clothes to shreds, attempting to snatch a relic of the sacred wardrobe.

The Fishers had been installed at the Villa Papa, less than ten minutes from Cinecittà. Set amid eight acres of parks and gardens, the ranch-style villa had seven bedrooms and six baths, terraces, living and dining rooms and an entire wing for the children and retinue. Five dogs and four cats roamed freely, and servants were kept constantly busy keeping the place clean. Not far away, in a smaller villa, were Richard Burton, his wife, Sybil, their children and his brother. "Nice family," observed Wanger, who did not think it unremarkable when Burton, at a Grand Hotel dinner party on October 14, asked that his place be moved next to Elizabeth's.

But the paparazzi, fully aware of Burton's reputation as the Don Juan of movies, were everywhere—lurking on studio catwalks, climbing trees near the Fishers' swimming pool, attaching long lenses to their cameras outside the Burton residence and waiting for whatever shot could provide a story. Reporters and photographers bribed the workers in the Fisher and Taylor villas, they stole costumes and slithered among the crowd scenes. Usually, producers welcome the press to a movie set and location, for of course stories in advance generate word of mouth and heighten anticipation for a movie; in the case of *Cleopatra,* Wanger and company very soon wanted to be left alone. That was not to be.

Throughout November and December, Elizabeth and Rex filmed their scenes with little rehearsal and great effect, working smoothly and with admirable mutual understanding and quiet professionalism. Their dialogue—alternately passionate, angry, full of wonder at how the love of Caesar and Cleopatra was changing the course of world history—was poetic but somehow naturalistic. Harrison, who could be a testy and irascible colleague, admitted that he

> loved working with Elizabeth Taylor on the film, because she is in every way the consummate film actress, and her professionalism on the set and in front of the camera is quite remarkable to see. She was, of course, practically brought up in the studios, and as a result she knows exactly what she's doing with the slightest movement of an eyelash or curve of a lip. She is always word-perfect, too . . . For those of us who had spent our youthful energies on the stage, Elizabeth's film technique is an eye-opener.

Mankiewicz, always his own worst critic, was pleased, and Wanger more optimistic each day.

In mid-January 1962, the papers for the adoption of little Maria were approved, but because the Fisher marriage was negotiating rough waters, they were not signed for several months. At that time, the baby was designated "Maria Taylor," and two years later she became Maria Burton. Several operations remained to be scheduled for the child, and before the final papers were signed, some of Elizabeth's friends urged her to reconsider, but to no avail. "She is my child. I want her all the more because she's ill. Maybe I can do something to help." In fact until February, Elizabeth dined every evening with Eddie, Michael, Christopher, Liza and Maria at the villa. Mankiewicz and Wanger knew that when one of the children was sick, Elizabeth raced to the telephone between every take on the set.

But in February, everything changed, and forever. At last the paparazzi had the big story they were waiting for. Elizabeth Taylor and Richard Burton filmed their first scenes together, and the rest, as the saying goes, is history. His initial reaction was unexceptional to the point of offense: "All this stuff about Elizabeth being the most beautiful woman in the world is absolute nonsense. She's a pretty girl, of course, and she has wonderful eyes. But she has a double chin and an overdeveloped chest and she's rather short in the leg." But this critique was soon replaced by a blazing passion that placed both of them onto more pages of more international newspapers than the Eddie-Debbie-Elizabeth triangle had ever occupied. "She gives you a sense of danger," Burton said. And for him courting danger and the lure of fame were the ultimate aphrodisiacs. "He was a very poor boy who suddenly found the whole world," said his daughter Kate after his death, "and he wanted it all."

The attraction is not difficult to understand: Elizabeth's sensuality was irresistible to Burton, and so was her awe at his talent, his erudition, his use of English, his preference for the good life over a good role. He had, for her, the appealing, brawling raunchiness often attributed to boozy, poetic Welshmen (Dylan Thomas, for example, who was his patron saint), but this was balanced by a stunningly resonant voice and impressive diction. Very soon, Elizabeth began to speak with an uneven but pronounced English accent, and life with Richard added to her storehouse of colorful expletives. She was, said Jack Brodsky, "an extraordinarily beautiful woman with magnetism, but I was put off by her language, which was foul, and her drinking. It was wine mostly, a lot of it consumed at lunch, and sometimes champagne or bourbon." And among Brodsky's responsibilities, it must be recalled, was the duty to prevent the press, any visitors or executives from the knowledge that Elizabeth (who quickly picked up the habit from Richard) was tippling at lunchtime.

After his death, the publication of his letters and journals indicated that under other circumstances Richard Burton might have been hugely successful as a writer. He was, in fact, a kind of arty Mike Todd—assertive, aggressive and extravagant, but also a terrific intellectual influence on Elizabeth, to whom he offered unpretentious little tutorials and on whom he urged the great books of the world, completing what Mike Todd had begun, the transformation of Elizabeth the child into Elizabeth the woman. Richard was a born teacher, she a dedicated student, and this was the most positive aspect of a relationship that was from the start deeply problematic. "I envied his Shakespearean background," she said, "and the fact that he was not a movie star but a genuine actor." The contrast with Eddie Fisher could not have been greater, although he and Richard were both addictive personalities.

Burton was forthright and articulate in his opinions; unreserved in his expression of them; completely, constantly confident with women and—oh, brave new world for her!—both literate and literary. Michael Wilding had meant serenity and gentleness after the pain of Nicky Hilton, and in an additional ironic twist, the script of *Cleopatra*—following the facts of history—makes clear that Caesar suffers from epileptic seizures. Cleopatra/Elizabeth first embraces Caesar/Harrison when he is overcome by a petit mal seizure: it would have been natural for Elizabeth to think of Michael Wilding. But there would be other kinds of weakness that made Richard dependent on Elizabeth.

Now, Richard meant extravagantly romantic and heroic emotions after what seemed to her the smallness and shallowness of life with Eddie Fisher. Eddie, too, had been Caesar for a time, but now that illusion was fading, only to be replaced by another, a greater. In Richard Burton, the aging Caesars of the past were replaced by the exciting, unexpected Antony. Henceforth, Elizabeth's life would be her most successful movie.

Another element was powerful in the Burton-Taylor affair: daring though he seemed, Richard also sent out a signal that he needed something from Elizabeth. Richard required and loved not only her adoration of his talent and his shrewd, often crude sexiness; he also needed her dependence on him—her need, since childhood, to rely on a man who cuddled one moment and cussed the next. And he rejoiced in her dependence: "She'll be on the set every fucking day I'm on," he said. The repetition-compulsion, to find a strong man who would demand, rule, reward, cosset—the cycle that had marked so much of her life—had found its clearest exponent in Richard Burton.

For her part, in addition to all the obvious talents, she was drawn to Richard's intelligence, his ability to quote Shakespeare by the yard, his casual sophistication. In joining her life with his, she was in fact taking on the most radically new role of her life. Here was the forceful European man to keep her in her place, adoring but in control: he was "Prince Charming kissing the sleeping princess," she said, which is itself a revealing self-designation. Each time she believed herself completely in love, this fairy-tale princess (weaned, after all, on movie scripts) expected to be swept away by Prince Charming—and if he was dilatory in so doing, well, she knew how to hasten the proceedings.

Elizabeth was also alert to Richard's evident neediness, for she sensed in him a man suffering constantly from wounds often self-inflicted, a man lacerated by his own remorse and by his own inconstancy and self-recrimination. The first day they worked together, Richard was hung over to the point of shaking tremors when he tried to drink coffee: "I had to help [lift the cup] to his mouth, and that just endeared him so to me . . . My heart just went out to him."

So did her body, whenever he wanted her; she became his willing servant. But even this was a complicated symbiosis in the Taylor-Burton relationship: according to Richard's biographer Melvyn Bragg, there was a repetition of some elements of the Hilton era "in her black eyes, cut lips, screaming matches and apparent willingness to dice with death." Their fights were often precipitated by his enormous intake of alcohol, which made him (thus his brother Graham) "argumentative and abusive" and evoked "wild bouts of temper"—characteristics she, too, developed in time.

Montgomery Clift, James Dean and Rock Hudson were objects of her patient, sisterly nurturing but not correspondents to her passion. Richard, on the other hand, was very soon everything to her: lusty, unpredictable, full of bravado and apparent independence— and terribly weak in a fundamental, more desperate way; weaker, even, than Michael Wilding. Capable of hurting, quick to mollify, lavish one moment, aloof the next, he was the ultimate father and lover of her life. From the time they worked on *Cleopatra* to his death twenty-two years later, each was the most important person in the other's life—but they were not, alas, the best for one another. Their love (for in its own way it was surely that) exemplified the conundrum expressed in an ancient couplet by the poet Catullus, a contemporary of Caesar, Cleopatra and Antony, in a lyric Richard and Elizabeth discovered that winter:

> *I love you and I hate you. "Why?" you may ask.*
> *I know not: I know only that it is so, and I am in agony.*

"You could almost feel the electricity between Liz and Burton," Wanger confided in his diary that January 22, 1962, the first day Taylor and Burton filmed together. "To have waited so long, to know so suddenly," whispers Elizabeth/Cleopatra to Richard/Antony, adding, "Without you, this is not a world I want to live in." He embraces her, saying, "Everything that I want to hold or love or have or be is here with me now." After Mankiewicz had called "Cut!" he often had to interrupt their love scenes: "You make me feel like an intruder," he told them. Very soon, the couple was meeting privately after the day's work, staying out together, driving off to God knew where, then next day sharing long, private lunches in her dressing room—except that the maid later found the food untouched.

Mankiewicz was the first to know that the affair had been quickly consummated. He was, he told Wanger on January 26, "sitting on a volcano" with this new development. "Elizabeth and Burton are not just *playing* Antony and Cleopatra!" Wanger had only to visit the set for himself: "It was hard to tell whether Liz and Burton were reading lines or living the parts."

"I behaved indiscreetly," Elizabeth admitted without pride or false shame. "I can't try to justify myself, and I can't expect the whole world to understand. The people directly involved understand, and I hope my friends understand." As it happened, only some of them did—not because they took a high moralistic attitude, but because they rightly foresaw the Taylor-Burton relationship as hazardous for both.

If she had hoped to deflect attention by unadorned frankness, Elizabeth was misguided. The press swung into action with a vengeance, and Jack Brodsky knew he had either a catastrophe or the greatest publicity coup on his hands. "It's no rumor, no guesswork, about what Burton is doing to Taylor," he wrote to his boss Nat Weiss in New York on February 15. Thenceforth, Richard-Elizabeth-Eddie made any memories of Debbie-Eddie-Elizabeth seem tame.

> It started about three weeks ago and is now the hottest thing
> ever [continued Brodsky]. It seems that Fisher found out about
> it and started squawking, so Taylor said, "I love him and I want
> to marry him."

Things then happened quickly. Fisher, livid, sped off to nurse his wounds on a brief holiday in Switzerland and Portugal, while Sybil, equally vexed, prepared to leave for New York. Elizabeth, as much eager for a new life as Cleopatra when Antony came on the scene, decided she would marry Burton: no one could withstand so destined, so ordained a love. But Burton was in no way ready even to discuss such a step: his wife and children were not so dispensable for him and, as he told Wanger, "I'm a selfish man. I don't want anything to interfere with my acting career. I'm happy with Sybil, who I know will help me in my career." That was a short-lived conviction, however, for very soon it was evident that association with Elizabeth had, among its advantages, increased fame and therefore greater bargaining power for future work. Already, his agent, Hugh French, was capitalizing on the delicious scandal and talking to producers about the next Taylor-Burton picture. "Jack," Burton told publicist Brodsky, "how did I know the woman was so fucking famous? She knocks Khrushchev off the front page." Her celebrity, indeed, was an important element in the aphrodisiac: discussing it, Richard told Joe Mankiewicz, "I fall more in love with her each day."

Even Rex Harrison, whose own dramatic and rambunctious sex life made him a good sport about such behavior, had to admit that the Taylor-Burton affair changed everything at work: "At the height of it, Elizabeth and Richard kept hitting at each other and giving each other black eyes and not turning up at the studio," he recalled—which, had he known, recalled something of the thorny times of Taylor-Hilton and Taylor-Todd. When exaggerated talk of just such violence began to circulate around Cinecittà, the publicists had an added complication. "What we clearly must do is to bottle up [the scandal] as long as we can," advised Brodsky, whistling in the dark.

For a short time, in fact, everyone thought the entire affair would pass. On Friday, February 16, during an interval in filming, Richard took Elizabeth aside and told her that the affair—after little more than one passionate month—had been great fun, but it was just one of those things. He could not have anticipated her reaction. She did not report for the next day's work, and when Mankiewicz and Wanger went to her villa (Fisher was still away) they found Elizabeth pale and neurasthenic, confused and apologetic. That Saturday night, February 17, she took an overdose of sleeping pills and was rushed to Salvator Mundi International Hospital. In his published 1963 account, Wanger called this apparent suicide attempt "a minor incident," probably the result of bad food rather than drugs. But this was a version sanitized for publication, as a flurry of cables from New York and Los Angeles revealed at that time, and as the Brodsky-Weiss correspondence makes clear: "We devised the food poisoning story and it seemed to go over." (Burton described the suicide attempt in considerable detail in a 1971 notebook entry, published in his biography.)

Other stories were put forth—or at least allowed to circulate without correction—in a desperate attempt to staunch the flow of potentially adverse publicity. One Italian newspaper trumpeted the news that it was Mankiewicz and Elizabeth who were in love, and that Burton, the man with the Don Juan reputation, had been dragooned as a decoy. To this report, Burton reacted stone-faced: "Mr. Mankiewicz," he asked loudly on the set one morning, "do I have to sleep with her again tonight?" And Mankiewicz, in his own way as good an actor, turned to the entire cast and crew: "The real story is that Richard Burton and I are in love, and Elizabeth Taylor is being used as our cover-up!" This announcement he sealed with a kiss full on the lips of Richard Burton.

But any wicked humor was quickly overshadowed when the Taylor-Burton affair became front-page news worldwide on February 20, and Richard Burton—merrier and more self-confident than ever—realized that suddenly he was internationally famous, not just another British actor. Eventual public discovery was of course inevitable, but it was much aided by Richard's attitude of confrontation.

"I just got fed up with everyone telling us to be discreet," he told Jack Brodsky. "I said to Elizabeth, 'Fuck it! Let's go out to fucking Alfredo's and have some fucking fettucine.'" Spicy language or no, Richard was now followed constantly, asked for comments, interviews, statements on everything. And, his agent Hugh French reported, offers for films came in at the rate of several a day, at double the salary he had been receiving. "The romance has changed his life," noted Wanger tersely, unsure of what it and Elizabeth's precarious emotional health meant for the future of his picture.

Certain things were immediately clear. The Fishers' marriage was over, the Burtons' was threatened as never before, the film was imperiled worse than ever—and Elizabeth Taylor, so recently the serene star who took it for granted that she was cast in the mold of Queen Cleopatra herself, longed once again to recommence her life. On her thirtieth birthday, February 27, 1962, Eddie Fisher (back from his journey to Switzerland and Portugal) tried to put a good face on his status as the fading Caesar: he threw a party for his wife at Rome's most famous night spot (the Borgia Room, with its sinister connotations), and with a great flourish he presented Elizabeth with an enormous diamond ring and an antique mirror. But when she regarded herself, her husband and the ring in the glass, her cool gaze implied that she saw only herself and her jewel: determinedly royal, apparently unable to stop herself from replacing Caesar/Eddie with Antony/Richard.

"She was the reverse of most other stars," said Mankiewicz. "For her, living life was a kind of acting." And the life she was now living was astonishingly like that of Cleopatra. Acting for Richard Burton meant finding and speaking the right voice; for Elizabeth, it was a nonintellectual but complete involvement: no role was more seriously assumed than that of the Queen of the Nile. From childhood, the cyclorama against which she had played out her life was the fantasy of her movie scripts, and none was more potent—or more enduring—than that of Cleopatra.

In a way, Elizabeth Taylor was becoming very like one of the *hetaerae*, that group of ancient professional courtesans that flourished long before Cleopatra. Beautiful, cultivated and privileged, the *hetaerae* enjoyed wealth and fame not accorded to normal women, and they were visited privately by married men, for whom they donned various exotic costumes. But these women were not shunned or condemned by society, and in fact they were often engaged as public entertainers. Their class may not have had a clearer modern counterpart than the sumptuous and forthright Elizabeth Taylor.

In Rome, for example, Elizabeth's regal lifestyle was forever confirmed, and not only in the fourteen-room villa off the Appian Way. "My home away from home is the House of Dior," she said, "and my favorite hobby is collecting *real* jewels." Admiring a bracelet in the form of an asp, perfect for Cleopatra herself, Elizabeth said, "My old man [Eddie] wouldn't buy this asp bracelet for me, but he came through later with a bracelet of sapphires, diamonds and green stones, set in gold and platinum, designed like a delicately woven coronet. He knows how to please me"—at least, she might have added, with such treasures and trinkets as temporarily postponed the inevitable finale.

Richard learned the same lesson: since childhood Elizabeth had expected the treats, blandishments and signs of movie-star luxury: now that she was at the peak of stardom and was paid more than anyone in the world for a single job, she did not consider any gift too extravagant for her position in life. After days of hints from Elizabeth and two visits to the expensive emporium Bulgari, she persuaded Richard to buy her a diamond and emerald brooch costing $150,000. Joking about her growing addiction to fabulously expensive clothes and jewels, she explained years later, "'The more the better,' has always been my motto."

Sara and Francis Taylor were visiting Rome at the time, and when Elizabeth showed off her latest acquisition, her father was "furious [thus Sara] and lectured her and told her she could not keep it, that she had to give it back. Her heart was broken and she burst into tears, but Daddy went on and on, demanding that she send it back immediately. It was a horrible after-dinner scene." Indeed, Elizabeth, in childish, angry pique, refused to work the next day. Briefly, she returned the brooch to Richard; she wore it again within a month.

As for her wardrobe, Elizabeth decided, after wearing the wonderfully elegant robes Irene Sharaff designed for Cleopatra, to buy only things that "give a woman a regal feeling. I think Egyptian dress and makeup are very becoming to a woman. We're doing things with eye makeup that are more accentuated, more colorful, more fantasy-like than ever before—to give a catlike look." Indeed, for the rest of her life, Elizabeth Taylor tended most often to apply the excessive blue eyelid makeup designed for *Cleopatra*.

The fantasy of queenship went more than skin-deep, as the

movie queen took on the aura of a benevolent, passionate dictator. In her goal of landing Richard/Antony, she was not deflected by the sudden arrival of Pat Tunder, a Copacabana performer from New York whom Richard had romanced during the run of *Camelot*— "another complication," as Wanger observed. By March 3, Elizabeth was muttering snide remarks about Tunder to Richard on the set, he was pushing Elizabeth around a bit too roughly and Joe Mankiewicz, almost crazed with fear for the production, was observing of Elizabeth and Richard, "When you're in a cage with tigers, you never let them know you're afraid of them, or they'll eat you."

Around March 15, 1962, after a long day's shooting, Richard joined the Fishers at their villa for dinner; after the children were in bed, the spirits and wine flowed freely. "Who do you love?" Richard suddenly asked Elizabeth, who made no reply. "Who do you love?" he repeated more loudly, his normally meticulous grammar impaired by alcohol. She looked at Eddie, then at Richard and said, "You."

"That's the right answer," Richard muttered. "But it wasn't quick enough." The exchange was very like Mankiewicz's dialogue from the film they were making: to the director, indeed, Elizabeth and Richard "were just two actors who did not know when the show was over."

Then, after work on the night of March 18, Richard and Elizabeth dined at a small inn—without Eddie—and by the time he drove her home it was nearly dawn. For ten days, the world's press had been blaring the news that the Fisher marriage was history: ROW OVER ACTOR ENDS LIZ, EDDIE MARRIAGE ran a typical headline. Eddie was awake, poring over the latest newspaper story on his life and his wife, when she entered their bedroom. He told her, quietly and simply, that he was leaving for New York later that day. "If you leave," she said coldly, "you'll never see me again."

In fact, he did not see Elizabeth for two years. "I had to get out," he explained later, "[because] the humiliation was too great." Unfortunately, the humiliation drove him to the liquor cabinet and to the unhelpful ministrations of Max Jacobson. Within a week,

Eddie, in emotional and mental collapse, was in a New York hospital; several friends and Milton Blackstone, Eddie's manager, always believed the immediate cause was a dangerous mixture of vodka and amphetamines. "Do you think Eddie will divorce me?" asked a hopeful Elizabeth of Jack Brodsky when news of Eddie's condition reached Rome.

She had her answer sooner than expected. The international press, radio and television were reporting daily the details of the various moods, travels and dinner menus of Eddie Fisher, Elizabeth Taylor and Richard and Sybil Burton, and after considerable subterfuge on all sides (including traditional denials from all parties), attorney Louis Nizer—acting on behalf of both Fishers—announced on April 2 that the couple would divorce. Contacted by a Hollywood reporter for her reaction to all this, Debbie Reynolds declined to comment.

There was, however, a loud statement made in Washington, where Elizabeth (in a situation directly recalling the public vilification of Ingrid Bergman in 1949) was the subject of a congressional moment. A member of the House of Representatives named Iris Blitch rose to say it was the right of Americans to bar from the country

> those who show no concern for either the Flag or people and show no respect for cherished institutions or God. It is my hope that the attorney general, in the name of American womanhood, will take the measures necessary to determine whether or not Miss Taylor and Mr. Burton are ineligible for re-entry into the United States on the grounds of undesirability.

Mrs. Blitch—one can only imagine what Elizabeth and Richard did with her name—received considerable support that spring of 1962. Congressman Hjalmar Nygaard of North Carolina rose to say that the nation's morals were decaying because of the Taylor-Burton scandal, although the logic of this was not entirely clear. New York Representative Joseph Addabbo climbed aboard the moral bandwagon, reckoning that "Antony and Cleopatra are angels compared to what is going on between Elizabeth Taylor and Richard Burton." The influence of this couple was so pernicious, several southern newspapers reported, that people were accepting any kind of popular immorality: why, even those sordid plays by that decadent writer Tennessee Williams were being exported for foreign production! There was simply no telling what the rest of the world would think of America when things like that happened.

To many, the collapse of Western civilization, if not the apocalypse itself, was at hand; thus the self-appointed guardians of public morality had to be vigilant. A year later, when *Cleopatra* opened with gala premieres in New York, Los Angeles and Washington, the reception in the capital was almost funereally muted. California and New York had formal parties, celebrity appearances and interviews at the time of the film's release, but no decent Washingtonian, it was said, could demonstrate support for the likes of Elizabeth Taylor and Richard Burton. Such sentiments were echoed in very many American cities, where newspapers endorsed the virulent sentiments of a letter published in the Vatican weekly *Osservatore della Domenica*: Elizabeth's life of "erotic vagrancy," it was stated, made her unsuitable as a foster mother for little Maria.

On June 23, Elizabeth's last scene as Cleopatra was filmed. "I watched her mature as an actress as well as a woman," wrote Walter Wanger in his diary. "I have nothing but admiration for the way she stood up under fire for her personal and professional beliefs. Despite unprecedented personal criticism, she has emerged as the most important star in pictures today. There will never be another motion picture like *Cleopatra*, just as there never will be another woman like her—or Elizabeth."

And what of the movie, which in the final cut ran four hours, eleven minutes? *Cleopatra* was nominated for the Academy Award in four categories (including Best Picture and Rex Harrison as Best Actor), and won statuettes for Leon Shamroy's splendid color cinematography and John DeCuir's art direction. But in general the critics were merciless, refusing to take seriously a picture that had already been a cause and had enjoyed the longest free publicity in history.

Regarded dispassionately years later, the overwhelming negative judgments seem myopic: Mankiewicz's dialogue is crisply ironic, the production values are everywhere first-rate, and the performances are uniformly compelling. Mankiewicz had no control over the final cut and had tried to have his name removed from the film, which he wanted released in two parts totalling seven hours. His objections remain comprehensible: characters' motivations seem often muddy and capricious (how *does* Octavian regard Caesar?); heavily edited conversations seem paradoxically leaden and purposeless, their centers removed or an important prelude omitted; and the Roman senators are not clearly defined—a serious *lacuna* in a story so thumpingly political. For all that, *Cleopatra* is a picture about the conflicts of public life against private passion, and in a way about Cleopatra/Elizabeth and the end of the golden age of Egypt/Hollywood:

> CAESAR: I seem to recall some obsession you have about your divinity. Isis, is it not?
> CLEOPATRA: I shall have to insist that you mind what you say. I am Isis. I am worshipped by millions who believe it.

And as for her performance: it was flawless, full of confidence, a serene, dark beauty and a knowing alertness about human foibles. Passionate, mercurial, meditative, her Cleopatra joined her own personality to a character, and the result was a whole, credible person—"a woman of force and dignity," as *The New York Times* critic wrote.

With *Cleopatra* complete, Richard returned, for the time being, to his family: he could not make an immediate decision about life with Elizabeth, and Sybil would not grant a divorce for some time. Elizabeth, meanwhile, took her parents to Switzerland, where she and Eddie had purchased a chalet in Gstaad. As part of her divorce settlement, this house would eventually be deeded to her. Eddie, whose life was in disarray, often turned to her for help at the end of that fateful year. "I need $225,000 immediately for an overdue gambling debt," he said anxiously on the telephone from Las Vegas one night. She wired the funds.

Chapter Ten

1963–1965

HE PROTRACTED EXPERIENCE OF
playing Cleopatra put Elizabeth Taylor firmly under the spell of a
majestic romantic tradition. Love and the risk of death, love found
with one man, love snatched by death, love offered by a new man—
the entire complex of the romantic fallacy was present in the story
of Cleopatra. There was a modern version of that story in the contours of her own life. Whether Elizabeth chose consciously to read
it there does not matter: she lived, thenceforth, according to the
pattern idealized in the account of the ultimate classical femme
fatale. And becoming a character is, after all, the goal of every actor.

All her life, using her movie roles as model and inspiration, Elizabeth had longed to be transported out of herself, carried away by a
great and definitive passion. This, she believed, she found with
Richard, for whom she was indeed the epitome of the femme fatale.
That designation means not that a certain woman is primarily
deadly to others, but that she longs for death and eternal life with
the beloved; thus, in music, art and literature, from the grandeur of
ancient myth (*Tristan and Isolde*) to modern weepy soap opera (*Love

Story, Ghost), the interplay of love and death is irresistible.

Properly understood, the femme fatale not only captivates others: she is herself captivated by the charm of loving, obsessed with the vocation of being a lover as much as a beloved, and here, too, the association is apt for Elizabeth. Trying out various roles, she found that the only suitable women for her to play were those whose lives were defined by passion: she could never imagine herself as Madame Curie or Sister Kenny. In her craft as in life, she always sought freedom and power, passion and poetry, and it was Richard's fate to be caught up in the web of her enchantment.

Elizabeth Taylor's approach to life, from the time of *Cleopatra* onward, suggests that in some way, however unconsciously, she saw herself as a modern incarnation of that kind of femme fatale, a beautiful, historic, fateful lady whose commitment to an ideal of love placed her outside the pale of conventional morality. Having spent her entire life since the age of nine assuming more and more romantic roles, how could she regard herself otherwise? She heard the gasps wherever she went. She was always being asked questions about the great roles—Angela Vickers, Maggie the Cat, Catherine Holly, Cleopatra. She felt the heat of flashbulbs popping; she was applauded, recognized, hailed everywhere. At any time, she could scarcely survey a magazine rack anywhere in the world and not find a story about herself or (more and more often) about herself and Richard, the prophets of a new freedom from convention and the flouters of the old morality. In this regard, it is no exaggeration to say that Elizabeth Taylor's relationship with Richard Burton—both the two-year affair and the subsequent marriage—was the most insistently publicized private matter of the 1960s.

There they were, Elizabeth and Richard, defying the acceptable norms, making "illicit sex" unshameful. They cared only that the public supported their work: smugly moralistic condemnations of their love did not affect them at all. In a way, she represented the romantic imagination and aspirations of a generation, although she may not have recognized that function.

Like the Duke and Duchess of Windsor but ever more present in the world's press, Elizabeth and Richard (Liz and Dick to everyone except those who knew them) epitomized the new era's standards of beauty, style, passion, abandon and scorn of the world's judgment. And like the Windsors—not to say Tristan and Isolde or Abelard and Heloise—their story seemed to follow the mythic pattern: the accidental encounter, the voyage, the unavoidable stroke of romantic enchantment, the turbulence—all of it promising both fulfillment and the risk of doom. They cannot help it, say history's great lovers: the grand passion is beyond their control. With the ecstasy came furious, legendary confrontations, angry, half-understood letters, tantrums, eruptions of guilt, acts of contrition and penitential resumptions of the affair.

For Elizabeth, a woman unable to speak or act dishonestly, her love was never to be hidden from the world: that, after all, would be to compromise and betray it. "Let them rage against us," cried the lover in Dryden's adaptation of the Antony and Cleopatra story: "It will only purify our love." And so with Richard (as before with Eddie and Mike), she would face a sometimes hostile world with only the armor of her love. Necessarily self-absorbed by the overwhelming demands of that love, she became ever more centered on the fact of loving, ignoring the consequences of her actions for any other except the needy beloved. "To stand in her way was to risk being hit by an avalanche," according to Richard's brother Graham, who recalled a conversation with her:

"Will you marry Richard?" Graham asked.

"What do you think?" countered Elizabeth.

"I think he's a troubled man."

"He needs someone to look after him," Elizabeth continued.

"Isn't Sybil supposed to do that?"

"Sybil was yesterday."

Elizabeth, she implied of herself, was today and forever. And that was that. Or would be.

Consistent with those of the legendary lovers of history, the Taylor-Burton affair from 1962 to 1964, and the ten-year marriage that followed, was intensely dramatic—melodramatic, some might say. They remained at a fever pitch of self-induced excitement—rushing hither and thither; making this film apart or that one together; buying jewelry and clothes and luggage; enlarging their retinue of retainers; collecting this child in Los Angeles and depositing that one in a London school; granting more interviews than they wished but enough to keep their names before the public and the producers; and, everywhere, drinking and brawling, generally leading the way into the freewheeling, self-indulgent 1960s and 1970s, and fighting heroically in public and private. "I adore fighting with him," she said. "There are all sorts of screaming matches, shouting and yelling, and it's rather like a small atom bomb going off— sparks fly, walls shake, floors reverberate."

But their situation was made more complex for the reporter, sociologist and cultural historian by the fact that Elizabeth Taylor and Richard Burton were not shallow, stupid people—their occasional actions to the contrary notwithstanding. They took seriously the things of the mind, they read and respected serious literature, they longed to meet people of accomplishment. Nor were they flippant with their friends, to whom they could be as generous as they were to themselves. But their love of luxury and their insidiously expansive and expensive addictions to the trappings of extravagant wealth, to drink and, eventually, to drugs was perhaps symptomatic of the fact that they were not, in the final analysis, good for each other. They fed each other's weaknesses and demanded little of their strengths, and the unquenchable thirst for excitement and the ceaseless desire to acquire things exemplified their desire to avoid being bored.

Thus they constantly created their own interdependence. When separated even for half a day, they grieved, telephoned each other incessantly, and became ill or inebriated or both, which was but a variation on the suicides of great historic lovers from the ancients (Tristan and Isolde, Romeo and Juliet) to the moderns (Archduke Rudolf and the Baroness Maria Vetsera).

The inebriation was evident for anyone who got near them after a meal: tippling got them through the anxieties of publicity, formed a wistful, bleary bond between them, lowered their defenses against bitter recrimination and, afterward, eased a weepy contrition. At no time was this more evident than during the whole of 1963.

Even before *Cleopatra* had wrapped, Elizabeth and Richard were signed by producer Anatole de Grunwald for a film at first called *International Hotel*, then *Very Important People* and finally *The V.I.P.s*. The script was written by playwright Terence Rattigan, and—the better to capitalize on the publicity surrounding *Cleopatra*—it was to be filmed quickly in England and released shortly after *Cleopatra*. Thus it was that the notorious couple came to London in early December 1962 and, with a formal but empty nod to propriety, took adjoining suites at the Dorchester Hotel.

The movie is a not very engaging series of vignettes about glamorous and influential people whose flight from London is delayed by airport fog. Elizabeth played Frances Andros, a wealthy, bored socialite who intends to leave her boozy, emotionally distant husband Paul (Burton) for a frivolous admirer (Louis Jourdan) who is something of a gigolo. But the best of her intentions is scuttled by some of the worst: her character's belief that pity can support love, for example. At the finale, the couple reconcile on-screen and head for home, Elizabeth and Richard snuggling down in the back of their chauffeur-driven Rolls-Royce. It was the first of many films in which audiences were not sure which sequences might be a documentary news clip from the lives of Elizabeth and Richard.

They worked quickly for about a month beginning in mid-January, but in the finished film they seem detached and disinterested. There must have been some comfort from their salaries, however: she received a million dollars and Richard half that, and together they received 20 percent of the gross receipts, which totalled $14 million. Thus together they took in from *The V.I.P.s* alone a total of more than $4,300,000. As for her uncharacteristic lack of emotional involvement in this underwritten, unsympathetic role, it may well have been explained by the fact that Richard frequently scurried from the Dorchester to Sybil and his daughters for a weekend, and more than once he told reporters that he had no intention of marrying Elizabeth. For the first time, such a statement from a man threw her into panic. The venerable character actress Margaret Rutherford, their costar in the film, considered Elizabeth "a much misunderstood girl whose only fault was that she loved [Burton] too deeply."

Contrariwise, a new tradition began that winter when they filmed at the MGM Studios outside London. Elizabeth and Richard separated themselves from the cast and crew to lunch privately at a local pub, where they consumed a bottle or two of champagne and a few brandies before returning, somewhat the worse, to the set. Following his half-dozen Bloody Marys at breakfast, Richard's noonday imbibing made for a somewhat haggard, pink-eyed appearance in *The V.I.P.s*, despite elaborate makeup and careful lighting.

Such rounds of hard drinking were new for Elizabeth, and an increasing part of life with Richard. She admitted as much in a magazine article the following year, after the press captured a colorful scene in which she joined her lover at a bar, slammed her hand down and turned to him: "Now, you shit-faced bastard, give me a drink!"

But Elizabeth remained stunningly photogenic even after liquid lunches, her splendid looks a testimony not only to her essential vitality but also to the unprecedented control she had won, by 1963, over her image in the movies. Elizabeth had the right to approve her own costumes, hairstyles and makeup designs; no publicity stills were released without her permission; she had the right to accept or reject the final version of the script and the producer's choice of director; and if she objected to certain takes or sequences, her resentment would not be risked by any studio. Thus the Elizabeth Taylor whom the public saw from 1963 was only the woman she wanted to reveal: the person who looked, dressed, acted, reacted and moved in a particular way in each picture. It is no exaggeration, therefore, to say that it was Elizabeth playing out precisely those aspects of herself she wished the public to see.

Happily, this did not cause grief to the other players, nor to her directors, nor did it affect her genial approach to collaboration. "She was always on the set in time and always word-perfect," said Anthony Asquith, her director on *The V.I.P.s*. "She is a director's joy, [with] a natural, instinctive acting talent." More was the pity, then, that this talent was wasted by a kind of agonized repression in *The V.I.P.s*.

They remained in England until September 1963. Burton played the title role in the film *Becket*, with Elizabeth on the set and on location every day—applauding him, nursing the wounds of ego or hangover and keeping him forever in her sight line. Her only days absent from the production of *Becket* were those during which she too was before the camera, as a tour guide for the television documentary "Elizabeth Taylor's London," broadcast in October 1963. Grace Kelly, by then Princess of Monaco, took viewers on a tour of that principality, and Jacqueline Kennedy gave the world a visit to the White House. Elizabeth was not to be upstaged. Besides, she could hardly turn down the fee of $250,000. But that was only one quarter of her next salary, for *The Sandpiper*—her second film with Richard, and her third with a $1 million fee.

That was not scheduled until 1964, however, and so Elizabeth again accompanied Richard to his next job, as the defrocked minister in John Huston's film of Tennessee Williams's play *The Night of the Iguana*. This was produced, with astonishing speed, in Mexico City, around the then-isolated Pacific coastal town of Puerto Vallarta, and on the rough peninsula known as Mismaloya. For over two months, Elizabeth endured tropical heat, scorpions, snakes, giant land crabs and chiggers that had to be extracted with scalpels. All this to attend Richard.

They arrived on September 22—"not quietly," as production assistant Thelda Victor noted. A vast crowd awaited them at the airport in Mexico City, and Elizabeth refused to leave the plane until she could be guaranteed the people would be kept at a distance. Nonsense, said Richard, we will do what we have to do and that is to get to our hotel, crowds or no crowds. That began a shouting match that ended only when a publicist dragged them off, both cursing and screaming. The press cleaned up Elizabeth's diction to: "I have always wanted to come back to Mexico—I like Mexico," but there was an unprintable adjective before each "Mexico."

Huston, who loved to ignite little furors among his players and visitors, appreciated that he had a colorful cast and anticipated some drama. Besides Burton, there were the fiery Ava Gardner, the youthful nymphette Sue Lyon, the sedate and elegant Deborah Kerr and a crew of hot-blooded young Mexican and American men in their midtwenties. The first day Huston gathered his company together, he presented Burton, Kerr, Gardner, Lyon and Taylor with gold-plated revolvers and five gold bullets: which of them would first be incited to violence? he asked. It was, after all, not beyond reason that by the time they got to remote Mismaloya, a peninsula accessible only by canoe or speedboat from Puerto Vallarta, violent passions might erupt. And everyone's patience was already sorely tried: there were no telephones, only erratic plumbing and electricity, not much good food except for what they could get flown in, and uncountable millions of annoying insects and the ubiquitous iguanas, which slithered about hungrily. The atmosphere was indeed torrid and uncomfortable. But every day, as Thelda Victor recalled, "Elizabeth was there—watching."

She had good reason to be suspicious. Kerr had once been pursued by John Huston; her husband, Peter Viertel, was present, and he had once been an ardent admirer of Ava Gardner. Sue Lyon's boyfriend was a young married man whose wife unexpectedly arrived. Then, in a poignant twist of fate, came Richard Burton's agent Hugh French with his new assistant—none other than Michael Wilding, who could not find work as an actor and hoped to succeed as a press agent.

With him was a beautiful and charming Swedish actress named Karen von Unge, with whom Wilding had a close, serious intimacy in the early 1960s, between his marriages to Susan Nell and Margaret Leighton. Thirty years later, von Unge recalled details of that autumn in Mexico. "Michael never liked Hollywood," she said, "and Hollywood didn't know what to do with him. By the time he was fifty-two, he knew he had to find something new, but being Hugh French's assistant wasn't it. Michael was a dear, sensitive man who should have been a great painter, and here he was, carrying suitcases full of special chili and beans to Elizabeth from Los Angeles because she asked for them. She wasn't imperious or demanding. She simply asked, and men did—it was as simple as that. It hadn't ever been any other way, and this co-existed alongside an enormous kindness she had."

Von Unge also recalled that Elizabeth had her three children with her (Maria was still in European clinics), and that she took enormous trouble to keep them from the prying lenses of the press. "Whatever else I do for [the children]," she said at the time, "I will never expose them to the kind of life my parents exposed me to." When she spotted a cameraman that season, she shouted, "Get away! Get away, you son of a bitch! Stop following us! I'll break your goddamn camera!"

The two Wilding boys were to have been with their father for a year—"but although he loved the boys," according to von Unge,

> he didn't really know the mechanics of being a father, and Eliza-beth filled their emotional needs as she could. But I do give him credit for seeing that their gypsy life was a little unnatural and trying to offer them some remedy for it. "What can we offer these boys?" he used to ask. "They're accustomed to the finest restaurants and hotels—breakfast in Rome, lunch in Paris and dinner in New York!" And then we found out that they liked nothing better than to munch raw carrots they took from the refrigerator.

As for Liza Todd, then six, she was precocious and articulate about her odd upbringing. "Did you see *Around the World in 80 Days?*" she asked another little girl. "My first daddy made that. My second daddy made a movie, too, and Richard makes movies and my only mommy makes movies." There was, to the bystanders, something terribly poignant about this proclamation from a child who had so little stability in her life. But when Liza expressed the presumption that Richard would be her next daddy—and jumped onto his lap calling him that—he said, "Don't ever call me daddy again. I am *not* your daddy. Your daddy was Michael Todd, and he was a very wonderful man, and don't you ever forget it." But such logic was lost on the poor girl, who had not a single memory of her father; she crept away sadly. She and the Wilding boys spent Thanksgiving Day, according to Thelda Victor, "watching their mother and Burton swilling tequila with beer chasers."

"My children are remarkable people," Elizabeth said, adding with her usual frankness that "my life should have been murder for them. We've lived like gypsies and—well, there's the obvious fact that I've been married too many times. They loved Mike. They loved Eddie as a friend, but when Eddie left they didn't even ask where he had gone." But the swift changes in the children's affiliations were leaving them with a gaping insecurity, a hesitancy to place their trust in someone who might not be present within a year; later, this peripatetic emotional life would profoundly affect the Wilding boys.

Elizabeth, never out of sight, turned up at the shooting location each day at noontime with a picnic hamper and bottles of wine. Her bikinis were vivid, and she kidded herself as a love goddess. Well might she have such a sense of humor about herself that season, for—idle and inclined to eat and drink too much—she was swiftly gaining weight: the bikinis looked tinier and more tragicomical by the day. "Look at her," said Richard acidly more than once. "She walks and looks just like a French tart."

At such harsh treatment, she only laughed and leaped to his demand for another drink. "The only thing in life is language," cried Burton one night in his cups, "not love—not anything else but language." At that, Elizabeth fell into a fit of weeping—which evoked from him an even more embarrassing humiliation of the woman he claimed, in his fashion, to adore. "It is ridiculous to get married or have a contract of any sort," he said on another occasion, "because you feel tied and want to get away from it—whereas if you feel you can walk away from anything, it's better. I'm not going to marry Elizabeth. Of course, I haven't told her that yet."

Nursing the bibulous Burton and monitoring whatever attentions he might want to direct to another woman was a full-time occupation for Elizabeth that autumn of 1963. "My best feature is my gray hairs," she said that season. "I have them all named. They're all called Burton."

She rented Casa Kimberly, a four-story villa in Puerto Vallarta that she and Richard eventually bought and linked by a footbridge to another across the street, and there she installed her secretary, cook, chauffeur and children, two maids and a masseur for Richard. The house was built around a picturesque courtyard with papaya and banana trees and coconut palms, and the interior was lavishly decorated; inside, there were six bedrooms and (marvelously, given the location) six baths.

But relaxation and toning sessions with his masseur were no remedy for Richard Burton's alcoholism, which was already life-threatening by 1963, as his brother Graham recognized: "To be in his company was to play life dangerously, [and] the fun times were interrupted by terrifying bouts of depression and ill temper when he became a stranger to us all. No one could tell when the storm would break." Ava Gardner was not easily shocked nor was she a teetotaler, and to her Burton was "a ferocious drinker" whose binges during production made her quite anxious. Thelda Victor watched Richard consume "what must have been his twenty-second tequila" one afternoon, and next day said he knew not how he got home. "Oh, we got you home, all right," said Elizabeth—and, added Victor, "She sounded a little bitter." But Richard had an answer for everything: "I'm a Method Actor," he explained to the press, "and I prepared for this [drunk] scene today by drinking boilermakers for five hours last night."

In such situations, Elizabeth was mother, nurse, a mate locked in the dreadful embrace of codependency, needing to be needed by him and needing to assume the burden of his abuse. Sometimes, quietly, she warned him that he might harm her physically: this would reduce him to incomprehensible sobs.

The production of *Iguana* complete, the lovers remained at Casa Kimberly for the winter holidays. Richard invited ten visiting reporters there two days before Christmas, and a four-hour drinking bout ensued: he downed a dozen glasses of Scotch, and Elizabeth tried to keep pace with four gins and tonic. The merriment, it seems, was inspired by the news that exactly a week later Sybil Burton, charging "abandonment and cruel and inhuman treatment," would formally be awarded a Mexican divorce in absentia. Elizabeth was only alluded to: her husband, Sybil complained, had been "in the constant company of another woman."

With that, Elizabeth sprang to action. "I genuinely do not believe in divorce," she said at the time: "I know that must sound pretty funny, coming from me." She was, in fact, serious about every marriage she contracted, fully intending it to last forever. But this remark did provoke amusement, especially when she filed for a Mexican divorce on January 14, 1964, pleading that Eddie had abandoned her in March 1962—a suit she handily won when he failed to appear six weeks later. She also gained custody of Maria, who took the name Burton. "What Elizabeth wants, Elizabeth gets," Eddie told a reporter, and with that he was out of her life forever, with a sadly prophetic exit line: "There'll be someone after Burton. That's the way she is. Elizabeth is beautiful—the queen. But she uses up men." His own life in the years after Elizabeth were often confused and unhappy. The public tastes in pop singers had changed radically, his addictions would require years to treat, and because he never regained anything like the popularity of his twenties, he was forced, in 1970, to file a bankruptcy petition.

Sara and Francis Taylor arrived on Christmas Eve in Puerto Vallarta—she beaming and prattling on as usual in her little girl's voice, he with his cool, uncertain expression. Elizabeth's brother and sister-in-law came, too; and Maria and a yapping Sealyham joined the three older children and a nanny. Richard had the last word before the family retreated from the press behind the walls of Casa Kimberly. "We will wait a month before marrying, for the sake of decorum—what little decorum is left now."

In a crushing, mad mob scene that suggested nothing so much as a sequence from Fellini's La Dolce Vita, Elizabeth, Richard and their vast retinue arrived in Los Angeles from Mexico on January 22, 1964: two hundred photographers, reporters and gate crashers poured onto the tarmac as the plane touched down and nearly tore them to pieces in a frenzy of relic hunting—a lock of her hair or his, a snatch of clothing, a bracelet, a handkerchief—or just a touch of the divine celebrities. A limousine whisked them off (at Richard's insistence) to a hotel bar near the airport, where they downed a pitcher of martinis; then they were deposited in the Presidential

Suite of the Beverly Wilshire Hotel. "The queen was home," as one reporter observed; next day, the monarch visited with her children, whom she had not seen since they departed Puerto Vallarta the day after Christmas: Michael, Christopher and Liza had been installed with their nanny in a bungalow at the Beverly Hills Hotel, while Maria was with Sara and Francis in West Los Angeles. But the separation between mother and children would be at its most poignant throughout 1964, perhaps the most peregrine year of her life thus far.

The following Tuesday, January 28, they flew to Toronto, where Richard began rehearsals, under John Gielgud's direction, for his *Hamlet* (part of the theater world's celebrations of Shakespeare's four-hundredth birthday); this would tour briefly that spring before performing to sell-out crowds in New York. Elizabeth, who had not worked for over a year, would remain idle for almost another, just to be at Richard's side for his third role since they completed *The V.I.P.s.* "Richard and I love each other," she told a reporter, "and we want to get married as soon as possible. I go where Richard goes. We want to be like other people and we don't enjoy being stared at. But there's nothing we can do about it now." She was quite right: after hysterical crowds at the Toronto airport had forever laid to rest any legend about unflappable Canadians, the couple had to post round-the-clock bodyguards outside their three-bedroom Royal Suite at the King Edward Hotel.

In a way, the scandal diminished—but not the attention—when Elizabeth and Richard finally became the Burtons on Sunday, March 15, in a hotel suite in Montreal, where they escaped to avoid the press. Eager to look her best, she was late to the ceremony, prompting Richard to scowl, "Isn't that fat little tart here yet? She'll be late for the Last bloody Judgment!" He had started a marathon drinking session earlier that morning—perhaps he was uncertain and even guilty over what he was doing, as some friends maintained—and his anxiety prompted Elizabeth's casual dismissal: "I don't know why he's so nervous. We've been sleeping together for two years." As they stood before a hastily corralled

Unitarian minister, Richard looked older than thirty-eight, Elizabeth younger than thirty-two.

"And they said it wouldn't last!" said Elizabeth three weeks later. Then, rather indelicately, Richard offered a résumé of her earlier husbands: "Her first marriage was a complete mistake. Her second was handicapped by an enormous difference in ages. Her third was perfect, but the husband is dead. The fourth is deplorable. As for the fifth—that's me—let's hope it won't be [deplorable]."

Elizabeth simply said she had everything she wanted: "Richard has given me a sense of reality. . . . I rely on him totally, [I] ask him about everything." She then repeated what had become traditional Taylor axioms, revealing the same odd dichotomies: "I am now above and beyond anything else a woman, and that's infinitely more satisfying than being an actress."

And then she added two curious statements.

"I'm a woman who needs to be dominated," which she now hoped to be by Burton, whom she often called "Dad."

The second remark suggested that her sense of self, long submerged in assuming other identities, was very much unformed: "I love not being Elizabeth Taylor, but being Richard's wife. I would be quite content to be his shadow and live through him." Confirming the state of this union, Richard added, "I have the last say in everything with her now."

Every love affair and marriage had been a scenario in which Elizabeth had to assume a new role; she had, in other words, to test and try a bond through which she confirmed her belief in herself. Now, she had landed the most challenging role of her career—that of Mrs. Richard Burton—and she had done it against considerable odds. Henceforth, she had to play it out, against equally daunting handicaps.

The demands began when *Hamlet* started its American tour in Boston, where the Burtons arrived on March 22. A thousand fans stormed the Sheraton Plaza Hotel, where Elizabeth was pushed and pulled from one corner of the lobby to the other, hair was torn from her head, and she suffered bruises to her back and arms. Apparently she was sufficiently upset by this that a physician (perhaps overzealously) sedated her and she took to her bed; perhaps, too, her confinement and her statements to the press about being so overwhelmed provided her with a minidrama of her own as the spotlight shone so brightly on Richard—and reminded her public that she was part of the excitement.

Even more scenes of near-lunatic public adulation surrounded the Burtons in New York, where *Hamlet* ran from April to August, and where, outside the Lunt-Fontanne theater, crowds swarmed each night beginning at eleven o'clock, when the final curtain fell. Mounted policemen had a job to keep crowds at bay, as fans and the merely curious waited for a glimpse of the most famous couple since the Duke and Duchess of Windsor. Elizabeth wore yellow last night when she met Richard at the stage door, ran the news reports . . . Thursday she wore violet . . . Monday she wore green . . . They slipped into their limousine . . . She waved royally to the crowds, and the car snaked its way to the Regency Hotel on Park Avenue—where more crowds awaited a glimpse of the royal couple before they were whisked up to their ten-room suite, which cost them $10,000 a month.

"Backstage and out front, I saw *Hamlet* some forty times," Elizabeth said. But she was always there to meet him after the performance, a loyal and supportive wife who also wished to assure that he would have no distraction after a performance, that he would be with her. And by arriving at the Lunt-Fontanne each evening, she was of course keeping herself in the public eye: movies or not, it was vital to maintain her identity, and much of that was drawn from her public. "If I get fat enough, they will not ask me to do any more films," she said of her expanding waistline. Or perhaps she would be offered a role requiring some heft? Indeed, one such was just around the bend.

The public pressure was enormous then, for the Burtons were always on display. Like Richard, Elizabeth was soon using liquor to cope with the pressure, with the tension and anxiety of constant scrutiny from the press and the public. To complicate their life further, she was idle while he was an idol, and constant togetherness made her the more dependent on him and him the more chafing for freedom. And there was, perhaps inevitably, competition.

The first sign of it emerged subtly, during the run of *Hamlet*. On June 22, Elizabeth faced a theater audience for the first time, with her husband as leading man. For the benefit of the American Musical and Dramatic Academy, then managed by Richard's old mentor, Philip Burton, they appeared in a single performance of poetry and prose readings—selections from Marvell and Yeats, Hardy and Eliot, both Brownings, Shakespeare and Lawrence.

Some of the selections were coyly chosen to spotlight the couple. Elizabeth, for example, read from Thomas Hardy's "The Ruined Maid":

> *And now you've gay bracelets and bright feathers three!*
> *"Yes, that's how we dress when we're ruined," said she.*

As if in response, Richard filled the theater with his resonant baritone, reading from Eliot's "Portrait of a Lady," which begins with a citation from an Elizabethan play:

> *Thou hast committed fornication,*
> *but that was in another country . . .*

His wife then read from Elizabeth Barrett Browning ("How do I love thee? Let me count the ways") and from Philip Sidney ("My true love hath my heart, and I have his"), and by intermission it was clear she was at ease, and her voice, although thin, was full of feeling—tender when that was called for, full of spice and vinegar if that was appropriate. "Sorry," she said once, smiling over the footlights, "may I start again? I got all screwed up." The audience loved her for it, and even those who might have been waiting for her to reveal her limitations had to admit that she read without false gravity and even with distinction. She had rehearsed for weeks with Philip Burton, and her preparation had paid its reward. "Well," said

Beatrice Lillie to a friend as Elizabeth completed one set of poems, "unless she starts to get bad very soon, people are just going to walk out!"

"I didn't know she was going to be this good," said Richard at one point, and there was nervous laughter in the theater: this was doubtless supposed to be a proud compliment, but it had the opposite effect. He smiled and kissed her at the conclusion, but to many there was an unmistakable if mild atmosphere of rivalry. "Another show stolen from me!" Richard said lightly backstage as they posed for photographs with well-wishers from the celebrity audience (Montgomery Clift, Lauren Bacall, Carol Channing).

In mid-August, the Burtons, their four children, two nannies and two secretaries were on holiday at Casa Kimberly, and in September Elizabeth and Richard were in Northern California for their third film together. Vincente Minnelli had directed Elizabeth twice before (in *Father of the Bride* and *Father's Little Dividend*), but those happy memories quickly faded during production of a very sorry business called *The Sandpiper*. "I don't know how I'd feel about it with other casting," said Minnelli, suggesting what everyone in the movie soon realized: the story and script were woeful. As a beach-dwelling artist, tending wounded birds and painting up a storm, Elizabeth was cast opposite Richard, as a married clergyman who tumbles into a steamy but disastrous affair with her.

This seemed to be a deliberate chip off the block of *The Night of the Iguana* (Burton as renegade clergyman, Deborah Kerr as sensitive artist), but the script was turgid and cliché-ridden to the point of hilarity ("I never knew it could be like this—being with you is like having the whole world in my arms," and so forth). Elizabeth was outfitted mostly in caftans, and when she was not, a change in her appearance was at once evident: whereas before there was an occasional slight dumpiness to her young figure, she was now downright overweight, and long hair, careful lighting and flowing gowns could not conceal the fact. Objections from Richard notwithstanding, Elizabeth was content: after all, she was paid $1 million, and he got half that amount—and they both took percentages of the gross receipts. "For the money, we will dance," he said. And so they did, in California for four weeks and then, for the interiors, in Paris (for tax reasons).

Sailing from New York (appropriately on the *Queen Elizabeth*), the Burtons booked five of the six suites in first class for themselves and their retinue; the remaining quarters had been booked by none other than Debbie Reynolds and her new husband, Harry Karl. The ship was soon buzzing with gossip, and everyone with a camera hovered as close as they could get to potential action. "Let's have cocktails, say hello, and get this over with," wrote Debbie in a note to Elizabeth—who had only moments before sent a similar note to her. When the Burtons and the Karls clinked glasses of champagne, Elizabeth said cheerily, if inaccurately, "Just look how you lucked out and how I lucked out! Who the hell cares about Eddie?" The foursome dined together twice, very like old friends on holiday.

The Sandpiper was not pleasant for anyone—least of all for audiences who submitted to it. When Richard missed a cue or blew a line, Elizabeth giggled.

"Oh, I'm so henpecked," he sighed, tossing her a wounded glance. "I don't know why I bother to act."

"You don't," she retorted, and he said that he could obtain a divorce on the basis of that remark alone. And so it went, to the end of the year.

"The film was so bad it nearly broke up our marriage," said Richard a few years later. "But the truth is, we couldn't get any other work"—a remark certainly open to question. As for Elizabeth, she later heard the news of a good review for her performance in *The Sandpiper*, and she replied that she intended to sue for libel: she was surprised that anyone could find the film remotely interesting, let alone intelligent or laced with human feeling. With the honesty typical of her, she said she had made the film for the money, and she had nothing but contempt for it. Years later, that was a critique many would share. However sour the experience, it must have been at least partly sweetened by the compensation: although a critical disaster, *The Sandpiper* drew more than $10 million at the box office, hugely benefiting both Metro-Goldwyn-Mayer and the Burtons.

Thus began the custom whereby the Burtons made most of their films abroad, and soon Elizabeth renounced her American citizenship as well—"not that I love America less, but I love my husband more." But there were also prudent fiscal reasons for her expatriation. As British citizens whose legal residence was Switzerland, they had to pay only the substantially lower tax rates of that country on their British and American earnings. Contrariwise, all earnings abroad would have been taxable for an American, and as a British citizen, full tax would be paid on work done in Britain. "Money is more valuable than citizenship or patriotism," Elizabeth said at the time, according to columnist Sidney Skolsky. "Down in your hearts, you know I'm right." Added her New York publicist, John Springer, in 1965: "As far as Miss Taylor is concerned, she is no longer an American citizen."

While working on *The Sandpiper*, the Burtons met with Ernest Lehman, who had written some of Hollywood's finest films— among them *Sweet Smell of Success*, *Somebody Up There Likes Me* and *North by Northwest*, and he had just completed the screenplay for *The Sound of Music*. He had been deeply touched at a performance of Edward Albee's prize-winning drama *Who's Afraid of Virginia Woolf?* and was preparing to adapt and produce it for the screen. As it happened, this was a courageous undertaking, for the four-character play consists of a series of raw, tragicomic conversations in which an embittered couple provocatively named George and Martha (a history professor and his wife) bicker, tease and openly wage war against one another and against a young couple who come to visit during one long and boozy night.

Virginia Woolf is not, however, merely a series of emotionally charged diatribes and dialogues: it is, among other things, an extended exploration of the entrapment of illusion that threatens all relationships in general and marriage in particular. Onstage, the play had taken place in the living room of George and Martha's house: not the least of Lehman's challenges was the task of sustaining the claustrophobic atmosphere while making *Who's Afraid of Virginia Woolf?* a film, not simply an expanded play. An additional task was the play's raw language: the text contained a number of words and phrases never before heard in an American film up to 1966. Lehman was undaunted and set himself the job of writing and producing for Warner Bros. what would be an historic motion picture—one in which every scene and sequence reveals not only the talents of the playwright, the cast and director, but most of all the unifying vision Ernest Lehman brought to it. Throughout the filming in 1965, he was an active, ever-present and consistently creative producer, making difficult and daily esthetic choices that transformed a stunning play into a movie as remarkable for its brilliance as for its commercial and critical success.

"I had seen a photograph of Elizabeth angrily pointing her finger at Mike Todd in a manner I immediately saw as 'Martha-like,'" recalled Lehman. He knew that she was a brilliant actress who could handle the difficult and complex role of a harridan in her late forties who must be no cliché: neither demon nor angel, she must reach the audience as a fully recognizable, pained and painful, terrifying yet oddly sympathetic creature. "I remember standing on line to watch the film of *The Night of the Iguana*," Lehman continued, "and the thought came to me, 'How would all these people feel if they could see Elizabeth Taylor in *Virginia Woolf?*'"

And so, with Jack Warner's approval (if not, at first, his encouragement), Lehman approached Elizabeth, who had read the play but not seen it onstage. She was hesitant, but Burton—acting on a hunch as inspired as Lehman's—insisted she do the role: it would be, he said, her *Hamlet,* her ultimate achievement and vindication as a serious actress. "Elizabeth took me aside," Lehman said, "and asked me point-blank, 'Why do you think I should play this role?'" He told her the obvious reason: it was the chance of a lifetime, and she had every talent for it.

Although Elizabeth finally agreed to play Martha, she was terrified of the demands on her voice and her range, not to say the requirement that, at thirty-three, she appear to be a slattern a dozen or fifteen years older; indeed, throughout filming Elizabeth resisted the makeup, wigs and costumes that made her appear an unkempt forty-something, and what concessions Lehman won were not done so easily. Elizabeth might have been a bit plump that year, but she was certainly not obese: therefore, when she gained twenty-five pounds for the part, she insisted that the press be told that the added pounds were for the movie, and that she did not have an eating disorder. She was, realized Lehman, not only beautiful and talented but also a shrewd manager of her own publicity.

Throughout production, Ernest Lehman learned in many ways the truth of a warning conveyed to him by Irene Sharaff, who had designed Elizabeth's wardrobe for *Cleopatra* and *The Sandpiper.* Lehman confided that whenever he had even a slight disagreement about something with Elizabeth, she rather overdid her reaction: it was as if she saw her producer as a threatening figure. Well, said Sharaff, Lehman's reaction was on the mark: Elizabeth needed to break down any man who was anything like a father figure—to shatter him and then replace the pieces into some kind of relationship. This was, perhaps (whether Sharaff knew it or not), Elizabeth's method of working out her distant relationship with Francis Taylor. Very soon after rehearsals began in early July, Lehman had the impression that Elizabeth regarded him not only as her producer, but also as a representative of all the producers she knew in her career. For someone less sensitive to actors, this might have been a disaster; Lehman somehow made her ambivalent attitude work toward the fullest realization of Martha and the success of the picture.

As for Richard, he was not anyone's first choice to play George: but after she had approved Arthur Hill (who had played the role on Broadway), Elizabeth then suggested Richard. Lehman needed no convincing about that, but Jack Warner did, and so Lehman drafted one of many crucial letters in the history of the production, advising Warner that Burton's presence in the film would be a steadying influence on Elizabeth as well as an artistically justified bit of casting. "Oh, I'm so henpecked," he had said; "I *am* George," he would say later, during rehearsals.

The last major decision, after casting George Segal and Sandy Dennis in supporting roles and the gifted Haskell Wexler as cinematographer, was the choice of a director, and here the Burtons were very much influential. They knew thirty-four-year-old Mike Nichols socially and respected his work as a Broadway director, and although Lehman had considered others (among them Alan Schneider, who had staged *Virginia Woolf* in New York), he agreed with the suggestion and signed Nichols. Fees were negotiated—$1.1 million for Elizabeth and $750,000 for Richard, plus, again, a healthy percentage of the gross receipts: they eventually realized over $6 million for this one film. A starting date was set for summer 1965, after Burton completed a role in the film *The Spy Who Came In From the Cold*.

But before Elizabeth arrived at the triumph of *Who's Afraid of Virginia Woolf?*, she endured a series of distressing events during the winter and springtime of 1965. First, Elizabeth accompanied her chauffeur, Gaston Sanz, to Paris, for the funeral of his sixteen-year-old son, who had been killed in a shooting accident. While there, thieves at her hotel made off with $50,000 worth of her favorite jewelry. Then, back in Dublin to attend Richard during filming of *The Spy,* she was riding with Sanz when he accidentally hit and killed a pedestrian. Days later, on March 12, her father (then sixty-seven) suffered a serious stroke, and she spent a week in Los Angeles to comfort her mother, then hurried back to Ireland a week later. (One thinks of Birdie [Thelma Ritter], on the catastrophic life of Eve Harrington [Anne Baxter] in Joseph L. Mankiewicz's *All About Eve*: "Everything but the bloodhounds snappin' at her rear end!")

By this time, it was as if the Burtons were rehearsing their forthcoming roles in *Who's Afraid of Virginia Woolf?* "I can't go to a pub anymore," Richard complained to John Le Carré. "Elizabeth is more famous than the Queen!" And then came a dreadful statement: "I wish none of it had ever happened," by which he meant the affair and marriage to Elizabeth. "They were living out their marriage in public," added Le Carré. "There were shouting matches in restaurants." Worse, as Le Carré waited in an adjacent room of the Burtons' hotel suite, he heard them have a terrible fight: "sounds of slapping—all of that."

* * *

"I love four-letter words," said Elizabeth—which was fortunate, since she had a fair number of them in her dialogue as Martha. Acting Martha that fall, she threw herself with complete abandonment into the complexities of the role, and the result was a performance that surprised even herself. "With Richard Burton," she said years later, "I was living my own fabulous passionate fantasy. In time it became too difficult to sustain . . . We were like magnets, alternately pulling toward each other and, inexorably, pushing away."

Which is exactly the character and attitude of the woman she portrayed in the film, a woman bound to a man full of contempt for himself. Why did Richard accept a role that essentially supported Elizabeth? asked Sidney Skolsky. "Half the fun of being an actor," replied Richard, "is getting away from your own disgusting self." This he could not do, nor could he prevent Elizabeth from addressing that self even as she played the role.

Angrily immersed in fantasy, poking and badgering her unroyal consort of a husband, pleading with and mocking him—yet all the while terrified of the truth about the emptiness of her life—Elizabeth exploited her own womanly wiles and drew on her own human needs. As Richard played every moment to her, granting her the superiority in every scene and submerging any nuance of scene dominance, so Elizabeth invented a walk, a stance, a lowered, modulated voice as never before. In one brilliantly harrowing scene, Martha and George confront each other in a parking lot, a distant street lamp glowing behind them and shot in the ominous mushroom-cloud shape of an atomic bomb exploding:

MARTHA: You're gonna get it, baby.
GEORGE: Be careful, Martha, I'll rip you to pieces.
MARTHA: You're not man enough—you haven't the guts!
GEORGE: Total war?
MARTHA: Total!

It was astonishingly like the exchange John Le Carré overheard in Dublin.

After filming was completed, both Elizabeth and Richard told

Lehman that making this picture had been the smoothest and most rewarding experience they had in their careers, and of the four they had made together, this alone was accomplished without their relationship suffering. More to the point, they confided that they had a curious reaction: when the production was over, they missed it, seemed lost on rising in the morning, and could not quite adjust to being Martha and George no longer.

The reason for this may well have been that *Who's Afraid of Virginia Woolf?* resonates with such tragic truth precisely because of real-life couples like the Burtons, locked in a collusion of love and hate and codependency from which they could see no escape. In fact, the calm at home that year seems to have prevailed because so much of the darkness in their own marriage was confronted at work. "I cannot stand it!" George shouts at Martha. "You can stand it," she retorts. "You married me for it!"

In their long and difficult fight scene outside the roadhouse, for example, Elizabeth and Richard are terrifying on-screen. As Martha attempts to strike George and he hurls her away, she continually cracked her head against the car. One take, in fact, was so realistic that tears came to her eyes, and the company doctor had to examine her. They were, Lehman recalled, so committed to giving their best performances that when Nichols was satisfied with this sequence, she was not: one more time, she asked the director, and so one more time it was—and much the best performance, too.

"We both have feelings of insecurity," admitted Richard, adding that when they felt uneasy they drank together—"to kill the feeling of icy isolation."

Martha and George, very like Elizabeth and Richard, had dubious alternate names for each other. Martha calls her husband a "klutz" with such contempt that the word sounds almost obscene. Yet in her final moments at dawn's first gray light, Martha responds to the tired joke ("Who's afraid of Virginia Woolf?"), whispering, "I am, George—I am." Tears stream down Elizabeth's face, she is hoarse from the anxiety of the night just ending, and her terror is palpable. Admirable actresses have undertaken Martha onstage. Elizabeth Taylor's rendering is perhaps her greatest performance; it is, in any case, certainly one of the most fully realized of her era.

"I'm wonderful at playing bitches," said Elizabeth years later. But this is much more: it was, in the final analysis, an almost miraculous achievement on her part, a role perfectly counterpoising humor and horror; for it, she was voted best actress of the year by the Academy of Motion Picture Arts and Sciences, by the New York Film Critics and by the British Film Academy. And Lehman's production, entirely faithful to the play yet a stunning motion picture on its own, deservedly received thirteen Oscar nominations and won a total of five statuettes.

Elizabeth Taylor was in her thirty-fourth year at the end of 1965, and she had appeared in thirty-four films. No role had been as challenging for her as Martha in *Who's Afraid of Virginia Woolf?*— and in fact nothing remotely this good would ever be offered to her again.

Chapter Eleven

1966–1973

THE NEW YEAR 1966 FOUND THE Burtons in Oxford, where for a week they appeared onstage in a university production of Christopher Marlowe's *Doctor Faustus,* staged in honor of Professor Nevill Coghill, with whom Richard had studied briefly years earlier. They took no salary, which many in the audience thought was appropriate: as the doomed philosopher, Burton raged without nuance, while Elizabeth, as the seductive Helen of Troy, simply drifted onstage in flowing chiffon for two minutes and uttered not a word. Later that year, Burton and Coghill co-directed a film version, full of color, smoke, atmosphere and bone-crushing tedium. Part of the problem was the generally wooden delivery of the sixteenth-century text by the student cast; another was the overbearingly solemn, academic tone with which Burton enveloped the character.

Beginning with this unfortunate production, it certainly seemed that the Burtons were embarking on an ambitious program to be taken as Serious Film Actors. After *Doctor Faustus,* they went to Rome and filmed *The Taming of the Shrew* with director Franco Zeffirelli; while there, they cut a deal to appear in *The Comedians*, which Graham Greene would adapt for them from his novel, and which sounded like a nicely prestigious enterprise. There were also discussions for John Huston's film of Carson McCullers's novella *Reflections in a Golden Eye* and of Tennessee Williams's play *The Milk Train Doesn't Stop Here Anymore*.

These looked like impressive literary works, designed to put the Burtons in the front ranks of a new wave of popular but serious artists. But in fact they were not wise choices, and as it turned out, the Taylor-Burton collaborations were, after *Who's Afraid of Virginia Woolf?*, woefully disappointing for audiences and critics. The basic reason for the failure of the partnership, however, was the obvious one: Burton's fierce alcoholism, a tragic dependency that dimmed his judgment, diminished his talent, poisoned his spirit—and, in 1966, began to afflict Elizabeth, too.

The failure of these projects was especially sad because she already had a highly refined intuition about movie acting. Richard was less comfortable, both before the camera and in the face of life, but as he admitted during the filming of *Becket*, Elizabeth had "taught me subtleties in film-making I never knew existed . . . [such as] the value of absolute stillness and that my very penetrating voice need not be pitched louder than a telephone conversation. But chiefly she taught me to regard the making of a film as exacting and as serious as playing Shakespeare on stage."

But Elizabeth and Richard were, under special circumstances like a Shakespearean project, well matched. He needed to learn the technique of film acting, she needed to learn about speaking verse; he had to tone down his expansive gestures, she had to understand the rich ironies of Shakespearean dialogue. *The Taming of the Shrew*, filmed in Rome from March through July, was the first film for which the Burtons put up their own money, deferred their salaries and finally went to the bank with a multimillion-dollar profit. As the ultimate macho lover, Petruchio was the perfect role for the once randy, now faithful Burton; as the termagant Katharina, Elizabeth showed why the character was often called "Kate."

Howling her rage, strutting crudely, running carefully dirtied fingers through a wig and spitting out the pentameter with fiery vividness, Elizabeth conveyed the spirit of both the verse and the shrew, although there are moments in the film when she seemed like Martha in a Renaissance bodice. Each evening, she rehearsed with Richard, and there were no late nights on the town, as they had during the time of *Cleopatra*. But the drinking on the set was Herculean: because it was Richard's habit to quaff while working, it became hers. "I am one of the few people I know who drinks only when he works," Richard said. The reason? "To burn up the flatness—the stale, empty, flat, dull deadness that one feels" after a scene.

Similarly: "Pure vodka," replied Elizabeth when asked why she felt unwell on the set one morning. It was a typical explanation for an increasingly typical condition—hung over in the morning, but somehow never appearing to be drunk the night before. "I had a hollow leg," she said later. "I could drink everyone under the table and not get drunk. My capacity was terrifying." But after their daily luncheon party, which began at one and ended at four, the work was sloppy and haphazard.

Zeffirelli, directing his first commercial film, believed that liquor and competition were at the root of the Burtons' "epic squabbles." Regarding himself as the nobler actor, Richard referred snidely to Elizabeth as a mere Hollywood Baby.

"A golden baby," she replied.

"Well, you certainly like gold," countered Richard, "and you're plump as a baby." And so it went, with bitterness and resentment now flashing around and between them, alternating with respect and mutual encouragement. Richard hated the Hollywood she represented, while Elizabeth deplored the snobbism of English contempt for movie acting. The tension, particularly acute during a difficult production like the lavish *Shrew*, was not helped by the Burton entourage, a court of a dozen lawyers, accountants, secretaries, hairdressers and dog walkers who were (so believed Zeffirelli) undeservedly influential with their employers, always muttering opinions and stirring up enmities and jealousies. The atmosphere was like something out of a Beaumarchais comedy.

Elizabeth regarded the intrigue with amused detachment, inviting this team or that from her retinue to join her for dinner at La Strega, a popular restaurant in the village of Practica de Mare. There, she held forth on whatever struck her fancy, and she ordered for herself and everyone at her table enormous portions of spaghetti with whiskey sauce, potatoes with coddled eggs and crepes with lemon cream. "I get a lusting, sensual thing about eating," she often said, and that year her figure did not belie her. Visiting reporters had the impression that Elizabeth was dedicated to self-indulgence: pounds of caviar and cases of champagne arrived at her villa in vulgar profusion and were quickly consumed.

Close to the end of filming, Elizabeth received tragic news from New York: her darling friend Montgomery Clift, after years of decline in the grip of multiple addictions, had died of a heart attack at the age of forty-five. "I'm in a state of shock," she said. "I can barely accept it. I loved him. He was my brother—my dearest friend." She longed to attend the funeral, but her professionalism would not allow her to throw the shooting schedule into disarray; instead, she went on, somehow able to confine her weeping to intervals between takes. "She gave us one of the funniest scenes in the whole film" the day she was most grief-stricken over Monty, Zeffirelli recalled.

Unable to perceive the danger that defined her attachment to Richard, Elizabeth was as responsive as ever to the heartaches of others—especially the emotional turmoil suffered by gay men like Clift. Zeffirelli was the object of her special, sisterly care in this regard: he had fallen in unrequited love with a blue-eyed lad that summer, and Elizabeth, hoping to put matters right, invited the young man for drinks and private encouragement on Franco's behalf. But Elizabeth was no blind romantic, Zeffirelli added: "When she told me what she had done, she also made it clear she thought it was hopeless and handed me a set of gold cuff links with two cupids in turquoise." Elizabeth was equally affectionate and generous with her dedicated gay secretary, Richard Hanley, who had been with her since the time of Mike Todd, and who was now suffering from heart disease that would soon claim him at the age of sixty-one.

That autumn, producer Dino de Laurentiis loaned Richard some space in his Roman studios for his Oxford University film of *Doctor Faustus*. No one was surprised, then, that Elizabeth insisted on the de Laurentiis Studios for the interiors of her next picture, John Huston's tenebrous production of *Reflections in a Golden Eye*, which was set in the American South. When plans for the film had first been discussed two years earlier, she had wanted Burton to direct and had chosen Monty Clift for her costar in this lurid little tale. She would play the sex-starved wife of a repressed homosexual army officer who is obsessed with an enigmatic soldier—who is in turn obsessed with the officer's wife. But Monty had refused to work under Richard, who, he thought, disapproved of and disliked him. Though the assignment then went to Huston, producer Ray Stark reminded Elizabeth that Clift was uninsurable. By the time of production, Clift was dead, and the role went—at Elizabeth's suggestion—to Marlon Brando: he loped with square-jawed detachment through the film's arty sequences, full of pregnant pauses and Freudian innuendoes. This ought to have made for an interesting pair of performances, but the result was very much otherwise: *Reflections in a Golden Eye* evidently fired the imagination of no one. Critics were divided, audiences bored or confused or both. But to see Elizabeth in *Virginia Woolf*, *Shrew* and *Reflections* is to understand how she could turn harridans into three-dimensional women—characters with very different backgrounds, however similar their angrily sensual needs.

The Comedians and *Boom!*, which the Burtons filmed in 1967, also promised more than they delivered. In the first, perhaps because Elizabeth's accent varies widely from French to German to strictly Mayfair, it is difficult to know if her supporting role—as the ambassador's wife—is cosmopolitan or merely schizophrenic. An additional problem was Graham Greene's meticulous fidelity to his novel: including virtually every character and incident gave the picture a confused density rather than the sharp moral center for which his writing was often distinguished. As a dutiful but (again) sex-starved wife whose lover (Burton) provides her only reason for living, Elizabeth acted with a kind of pathetic nobility. And although her tight, modish wardrobe was ill-fitting (the pounds were going on rapidly that season), she somehow seemed all the more emotionally unkempt, imprisoned by the clothes rather than merely constricted by inadequate sizes.

Unfortunately, the children endured a time of benign neglect. Elizabeth adored them, and if they were ill she went to them or flew them to herself at once. Their anxieties were hers, their pleasures made her proud. "Elizabeth loved her children," said Raymond Vignale, one of the Burtons' staff, "but she wasn't like an ordinary mother. She really wasn't that closely involved in their lives. When Liza had her first period, she came to me, and once, when Maria had to write her mother a letter of apology, she began, 'Dear Mrs. Burton.' She wasn't joking. I always felt sorry for Maria. She was a little apart, the outsider." Happily, Maria's marginality would alter in time. As for Michael and Christopher, they briefly attended school in Hawaii, where they lived with Elizabeth's brother, Howard, and his family.

But Elizabeth was also growing weary of her peripatetic and actually rootless life, although she seemed not to know that a major overhaul was in order. She drank and ate excessively, inclinations perhaps at least partly resulting from the professional inferiority she felt alongside Burton: "I am just a broad," she told director Peter Glenville during production of *The Comedians*. "But Richard is a great actor." Glenville needed no reminding: he had directed Richard in *Becket*. He did not, however, agree with her dismissive self-assessment. She was, recalled Glenville, bored with her own fame and success but obsessed with Richard's—as was Richard himself.

Boredom, restlessness, the exhaustion that follows various excessive indulgences, a fear of aging, of becoming anachronistic and unfashionable amid a new wave of younger, more socially and politically aware actors—all these created anxieties for the Burtons, who from 1967 onward took refuge in an orgy of getting and spending. No couple in the world exemplified conspicuous consumption more than they. By the late 1960s, Elizabeth Taylor no longer had to have great starring roles: she had only to live like a star. Her offscreen life was far more glamorous and fascinating to admirers and detractors than any script submitted.

Everywhere, they seemed to flaunt their extravagant wealth: together, over the decade, they earned more than $88 million and spent more than $65 million. They joined their names to form Taybur Productions for international movie-making, but after *Shrew* they never made any movies: Taybur was merely a holding company. They invested in Paris boutiques and in Mexican, Irish, English, Swiss and Caribbean real estate. They booked entire floors of luxury hotels. They bought a fleet of Rolls-Royces. They bought paintings by Monet, Utrillo, Picasso, van Gogh and Rembrandt. They bought a yacht named the *Odysseia* for $192,000, rechristened it the *Kalizma* (for their three daughters: Kate, Liza and Maria), refurbished and redesigned it to include fourteen bedrooms for guests and quarters for a crew of nine, filled it with Chippendale mirrors and English tapestries, sailed it round the Mediterranean, and later sold it for $6 million. When Raymond Vignale asked them his duties aboard the yacht, Elizabeth smiled and replied, "I drink Jack Daniel's, my husband drinks vodka. All the food and entertaining I will leave to you. Just make sure there is a cold buffet every night—salmon, caviar and chicken."

They paid $1 million for a private de Havilland jet and $500,000 for a French helicopter. They bought a seventy-two-piece set of matched luggage to hold expensive clothes they rarely wore. Richard smothered his wife in a $125,000 Kojah fur, which was mostly wrapped in mothballs. They bought precious gems, which were like favorite, childish toys for Elizabeth, who was accustomed to ever more lavish indulgences since childhood. Richard (or the Burtons together) paid $37,000 for La Peregrina, the pearl King Philip of Spain had given Mary Tudor in 1554; $65,000 for a 40-carat blue sapphire brooch; $305,000 for the 33.19-carat Krupp diamond; $1.5 million for the 69.42-carat Cartier diamond. And so it went, year after dazzling year. Princess Margaret, seated beside Elizabeth at a London banquet, glanced at the Cartier gem. "Is that the famous diamond? But it's so large—how very vulgar!"

"Yes," Elizabeth replied, proudly lifting her hand to the light. "Ain't it great?"

There was a slight pause before Margaret continued: "Would you mind if I tried it on?" She did so, and her eyes widened.

"It doesn't look so vulgar now, does it?" Elizabeth asked.

At Tiffany and Bulgari (and elsewhere), they bought emeralds and rubies, turquoise and jade, gold and silver, and heaven only knows how much they paid to insure it all. It was all very wise investing, friends said, defensively. Well, yes, but—they would have sold their bread for marmalade, as the French writer Théophile Gautier once said of thoughtless excess. They bought and bought and bought, in the manner of nouveaux riches, with monstrous immodesty.

"In this Age of Vulgarity marked by such minor matters as war and poverty," ran a *New York Times* editorial condemning the Taylor-Burton roadshow, "it gets harder every day to scale the heights of true vulgarity. But given some loose millions, it can be done—and worse, admired."

Elizabeth responded with a frontal attack. "I know I'm vulgar, but would you have me any other way?" It was as if she were speaking with a director about a part in a movie: vulgarity was now part of a role assigned her, and she would play it fully—playfully, in fact. But fame and ostentation italicized the unreality of their lives. The Burtons were confined, overprotected by an entourage of bodyguards and lackeys, and they had few true, intimate friends, for people were of course intimidated by it all. This was singularly tragic for Elizabeth, whose gift for friendship was well established among those fortunate enough to enjoy hers.

As the Burtons' excesses proliferated, their work, perhaps predictably, suffered. That summer and autumn, director Joseph Losey tried to improve *The Milk Train Doesn't Stop Here Anymore*, a Tennessee Williams play about an aging woman and a mystical (but poorly defined) interloper that had twice failed on Broadway; but not even the playwright's presence during production could redeem *Boom!* Nor (according to Losey) could the two stars save it, for the Burtons arrived "screaming, drunk and abusive, and it was unimaginably awful." Filming a confused and pretentious script full of aphorisms about The Meaning of Life was not facilitated by Bur-

ton's nearly constant state of inebriation, by Williams's drugged stu-
por and, conversely, by Elizabeth's inability to look as frail, ill and
dying as the story required. The Burtons were paid $1.25 million
each plus expenses, which were considerable.

But like every director who worked with her, Losey found Elizabeth thoroughly professional and downright endearing, and they
agreed to work together on her next picture, an equally dreadful
thing called *Secret Ceremony*. This was produced in London in early
1968 while Richard worked nearby in *Where Eagles Dare*, and the
jobs created a sudden problem. British quarantine laws prevented
the Burtons' dogs from entering the country. Solution: they char-
tered a two-hundred-ton yacht at $20,000 a month and turned it
into a luxurious floating kennel for their pampered puppies. This
huge dockside doghouse, known as the *Beatriz,* was anchored in the
Thames near the Tower of London, and, presumably with the animals' permission, the Burtons occasionally used it for parties.

Secret Ceremony kept its secrets from the cast and the audience,
too, although it seemed to have something to do with a demented
girl with a tendency to incest (Mia Farrow, straight from her ordeal
in *Rosemary's Baby*) who kidnaps an aging prostitute (Elizabeth) in
the mistaken notion that she is the girl's mother. Like the *Beatriz*
years later, the film sank without a trace. As with her notices generally since *The Comedians*, Elizabeth received mostly polite or dismissive reviews: never less than competent, she could not rise above
inferior material. The state of film criticism, however, was such that
very few with that occupation bothered to distinguish the role or
the project from the actress so willingly trapped within them.

During the making of this baffling movie, Elizabeth suffered sharp
abdominal pains, and after a series of tests early that summer, she
entered a London hospital for a hysterectomy on July 21. "I have
just spent the two most horrible days of my adult life," wrote
Richard in his notebook two days later, describing Elizabeth's unexpectedly complicated surgery followed by her "screaming agony,
hallucinated [sic] by drugs, sometimes knowing who I was and
sometimes not, a virago one minute, an angel the next." Her recov-

ery was painful and retarded by a severe depression: she had often spoken of giving Richard a child, and now, at thirty-six, sterility must have made her feel prematurely old and useless.

It was back to work that autumn of 1968. With Rex Harrison, Richard signed to act in *Staircase*, directed by Elizabeth's old flame, Stanley Donen. By that year, the Burton's contracts stipulated that they never had to work more than an hour's distance apart. And so, as David Brown (then Twentieth Century-Fox's executive vice-president) later recalled, "Elizabeth and Richard demanded Paris— never mind that his film was set in London, and that hers, based on Frank Gilroy's play *The Only Game in Town*, was set in Las Vegas!" Thus the scenery for *Only Game*, constructed in a Paris studio, sent the budget skyrocketing.

Again, there were unrealistically high hopes for the project: her old friend George Stevens directed, her costar was Warren Beatty, and Twentieth Century-Fox again went over the top, paying her $1,250,000 ("They must be out of their tiny Chinese minds," she said). But this story of a tired Las Vegas showgirl and a compulsive gambler had neither wit, style nor dramatic purpose, and in many scenes Elizabeth looked simply exhausted and aloof. Hopeful movie-goers lined up patiently to leave the theaters; most stayed away in droves. It was two years and seven films since *Who's Afraid of Virginia Woolf?*, and everything had been a disappointment: if Elizabeth began to think she was an anachronism, she was correct—at least in this stonily aloof performance. "I just came out when I was called and read my lines," she admitted years later. Nor were her feelings lightened by the news that Richard was to act Henry VIII in *Anne of the Thousand Days*, but that she was judged too old to pass for Anne Boleyn.

There are other explanations for her disaffection during filming at the end of 1968 and into early 1969. Her chronic back pain worsened, and for several days she panicked when there was numbness spreading in her hips and legs; this turned out to be a severe case of sciatica, aggravated by anxiety, overwork and overweight— but doctors, to keep their famous patient comfortable, prodigally overprescribed painkillers. These she washed down with liquor, to avoid even the possibility of discomfort: "A Jack [Daniel's] on the rocks," she often called to a servant. "I feel a headache coming on!" At work on *Only Game,* recorded Burton in his notebook, she was indifferent to the point of apathy.

Her imprudent consumption of drugs and alcohol was neither new nor, for the time, of much concern to many people who thought they could monitor and control the debilitating, addictive effects. In 1962, Eddie Fisher—who knew such danger signs when he saw them—was "more concerned than ever by her drinking in combination with the many pills her various doctors prescribed, including Demerol, a potent painkiller and sedative. A well-meaning doctor or two had tried to give her substitutes, but Elizabeth could always tell the difference. Nothing but Demerol seemed to offer her any relief." Naturally, her need for pills and injections increased with her tolerance of their effects, and so Fisher himself administered the drugs. "It was very simple," according to Fisher: he gave her what pills and shots she needed to sleep. Now, with Burton, she managed it herself—although her drugs were limited to pills.

By 1968, this dangerous regimen was exploited for anxiety and for grief—both of which afflicted her when she received word that her father died in his sleep at home in Los Angeles on November 20, a month short of his seventy-first birthday. With Richard, she departed Paris, flew home, attended the funeral and burial, and was back at work six days later—cheerfully and energetically, her colleagues noted.

But there must have been some very confused feelings to blunt. Sara returned with Elizabeth to Paris, and by December, Richard was frantic about his wife, whose back pain, now worse than ever, forced the shutdown of *Only Game* for a week. "It can't be alright for her to drink *and* take the doses of drugs that [her nurse-companion] is forever pumping into her . . . At this rate, her malady will never never [*sic*] get better. And talking to her about it is like talking to a wall."

As the year ended, she was falling down constantly, "sipping away at the drinks," according to Burton. "I dread it at night, when she has had her shots of drugs and is only semi-articulate . . . The most frightening thing is that as a result of E.'s total self-indulgence when she moans and groans in agony I simply become bored. And what is more frightening is she has become bored with everything in life. She never reads a book." The situation, of course, intensified Richard's own problems: "I have always been a heavy drinker but now as a result of this half-life we're leading I am drinking twice as much." His final word on the subject was a tragically accurate prediction: "The upshot will be that I'll die of drink while she'll go blithely on in her half world." Burton's notebooks for 1969 and 1970 continue with a litany of horror anthems about his wife's addictions to alcohol and drugs.

Despite her frailty, *The Only Game in Town* was at last completed in early 1969, after location photography at Caesar's Palace in Las Vegas. She then checked into a Los Angeles hospital—for a thorough back examination, the press was told, but it was actually for a feeble attempt at drug detoxification. The back trouble, it turned out, would be a minor though chronic problem; the bad news was that her liver was seriously damaged by alcohol. For too long, noted Burton in his diary, Elizabeth was wildly drunk every night—"stoned, unfocussed, unable to walk straight, talking in a slow, meaningless baby voice utterly without reason, like a demented child." He tried to imagine life without her, he added, but he could not.

The Burtons were, then, a living definition of neurotic codependency, and perhaps the most tragic element in their sicknesses and unreason was that they were both essentially good and kind people, never deliberately cruel to anyone but themselves. They admired talent in others and praised it lavishly; they were loyal to friends (when friends were permitted access to them); they were generous when they saw ill fortune; they wept with the needy and rejoiced in others' happiness. And they longed to do good work: part of the reason they did not was their own demons, to be sure—but another part had to do with the distemper of the times, with the proliferation of shallow and silly screenplays and a culture that, less and less, took seriously the talents of people who had the audacity to have survived so long and still be eager to work.

Released from the hospital in March, She went with Richard for a holiday at Casa Kimberly in Puerto Vallarta, where the atmosphere between them—caused by both fear and resentment—was rife with what he called a "venomous malice," and where they had to deal with the adolescent problems of her sons, who visited from Hawaii. Living with the Burtons could never have been easy for youngsters, but at this time, it was perilous: Elizabeth had been told, to no avail, that she ought to stop drinking, while Richard claimed that he, at least, was only a tolerable companion when drunk nearly to the point of coma. Often unfit to be in the children's company, one servant or another would play companion to them. Alternately, according to Raymond Vignale, "When Elizabeth and Richard were drunk, the children simply retired to their bedrooms to watch TV."

Much to his credit, however, Burton remained sober and attentive whenever Elizabeth was ill—which was increasingly often, as she suffered conditions real and imagined. Lovingly, he could perform the most delicate and unpleasant nursing duties for her—as well as coping with her anxieties about premature aging, though she was only thirty-seven. Such tasks much occupied him during the spring and summer of 1969, when they were in London while he filmed *Anne of the Thousand Days*. Elizabeth was afflicted by idleness, a fear of being abandoned by Richard and an irrational jealousy: he had been entirely faithful to her since their marriage, and she knew it; nevertheless, that season Elizabeth was quite wrongly convinced that her husband was having an affair with his costar, Genevieve Bujold.

The remainder of the unhappy year 1969 was (if one trusts Burton's detailed notebooks and the accounts of friends and employees) a constant cycle of verbal and physical battles: "We are fighting & have been fighting for over a year now over anything and everything," he noted in August, adding that they were committing slow suicide with liquor. Desperate combat was temporarily interrupted by the mutual presentation of expensive gifts: that year, for example, he bought her the Cartier diamond, and she presented him with the Everyman Library, a thousand uniformly leather-bound editions of great literature.

But soon the war between George and Martha resumed to the point of a wild pummeling she inflicted on him: full of guilt and self-loathing, Richard accepted her almost psychotic assault and her accusations of every fault and sin in the history of the world. It may be close to the mark to suggest that in her latter years with Richard, Elizabeth was counting on him—her new "Daddy" as she sometimes said—to play the role of just that man in her past life with who she had so distant and unfulfilled a relationship: her own father.

Nineteen-seventy began without much prospect of creative pleasure: the Burtons hoped for a sabbatical and instead got a taste of purgatory, if not worse. "Except when we were alone, we have bickered and quarreled incessantly," noted Richard at the end of March, the day after, in the company of friends, he had pointed at Elizabeth and said, "There's someone who could never give up drink."

Whereupon [he continued] she said she hated my guts . . . and said, "I wish to Christ he'd get out of my life." She has said all those things, and I to her, but never before, as I recall, when sober and in front of people . . . She has had [this] outburst so often recently—going back about a year, I would say—that it undoubtedly smacks of the truth. The eyes blaze with genuine hatred and contempt, and her lovely face becomes ugly with loathing.

There were a few days of cease-fire, however. The Burtons showed what terrific comedians they could be, with impeccable timing and graceful nuance, when they filmed an episode of Lucille Ball's television show, broadcast that September; the concept was that Lucy, having tried on Elizabeth's enormous diamond ring, couldn't remove it in time for a press reception.

Otherwise, domestic issues were not so comical. She fought violently (but only verbally) with her mother, and after years of pain and chronic bleeding, Elizabeth underwent surgery for hemorrhoids—a procedure from which she had a long and unusually complicated recuperation, and which pitched her back into the cycle of narcotics from which she had for once tried to extract herself.

For neither the first nor last time, Elizabeth recovered fitter than ever and (thus Burton in a notebook entry dated July 13) more sexually eager than a teenager, which was for once a desire not met by her husband. He was, to his astonishment, left less rather than more inclined to sex by a protracted time of sobriety. Against doctors' orders, she insisted on traveling to London, where in October her seventeen-year-old son Michael married Beth Clutter, a nineteen-year-old from Oregon. Elizabeth gave them a new Jaguar and a London town house, both of which lasted much longer than the marriage Elizabeth arranged at Caxton Hall, where she had wed Michael's father.

The year 1971 began sadly, with the death of her secretary and good friend Richard Hanley, and she was not at all cheered when she went to work later in January on a fourteen-week shoot for one of the worst films of her career, *X, Y and Zee* (in Britain, *Zee & Company*). Forever after, author Edna O'Brien rightly felt cheated: her script had been rewritten, scenes removed, sequences added—the entire effort "butchered and killed," she said, and the relic was too mangled and dead to contemplate.

The story concerned Zee (Elizabeth) who resorts to cunning in her attempt to scuttle an affair between her husband (Michael Caine) and a young widow (Susannah York). When he leaves Zee, she attempts suicide but recovers, and in the fullness of time exploits the rumor of a past lesbian episode in the widow's life to seduce her. Taking full advantage of the cinema's new freedoms of raw language (by now firmly imbedded in movie culture since the worldwide acceptance of *Who's Afraid of Virginia Woolf?*), of brief nudity and of explicit indications of lesbianism, *X, Y and Zee* had no idea what to do with those freedoms. The result was a tangle of trendy hokum.

For the role, the now frankly zaftig Elizabeth exaggerated her makeup, wore mammoth fright wigs, and generally created a parody of Martha. Director Brian G. Hutton gave her full rein to storm through her scenes with hysterical bitchery, but the story was so thin and the characters so shallow that her energy was wasted. "She was smashing to work with," according to Michael Caine, but Elizabeth's expanding and difficult retinue was not, especially since the trusty Hanley was no longer present to keep the peace. As usual, she required hair and makeup artists, secretaries, messengers, dog walkers and chauffeurs, but these courtiers placed Elizabeth in a cocoon from which she was unable to have the normal give-and-take of working relationships. "When you work with her," added Caine, "the people around her make it seem as if you're working with the Statue of Liberty!"

To keep surveillance on his health, to have access to his critiques and from simple possessiveness, Elizabeth demanded that Richard be on the set with her as much as possible; and he was there, until he began a fifteen-month-long marathon of his own mediocre films, two of which included his wife. One of these was an adaptation of *Under Milk Wood,* Dylan Thomas's valentine to simple Welsh country folk, and that spring and summer Elizabeth attended Richard and worked briefly in the picture as the tarty Rosie Prebert, a girlfriend of the narrator's memory. In a few quick flashback sequences, she had little to do but roll on a bed like a merry wife of Cardiff, cackling and giggling (which she did not much do in real life that year).

From there, the Burtons were off for a brief holiday, first to Gstaad, where they learned that Elizabeth, at thirty-nine, was a grandmother: on July 25, Michael and Beth had a baby girl they named Leyla. Elizabeth flew back to London, but only for a few days, for the handsome $70,000 house she had bought the young Wildings was now in shambles, a crash pad for their hippie coterie. Michael would accept no gifts on the occasion of the baby's birth, for he was a lad of his time, and he regarded his mother as an unjustly rich woman, famous only for her beauty and therefore one of the dreaded "Establishment" so popularly reviled in 1971. "Mother's life seems just as fantastic to me as it must to everyone else," he gracelessly told the press. "I really don't want any part of it. I just don't dig all those diamonds and things."

Later, long-haired, bone-thin and glassy-eyed Michael moved to

a stone cottage in Wales, intent on growing natural foods and form-
ing a rock band, and eventually he and his wife divorced. Elizabeth,
anxious but powerless to intervene in the lives of children who were
for the most part ever more distant from her (Maria now excepted),
was realistic: "Though I would do anything at all for [my children],
it is they who must live their own lives."

No doubt about it, Elizabeth Taylor's film career was withering to
the point of annihilation. During autumn 1971, the Burtons somehow found themselves in a ghastly picture called *Hammersmith Is Out*,
directed by and costarring Peter Ustinov. (The Burtons got their
usual inflated fees, for their very presence in a film guaranteed audiences worldwide.) Elizabeth played a slatternly waitress (another
Martha variation) careening around with a madman (Richard) who
thinks he is the devil—and to prove it, he turns Elizabeth into a
movie star.

   The movie showed the Burtons blank-faced with boredom and
unfocused from drink and drugs: the most skilled cosmetician and
photographers had their greatest challenges. Richard, in the bargain,
was particularly angry because his sporadic attempts to avoid alcohol were sabotaged by Elizabeth: unwilling to drink alone, she
pressed lunchtime martinis on him, too. By the end of 1971, she
was listless, bored, too often drunk, and finally in a state of catatonic apathy.

   In February 1972, Elizabeth turned forty. For the occasion, she
was in Budapest with Richard, who was filming *Bluebeard,* and for a
weekend of parties at the Inter-Continental Hotel they invited over
eighty friends—among them, Princess Grace of Monaco, Ringo
Starr, Michael Caine, Susannah York and David Niven. Richard gave
her a $50,000-diamond pendant designed by the man who had
built the Taj Mahal and, marvelous to relate, he kept with religious
fervor to a fresh attempt at sobriety: while most around him were
pink-eyed and boozy that weekend, he restricted himself to mineral
water. But his abstinence ended (as it happened, forever) when a
beloved brother died. After four years of total paralysis following a
freak accident, Ifor Jenkins had finally succumbed. Thus began, as

Bluebeard director Edward Dmytryk recalled, a long nightmare.

Dmytryk very much liked and admired Burton when they met; Elizabeth he had known since 1956, when he guided her through the rigors of *Raintree County.* For the rest of the filming that Hungarian winter, Burton was a wreck, unable to work more than a few hours, often drunk on arrival at the studio, invariably drunk when departing, and causing constant havoc to the production.

Just so, both Burtons were completely inebriated when David Frost interviewed them in Budapest for his American television show. Elizabeth approached these talk sessions, filmed on one of Dmytryk's sets, with fear and loathing. She also resented the sketchiness and distortion usually evident in the final cut of broadcast interviews.

False courage was nearby in a beaker of Jack Daniel's, placed just out of camera range and duly refilled by one of her courtiers as the interview progressed. Broadcast later that year and extended to two hours—the better to linger gleefully over the Burtons' drunken state and the long pauses in their replies—the Frost interviews show Richard far gone and Elizabeth slow of speech, increasingly diffident, eventually almost supine. Everyone present that day in Budapest expected that Frost and his producers would judiciously edit the interviews and save his guests international embarrassment. But television, of course, prefers the sensational, and so viewers saw the Burtons incapacitated by drink. "I made a fool of myself, as usual," she said a few years later; the show was unfortunate, but such an appearance was hardly "usual."

Embarrassments followed serially. Losing all discretion with the actresses in *Bluebeard*, Richard fondled and flirted outrageously. One of the actresses received a punch in the face from Elizabeth, but another avoided any confrontation by simply yielding to Richard's invitation to meet quietly for a two-day romantic tryst: it was, according to his own insistence and all other accounts, the first infidelity of the eight-year marriage. "Once I started being attracted to other women," said Richard, "I knew the game was up."

Furious, Elizabeth flew to Rome, where she and Aristotle Onassis (without his wife, Jacqueline) attracted a horde of paparazzi and scandal-famished reporters when they dined at a popular restaurant. This was no romantic encounter: the Burtons and the Greek tycoon were standing members of the same international crowd of sybarites and had often met socially. Never mind: the world's press wires buzzed with implications about Ari-and-Liz. What she wanted, however, was paternal comfort, and she got it in the form of a stern exhortation. That evening, Elizabeth telephoned Richard and ordered him to "get that woman out of my bed!"

"How did she know?" he asked Dmytryk hours later.

"Don't you know by now that you're surrounded by her spies and agents? You can't get away with anything, no matter where she is!"

That fall in London, Elizabeth quickly completed a stylish but weak thriller called *Night Watch*, in which she brooded fitfully, wrung her hands and ran about nervously in a collection of Valentino dresses. Immediately after, the Burtons filmed a dreadful two-part television drama, written for a London setting but swiftly altered and filmed in Munich so that the Burtons could avoid paying British taxes. *Divorce His* and *Divorce Hers* turned out to be their last collaboration, and the titles indicated the theme, the breakup of a marriage seen from the perspective of husband, then of wife.

But Elizabeth and Richard seemed merely a well-dressed, poorly written version of George and Martha: themselves, in other words. Richard's insobriety and Elizabeth's stolid temperament, now perpetual, poisoned the production. "In an odd way, the script echoed the chaos of their lives," said director Waris Hussein, who recalled the experience as one of the worst of his life. So did viewers: watching the finished episodes had all the charm of observing an autopsy.

As they were putting this sorry business on film, their own marriage was rapidly unraveling—as was that of her son Michael, whose wife, Beth, decided that living in a Welsh commune did not suit her and her baby. One rainy morning, she wrapped Leyla up in a quilt and sped off to Hawaii's more hospitable climate. As for Michael, he soon had a new girlfriend, Johanna Lykke-Dahn, who bore him another daughter they named Naomi; he also had a police record after he was fined for growing marijuana near his Welsh farmhouse. His brother, Christopher, meanwhile, would marry the granddaughter of John Paul Getty—but this, too, was a doomed marriage.

In the new year 1973, much in Elizabeth Taylor's life was dark and confused. It was clear that the Burtons were no longer working together, that in public they bickered and baited each other, and that their travels—from London to Gstaad to Rome to New York to Los Angeles to Puerto Vallarta—were not purposeful journeys but mere treadmills to oblivion. *Ash Wednesday*, which she appeared in that year, evoked all sorts of troublesome motifs and images.

In this movie, she played Barbara Sawyer, a fifty-something woman driven to plastic surgery in an attempt to keep her husband (Henry Fonda), who wants a divorce despite results so marvelous that Barbara can attract a handsome young lover. Not the least of *Ash Wednesday*'s problems was the fact that Elizabeth looked slim, stunning and elegantly turned out, and her character would apparently die to please any man: how, one wonders, could her husband boot her out?

As for herself in a situation like Barbara's: "I don't worry about growing old," Elizabeth said at the end of filming, as confidently as if she believed it. "We can't stop the inevitable, so why try? I'm forty-one and have never felt better. Plastic surgery isn't for me— simply because I don't base my happiness on the physical aspects of life." That was a noble ideal at her age, but (as she would learn) unrealistic for Elizabeth Taylor twenty years later. In any case, by late spring 1973 she was miserable, especially after she visited her old friend, ninety-three-year-old Donald Crisp, with whom she had appeared in *Lassie Come Home*, who had played her father in *National Velvet*, and who was then close to death. Leaving his room at the Motion Picture Country Home, she was unable to hold back tears.

Reunited with Richard for a brief holiday in Rome, Elizabeth was still melancholy. In a fit of pique—over what, he could not recall—Richard asked Elizabeth to leave: "I told her to get out, and to my surprise, she went. I couldn't believe it! I thought she would be back next day, but not a bit of it."

Instead, next day she went back to finish the looping of dialogue on *Ash Wednesday* which, like all the other post–*Virginia Woolf* movies, made her considerably richer: she was still earning over a million dollars per picture, had a generous expense allowance, and enjoyed a percent of the profits, which somehow even these disappointing pictures managed to realize.

After her work was completed, she flew to Hollywood—ostensibly to visit her ailing mother, but really to confer with friends about the route her life should take. Roddy McDowall, as usual, was attentive and concerned, but when she rang Peter Lawford he was mired in problems of his own: another failed marriage and an addiction to drugs that would eventually kill him.

Through Lawford, however, Elizabeth met Henry Wynberg, a tall, handsome Dutch-born businessman five years her junior, then a divorcé and a shrewd Hollywood used-car salesman much appreciated by certain women. She liked not only his looks but, as her secretary Raymond Vignale said, Henry was "more fun—he could dance all night, while Richard preferred to sit at home. Going out was *life* for Elizabeth then," and Henry was (thus Elizabeth) "cute and amusing." By early July, they were lovers.

"It wasn't love at first sight, it was infatuation," said Wynberg later, "and there was only one place to go"—by which he seems to have meant upstairs and to bed. "We began dating openly, and she started calling me at all hours of the day and night, confiding in me about her marriage problems with Burton. Before I knew where I was, I was in deep." The Wynberg affair was once again a case of Elizabeth Taylor living out the role she had just played on-screen. Fearful of time, age and loneliness and desperate for companionship, the character Barbara and the woman Elizabeth—both separated from their husbands—take lovers.

"I think she suddenly saw all the empty seasons and lonely lands ahead," said Edith Head, at whose Hollywood home Elizabeth stayed briefly that year. And so Henry Wynberg, confident and evidently comfortable in being her companion on whatever uncertain terms, was soon slaving triple-time to provide jewels: "Make it bigger," he demanded of a jeweler who showed him a coral necklace for Elizabeth. How the jeweler might accomplish this feat of magic Wynberg did not explain.

Richard, meantime, was convinced that she had taken on Henry as revenge, or to incite jealousy. He complained that Elizabeth's wily techniques of possessiveness were insufferable, that her constant demands for attention were tiresome, and that her own addictions were beyond his ability to resolve. She had to know that she was primary in a man's life, yet every fiber of her being suspected she never was. "When Elizabeth loves you," Richard said that year, "she is not happy until she owns your soul. Our natures do not inspire domestic tranquillity." For years, there had been, of course, precious little serenity in their professional and personal lives. Without some occasional distance from the pressures of publicity, there can be no tranquillity, and without that, no reflection—and therefore no real inner life, no movement forward. And perhaps, too, the slow loss of that tenderness which is the rein of otherwise reckless craving.

Further complicating the Burtons' life was the curse of fame, the simultaneous need for and recoiling from adulation that marked their lives—and the constant attention to which she, especially, had been accustomed since childhood. To the spurious blandishments of praise and presents, they made of themselves willing sacrifices. Their talents, in other words, were being choked by an abundance that failed to satisfy; they knew the price of everything but the value of very little, and they enjoyed nothing.

In a moment of admirable clarity such as would later be her saving grace, Elizabeth diagnosed the disease:

> Our marriage has turned into a gigantic commercial enterprise . . . I've worked since childhood and I'm afraid I've been strong and willful at times. I must have been awful to live with because I've always wanted to be independent, even though I knew that more than anything else in the world I wanted a man who could control me.

Richard, of course, could not control her, partly because he could scarcely control himself, partly because it was important for her to triumph over precisely the man from whom she thought she craved control. "I have been totally dependent on love," she told a sympathetic journalist. She meant "on passion," which soon became her favorite word—but it was not yet clear whether she would understand that such a dependence could kill.

And so, on July 4 (an ironic coincidence or not, depending on the viewpoint), she issued a press release from her suite at the Regency Hotel in New York:

> I am convinced it would be a good and constructive idea if Richard and I separated for a while. Maybe we loved each other too much. I never believed such a thing was possible. But we have been in each other's pockets constantly, never being apart but for matters of life and death, and I believe it has caused a temporary breakdown of communication. I believe with all my heart that the separation will ultimately bring us back to where we should be—and that's together.

In 1936, the King of England broadcast a statement to the world, explaining that he was abdicating his throne to marry an American divorcée. More than half a century later, the Queen of England's children issued similar statements when their marriages were troubled. Otherwise, it is difficult, in modern times, to enumerate similar public utterances by famous people about their separations or divorces. But in 1973, the Burtons *were* America's troubled royalty—rich and famous, regarded with awe by some and with contempt by others. Elizabeth, for one, believed she owed her people an explanation—or at least a gracious statement, without rancor or bitterness or justification, and with the faintest hope for reconciliation. She concluded royally: "Pray for us." Perhaps millions did. But the curators at Madame Tussaud's Wax Museum in London gravely separated the effigies of Elizabeth Taylor and Richard Burton.

* * *

Elizabeth then returned to Rome and appeared in *The Driver's Seat*, a film that at first viewing seems absolutely impervious to comprehension, not to say reasonable analysis. At times it seemed to have something to do with a promiscuous woman named Lise, hell-bent on paying for her sins by finding a man to kill her during lovemaking, but that is never certain; in any case, the lady has problems. So did the production: "We are shooting it differently, without a proper script," Elizabeth told a visiting reporter.

But *The Driver's Seat* (very freely adapted from a story by Muriel Spark) makes perfect sense when seen—just as it was made—as a veiled piece of autobiography, for it was concocted as filming proceeded, with the star improvising her way through a kind of confessional memoir she virtually wrote and directed. "I sometimes worry that I've used up all my happiness," Elizabeth told a friend that summer of 1973, "and that I'm going to spend the rest of my life on planes searching for a new hoard of it." This statement, only slightly altered, found its way right into *The Driver's Seat*. Just so, the actor Guido Mannari—who bears an astonishing resemblance to Henry Wynberg—played a randy masher who tries to have his way with Lise in a car: in Henry's presence, Elizabeth chose Mannari for the role. "Henry acquired the charisma of a perfect lackey," one heard during production.

In Rome, Richard was nearby at another studio, making a picture with Sophia Loren. Elizabeth, needlessly suspicious of an affair blossoming, made feeble attempts to spend a few graceful hours with him. The truth was that neither of them had the remotest idea of what they really wanted from each other or themselves. The matter was further complicated by the peripheral presence of Henry Wynberg, who had stayed on at Elizabeth's expressed demand. "Poor Elizabeth," said Henry injudiciously. "She needs much comfort at this stage, and I am able to give it. She really needs me."

Alas, perhaps not: things were evidently as unclear as the plots of her recent movies. Two weeks after he had spoken, as Elizabeth was darting like a hummingbird from him to Richard and back again, Henry's mood was cautious: "Three months from now, we may no longer be such good friends—or perhaps we'll be something much more than that. Only God and Elizabeth know." She then accompanied Henry to Amsterdam to visit his parents: "I know how different we are," she said, "but Henry puts himself out to understand me. He brings me comfort."

Which she then tried to bring her old friend and colleague Laurence Harvey, her costar in *Butterfield 8* and *Night Watch*, who was dying of cancer at his London home. Her bedside manner was, according to Harvey's companion Paulene Stone, "brooding and dramatic" as Elizabeth spoke to him about an operation she would soon have in Los Angeles: she, too, might have cancer! She then turned to Henry, who turned to Paulene, as if on cue: "Elizabeth drinks Jack Daniel's on the rocks." It was fetched at once.

To give the family saga just the right touch of comic relief, an elderly widower named Elmer Tammist, the Estonian vice consul to South Africa, announced that he was going to marry Sara Taylor at Christmas 1973, just as soon as she recovered from a tiny touch of pneumonia. Sara was then seventy-seven and Mr. Tammist a decade younger.

The couple, it seems, had met on a cruise, and on discovering that they were both mad about country western square dancing, they fell in love, or at least in step. To make everything completely psychedelic, the wedding was to take place at her son Howard's home on the island of Oahu, to the strains of "Hawaiian Love Song," which is not easily adapted to the beat-beat-beat of a square dance. But then Sara's autumn fever passed, and with it Elmer Tammist, too. Elizabeth, who was also confined briefly to the UCLA Medical Center in November—her problem turned out to be a benign ovarian cyst—never met the vice consul, but she was apparently much relieved when told of her mother's decision.

And so Sara remained the Widow Taylor. Eventually she moved from Los Angeles to a condominium at the Sunrise Country Club in Rancho Mirage, near Palm Springs. There, she cheerfully presided at rustic hoedowns and country shindigs for senior citizens.

Chapter Twelve

1974–1978

I N JANUARY 1974, WORKMEN AT Madame Tussaud's scurried about, pushing the images of the Burtons closer together—"but not quite so close," as a supervisor prudently advised. The reason for the frequent moving of the wax effigies was simple. Elizabeth rang in the new year 1974 with Richard, who had escorted her from the hospital in December and whisked her off to Rome (where he had to complete *The Voyage*, his film with Sophia Loren). "We are back together again," Elizabeth told reporters triumphantly. "We've been through far too much together to see it all disappear in flames."

The Burtons were nothing if not unpredictable, and so the reporters had to get a statement from Wynberg, who announced that he had been drafted by Elizabeth only as a friend, to play the part of a lover without actually being so, and thus to make Burton jealous and so win him back to Elizabeth. "I agreed to the conspiracy," said Henry with a straight face, "on condition that my real girlfriend, Helen, could always be near." Nobody close to Henry knew anyone named Helen.

That March, after a respite at Casa Kimberley, the Burtons celebrated their tenth wedding anniversary in rural northern California, where Richard was filming *The Klansman*—and downing eight-ounce tumblers of vodka for breakfast and thrice that amount before the end of the day's work with his costar, the equally boozy Lee Marvin. Elizabeth, often enough, tried to keep pace with the boys—to show that she was a trouper and could cuss and drink with the feistiest of them. But the result was messy in more ways than one. Richard yielded to the advances of a nubile eighteen-year-old, a former local "Miss Pepsi" whom he presented with a diamond-and-ruby ring in gratitude for her favors, and there was a second bit of fumbling with an older married woman, whose husband actually loaded up the shotgun.

That did it. Elizabeth left Richard and flew to Henry Wynberg for more of his special kind of comfort. "My God, I can do no more for him," she said of Burton, "because there is nothing more he can or will do for himself. He's killing himself." And so he was: he very nearly died on location and was rushed to a Los Angeles hospital, where doctors told him his kidneys and liver were rotting away and that, if he did not stop drinking altogether, he would be dead in less than six months. But they did not take into account his obstinacy: Richard went on the wagon only sporadically and lived another ten years.

On April 25, a statement was given to the international press by the couple's New York lawyer:

> Elizabeth and Richard Burton have requested Aaron R. Frosch, their longtime attorney, to proceed to legally terminate their ten-year marriage due to irreconcilable differences. Frosch will seek the divorce in the canton of Berne, Switzerland, where the Burtons have been legal residents for many years.

The financial settlement was easily negotiated. Elizabeth kept the *Kalizma*, Casa Kimberley, $7 million worth of jewelry, all the art and anything she wished of their joint possessions; she was also awarded custody of Maria, whom they had formally adopted in

1964. Two months later, on June 26, after a forty-minute hearing in a Swiss courthouse, Elizabeth was no longer Mrs. Burton. She stopped at the house in Gstaad to collect some clothes and to rejoin Henry Wynberg, with whom she was already traveling. They resumed a season aboard the *Kalizma*. "The world knows Henry is with me," she said at one port of call. "We have not tried to hide ourselves."

And so, at forty-two, Elizabeth was playing, marvelously, her new role—that of an independent woman of the 1970s, heedless of public opinion, smiling and waving as she sailed round the Mediterranean with a handsome companion. Flinty but romantic, maternal yet lusty, she simultaneously showed the world a tough will and a vulnerable softness. She had been the studio-manufactured postwar ideal of the delicately beautiful virgin; now she was the unpredictable, ever youthful and vigorous woman, and the world waited to see how she would grow into the part. She was again a needy young woman, longing for a relationship on which she could depend. She had and spread an illusion of perpetual youthfulness, and this the culture found irresistible.

Each of her marriages had been an attempt to find another path to her own adulthood, and so in a way Elizabeth Taylor was a kind of dramatic proto-feminist, making her own decisions and living by her own code despite her obvious dependence on a man and her stated need to be dominated. But like many of both genders who proclaim their desire to be controlled, this was only half the truth: a strong part of her wanted to do the commanding, too.

Nicky Hilton was a dashing, rich gambler who represented freedom from her parents and the studio. But she had quickly learned that he was a bad choice, that such forceful domination and humiliation could ruin her. And so, whatever personal compulsions caused her at first to submit and whatever social considerations encouraged her to keep a discreet silence (which was much the custom of the time about physical abuse), she knew she had chosen badly, and she ended the marriage. Since then, whatever mistakes she had made were eventually acknowledged and repented.

Michael Wilding, so different from the youthful, abusive Hilton, was a senior Englishman: surely he would be the Daddy and lover she so desired, the kind she might have married had she not emigrated to California from London. Wilding was a sensitive artist, a chronically impecunious, dependent, somewhat weak man who supplied the gentle attentiveness she had missed in her father and Hilton. But Wilding could not provide the toys with which she had become obsessed—the riches and baubles a movie queen expected, and which Elizabeth needed, perhaps to prove to herself that she was worth something.

And so she went over to the brash, generous Mike Todd, who spoiled her and kindled her imagination. Unlike Wilding, he was unrefined, raw, strong—and he made Elizabeth his ultimate showpiece, doting on her as the doll she considered herself to be.

The choice of Eddie Fisher was almost inevitable: he was Todd's shadow and surrogate son, the boyish charmer who resurrected Todd's swagger, his cigar-chomping, his language, his flamboyant style. But after Todd, he had neither the fiery intelligence nor the strength to possess her—and therefore he was not, for long, someone she wanted to possess.

When Richard Burton came on the scene, there occurred the single most dramatic turn in her life until the end of 1983. She and Richard Burton were obviously not good for each other, although each was in some ways instructive and useful for the other's careers. But with Richard, Elizabeth had turned (as before with Wilding after Hilton) to a smooth, confident, sophisticated, literate British actor as her mentor. He was (like Todd) a swaggering man who answered only to himself. But he was also described and hailed as one of the potentially great actors of his generation, and with him she saw the opportunity to mature as an actress—perhaps even to become a great one—and to form an historic partnership on stage and screen. But apart from *Who's Afraid of Virginia Woolf?*, the collaboration was a failure.

They were perhaps too strong for each other, too competitive with both their quickness and their indolence. Which of them could conquer the world in acting? Which of them could brawl better or command more imperiously? Who could swear more colorfully and, tragically, drink more robustly? Burton's character had a fatal flaw: somewhere he had a deeply ingrained self-distrust (even a self-loathing) that was manifest in carousing and drinking and neglect of his gifts—and thus began a dangerous new habit for her. But she was a survivor; he was not. He reveled in his vices; when she finally acknowledged her own, she resented and strove to overcome them.

In 1975, Henry Wynberg was cast in the supporting role of her new life-drama. "She was indeed one of the most famous women in the world," he said years later, "if not *the* most famous at that time"— and there was a bittersweet wondrousness about it all. It was like starring in a movie—*Our Life Together.*

But her life was not their life together: that was still inextricably linked with Richard. "Twenty minutes after our divorce," according to him, "she phoned me and asked, 'Richard, do you think we did the right thing?' We talked at least three times a week, called each other almost daily."

But circumstances separated them for half that year. Elizabeth had agreed to act in the first Soviet-American coproduction, a lavish remake of the Maeterlinck allegory *The Blue Bird,* to be filmed in Russia in early 1975. Before she departed with Wynberg, there was a reunion with her old acquaintance Karen von Unge (Michael Wilding's by-now former companion), who was a real estate agent in Los Angeles. Elizabeth wished to rent out her house during her forthcoming absence, and von Unge had, as her client, another Swedish-American: Ingrid Bergman, who was performing onstage in Maugham's *The Constant Wife* before taking the play to Broadway. "The rental agreement between them did not occur," von Unge recalled, "but I shall never forget the meeting of these two women, at a small table in the maid's room of the house. Normally, the homeowner keeps out of the way during a showing, but Elizabeth wanted to be there. It was really very touching—she was certainly no less famous than Ingrid, but she was absolutely star-struck and so impressed to meet her!"

At first, it was not at all clear that Wynberg would accompany Elizabeth to Russia, for he had been indicted for fraud. Pleading no contest to the charges that he had turned back the odometers on four cars he had sold in 1972 and 1973, he was put on three years' probation, fined $1,000 and at last left for the airport with Elizabeth.

They joined director George Cukor and the rest of the cast (among them, Ava Gardner, Jane Fonda and Cicely Tyson) at the Leningrad Hotel in February, where Elizabeth arrived in a scene that recalled Marlene Dietrich as Catherine the Great, coming to the Winter Palace in *The Scarlet Empress.* She swept in with 2,800 pounds of luggage (which required that several passengers be bumped from her flight), her secretary Raymond Vignale, a maid, two Shih Tzu dogs, a Siamese cat and, like Catherine's Emperor of the Night, Henry Wynberg.

In *The Blue Bird,* a tale of two spoiled children who are taken to a fantasy world in search of the blue bird of happiness, Elizabeth played four roles: the peasant Mother, the Witch, Light and Maternal Love. In each she was credible to the point of being unrecognizable—especially as the Witch, with her heavy makeup, a bent back and a chillingly wizened voice. But her scenes were delayed two weeks, for immediately after her arrival she came down with influenza and was put to bed with antibiotics. Other scenes were interrupted again later when she contracted amoebic dysentery, for which she flew to London for treatment.

"I don't know how I got into this mess in the first place," Elizabeth said when she returned to the production and explained why she did not simply bolt.

I was told Shirley MacLaine and Jane Fonda were doing it. Meanwhile, they were being told I was doing it. So I was the first sucker to sign . . . The days of getting a million dollars a film are over. If this film isn't a big success, I've wasted a year of my life and spent my own money instead of the usual expense money I get when I'm working. That's why it's in my interest to see that it's made, so maybe I'll see some money out of it.

Filming was at last completed on the difficult and ultimately bankrupt *Blue Bird* on August 11, and Elizabeth hosted a gloomy party in her hotel suite. The filming had been, she said later, "a disaster: in five months, I did about a week's work." That same evening, she received a telegram from Richard in Gstaad: would she please come to Switzerland for an important discussion? Three days later, Elizabeth and Henry arrived in Geneva, and the day after that, he was on his way back to California and she was with Richard. "Then for two days," said Burton, "we circled each other—very wary, very polite. On the third day, we had a fight. Then we knew that we were ourselves again."

And so on August 20, Elizabeth and Richard announced plans to remarry: "We really cannot keep away from each other," he said. According to their press agent, John Springer, Elizabeth was persuaded by Richard's sworn oath that he would give up drinking. The reunion, photographed formally for all the world to see, was very romantic and very unrealistic. Introducing him to acquaintances, Elizabeth began, "My former husband—oh, I mean, my *future* husband—oh!—I don't know *what* to call him! I can't say, 'my fiancé' or 'my roommate!'" Life is full of ironies.

"It was a bombshell for Henry," said his friend Peter Lawford, although at the time Wynberg (probably like many others) was not at all sure this reunion would last. "I was her lover," he said, "and people always assume that when a love affair is over, the lovers become enemies, not friends. I will always be her friend."

For a very brief time, the Burtons seemed like their old selves, toodling around the world from Switzerland to Rome to Israel to South Africa. They then proceeded to the Chobe Game Reserve in Botswana, and in that unlikely place, before the district's commissioner, Elizabeth Taylor and Richard Burton were remarried—her sixth marriage ceremony, contracted to her fifth husband (or sixth, depending on the counting method). The witnesses, kept at a safe distance, were two hippos, a rhino, a cheetah and some exotic birds. That night, Richard fell off the wagon with a resounding crash. Elizabeth was not so much angry as worried: the rage would come soon enough.

From Botswana the newlyweds headed for Johannesburg, where Richard bought and slipped on his wife's finger a seventy-two-carat-diamond wedding band. "We are stuck like chicken feathers to tar," wrote Elizabeth in a note to Richard—to which he replied, "Without you, I was a ghost." Journalists were busy scribbling, too, one American wit noting that "Sturm has remarried Drang and all is right with the world. In an era of friendly divorces and meaningful relationships, they stand for a marriage that is an all-consuming affair, not a partnership. None of this respecting each other's freedom, but instead saying, 'I can't live without you.' Wow."

But it was all too fantastic—"like a huge dream . . . an extraordinary adventure, doomed from the start, of course," Burton said later. "I remember thinking: what am I doing here?" Then he fell ill with what seemed to be malaria, and an Italian-Egyptian pharmacist named Chenina Samin (always called Chen Sam) was flown in to care for him. Twenty years later, she was still working for Elizabeth Taylor, as her New York–based publicist.

Ill and weary, Burton agreed to a fiftieth-birthday celebration in London that November, and there he accepted the good wishes of their friends and sipped mineral water while Elizabeth gulped down bourbon. When she went briefly into a London clinic for physiotherapy on her back, he refused her demand to spend the night in her room, and this made her furious. She may have been dependent, but she was also obdurate, and not a woman to be lightly refused.

In Gstaad for the Christmas holidays, Richard was depressed and anxious—until he met a tall, blond English model named Suzy Hunt, then being divorced. When he went to New York in January 1976 to begin rehearsals for the play *Equus,* he cabled Suzy to join him. Elizabeth, who had remained in Switzerland with her visiting children, learned at once what was happening in New York, and before she could cry "Revenge is sweet!" she rushed to the local discotheque and swept down on a flaxen-haired, square-jawed, thirty-seven-year-old Maltese advertising man named Peter Darmanin. They danced, she invited him home for the night, and next day he moved in—thus becoming, for about a month, Henry Wynberg's stand-in.

There was one crucial difference: this time, Elizabeth seemed almost deranged with anxiety and given to senseless fights with her new lover. After a stormy four-week affair, Darmanin had a perma- nent memento—a scar over an eyebrow, marking the spot where, as she lashed out at him, one of her huge rings sliced off a bit of his flesh. "Romance with Elizabeth?" Darmanin replied to a writer's inquiry. "Man, it isn't easy!" The last straw was a bite on his hand from one of her dogs. With that, Peter Darmanin sped off to the peace and quiet of Malta, where he had a kindly widowed mother and a modest business, and there he nursed his various wounds.

There was no precedent in Elizabeth Taylor's life for this kind of capricious and unruly conduct; indeed, her actions indicated the first signs of frank alcoholism. Like very many alcoholics, she would, over the next several years, somehow pull herself together for the press, for an interview or for a social gathering. But more and more often, there were all the signs of decay, and her children and her old friends grew anxious. She could, for example, be unac- countably rude and indiscreet: What was the lovely pendant adorn- ing her neck? asked a dinner guest seated next to her at the home of George Cukor one evening. "That's the Taj Mahal diamond, you dumb shit!" she replied with a tight smile. Elizabeth was fortunate that her candor was sometimes taken for wit.

And so it went: when Darmanin exited in February, she flew alone to New York, exchanged insults and accusations with Richard backstage at the Plymouth Theater and in his suite at the Lombardy Hotel, and stormed off to California, right into the arms of Henry Wynberg. She had never seemed so furious with herself; the resem- blance of Elizabeth and Richard to Martha and George (with Wyn- berg as the willing Nick) was by now too perfect.

Wynberg ran interference with the press on her forty-fourth birthday that February 27, explaining that she was too tired to emerge from her suite at the Beverly Hills Hotel. Instead, he hosted a private dinner at his rented house at 400 Trousdale Place, Beverly Hills.

"My life is a little complicated," Elizabeth said sadly to journal- ist Gwen Davis.

"Oh, come now, Elizabeth," Davis replied, adopting precisely the mentorial tone Taylor could not sustain. "Anyone can find peace, but not many have it in them to carry off a really rip-snorting drama!"

"Well, wa-a-*hooo*!!!" cried Elizabeth, coming to life.

That season, as it happened, was her last fling with Henry Wynberg—and none too soon, as she must have thought when she heard the news a year later. Wynberg, still on probation from the odometer fraud case, had been arrested on serious moral charges that appeared in all the Los Angeles newspapers and some beyond the county borders:

Actress Elizabeth Taylor's ex-boyfriend, Henry C. Wynberg, was scheduled to be arraigned today in Beverly Hills Municipal Court on ten counts of misdemeanor . . . of contributing to the delinquency of four teenaged girls [by] allegedly providing drugs and alcohol, engaging in sexual acts with them and taking lewd pictures of them.

Later that year, after admitting sexual misconduct with one sixteen-year-old, he was sent to the county jail for ninety days, fined $1,250 and ordered to a five-year probation thereafter (the longest period allowed by California law). With that, he lost his place in the sun of Elizabeth's life.

By that time, her life had altered dramatically. In Washington, D.C., that spring of 1976, she was invited to attend a series of fundraising benefits, cultural events and Bicentennial receptions. There she was, the reigning queen of America's celebrity royals, the slightly dumpy, slightly outrageous "Liz," photographed on dance floors with senators (Edward Brooke, for one), dancers (among them, Mikhail Baryshnikov), designers (Halston) and diplomats—notably, Iranian Ambassador Ardeshir Zahedi. With Elizabeth in the capital, Secretary of State Henry Kissinger was, for once, outshone at the best social events.

One of the reasons for her several visits to Washington was

the world premiere of *The Blue Bird,* to which she was escorted that June by none other than Ambassador Zahedi. Two days before, he hosted a luncheon for her, and that evening escorted her to a dinner party. The day after the screening, he drove her out to a horse race in Maryland; next evening, they were at a sleek new nightclub. Zahedi—forty-eight, dark-eyed and intense—was known in the capital as a skillful diplomat and an indefatigable partygoer. "I just laugh at stories we are in love," he said, which did not exactly deny rumors buzzing round Washington and soon filling the nation's gossip columns. How serious the Taylor-Zahedi relationship became is difficult to say, but after they were seen holding hands and kissing in public, the despotic Shah sent clear warnings to the ambassador's town house. This was not the image to be conveyed to America by a diplomat once married to the Shah's daughter.

To staunch the hearsay—and, some said, to show Elizabeth Taylor's innocent friendliness to Iran in that era before revolution and terrorism—she headed the guest list of 150 people who jetted off to Teheran, thus glamorously inaugurating nonstop US-Iran air service. Attended by the ambassador's cousin, Firouz Zahedi, she was installed at the Teheran Hilton, visited a mosque, lunched with American Ambassador Richard Helms, and dined at the Zahedi palace, where she washed down generous portions of caviar with Burtonesque gulps of vodka.

By midsummer, some reporters observed that despite Elizabeth's strenuous socializing and late-night dancing, she seemed heavier than ever. The truth was, as she later admitted, that in private she had turned to food and drink for comfort. And if late-night snacking and tippling did not induce sleep, it was easy to find doctors to prescribe sedatives and hypnotics. What physician, anywhere, would refuse to make Elizabeth Taylor happy?

Also that summer, two decisive events occurred.

On July 29, less than ten months after their second marriage, Richard Burton and Elizabeth Taylor's attorney delivered their signatures to a judge in Port-au-Prince who forthwith granted them a divorce. "I love Richard Burton with every fiber of my soul," Elizabeth said. "But we can't be together. We're too mutually self-destructive."

They did not wish to be that for others, however, and although Elizabeth got almost everything the Burtons had owned in common, a complicated and generous trust fund was devised for their children, none of whom was surprised at the dissolution of the marriage. Maria, fifteen, was at the International School in Geneva; Kate, eighteen, was at Brown University; Liza, nineteen, was studying sculpture in London; Christopher, twenty-one, attended the University of Hawaii; and Michael, twenty-three, played saxophone and flute with a rock band in London and Wales. Jessica, consigned to a Pennsylvania institution, would also be comfortably supported, despite the darkness of immutable mental illness.

Thus ended, with payment of a seven-dollar fee and the ceremonial bang of a gavel, the bond between the most celebrated married couple since King Edward VIII left the British throne for the American divorcée Wallis Simpson. A few weeks later, Richard married Suzy Hunt.

But Elizabeth was largely distracted from the publicity surrounding all this, for there was a glamorous new man in her life who eclipsed all thoughts of spirited Welshmen and exotic Iranians.

She had been invited by the British Embassy to a Washington reception honoring the Queen of England, President Ford and America's two-hundredth birthday. "But I can't walk in by myself," she replied. "I really feel terribly sort of shy." Well, then, an escort would be found: of course, he would have to be a respectably single and singularly respectable gentleman. Who better than the chairman of the Bicentennial Administration himself, John Warner? The name rang no bell with Elizabeth. Needing a quick take on her blind date, she telephoned Zahedi, who reminded her that she had met Warner at least twice, once at the Iranian Embassy and once at a Georgetown dinner party. Oh, yes . . .

John William Warner, Jr.—six feet tall, with a distinguished touch of gray hair and a patrician face and form—was by this time strictly Main Line, Hunt Country, Virginia Republican. Born February 18,

1927, to a prominent but not immensely wealthy family (his father was a doctor), John had served in the navy during the last two years of World War II and later with the marines in Korea. In 1956, he took a law degree from the University of Virginia, and the following year won a position as an assistant U.S. attorney in Washington.

Also in 1957, after cross-referencing the characteristics and assets of the most eligible debutantes in the *Social Register*, he courted and married Catherine Mellon, of the legendary, philanthropic Pittsburgh family. Her father's wealth was conservatively estimated at $1 billion. The Mellons were ardent Nixonian Republicans, and it was believed that their influence was critical in obtaining for Warner his positions as Secretary of the Navy (1972) and director of the American Revolution Bicentennial Administration (1976); indeed, cynics dubbed him "John Warnermellon."

The marriage was troubled. "My first marriage broke up over politics," he said. "When I was Secretary of the Navy, my wife had to be involved in all kinds of political functions, but she was very shy and couldn't stand it. We disagreed on Vietnam. I was in the administration and thought we had to finish something we had started. My wife was almost a student radical." Not quite: she was simply unafraid to think for herself. According to Catherine (a sensible, unpretentious woman), John's insistence on getting into "the horse business" as a prop in the setting of social-political ambition "seemed a little too much like what people would expect." She told him, "If you're going to run for the Senate, don't expect me to give those teas," and he replied, "All you have to do is sit there while I'm on television and look pretty." The couple divorced in 1973.

Restored to single life, Warner was a desirable escort and appreciated by socially prominent women. "You are such a terrific woman," he told one of them, news anchor Barbara Walters—and added, "You could make me a Senator!" Walters passed up the chance, thus leaving that achievement for another.

By the time he met Elizabeth, Warner was living in considerable luxury at Atoka Farms, his 2,000-acre estate in Middleburg, Virginia, and in a comfortable Georgetown house: he had, it was said, a divorce settlement that gave him assets in the neighborhood of

$7,500,000, which is not a bad neighborhood. Acknowledging his ownership of more than 3,000 acres of farmland in several Virginia counties, with a heated swimming pool in the modernized barn at Middleburg, Warner said with exquisite understatement that he was only a simple farmer. But his British tweeds, his pipe, his livestock, his paddocks and memberships in the right clubs indicated that he was no rustic bumpkin. One of the most attractive and active bachelors on the Washington social scene, he was thus described by a friend: "John should have been born an Englishman—no, he *became* one."

But some Britons might not have appreciated the allusion, for although Warner was admired for his polished cordiality and political skills, he was considered by some to be a trifle dull. "He is not intellectually demanding, he is just—pale," said one colleague. Another, who liked him, praised him with a faint damn: "He made a serious effort to keep in touch with naval developments. I have never heard him say anything earth-shaking—but that is not required. Very few senators will use their time to learn something." *Touché.*

Alas, Warner's public statements sometimes reinforced the impression that he suffered an incredible lightness of knowing.

On his recent career: "Being head of the US Navy is without parallel. It has everything all the others have. Even part of the space program. War is a terrible thing, of course. I went several times to Vietnam. It was like it was in M*A*S*H, without the humor. But life was so full in those days!" Fuller for some than others.

On his family: "My children suffered from their father's public involvement with the war in Vietnam"—in which he ardently supported Nixon—"so the Bicentennial was a counterpart." *Sic.*

On education: "Not everyone wants or needs a four-year college education. Some of us are at our best working in the fields or forest under God's great sky." This assertion he then backed up with a strange logic—by voting to cut government loans for college students, thus enabling many of them to enjoy such refreshing outdoor activities as he had recommended.

* * *

Very soon after the royal reception in July, John and Elizabeth became the hot new Washington couple, dining and dancing, turning up after midnight at a Manhattan discotheque, bumping and hustling on the dance floor to the delight of the press and those celebrity-watchers who feared that Zahedi and friends were not the best company.

Her attraction to Warner is not difficult to understand. At forty-four, she was no longer receiving interesting movie offers, and she had no need to work in any case. And so the pattern of past relationships resurfaced—the sine curve according to which she alternated styles and men. After the turbulent Richard Burton era, which almost destroyed her, she was now no longer sustained or enchanted by the gypsy life of mere jetting and spending—she longed, in other words, for smoother air and calmer days.

Elizabeth visited John Warner's estate that July, fed carrots to his stallions, rode around his farmlands, dined at his town house—and spent hours with his children (ages eighteen, seventeen and fourteen), frying them hamburgers, listening to them, riding on motorcycles with them. She felt renewed, her innocence restored. "This reminds me of my childhood home in England," Elizabeth told John on her first visit to his farm. More to the point, it was as if Elizabeth had been given back her best and most beloved maidenly role: she was Velvet Brown again, a gentle country girl, right there among the local gentry in the misty blue hills of Virginia.

There was only one protracted separation that summer, when Elizabeth had to fulfill a contractual obligation to appear in the movie version of Stephen Sondheim's musical *A Little Night Music*, to go before the camera in Vienna that summer and early autumn. Her costars were mostly stage actors, insecure about film technique. "She knows what she's up to," said the veteran English actress Hermione Gingold, who gave no quarter, was awed by neither human nor animal and, to her surprise, liked Elizabeth enormously. "She knows about the lighting, what she should do, when she's in shadow. Elizabeth was a dream to work with, really. Of course, she's a naughty girl, late and all. But she was divine to work with." So said the others, who found the star undemanding, untemperamental and entirely one of them.

"I was petrified," Elizabeth said of her singing, especially the show's signature tune, "Send In the Clowns."

"Every great singer has done it—and now, here comes Chunko. I decided to sing-act rather than sing-speak." Her frank self-critique was refreshing; the film was not. *A Little Night Music* may well have clinched her desire for an unofficial retirement, for this brilliant and prize-winning Broadway show somehow became a distended and deeply uncharming picture. Cast as Desirée Armfeldt, an actress bored with her late Victorian life who at last settles down with a former beau, Elizabeth gamely but drily recorded a number of songs and then squeezed into a form-fitting, alarmingly unbecoming wardrobe. In the finished picture, she seems comically forlorn, too much like Miss Piggy longing for Kermit—which was, in fact, rather close to real life, for Elizabeth yearned to get back to John Warner. Otherwise, as she told several friends, there was no real place she could call home.

She did not have to yearn for long. On October 1, Warner resigned his Bicentennial directorship, and a few days later he flew to Vienna and formally proposed to Elizabeth. Their engagement was announced on Sunday, October 11. At the same time, Warner said that yes, he would consider running for the governorship or a Senate seat. "John knows what he's going to do and I want to be by his side," said Elizabeth. "I want to make my contribution to Washington."

Back in Virginia just before the presidential election of 1976, John and Elizabeth sped to a stock-car race, where they were cheered by a crowd of 35,000. With Elizabeth at his side making her unofficial political debut, he made a short speech on behalf of Gerald Ford's candidacy and introduced Miss Taylor as his fiancée: "I lean a little to the right and Elizabeth leans a little to the left, and we both consider ourselves progressive-thinking people." Never mind that she was not an American citizen and therefore could not vote: John said he wanted to make Elizabeth "a citizen of our state," a remark that evoked the response, "Virginia needs Liz!" Years later, she wrote that this was when she became "fully aware that he had political ambitions." For the present, she was happy to try on this new role—even though she had attended an important fund-raiser for Jimmy Carter and was rightly considered to be anything but a conservative on issues social, political and moral—nor a party person, as she said. "I've never voted. There are so few honest men in politics."

To Warner's evident delight, Elizabeth also brought out the crowds on November 11, when he spoke at the Virginia Military Institute's Founder's Day and she answered drama students' questions at a seminar in the campus theater of Washington and Lee University. She proudly showed her engagement ring, a blinding thing in red, white and blue, fashioned from rubies, diamonds and sapphires. When asked if he could support Elizabeth in the style to which she was accustomed, Warner said that frankly he was not sure: "But if I can't," he added with a smile, "perhaps she will support me."

During the next three years, Elizabeth met several times with drama and film students in Richmond or Charlottesville, answering questions and speaking without affectation about herself and her career. "I've never had an acting lesson in my life," she told them, adding with a wink "which may be clear to some of you." Did she miss the glamorous life? "No, I don't want to go out much anymore. I want to stay home and feed the chickens and watch the cows. Does that mean I've been put out to pasture? Let's just say I'm not as active now." By all accounts, she was sincere—but a dangerous illusion could often be heard that year, too: "I've always loved the basic, simple life." Could listeners refrain from smiling? Only because she seemed so desperately to mean it.

Her work was indeed drastically curtailed, although that November she flew to Los Angeles, where she picked up several hundred thousand dollars for a few minutes' work in *Victory at Entebbe*, a television movie. She also approved the advertising copy that would allow her name to be used for the first time in a commercial venture outside the entertainment world. Harry Shuster, founder of the Lion Country Safari, an animal park south of Los Angeles, had made a deal with her attorney in early 1976 to form the Florida-based Elizabeth Taylor Diamond Corporation, which would market gems for under $200 to $3,000 and give her a substantial portion of the profits. She had nothing to lose—and, as it happened, nothing to gain. In early 1978, Elizabeth filed a lawsuit against Shuster, seeking $1.43 million in compensation and $10 million punitive damages. He had guaranteed her a $250,000 commission for the first year and at least $200,000 twice annually for the use of her name and photograph to advertise the jewelry. She had received not a penny.

At sunset on Saturday, December 4, 1976, Elizabeth and John were married on a hilltop at Atoka Farms; only employees and a few friends attended the fifteen-minute Episcopalian ceremony. Two days later, they departed for Jerusalem, where she was honored at a hospital fund-raising dinner, and he planted a bicentennial tree. From there, she took her husband to London to meet friends and to collect her children for a snowy Christmas in Gstaad. Virginia Republicans, meantime, were drawing up a short list of names to succeed Senator William Scott, who had just announced that he would not seek another term in the next election.

Back in Virginia early in 1977, there was little for Elizabeth to do but what was expected of her: John set out to test the political waters and to gather support for his Senate candidacy, and Elizabeth was at his side, converting conservative Virginia Baptists who raised their eyebrows over a much-married movie star as the wife of a senator. The initial antipathy was in fact made concrete by the bluebloods: the 1978 *Social Register* no longer included John Warner's name, for its advisory committee looked coolly on both actors and divorce—although Catherine Mellon Warner's name was important enough to keep her on the list despite her remarriage.

"I feel at last I've come home to nest" was a refrain she repeated over the next year: "I've never felt so much at home, and I just know my long search for roots is over." But the nest, unfortunately, would soon seem cramped and uncongenial, and the roots would again have to be torn out.

From the start, there were small but ominous abrasions.

ELIZABETH: "We've made a deal to go everywhere together. He
can make me do whatever he wants—except make me pregnant. I don't have the tubes."
JOHN: "We're going to find a way around that problem, too."
E: "You don't own me like your cattle."
J: "Oh, yes I do! I'm a Virginia farmer to the hilt—you're my
property!"

There were also statements by John, repeated astonishingly
often, that must have been uncongenial, no matter how much she
thought she wished to be dominated: "I would never have married
Elizabeth," he said, "if she hadn't been willing to fit into my life. All
those days of big jewelry and that stuff are over. It's not my bag."
He also called her his "little heifer," and referred to her as his "little
woman," for all wives, after all, were "the little women."

Little by little, the new role failed to attract the emergence of a
new self at all, and Elizabeth's drinking, so often desperate and
angry with Burton, was now a means of avoiding the sad realization
that she was indeed swiftly becoming chattel, the "property," as he
had said, of a benevolent but presumptuous politician. "She likes to
have a little nip of Jack Daniel's," he said nervously as bystanders
stared at the pewter whiskey flask she took from her purse.

The deal to go everywhere together was honored in February, when
the Warners flew to Los Angeles. Elizabeth had been offered over
$200,000 for an unbilled cameo in a political thriller called *Winter
Kills*, in which she was to appear as Lola, a hard-boiled madam who
tries to blackmail her top client, the president of the United States.
She was on-screen less than half a minute for a role that was word-
less—to the final shot, in which she silently mouthed the words
"Son of a bitch!" The object of her wrath, the president, was
unseen, except for his right arm—it was none other than John
Warner's. As in *Victory at Entebbe*, Elizabeth did not so much perform as appear—and, audiences and critics noted, she appeared
larger than ever. "I enjoy eating and I love to cook," she said defensively. "Eating is one of the great pleasures of life—but I can hardly

get into my clothes." And later, as she sipped whiskey and spoke to a reporter at home: "For the first time, I'm not worrying about growing older or even being able to get into any of my clothes, because I'm eating too much. I'm so happy and contented"— which, of course, she was not.

Throughout 1977, she forced herself with admirable energy into the completely new and untried role of the candidate's wife, which meant kissing babies; shaking hands; enduring rude questions from strangers about her life and career when the attention was to be focused on her husband; gazing admiringly up at him as he spoke; riding from town to town in a Greyhound Bus (for the first time in her life); munching corn on the cob and fried chicken at rally after rally; signing autographs; laughing at unfunny jokes; dancing with students at junior political fund-raisers; patiently sustaining surprising comments:

"My husband even put on clean shorts for you!" said one housewife.

"How nice," replied Elizabeth.

"Gee, you're large—but you're lovely!" cried a workman.

"I'll look a lot lovelier when you have elected John, and I don't have to get crushed to death campaigning!"

By year's end, her equanimity was sorely tried: "If I have to make one more campaign speech or kiss one more baby, I'll go mad!"

She did not lose her sanity, but her fundamental instinct to survive was severely tested in June 1978. At the GOP convention in Richmond, Warner lost his party's vote to run for the Senate: that victory went to Richard Obenshain, once the state's party leader and a national committeeman. (A few ungentlemanly Virginians cast floor votes for Eddie Fisher and Richard Burton.) "We're not quitting," said Elizabeth. "I don't know what [political] office it will be, but I'm sure something will come up."

This statement she made in Los Angeles, where she appeared in her first taped, starring role in a television drama, *Return Engagement.* Improbably cast as a college ancient history professor who falls chastely in love with a troubled student, Elizabeth was clearly

With Paul Newman, in *Cat on a Hot Tin Roof*: 1958. (Culver Pictures)

With Francis and
Sara Taylor, at Eddie
Fisher's Las Vegas
engagement: April
1959. (Courtesy of
the Academy of
Motion Picture Arts
and Sciences)

Mr. and Mrs. Eddie
Fisher: 1959.
(Movie Star News)

OPPOSITE: Eddie
Fisher accompanies
Elizabeth and sons to
Disneyland: January
1959. (Courtesy of
the Academy of
Motion Picture Arts
and Sciences)

In Spain, filming
Suddenly, Last Summer: 1959.
(Movie Star News)

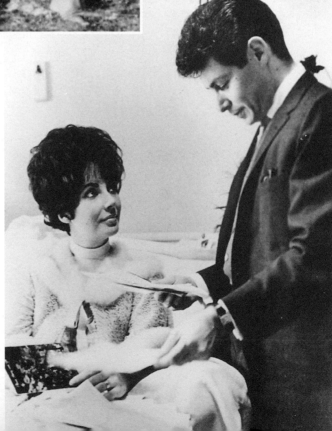

Daniel Mann directs the Fishers in
Butterfield 8, her first Oscar-winning
role: 1960. (Courtesy of the Academy
of Motion Picture Arts and Sciences)

OPPOSITE: At the London Clinic,
recovering from pneumonia: March
1961. (Associated Press/Courtesy of
the Academy of Motion Picture Arts
and Sciences)

With Richard Burton in Rome: 1962.
(Courtesy of the Academy of Motion
Picture Arts and Sciences)

With Burton, leaving a bar in Puerto
Vallarta in 1963, the day after his wife
was granted a divorce. (Courtesy of the
Academy of Motion Picture Arts and
Sciences)

During the filming of *Cleopatra*: 1962. (Movie Star News)

In New York, backstage after giving
a poetry reading with Burton: 1964.
(Movie Star News)

The Burton entourage, heading for a beach scene for *The Sandpiper*: 1964.
(Courtesy of the Academy of Motion Picture Arts and Sciences)

July 1965: Elizabeth before makeup and padding, during a rehearsal for *Who's Afraid of Virginia Woolf?*, with director Mike Nichols, Burton, costar George Segal and writer-producer Ernest Lehman. (From the collection of Ernest Lehman)

. . . And next day (July 1965), during a break in filming, with Nichols, visitor Andre Previn, Burton and Lehman. (From the collection of Ernest Lehman)

The final scene of her second Oscar-winning role, as Martha in *Who's Afraid of Virginia Woolf?*: 1965. (Culver Pictures)

In Sardinia with Burton, filming *Boom!*: 1967. (Movie Star News)

Wearing her sixty-nine-carat diamond with
a double strand of additional diamonds: 1969.
(UPI/Courtesy of the Academy of Motion
Picture Arts and Sciences)

Arriving in London after the birth of her first
grandchild, Leyla Wilding: 1971.
(UPI/Courtesy of the Academy of Motion
Picture Arts and Sciences)

The Burtons with Princess Grace, at a Monaco charity gala: 1971. (UPI/Courtesy of the Academy of Motion Picture Arts and Sciences)

Awaiting a call to the set of *Ash Wednesday*: 1973. (Courtesy of the Academy of Motion Picture Arts and Sciences)

With Henry Wynberg, during a break in filming *The Blue Bird*: 1975. (Brenard Press/Courtesy of the Academy of Motion Picture Arts and Sciences)

During production of the teleplay *Return Engagement*: 1978. (Courtesy of the Academy of Motion Picture Arts and Sciences)

Senator and Mrs. John Warner: 1979.
(Movie Star News)

With nightclub owner Steven Rubell:
1979. (Ron Galella)

Mr. and Mrs. Larry Fortensky: 1994. (Book City, Los Angeles)

unhappy. "This face has been around a lot of years," she told a reporter. "People are looking for wrinkles and pimples, and I don't disappoint them. They want to see if my eyes are really violet or bloodshot or both. Once they check me out, they can go home and say, 'I saw Liz Taylor and you know what? She ain't so hot!' And you know what? They're right. She ain't."

Elizabeth had seen the first cut of the show, in which she and her costar, Joseph Bottoms, had to do a vaudeville soft-shoe in a school pageant, and she saw how awkwardly overweight she looked. In the months following, Elizabeth sounded more and more disconsolate about her appearance, which camouflaged only a stymied life. Nor was she comforted by what was really an enormously appealing performance, shaded with tenderness and frustration. She could neither dance nor sing when that was called for, but subtle emotions flickered over her features; in fact, her heft gave the role of a lonely teacher a certain poignancy and credibility that a slim, elegant actress would not have earned.

In July, she rejoined Warner in Virginia, where his political career seemed drowned in the tide of his opponent's party victory. But on August 2, Richard Obenshain was killed in the crash of a light airplane, and eleven days later John Warner inherited the nomination. He had wooed convention delegates with a half-million-dollar primary campaign, he had been a graceful loser, and he had worked for Obenshain during the summer. Now he had three months to convince voters of both parties that he would be the right senator for Virginia.

In this effort, he spent $1.2 million in three months, but even more important was Elizabeth's presence. She traveled tirelessly, smiled, signed autographs, was endlessly charming—and never seemed to be anything but the blissfully happy farmer's wife. She kept to a killer schedule, keeping eight and ten appointments daily and everywhere disguising her discomfiture before the public. Answering questions before over a hundred members of the Washington Press Club in October, she was as adroit at deflecting political questions as she was in offering a critique of contemporary movies: "I'm getting kind of sick of sequels and disaster films. If I see one more *Airport*, I'll scream. Why go to be entertained by someone else's disaster? I want to be entertained!" Many agreed, then and later. With such candor, lack of pretense and her down-home, matronly support of her husband, she appealed to many rural (and more than a few urban) voters.

On November 7, 1978, the people of Virginia elected John Warner to the United States Senate, although he won by less than one percent, the slimmest margin anyone could remember, a mere 4,271 votes, out of 1.2 million cast. Elizabeth smiled but had nothing to say: two weeks earlier, nervous and tipsy, she had choked on a chicken bone at a political buffet and was confined to a hospital. On election night, warned not to strain her voice, she had just been released. "I'm just so thrilled because I know you did the right thing," she whispered into a microphone of the ballroom of the Jefferson Hotel in Richmond. "It is so marvelous for all of us."

Her eyes glistened with tears, and the room went wild. It was one of her finest performances, for she had, she said later, never been unhappier in her life.

Chapter Thirteen

1979-1983

*S*HE HAD PERHAPS SENSED THAT
things were not going to have a happy ending when a delegation
from the Republican Party advised that her clothes were inappropriate—well, not the entire wardrobe exactly, but the color purple.
Various shades of violet and lavender had been her favorite colors
since childhood, Elizabeth said. That was too bad, replied the ladies
and gentlemen: purple denotes passion, and sometimes people
associate it with royalty—and neither of these was an impression
the Party wished to convey. She would have to modify her wardrobe,
at least at political events. And so she put aside her own tastes and
chose acceptable Republican garb. Only later did she realize that
this was a crucial moment: "I was losing my own sense of self."

The loss had a single, clear explanation: since the age of nine
she had a purpose, a function—and she was the center of very
many people's attention. Even during the campaign, Elizabeth had a
role to play—the international celebrity in support of a handsome
politician, the movie star bringing her fame to bear in causes her
husband endorsed. But the day after John Warner was sworn in as a

Virginia senator that cold January day in 1979, she had no job, no movie or television show to anticipate, no people with whom to discuss what she would do or who she might become. Not yet fifty years long, her life ground to a halt, and because she had never been encouraged to develop any inner resources, anything that might be called in the broadest sense an intellectual, esthetic or spiritual life, Elizabeth Taylor found herself in a condition of stasis, empty, forlorn and desolate. She was, in other words, a fabulously wealthy woman in the throes of a profound and desperate poverty.

As she later wrote in her book *Elizabeth Takes Off*, she never felt so lonely as in those early months of 1979: she was isolated and imprisoned, as if in "a domestic Siberia" as her husband devoted his entire life to his tasks as a senator. From breakfast to dinner she did not see John—and often enough, because he was away lecturing or presiding at civic and political events, she did not until late at night. By that time, she had dined alone and, more and more frequently, she had fallen asleep with the help of sleeping pills (which she admitted she had been taking for years). When he was at home in the evening, he retired to his office to work and sent her, like a child, to watch television—a telling indication of his benign contempt for her capacities.

"The principal role in Elizabeth's life has always been as the wife of the man she's married to," said Joseph L. Mankiewicz. "Whatever the script called for, she played it. Therein derives her identity." But since her husband saw her as little other than a pretty adjunct to his career ("You are a wonderful woman—you can make me a senator!"), Elizabeth in fact had no identity. And Washington was no help. With no personal history on which to rely as Warner sprang to his new political prominence, Elizabeth was cast adrift.

In some way even then she knew what later became resoundingly clear: a surfeit of food and drink and pills was the path to oblivion. As she felt unnecessary to anyone and anything, Elizabeth lost all sense of her possibilities, and as she lost hope of the future, so she abandoned all concern for the present. Invariably, this led to a neglect of her health: redundancy, the overwhelming sense of blankness and senselessness of life led in fact to subtle forms of slow self-destruction. It was suicide on the installment plan, and deposits were made between meals, at dinner and before bedtime. Often enough, in 1979 and 1980, she replied to questions or comments about herself with the snappish remark that she was content, so what the hell; her anger revealed how far she was from contentment. There were more frequent accidents, too, as she stumbled about, too often tipsily, in search of purpose: in the first six months of 1979, for example, she fell and broke a finger, then fell and broke a rib, then fell and sustained hip bruises—the cycle was dreary and slightly sordid.

"I was the loneliest person in the world. I didn't have a friend. I rarely saw my husband. My children were grown and had their own lives . . . I began drinking out of loneliness." And, perhaps as well, out of a desire for obscurity: she would not be offered roles to play, she would be left alone, confirmed in her belief that she was a nonentity and committed to oblivion.

Thus the more disconsolate and unhealthy she became, the more her husband rode the crest of his own popularity. Her jewelry was more cumbersome than ever, her rings—signs of a former life that now may have looked marvelous—no longer fit, and she had no reason to wear them; no one was surprised, therefore, when she put up for sale her 69.42-carat Cartier diamond, a gift from Richard. A dealer named Henry Lambert bought it for $3 million, thrice what Burton had paid. "It was large and very heavy," she said. "Anyway, I hadn't worn it for ages. It represented a different phase in my life, the fun and camp phase."

In June, however, the old spirit and resilience emerged for a time, just as it had after Mike Todd's death, when she had suddenly put aside her grief and returned to the set of *Cat on a Hot Tin Roof.* Elizabeth went to a Florida spa and lost twenty-five pounds; she then checked into a hospital for extensive oral surgery and what later appeared to be a new set of teeth: virtually her entire mouth seemed to have been recreated by 1986.

Her first opportunity to reveal a temporarily restored and renewed image was hardly what she might have expected. On July 8,

1979, Michael Wilding died after a fall at his home in Chichester, at the age of sixty-seven. She joined her children in England for the funeral, where Michael's coffin bore a single spray of yellow roses with the legend, "For dearest Michael—love always, Elizabeth." First Todd had gone, and then, in 1969, Nicky Hilton, whose death surprised but did not much affect her. But with Wilding there had been a longer history—and two sons as a legacy. She never forgot his gentleness, nor his unassailable gentlemanliness when she skipped off with Mike Todd.

He had been in wretched health for years, after the deaths of his third and fourth wives, Susan Nell and Margaret Leighton. His epilepsy was never properly controlled; he, too, drank excessively; and a postmortem revealed that he also had a long-standing brain aneurysm that might have killed him years earlier and certainly must have altered his personality.

Of Elizabeth, he had spoken only generously in the years since their divorce. Often asked to comment on the vagaries of her life, he refused to yield to the suggestions of tabloid journalists: she was a fine, honorable woman, he said, and a first-rate mother. So he believed, and in many ways it was an accurate assessment.

"In the old days," he said not long before his death,

> when I was doing well on the stage and in films, I'd have been mobbed if I walked along the pavement. Now, I suppose if they've heard of me at all, it's because I was married to Elizabeth—and not even that is sure. I was in America for the premiere of *Cleopatra*, and a reporter shoved a microphone under my nose and asked me whether I'd ever met Elizabeth Taylor. So much for the brilliant career of Michael Wilding.

Back home, she felt more lost than ever. "Washington is a very difficult place for a woman to live," Elizabeth said later. "I think there are more unhappy wives in that city than anyplace in the world. Why? You have to live through your men, and they don't pay too much attention. You help them get elected, and then the Senate becomes the wife, the mistress. That was one lady I couldn't begin to fight. She was too tough." But Elizabeth could be tough, too: Speaking of Hollywood in 1992, she said, "This town and Washington, D.C., are the biggest bullshit towns in the world! They both have picket fences surrounding them, and they live and feed off people."

At the same time, Elizabeth's temporary weight loss was soon reversed, and by early 1980 she weighed over 180 pounds. For the first time in her life, she was an object of ridicule. A particularly unflattering photograph of her appeared on the cover of *Hollywood Babylon*, an account of movie-lore scandals. And the humorist Joan Rivers had an ongoing series of Elizabeth Taylor one-liners:

- "Elizabeth Taylor wore yellow and ten schoolchildren got aboard her."
- "I took her to McDonald's just to watch her eat and see the numbers change."
- "Elizabeth Taylor went to Sea World and saw Shamu [the killer whale] and asked, 'Does he come with fries?'"
- "She has more chins than a Chinese phone book."
- "Elizabeth loves to eat so much that she stands in front of her microwave and yells, 'Hurry!'"

To ease the pain, she took Jack Daniel's, sleeping pills and painkillers—bogus remedies she often relied on for relaxation, or to overcome her normal shyness in public. At a Republican party conference in Easton, Maryland, in early 1980, she sparred publicly with her husband when the chairman invited spouses to participate in discussions. Warner urged that the military draft be reinstated, but only for men: "Congress, in my opinion, would never let women into combat, so why register them?"

Elizabeth was quick to reply. "I think women are willing to go into combat."

"I'm sorry," said Warner, raising his hand to silence her, "but on this issue you don't have a vote."

With that, Elizabeth's voice rose. "Don't you steady me with that all-domineering hand of yours." There was a momentary hush in the room.

Well, said Warner, trying to defuse the moment, even Abraham Lincoln, the Great Emancipator, would agree with him on that issue.

"Abe Lincoln?" cried Elizabeth. "How many years do you want to go back?"

Warner shifted the focus to himself. "I'm proud to say that when I was Secretary of the Navy, I opened up many more jobs to women than they ever held before!"

"Rosie the Riveter jobs," muttered Elizabeth acidly, leaning into her microphone.

Congressman William Dannemeyer of California tried to calm the waters, saying that he thought the issue of draft registration ought not to be confused with the problem of "alleged discrimination" against women.

"Alleged discrimination?" cried Elizabeth. "Did you say 'alleged discrimination'?"

Later, in an interview with a magazine reporter, she was asked how devout a Republican she was. "I am not a Republican," Elizabeth answered truthfully, since her lack of citizenship precluded party registration.

"Oh, my God, you are, too, a Republican," interrupted Warner. "Now you may have blown the whole thing!"

"I'll become a Republican," she said with her best movie star smile, "when you come out for the E.R.A.!" John Huston, speaking in another context, was right: "Elizabeth is really stronger than any of the men she has married!"

Warner rushed from the room as if he were suddenly ill.

"I was only teasing him," she told the reporter. "If you print what I said, I'll get my tit caught in a wringer."

Warner returned later, dabbing a slightly bloody chin: while shaving and thinking about an upcoming speech he had to give, he had been distracted and cut himself. "Well," she said, "you ought to think more about your face and cut your speech!" As Warner said later, "We have a very competitive relationship."

By early spring of 1980, the Warners were discussing the possibility of a temporary, friendly separation. That began almost immediately, when she went to Los Angeles to congratulate her son Christopher on his engagement to Aileen Getty, the oil tycoon's granddaughter. She then took the couple for a quick holiday in Puerto Vallarta, then off for shopping in New York, and then to Taiwan, where she helped inaugurate a film festival—anything to avoid life in Georgetown and Middleburg.

An offer to work in England that May provided further escape, and so Elizabeth accepted a role in a brittle comic thriller called *The Mirror Crack'd*, based on one of the Agatha Christie "Miss Marple" mysteries. This would be her fifty-third movie since 1942, and her first speaking part in almost four years. She looked forward to playing the wife of her old friend and *Giant* costar, Rock Hudson; to working again, after all the years since *National Velvet*, with Angela Lansbury; and to trading tart dialogue with Kim Novak, an on-screen rival. As so often in the past, Elizabeth was subtler than the movie. Surrounded by players evidently permitted to go over the top, she kept to an admirable even keel.

Inspired by a tragic incident in the life of Gene Tierney, the story's hook is the trauma endured by a movie star who contracts German measles during pregnancy, gives birth to a severely retarded child, suffers a breakdown and eventually attempts a comeback. But when she is accidentally reunited with the young woman who had accidentally infected her, she poisons her and attempts an elaborate cover-up before she is unmasked and poisons herself.

Elizabeth began working in London and Kent on May 19, just as screenwriters Jonathan Hales and Barry Sandler were putting finishing touches to a script laced with references to the lives of the stars, to old Hollywood—and especially, it seemed, to Taylor herself. "I'm so glad to see you've kept your figure," says Novak, "and added so much to it!" More: Elizabeth is described in the dialogue as a former MGM star of frequently "risqué films"—a two-time Oscar winner who is "under all that jewelry, a sad, insecure lady," often hurt by Hedda Hopper and now under the influence of pills and alcohol. "She'll be happy until she gets bored playing the lady of the manor," sighs one knowing character.

Bored is what she felt after returning home in late June, so she went, rather indifferently, to the Republican convention in Detroit and to read at a D. H. Lawrence Festival in New Mexico. That autumn, she received the first Simon Wiesenthal Humanitarian Award in Beverly Hills—"for converting to Judaism," said Wiesenthal himself, calling that "a courageous decision, for even in the best of times it has never been easy to live as a Jew." Holocaust survivors, so bravely defended by Wiesenthal, may not have appreciated the comparison to a movie star whose life had been one of uninterrupted privilege. Never mind: the award dinner was sold out and netted a tidy fortune toward the important Holocaust Museum in Los Angeles.

Now the laurels were coming in faster than the offers to work, and the movie-life was ending its run. "I couldn't have settled for a life without love—but I could have settled for one without marriage. Now, it has occurred to me that real love, given the number of husbands I have had, might not come again."

Remarks like that fed rumors of her disaffection with John Warner—as did her observation that "politics involves the same hanging around and waiting as filmmaking. I can hang around waiting for my husband to come home from the Senate and never know what time that will be if there is a vote. And if we're giving a dinner party, sometimes he might phone at the last minute to say he's been delayed, and I'll have to host it by myself."

Word of her restlessness finally reached producer Zev Bufman, who brought Elizabeth to New York to discuss her appearing in a Broadway play. He had sat next to her in September at his revival of *Brigadoon* in Washington and said how he would love to put her on the stage. "Why don't you call me?" she asked.

Bufman did not expect her to respond so quickly: yes, she said, she would try something new—but she would do it with something old. And so it was announced, that autumn of 1980, that Elizabeth Taylor would star on tour and then proceed to Broadway in a revival of *Who's Afraid of Virginia Woolf?* with, of all people, Burt Reynolds. This was quickly changed to a revival of Lillian Hellman's *The Little Foxes*—without Reynolds—which had provided such stunning opportunities for Tallulah Bankhead and Bette Davis. Elizabeth was also encouraged by Bufman's offer to pay her more than any stage actor had ever received: more than $50,000 a week.

After a tryout in Fort Lauderdale (where Elizabeth had again gone to drop twenty pounds at a spa), the play opened at the Kennedy Center in March 1981, before an audience including President Reagan, Vice President Bush and half the United States Senate—all guests of John Warner. It was, wrote one critic, "a robust and involving performance that pumps life and suspense into many of the critical passages of the play." As for the redoubtable Lillian Hellman, she dragged on her cigarette and said merely, "I think Elizabeth was good."

Although she was ferried to and from rehearsals and performances in a Rolls-Royce, was everywhere attended by a bodyguard and threw excessively lavish parties for the cast, Elizabeth's colleagues found her diligent, docile and genial. Director Austin Pendleton (who had played in a Mike Nichols revival of the play) praised her appreciation that she was part of an ensemble cast, her lack of movie star attitude, her willingness to benefit from criticism.

No doubt about it, this was a bold and brave step for Elizabeth, who must have known that vultures would be circling. She had played a number of roles written originally for the stage by Tennessee Williams, Edward Albee and even Shakespeare, and she knew how to build character and deliver exacting monologues—but in bits and pieces. She would have to project her voice and find a core to the character, a task that took time during the Fort Lauderdale tryout. Typical of the notices there was the critical review in *Variety:* although she was at first "defensive and uncertain," she acquitted herself more than honorably.

Just as her charming, avaricious and tough-minded Regina Giddens in *The Little Foxes* marked her first step toward a new kind of acting, so it was the first departure from her four-year run as Mrs. John Warner, the indestructible senator's wife. That decision was firm when he announced that he would sell the house in George-town and they would take a large apartment at the Watergate, and that she would have to give up her pets. Now, with endorsements from critics and live audiences, she was unwilling to accept such an arbitrary decision and its implicit condescension.

In this regard, an admirer at the Florida preview referred to her as Mrs. John Warren before apologizing, "I've got you married to the wrong man."

"I've done that myself!" replied Elizabeth with a laugh.

At the same time, just before the production went to New York, Elizabeth found the association between herself and Regina—a woman driven by healthy appetites that become greedy. "I want to give her a new aspect, a new dimension," she said. "She's a woman pushed into a corner. She's a killer, but she's saying, 'Sorry, fellas, you put me in this position.'"

On May 7, *The Little Foxes* opened at the Martin Beck theater in New York and, except for two weeks when she shut down the play with a respiratory infection, Elizabeth performed 123 times, until September 6; every performance sold out, even when word went round about a weakened voice resulting from what producer Buf-man called "the bronchitis that has plagued Elizabeth all her life," and which certainly was exacerbated by chain-smoking.

Occasional lapses or not, she toured two weeks in New Orleans and two in Los Angeles before taking *The Little Foxes* to London. "She kept growing in the role, growing into the ensemble," said Pendleton, adding that she adapted many moments in her perfor-mance to what the new supporting players did, and she modulated her gestures if she had earlier tended to exaggerate.

The critical reaction in New York was divided. *The New York Times*'s weekday critic adored her "charm, grandeur and sex appeal" and her ability to be both "stinging and funny at the same time . . . Her performance may just knock you out of your seat." *The New Yorker* agreed: her performance was "well thought out and skillfully modulated."

But many others agreed with Walter Kerr, writing on Sunday, who was less impressed: she brought no through-line to Regina, he noted, and the character's tone came out like her voice: "random, arbitrary, often entirely inappropriate." Bits and pieces of technique were fine, but "they don't attach themselves to a single intelligible person . . . It's a performance of scattered loose change, when of course what we want is a nice crisp dollar bill." *Newsweek* agreed: her performance was "underdeveloped, [with] a disquieting element of camp." But the critical notices mattered not at all: the run was sold out long before opening night.

Mixed reviews or not, Elizabeth had a new purpose: "I have a sense of accomplishment," she said, "a feeling of doing something useful in my life—and the applause is wonderful." The implication was clear: achievement and endorsement were lacking in life with John Warner, as she clarified later. "My life had no meaning, no responsibility. John was a worthy senator. But his life is his work—it's his wife, his mistress, his family. There didn't seem to be room for anything else."

Los Angeles greeted the return of the prodigal daughter that autumn with a riot of cheers and awards, including the Filmex Award from the local film society. She also managed to work for a day on "General Hospital," her favorite television soap opera, playing a character especially created for her: the rich widow of a mad scientist, whose fortune she magnanimously gives to the General Hospital. Her taping was neatly spliced up to be spread over five days, and in another closing of the gap between life and performance, Elizabeth announced that her $2,000 fee would go to two Virginia hospitals. "What a camp!" said she at the end of the day.

Then came the provocative news in December that she had negotiated to buy the former home of Frank Sinatra's first wife, a remodeled house at 700 Nimes Road in Bel-Air, that wealthy and secluded section of Los Angeles between Beverly Hills and Brentwood. Months later, a small squad of servants settled her in.

Enclosed behind iron gates and outfitted with security cameras, the $2 million home became her sprawling minichateau, its main rooms decorated in antique English furnishings, Aubusson carpets, parquet floors—and white walls, the better to highlight Elizabeth's collection of Renoir, van Gogh, Degas, Monet, Modigliani and several Utrillos. Everywhere was a wild profusion of exotic flowers and plants, always in full bloom. Her two Oscars and a crop of other trophies gleamed brightly, and photographs of Elizabeth with the rich and famous were perched everywhere—images of her presented to the Queen of England, relaxing with Reagan, chatting with Ford, laughing with Tito, welcomed by Zahedi, relaxing at Ascot, reminiscing with Grace (Kelly) of Monaco. Elizabeth's private rooms were arranged on the upper floor; a number of guest rooms, and a library, projection room and quarters for employees were soon furnished. A swimming pool rimmed with glorious potted plants, a sweeping view over the city lights below, and an Aston Martin Lagonda (price of the automobile: $153,000) completed the representation of gleaming opulence.

This purchase prepared for the next announcement, on December 21, 1981—that Mr. and Mrs. John Warner were separating. At Christmas, without Warner, Elizabeth was in Gstaad, going the round of parties with the likes of the Burtons (Richard and Susan), the Edwardses (Blake and Julie Andrews) and the Geros (Mark and Liza Minnelli). She was not alone in pouring herself generous drinks and arising late and groggy next day: it was the holidays, after all. But a few perceptive friends were alarmed by what seemed to be her constant haze of confusion, as if she was moving through life slowly, under water. By the time of her fiftieth birthday party, held in London in February 1982, Elizabeth Taylor was a serious drug addict and a confirmed alcoholic: even her escort, Richard Burton, recently separated from Susan Hunt, was alarmed at her manner and appearance.

"Drugs had become a crutch," she later admitted. "I wouldn't take them just when I was in pain. I needed oblivion, escape . . . I was," Elizabeth explained later, "hooked on Percodan"—a powerful painkiller she had once been given postsurgically. Drowsy, dizzy, in a mild state of euphoria, it also made her ever more susceptible to respiratory infections, which were more and more often reported to the press as the reason for her withdrawal from scheduled events.

I reached a point where I would take one or two Percodan mixed with booze before I could go out in the evening and face people. I thought it would help me, because that combination would make me kind of talkative. I felt I was being charming. I was probably boring as hell, but it gave me false courage. During the course of an evening—like every four hours—I'd take another two Percodan. And of course I had a hollow leg. I could drink anybody under the table and never get drunk [or so she thought]. My capacity to consume was terrifying. I didn't even realize that I was an alcoholic.

Apart from her dependence on Jack Daniel's, she was issued, from 1980 to 1985, more than 1,000 prescriptions for twenty-eight different hypnotics (sleeping pills), anxiolytics (tranquilizers) and narcotics (painkillers) by three California doctors who were later reprimanded by a medical board.

She was, of course, well insulated by her retinue, who issued polite reports to the press about colds and influenza, of sinus infections and respiratory distress, of back ailments and arthritis. And with the help of hairdressers and cosmeticians, of dressers and secretaries, she somehow managed to appear at the most important personal events—such as the wedding of twenty-one-year-old Maria to talent agent Steve Carson that February; in November, they made Elizabeth a third-time grandmother and named the baby for her. In 1984, Liza Todd married fellow artist Hap Tivey and they, too, began a family—as did Christopher Wilding after he married Aileen Getty, and Michael Wilding after his second marriage, to Brooke Palance.

Elizabeth was determined to resume the tour of *The Little Foxes*. When necessary, she could postpone drinking and put aside her pills until the end of the day, and that discipline was called for in March, when the play opened for a brief run in London. The critics were not so kind as in New York or Los Angeles:

- "Elizabeth Taylor sailed into London last night like some stately old galleon, almost submerging the play."

- "She suggests no scheming vixen, more of an apprehensive, cuddling bunny. We are left with a peep show. Most customers, to be brutally frank, are paying their money to gawk at a movie legend in the flesh."
- "She made an entrance worthy of Miss Piggy, trailing mauve lingerie."

Some offered mild commendation:

- "Miss Taylor is enough of an artist to build gradually to a climax in the big scene."
- "She has moments of real power: and if her performance is not good enough for unalloyed adulation, it is certainly not bad enough for crucifixion."
- "Miss Taylor looks in tiptop shape and has a strong line in reptilian Southern charm."

Burton's attendance at the London birthday bash had the gossips going full tilt, especially when Elizabeth and Zev Bufman announced their second production, a stage revival of Noël Coward's *Private Lives,* to tour and then go to New York next year. Perhaps sensing parallels in her own life, perhaps wishing to do a kind of penance-by-sympathetic-magic, Elizabeth had been negotiating to play the aging, faded, hustler-addicted Alexandra del Lago in Tennessee Williams's *Sweet Bird of Youth.* But there was a catch, as she said: there was no role for Richard Burton. Unwisely, they settled on Coward's deft, 1930 drawing room comedy—a play that depends on precisely the grace and subtlety, the milli-second-right timing, the gossamer-thin allusions of which neither Richard nor Elizabeth, ill and insecure, were capable, not to say miscast for. But it seemed a surefire thing: You've seen it in the gossip columns, the production implied—now see them live onstage, battling it out for laughs.

At a madcap press reception at the Beverly Hills Hotel on September 23, the ex-Burtons smiled for the cameras and answered the usual silly questions: How would they work together? Was there any possibility of a remarriage, now that they were both again single? The tone of the proceedings was set just before Richard and Elizabeth stepped to the microphones, when a publicist with the Runyonesque name Charlie Cinnamon called out, "Does anyone have a Valium?" But for once prudence overruled the flacks' wish for a great photo-op, and Cinnamon went back to his clients empty-handed.

But with Burton, things were strictly platonic. The fact is that by autumn 1982 Elizabeth had found a new beau: a wealthy, divorced Mexican lawyer named Victor Gonzalez Luna. They met that October at the memorial service of a mutual friend in Beverly Hills, and for the next months he was her regular escort and constant companion, more and more warmly treated in public by Elizabeth after the announcement of her final divorce decree from John Warner on November 5. That day, she and Luna departed Los Angeles for Puerto Vallarta.

Nothing like the seductive Burton or the jaunty Wynberg, the balding, paunchy Luna was a quiet, paternal gentleman of fifty-five, the father of four daughters and a man who lacked Warner's diffidence or preoccupations. Introduced to the press as Elizabeth's former financial advisor in matters of real estate south of the border, he was a quiet, courtly presence, but he spoke somewhat prematurely. "We're very much in love," he said, adding that a wedding early in 1983 was "very likely—I cannot deny that." This was a bit precipitous, even for the capricious Miss Elizabeth; nevertheless, she accepted a Christmas gift of a diamond-and-ruby ring.

Victor Luna accompanied Elizabeth for a Christmas–New Year holiday to Egypt, Lebanon and Israel, a journey that was suddenly announced to the world not as a vacation, but as one of the strangest (indeed, most outrageous) trips of her life—and one that made her almost a figure of exorbitant satire.

In December, looking dazed and frail, her voice barely above a whisper, she held a press conference at Los Angeles International Airport just before departing, with Luna and their entourage, on what she called a diplomatic mission to the war-torn Middle East. She was, Elizabeth said quietly, going on a ten-day mission, to meet with both Prime Minister Menachem Begin and President Amin Gemayel, "to try to create peace between Israel and Lebanon." Did she have specific things to say to these heads of state? Was there a specific plan to end the hostilities? Oh, yes, she replied, but it would be unwise for her to outline the plan then and there. Victor Luna sat expressionless and silent while Elizabeth fielded questions.

Just as before—when she jetted off to Moscow in 1958 with Mike Todd, saying "I want to have tea with Khrushchev"—so now Elizabeth caused immediate astonishment (not to say some anxiety) in Washington. Anita Stockman, speaking for the State Department, said she was unaware of the trip, that President Reagan was proceeding with his own efforts to remove American troops from Lebanon, and that Miss Taylor was certainly not acting in any official capacity. "We do have our own diplomats," said Miss Stockman, trying to suppress a sarcastic tone. "The President has Ambassador [Philip] Habib going back to the area early next week to continue the talks." Privately, another aide was blunter: "It makes her sound a little nuts. I can't imagine her sitting with Gemayel and talking troop movements, security zones and Lebanese banking."

No one should have been surprised. Marlene Dietrich had bravely entertained the troops during World War II, but she was mightily aware of her image (then eclipsed by a movie career in decline), and so Dietrich assumed a new role, assuring herself a front place in the march down the Champs-Elysées when Paris was liberated. After her stint as a politician's wife (Mrs. Warner) and then as a fiercely driven machinator (Regina Giddens), Elizabeth was once again blurring the distinction between art and life, creating a new role for herself as political strategist—in a way going for the ultimate competition with John Warner. In her, Golda Meir met Joan of Arc.

"I am Mother Courage," said Elizabeth Taylor, doubtless thinking that Brecht's eponymous character was a heroic figure of earthy strength, completely described by her name. But Mother Courage is a stern mercenary, blind in her self-determination, a pathetic and deluded soul whose livelihood depends on militarism and whose own life and those of her children are finally destroyed by her own illusions. Brecht's play postulates that even a simple soul like Mother Courage is partly responsible for war's horror: indeed, she contributes to it by depending on business dealings with the army. She is the worst casualty of all, for she learns nothing from her tragedy.

To be sure, no such stern judgment can be enjoined against Elizabeth Taylor, who in due course would indeed learn a great deal from her mistakes. But at the beginning of 1983, chemicals and alcohol had certainly clouded her reason, and with this trip she very nearly became an international joke (not to say a potential hazard), a woman far less amusing than the merely dumpy Virginia hausfrau of yesterday. A typical day at home began with Bloody Marys for breakfast, wine with lunch, Jack Daniel's at cocktail time, and perhaps a half-dozen glasses of wine with dinner.

She arrived in Israel on December 27. "All it takes," she said at the Tel Aviv Hilton (irony upon irony), "is love and understanding"—a noble sentiment, to be sure, but one that sounded more like a line from the Beatles or Rod McKuen. But did she have herself in mind as the recipient of love and understanding, even as she certainly was a woman of essential goodwill toward men?

Her visit with several hundred wounded Arab and Israeli children at the Hilton that day was nearly catastrophic. First of all, she was almost two hours late, and the actor Mike Borstein—fresh from his job playing P. T. Barnum in a Broadway musical, was asked to entertain the children beyond his repertoire. Elizabeth then swept in for a mere ten minutes—"and her behavior was odd," according to Borstein. Instead of distributing gifts, she simply tossed them in the air, and in a mad scramble for treats, three tiny tots were nearly trampled to death.

Only later was the real purpose of the journey revealed: the trip had been organized by Phil Blazer, the Jewish-American publisher of *Israel Today,* who hoped to challenge the Jerusalem *Post* with a good right-wing, conservative newspaper. Because she diligently supported the Wiesenthal Center, had narrated a documentary on genocide and duly supported Israel's freedom, Elizabeth was mistaken in undertaking what was essentially a commercial enterprise—just as she was surely beguiled by this new role of international diplomat. The journey, in any case, was a fiasco, despite her appearance with Victor Luna at a diplomatic ball in Tel Aviv on New Year's Eve, when she nearly blinded everyone with a few thousand of her favorite carats. Aborting her stay, the Taylor party flew home to America on January 6.

It was no coincidence that next day, on safer terrain, it was announced that, beginning in late January, she would travel to Canada to film a story for American pay television. Elizabeth would play a rich divorcée pursued by a boring vulgarian and saved from marriage to him by long—very long, indeed—dialogues with another divorcée, a bed-hopping friend played by Carol Burnett. "She's the nympho," said Elizabeth at the traditional news conference to announce the project, "and I'm the drunk." They played, indeed, two unsavory and self-absorbed women. Did they need the money? "A job's a job," said Burnett. But does it pay enough? "It'll feed my parrot," replied Elizabeth.

Between Friends was remarkable only for its anatomically explicit vocabulary, its very many scenes of the two actresses drinking excessively, and the implication that in matters of sexual behavior, women can be as nonchalant, unfeeling and exploitive as men. It is also noteworthy for its emphasis on the absolute necessity of a man in a woman's life: "I want to be in love," says Elizabeth, with her usual supple underplaying. "My life is too quiet. I can't stand the silence—and I like a man to be the boss! Some of us just need a man, and I'm one of those." She might have been speaking of herself on a television talk show.

By March 13, she was in New York for *Private Lives* rehearsals, borrowing Rock Hudson's apartment at the Beresford, overlooking Central Park. As Richard jotted in his notebook, rehearsals were a disaster. Elizabeth had neither read the play nor begun to memorize her lines—and she was drinking almost constantly while popping a variety of pills: there were lines of dialogue she could not pronounce properly even when she had the text in her hand. But eventually she managed to get most of the text down, and a wobbly production opened in Boston on April 7, then in New York on May 8, where—under the pretext of occasional bronchitis and laryngitis—Elizabeth missed more than a dozen performances.

Richard took advantage of one such absence to jet to Las Vegas, where he married Sally Hay, a former production assistant for the BBC, twenty-two years younger than the groom. "She can have him," sneered Elizabeth, who was scarcely speaking to Richard outside the theater. For the press, however, she agreed to pose backstage with the newlyweds, although she insisted that Victor Luna stand at her side to give the impression that Elizabeth was not without male attention. Days later, she announced her engagement to Luna at a party featuring flamenco dancers and Mexican musicians. It was "a white-tie-and-taco party," according to the Burtons, who were invited.

If the former Burtons had hoped for a play à clef, drawing audiences to see them trade barbs that could be interpreted as innuendoes about their own years as Liz and Dick, they planned badly. "When Taylor should be light and easy, she's dull and impossibly phony," wrote one critic, "and Burton moves with clumpy hesitation. But no one will care about this, right? They're Taylor and Burton, right?" Right: performances were heavily booked, and the pair made a tidy fortune, moving cross-country from April to November. "This production has all the vitality of Madame Tussaud's exhibit and all the gaiety of a tax audit" was a typical assessment.

On the national tour, there were weeks of dangerous indolence, the trouble coming from a stash of bourbon and an array of comforting tablets and capsules that were always at her side. This combination doubtless accounts for her frequent cancellations of many performances during the tour: a lifetime of professional conduct had been washed out of her by multiple addictions. Victor Luna, evidently powerless, escorted but could not help her. After Elizabeth missed the Chicago premiere, the run of the tour was cut in half.

Finally, the murky issue of Elizabeth Taylor's health reached critical mass. In late November, immediately after the brief Los Angeles run of Private Lives, Elizabeth entered a hospital to learn if abdominal pain indicated spastic colitis. She brought a bottle of bourbon with her, used it to wash down painkillers and was soon virtually incompetent. Finally, there was a classic intervention: her brother, Howard, her old friend Roddy McDowall, Christopher and Michael Wilding and Liza Todd came to her room and, with loving but firm candor, said that they had watched too much of her self-destructive behavior. "I had caused my children such pain," she admitted later. "They worried about me, had to pick me up off the floor when I'd taken sleeping pills on top of booze. How much pain I could see on their faces—and I caused that!"

They left her alone for two hours of solitary thinking, and then Elizabeth allowed them to take her to another, more specialized clinic. Her loved ones drove her south for hours that same night, making their way toward an oasis in the desert. On December 5, Elizabeth Taylor entered the Betty Ford Center in Rancho Mirage, near Palm Springs, California. There she stayed for seven weeks, beginning the long and difficult process of recovery. There, too, she began to confront at last the layers of illusion that enveloped her life. The role of an ordinary, needy patient among ordinary, needy people was one she never could have foreseen. In fact, it was not a role at all.

Chapter Fourteen

1983–1989

*T*HEY ARRIVED LATE THAT MONDAY evening. Her loved ones were not permitted to enter the hospital with her, nor to prolong their farewells: that is precisely the moment when some patients bolt.

A nurse's aide came out to guide her along the path to the eighty-bed Betty Ford Center, and along the corridors, hushed and dark for the night. "She was a bewildered, frightened child," recalled the nurse.

Elizabeth had imagined a place surrounded with barbed wire and iron gates on the windows—an asylum supervised by sadistic nurses. With no clothes except those she wore, no personal effects, no makeup, no books, she was at once led to a plain, twin-bedded room. "It was the first time in my life I shared a room with a woman!" she said later.

But the challenge went much deeper: "I was terrified," she recalled—and four days later, she began to keep a journal of her recovery:

Today is Friday. I've been here since Monday night, one of the strangest and most frightening nights of my life. Not to mention lonely. But I am not alone. There are people here just like me, who are suffering just like me, who hurt inside and out, just like me, people I've learned to love. It's an experience unlike any other I've known. Nobody wants anything from anybody else, except to share and help.

The Center was no snake pit, as she had feared. But the first ten days were perhaps the hardest of her life, as she endured the physical and psychological rigors of detoxification:

I feel like hell. I'm going through withdrawal. My heart feels big and pounding. I can feel the blood rush through my body. I can almost see it, running like red water over the boulders in my pain-filled neck and shoulders, then through my ears and into my pounding head. My eyelids flutter. Oh, God, I am so, so tired.

But there was no time for rest, nor was it allowed. Elizabeth was introduced to the other patients, who must have been astonished next morning to see their famous housemate, arguably the country's enduring example of celebrity. Now she was a shaking patient: "Hello," she had to say, rising to her feet at the Center's group sessions. "My name is Elizabeth, and I'm an alcoholic and a drug addict."

She could not recall a time when she was not famous—nor could millions of others. That factor—celebrity, renown, notoriety—was one of the key issues on which Elizabeth had to meditate during her introduction to what must be called, in the broadest sense of the term, a spiritual life, for the Betty Ford Center is based on the principles of the Alcoholics Anonymous program. A typical day at the Center is full of work in the inner life, for many believe that it is a stasis in the inner life that causes the illness of addiction. A meditation walk, household duties, lectures and group therapy, recreation and study time—these, along with professional help and medical care, are the regime of renewal.*

But it was her fame that she had to think about. "Fame," she said, "and the very nature of acting—it's schizophrenic. You become, in a role, somebody else. You're not yourself, but a character you portray." It had been the story of her life since the age of nine: role after part after illusion, an endless treadmill of finding and losing, of discovery and disillusionment, of rushing here and seeing disappointment there, of finding herself in a role rather than looking for a bit of the role in an established self.

That dilemma is, of course, the occupational hazard of every actor, of all who refine the gift of fancy, who depend on a kind of professional pretense. Many succeed, knowing from the start or finding along the way a core of themselves that is kept secret and in a sense hallowed, untouched by the disguises. Others, more or less like Elizabeth, take years before they learn that their lives have been, as she said, wrapped in illusion that had to be torn away like so many layers of onion skin.

She began, with slow and uncertain first steps, to return from the dead in the new year 1984—much more truly than she did from her pneumonia in 1961. Could it have been that this resurrection was watched by, documented for and reported to an entire culture precisely because so many within that culture were growing old and jaded and finding that something inside was dying—long before they were ill unto death? Did the world watch and wait because, recognizing the signs of inner mortality before the final mortality, people long for and even expect a kind of mysterious mercy?

On January 20, 1984, Elizabeth—exhausted but sober and serene—departed the Center after the initial seven weeks of recovery; during the next year, she would return regularly for a continu-

*Among many celebrities who have resided at the Betty Ford Center: Mary Tyler Moore, Johnny Cash, Tony Curtis, Peter Lawford, Liza Minnelli, Andy Gibb and Don Johnson. In 1983, the fee at the Center was $150 per day, far less than the charge for a luxury hotel room in Palm Springs.

ing program of outpatient therapy. She flew to Los Angeles and then went immediately with Victor Gonzalez Luna—now officially her fiancé—to Guadalajara. Grateful for the emotional security he represented, she at once began to plan trips abroad, to tell her friends the good news of her recovery—which was a bit premature, warned Betty Ford—and to prepare for her springtime wedding. She was, in other words, still Elizabeth Taylor, and she could not imagine life without constant diversion and a man. "I plan to be on vacation for the rest of my life," she said, which suggested that the recovery process would not be completed in a day. Their holiday began with a two-month-long journey to Southeast Asia, China, Japan, India and Switzerland. On her return to Los Angeles, Victor stood shyly in a corner when she worked for a week on the television series *Hotel*, playing an aging actress, a part written especially for her and costarring her friend Roddy McDowall. After a half-dozen rehearsals for a scene in which she was to walk along a corridor escorted by actor Shea Farrell, Elizabeth turned to him: "My God, this looks like we're walking down the aisle together—in which case, I'm very well rehearsed!"

By autumn the romance with Victor Luna had run its course. "Our problem" he told reporters, "was that we came from two different worlds. She wouldn't be happy in the strict, socially enclosed atmosphere of Guadalajara. A six-times-divorced [sic] woman would be a social outcast there. And my life isn't flying and cruising and mixing with the international jet set—the life Elizabeth enjoys."

But there was another, immediate reason why Luna ended the engagement. That August 6, Sally Burton (who had married Richard just a year earlier) telephoned with the news that Richard had died the previous evening after suffering a massive stroke at the age of fifty-eight. "I knew she would be devastated, shattered," said Victor Luna,

> but I didn't expect her to become completely hysterical. I could not get her to stop crying. She was completely out of control. I realized then how deeply tied she was to this man, how vital a

role he had played in her life. And I realized I could never have that special place in her heart she keeps for Burton. For me, the romance was over, and I told Elizabeth that.

She flew to Wales to condole the surviving members of Richard's family, and there two hundred villagers sang the old anthem "We'll keep a welcome in the hillsides." In London, Elizabeth could not restrain her tears at a memorial church service and ignored the cries and commands of reporters and photographers as she left St. Martin's-in-the-Fields.

Back in New York, she returned to Victor the quarter-million-dollar sapphire-and-diamond engagement ring. And that autumn, Elizabeth met Dennis Stein, a New York businessman exactly her own age who made a small fortune marketing faded blue jeans and who had once escorted Joan Collins and at least one Miss Universe. Gray-haired, barrel-chested, fun-loving and (like Luna) doting in a fatherly way, Stein was "the best-looking man, and even an *available* man," as Elizabeth told a friend. That year, he worked with a New York holding company whose subsidiaries included Consolidated Cigar and Technicolor, Inc. The reaction of old friends was decidedly mixed: "She has a knack for choosing men who are bothersome and hurtful," said Richard Brooks.

"Dennis is very Brooklyn," said Warren Hirsh, an executive who knew Stein. "He's a street guy. He's flashy, very much a seller of himself." By November, Elizabeth was wearing a twenty-carat sapphire engagement ring and discussing plans for a wedding gown; Stein was with her for Christmas 1984 in Gstaad.

Elizabeth returned from Switzerland and continued on to Los Angeles, where she picked up half a million dollars for three weeks of work on a television movie called *Malice in Wonderland*. This was a campy fashion show that tried to be a comedy about the brassier ladies of Hollywood's golden age; Elizabeth played the role of Louella Parsons to Jane Alexander's Hedda Hopper. The best one could say for the project was that Elizabeth was svelte in the waist and spiky in her wit—qualities not, however, associated with Louella.

Later that year, she worked for a day (and got $100,000) as a madam in *North and South*, a Civil War television miniseries epic not nearly so engaging as *Raintree County*. In 1986, she appeared to great effect in yet another television film—Mart Crowley's compelling teleplay *There Must Be A Pony*, in which she played a troubled screen star attempting a comeback after mental illness. Based loosely on James Kirkwood's novel, Crowley's script digs more deeply than the book into a network of complex relationships (mother-son, woman-lover, friend-son).

Although the character bore a vague resemblance to Marina Gregg in *The Mirror Crack'd*, the role of Marguerite Sidney in *There Must Be A Pony* was far superior, written with subtexts of delicate emotion to which she brought extraordinary shading and intensity. There were also, for alert viewers, plenty of allusions to Elizabeth's own life. Once a child actress, Marguerite is accidentally reunited with her old costar Mickey Rooney (playing himself) at a racetrack (shades of *National Velvet*); and hurrying to conclude a phone conversation, Marguerite's agent says, "Gotta run—it takes a while to get to Metro," to which she replies, "And a while to get out."

Similarly, her friends always call the character Marguerite: "those who *think* they know me, call me Rita." Just so, Elizabeth/Marguerite has known multiple marriages and divorces, an ex-husband who beat her, a history of instability and of romantic missteps. And the new project she hopes to film is a pastiche of *Raintree County*, *Cat on a Hot Tin Roof* and every Southern belle in Elizabeth's past career. At every narrative turn, a moment that might have become soap operatic was redeemed by sensitive writing and alert performances.

Elizabeth's costar was Robert Wagner, in the role of a charming cad; and a young actor named Chad Lowe played her son with querulous adolescent tenderness. "She was absolutely wonderful," according to Wagner. "There's a certain kind of danger about Elizabeth. She's unpredictable, and of course that makes for a fascinating work experience." Recalled Crowley, "Everybody on the production loved her and admired her. She was very respectful of the material and of the script, and she kept a wonderful sense of humor." An unruly dog, for example, kept missing cues in an important scene, thus taxing everyone's patience. Finally, Elizabeth spoke to the crew about Lassie: "I started out working with a dog," she said, "and believe you me, this will be the last time!"

By early 1985, after two months of intense courtship, Dennis Stein was talking rather too openly to the press about his new inamorata. "I have to constantly pinch myself that I'm really with Elizabeth Taylor," he said like a gushing fan. "She's the most beautiful woman I've ever seen. She's the most glamorous. And right now, I feel like the luckiest man alive." That did not quite fit Elizabeth's idea of a dignified engagement. "No interviews!" she cried. "No way!"

And so, at the end of January 1985, Dennis Stein was dismissed, and another engagement ring was returned to its owner. "I almost made a mistake," Elizabeth said. "I think maybe finally I'm growing up, and it's about time, too." But that would not mean a rocking chair and knitting needles: "No matter what happens, I'm loud, noisy, earthy and ready for much more living."

Nor was she afraid to speak out when a terrible epidemic began to destroy the lives of many—among them, Rock Hudson. "It was not considered a good idea to talk about AIDS in 1985," said Robert Wagner. "Hollywood was afraid to acknowledge the devastation." Just like Washington, said Elizabeth; like the rest of the country. She saw at once the absurd reason for the laziness and ignorance: the largest group then afflicted with AIDS was homosexual men. The country in general and Hollywood in particular, Elizabeth knew, were in the grip of an insane and inhumane homophobia.

"Never has a disease left so many helpless, leaving loved ones and families reaching out only to frustration and fear," she said that June of 1985, the first American celebrity to speak out when she announced plans for the first benefit dinner for APLA (AIDS Project/Los Angeles), to be held the following September. The event raised over a million dollars.

Elizabeth's commitment went even deeper and sterner after the news that Rock Hudson was dying. In August, just before the end, she went to visit him at UCLA Medical Center, but the disease had affected his brain, and he did not recognize her. The accepted creed in Hollywood and elsewhere enraged her: well, it's not our illness—it's only something they—that is, gay men—have to worry about.

"I was so angry!" she cried. "The attitude people had, the bigotry! Nobody was doing or saying anything, and that incensed me. I finally thought, I'll say something." She did, and to her everlasting credit, she never stopped—even to the point of reprimanding the President of the United States: "I don't think President Bush is doing anything at all about AIDS," she told the Eighth International Conference on the disease in Amsterdam in July 1991. "In fact, I'm not sure he even knows how to spell 'AIDS.'"

And so in her fifties, with no leading roles and no man leading her, Elizabeth Taylor found a purpose—a mission, really; and because of her boldness and efforts, celebrity support of AIDS research and against prejudice had a model patron. Even her passion for jewelry had a difference. For $623,000, she purchased a brooch from the late Duchess of Windsor's collection—not only because it was sentimentally linked to Richard (the Welsh, three-feathered emblem marking the Duke's earlier title as Prince of Wales), but also because the price she paid was donated to the Pasteur Institute, a leading AIDS research center.

"AIDS is not a sin," she said over and over. "It's a disease, a virus. How dare these so-called religious people use this illness to discriminate against homosexuals? This insanity has got to stop! We're all God's children. Whatever happened to compassion, and to caring, and to the Ten Commandments?" Well did she ask.

She was the first to hit Hollywood hard on the matter of its ingrained homophobia, too.

This offends my sensibilities and outrages my sense of fairness! I know so many homosexuals. There would be no art in America if it weren't for gays! Why are they stigmatizing these people? That was when I decided that my name could open certain doors, that I could take the fame that I've tried to get away from and use it to do some good. Well, now I'm doing everything I can. This work means more to me than anything I've ever done as an actress.

By the end of 1985, she had lost James Dean, Montgomery Clift, Rock Hudson and dozens more gay friends: her work in the years to come would be her testament to them, and to her own profound empathy for all who suffer—a character deepened as she, too, battled against the daily temptation to have just one drink, one pill. For this humanitarian cause, Elizabeth used every social occasion and the many times, beginning that year, that she was honored with lifetime achievement awards. Her message was always the same: "There is an urgent need for intensified, accelerated biomedical research," she said to a group of senators that included John Warner. In 1986, she was, in fact, the first witness to testify concerning appropriations for the National Institutes of Health.

By 1992, she had spoken out more often, raised more money and shattered more hypocritical prejudices than any celebrity. When urged to tone down her sometimes strident rage, lest people would think she was really overreacting and she might be accused of bad taste, her response was pure Elizabeth Taylor: "I don't give a shit what people think . . . If you have to fucking do it, you do it."

And she corroborated her goodwill with action, helping—in consort with leading medical researchers like Dr. Mathilde Krim—to form AmFar, the American Foundation for AIDS Research.

> The stakes are phenomenally high . . . We hope [the Foundation] will emerge as the national organization to support research, with the staying power to attract adequate financing and resources from the private sector. We plan to muster the talent and energy of America's brightest scientific and medical researchers, to solve the mysteries of AIDS. We are prepared to do what it takes to find a cure.

"At that time," said Mathilde Krim, "very few people were willing to speak up publicly for this cause. Elizabeth said she wanted to be head of it. Elizabeth is a smart, sincere, compassionate woman who commands enormous respect and prestige with the public. No one can match her."

In this regard, one of her most important appearances was before the Senate Committee on Labor and Human Resources in June 1992, to criticize the failure to utilize allotted funds for AIDS care in the nation's cities. "I am here," she began,

> to speak for all those people with HIV infection and AIDS and for those who love them . . . AIDS is devastating this nation. It is unmercifully impoverishing, torturing and finally killing young men and women—straight, gay, bisexual—in the prime of life and at what should be the height of their creative and economic potential. AIDS is sweeping through our inner cities and ravaging infants and children who cannot speak for themselves. AIDS is corroding our society at a time when so much is promised and so much left undone. I am here to speak for all of them.

Skewering the appropriation of only $275 million out of $875 million authorized for alternative housing for AIDS sufferers, she said bluntly,

> Two-thirds of that money authorized was not used to help people with AIDS. What happened to that money? . . . We must face our responsibilities to our citizens, whoever and wherever they are. We must provide our cities and states with the resources to provide these services. I ask, here and now, for the national leadership that is necessary to fully appropriate this bill. Because I will continue to come and ask for it—again and again and again— until this is done.

She paused and her eyes flashed toward Senators Thurmond, Hatch, Kennedy and the rest:

> And I will not be silenced. And I will not give up. And I will not be ignored.

In other ways, Elizabeth Taylor in her fifties was in many ways unchanged from the Elizabeth of decades earlier. She loved pretty, expensive things; she saw herself as a girl, perpetually on the threshold of unattained maturity; she rocked rooms with her raucous laugh and her earthy sense of humor; and she believed that if she did not save millions of dollars, she might be caught in sudden, grinding poverty.

As 1987 began and her fifty-fifth birthday approached, not many people were surprised when Elizabeth licensed her name to a perfume company. To great financial advantage, Sophia Loren had done that in 1980 with her "Sophia" brand, and now the Parfums International division of Chesebrough-Pond's, perhaps thinking of "Calvin Klein's Obsession," marketed "Elizabeth Taylor's Passion," doubtless inspired by her often-repeated statement, "I have a passion for life." (Later, other fragrances bore her name.)

Backed by a $10 million promotional campaign and priced at $200 an ounce, the luxury item was, by 1995, the fourth biggest-selling women's fragrance in America—and, with her share of the income, it made Elizabeth Taylor one of the richest women in America. With her investments, sale of various gems from the Burton years (which had become too expensive to insure) and residuals on the many movies of which she owned a percentage, her net worth was variously reported between $60 and $80 million.

Five hundred journalists and media representatives attended the press conference for Elizabeth Taylor's Passion in New York on January 14, where she was introduced by a new friend. Even though they were eager for details of the product, there was greater interest in her private life. For instance, would she marry George Hamilton?

"It's amazing," replied Elizabeth with a sigh. "Any announcement I make turns into a marriage. But I just married Chesebrough-Pond's! You don't want to make a bigamist out of me!"

The question about Hamilton was based on a silly rumor then swirling around, for with him she was about to start filming a television movie called *Poker Alice*, a light western comedy-drama about a slick poker player who wins a bordello in a card game. Filmed that February in and around Tucson, it was an unfocused story, nicely acted by Taylor, Hamilton and Tom Skerritt and full of atmosphere—but without an iota of narrative coherence or character sensibility. Elizabeth, in a variety of nineteenth-century gowns, looked stunning, but her gradations of feeling—toughness, vulnerability, tenderness, fear—were lost in a script that tried too hard and achieved little.

For Elizabeth, however, the experience achieved very much indeed, since as usual she expected and received presents as proper reward for her presence, much as a fractious child expected trinkets. "She's a little girl," said the director Arthur Allen Seidelman, who directed *Poker Alice*, "but don't be misled. This lady is no pushover. She knows how to take care of herself, but she still has that air of vulnerability."

Not to say downright cupidity. A total of $100,000 was added to the budget for twenty-three daily gifts from the production company to Elizabeth: a bejeweled Cartier stickpin, a travel clock from Van Cleef and Arpels, a gold necklace, diamond earrings and a gold cigarette lighter for her ubiquitous cigarettes (the one vice she had not overcome, she said). The purpose was not only to mark her birthday that February: it was also to keep her happy for the three weeks of filming, even to assure her arrival each day—just as one might bribe a willful child; still, she kept her own schedule, refusing to be rushed into the Arizona sun, not stepping from her trailer until the last hair was in place, the makeup perfect. "Filming moves at her pace," said a member of the crew. "She's there, but it's slow."

Elizabeth's appreciation of expensive baubles was linked to a preference for the society of wealthy men, and she had fewer friends wealthier than Malcolm Forbes, then sixty-seven, the tycoon and publisher of the monthly "capitalist tool" bearing his name. She was among eleven hundred guests at his New Jersey estate that June (Henry Kissinger also headed the list), celebrating the seventieth birthday of the magazine. All that spring and summer, she gladly accepted invitations to join him and a sprinkling of others (Walter Cronkite, Donald Trump, Henry Kissinger and others) for sprints on motorcycles, for Lucullan banquets and soirées at one of his many estates. There were also hot-air balloon excursions—shades of *Around the World in 80 Days*—in one of Forbes's fantastic devices. He commissioned one in the shape of his Normandy chateau, and others in the forms of bottles, light bulbs, cola cans, blue jeans and the London *Financial Times.*

Rumors to the contrary, there was nothing at all romantic in the Taylor-Forbes friendship: in intimate matters, Forbes (once married) evidently preferred gentlemen. "She knew he was gay," said Henry Wynberg. "Everyone did. Besides, she would never have risked AIDS to sleep with Forbes." Of greater importance was the fact that Elizabeth wheedled vast sums for AIDS research from Malcolm Forbes.

At the same time, alas, she rather enjoyed herself too much— and thus soon found herself right back in a style of living dangerously close to the Burton years—a life now undertaken because she was bored and unoccupied. Besides social jaunts from California to New York to France to the Far East, she accepted Forbes's offer of a private jet to take them to Rome for several weeks during the summer of 1987.

There, Franco Zeffirelli had asked her to appear in his film *Young Toscanini*—as, of all things, a Russian soprano in South American exile. The story concerned the maestro's fiery encounter with the singer during his tour of Brazil. (Elizabeth's "singing" was dubbed by diva Aprile Milo.) For a time, the doomed project was suspended for lack of funds, and, screened once at the Venice Film Festival, it was a resounding failure and remained unreleased. For much of the first half of 1988, things were happier: her successful efforts during 1984 and 1985 at rehabilitation and weight loss, so meticulously recorded in a best-selling book, took her on a world tour. Notable among her most appealing qualities was a refreshing candor: "I should be committed for having been married so many times!" she said without affectation or false shame.

Everywhere, comments were made about how wonderful she looked. Serious about recovery and earnest about keeping weight off, Elizabeth never lost her sense of humor. Dieting works, she said, "if you can fall in love with the same person over and over again— but of course that hasn't been my experience."

To questions about cosmetic surgery, Elizabeth replied that she had only a chin tuck, to remove fatty tissue after weight loss. But over the next several years, her appearance altered dramatically, and by 1994 her face was so unnaturally youthful, her cheekbones so high and full and her mouth so set that she seemed to have gone much further than the modest chin tuck. "The most beautiful creature in the world" she had been called, as Michael Wilding had said sadly: "Imagine bearing that title round your neck! What must that do to a woman?" For one thing, it often imposes the obligation to remain beautiful, even to the point of pain, even to the point of a futile attempt to stop the clock.

Like many people recovering from addictions, her success at sobriety was sabotaged. By July 1988, when she returned home to Los Angeles from the publicity tour for *Elizabeth Takes Off*, it was clear that the old weakness was dragging at her will. Weary of travel, her limbs aching from promotional trips, she was also drinking alcohol again, and overeating—not surprising in view of her frenetic life. In addition, decades of heavy smoking had induced incipient osteoporosis, a painful and potentially crippling bone degeneration that afflicted her pelvis and hips.

Thus that autumn she was back at home, resting, watching old movies on television, ingesting Percodan, Demerol, Tylenol with codeine and whatever painkillers she could obtain—and washing them all down with Bloody Marys. As she admitted, "A drunk is somebody who drinks too much. Somebody who takes too many pills is a junkie. There's no polite way of saying it."

On October 25, Elizabeth returned to the Betty Ford Center for another seven-week stay, and in a way this was more difficult than the first visit three years earlier. She was, reported a friend, "paranoid and disoriented" on arrival. "With all the drugs she's observed," said a staff member at the clinic (with permission to speak, it should be noted), "she's a female version of Elvis—and you know what happened to him!"

At the same time, ninety-two-year-old Sara was in the nearby Eisenhower Medical Center with bleeding ulcers. Elizabeth was allowed to visit each afternoon, a short trip she transformed into a royal visit after a journey to the Center's hairdresser each morning and an hour before the vanity mirror each noontime—to the detriment, perhaps, of more critical concerns. Sara, evidently quite indestructible, awoke from a coma and recovered quite nicely.

Her daughter's condition was more precarious. Elizabeth was off pills and alcohol, but she was wreathed in smoke—and, displeased with the Ford Center's cafeteria, she detoured each day to the Eisenhower's dining room, where she ordered take-out meals and a stash of candy. On December 10, when she left Rancho Mirage, she was sober and drug-free, but shaky and not slim.

Yet there was encouragement, and from a source other than the professional staff. "Patients develop strong bonds with their support groups," according to the brochure for the Betty Ford Center. "Each group becomes . . . a network of individuals, sharing love and experiences together." Romance was certainly not what the directors meant, but neither did they count on Elizabeth Taylor. One day in group therapy session, she noticed a tall, thirty-seven-year-old truck driver and construction worker. As it turned out, he had an arrest record for drug possession and was on probation for three years after a conviction for driving while intoxicated. "I drink and do a little coke now and then, but I don't smoke marijuana," he told an arresting officer.

With long, blondish red hair, bright hazel eyes and a workman's rugged, tight physique, he had somehow remained unravaged by his addictions. Elizabeth arranged to meet him, and by Christmastime her family and friends learned that there was this new man in her life. He was neither a dapper diplomat nor a shady entrepreneur, not an ambitious politician, nor a gay tycoon. As she said, he was something completely different.

Chapter Fifteen

1989–1994

*T*HE SCENE COULD HAVE COME from an old movie.

On January 20, 1989, an Aston Martin Lagonda pulled in to the driveway of Mr. Philly's, a roadside diner in Stanton, thirty-five miles south of Los Angeles. A few moments later, a short female customer tucked into one of the restaurant's famous cheese-and-steak sandwiches with grilled onions and mushrooms. May Najem, proprietor and cook, noticed the woman's elaborate silver and pewter jewelry; her spiked, black hair; her dramatic, arched eyebrows and heavily darkened lids; and her rhinestone-studded jacket. "Just look at those boots," said May to her husband, Moe. "They belong either to a drug dealer or a movie star."

The lady avidly eating the sandwich was, of course, Elizabeth Taylor, in one of her hip new outfits; she was returning to Los Angeles after an outpatient therapy session at the Betty Ford Center.

A few days later, the same car pulled up, and out stepped a tall, handsome man, bronzed and gleaming from a session at a local tanning parlor. Elizabeth Taylor waited in the Aston Martin while the man ordered take-out meals.

"Are you her bodyguard or her driver?" Moe asked.

"No, I'm her boyfriend."

Born in 1952, Lawrence Lee Fortensky was five when his parents divorced. He moved with his mother from Northern to Southern California, where he dropped out of high school and took odd jobs. At nineteen, he was married and drafted into the Vietnam War the same day. Discharged several months later, he and his wife had a baby girl; the marriage soon failed, and Larry took another wife. That union was also terminated, after his wife testified that Larry, who drank too much, had tried to strangle her during an argument. He seemed like a troubled fellow.

After a stint as a sanitation mechanic for the City of Los Angeles, he began to work in construction. As a member of Teamsters Local 420 in Los Angeles, he had a specialized driver's job, with a base pay of $18.50 per hour. "I like the work, I like the dirt, I like the mountains, I like the big machines," he said.

By early 1989, just weeks after they checked out of the Betty Ford Center, Larry (twenty years younger than Elizabeth) was staying often at her Bel-Air mansion. "She invited me to come up [from my home south of Los Angeles]," he said. "And I did, mostly on weekends. I didn't think I fitted in, but I kept on coming."

"You get to know someone real fast when you are in group therapy, in a recovery program," said Elizabeth. "All the bullshit is stripped away. We just started instantly to know each other. He knew I could see through him, and I knew he could see through me. They tell you in recovery not to get romantically involved for a year at least. But Larry and I did not wait a year." By springtime 1989, they were lovers, and before the year was out he was permanently installed at 700 Nimes Road. But he still held down his construction job.

Elizabeth understood Larry's desire to keep his employment. "People think that because he's got a rich wife, why work? It's like asking, 'Why maintain your balls?'" Proper old *Life* magazine, which not long before was deleting even a single *damn* from an interview, faithfully reproduced her colorful diction.

Elizabeth's attraction to Larry is not difficult to understand. At the outset, they were drawn together by their shared weaknesses and similar histories of broken relationships. In addition, Larry was a wounded "son" she could nurture, and thus in a way compensate for the pain she acknowledged causing her sons, Michael and Christopher, during times of distance and periods of addiction. Hilton, Clift, Fisher, Burton—many of the men in her life had been enslaved to various addictions. With Larry, it was as if Elizabeth could reenter the unhappy past and cancel the failures. And this she could do without professional competition, for Larry was an attentive acolyte without any connection to her professional or social world.

With him, therefore, she could enjoy a kind of parity previously absent in her romantic attachments. Larry was the prototype of the strong, silent type, a man whose sheer physical bulk was reassuring, protective, satisfying—and who confirmed that she was still vital and young enough to attract and keep a man twenty years her junior. When they married, it was the first time in her life she was joining her destiny to that of a man with no prior image to overcome; by 1995, the relationship had lasted longer than any in her life, except for the years with Burton. "Larry gives me a sense of security," she said. "I know I'm protected and he's there for me."

Little else was different for Elizabeth after 1989. There were award ceremonies tendered for her then and in the years to come, lectures and congressional testimonies on behalf of AIDS research, and travels to exotic ports for fashion shows, for perfume promotion and for parties—most notably, an appallingly tasteless, $2 million bash in Morocco for Malcolm Forbes's seventieth birthday that summer. The following February 24, he died at his New Jersey estate.

A month later, Elizabeth was further upset by the death of her friend the designer Halston, who had suffered from AIDS. Then that catastrophic illness came closer to home in 1991, when her personal secretary, Roger Wall, gulped down an overdose of pills rather than face the final ravages of the disease; and again in 1992, when Aileen Getty, by then married and divorced from Elizabeth's son Christopher, fell desperately ill with the same illness. "If it hadn't been for her," said Aileen, speaking of Taylor's emotional and financial support, "I would have had a really, really hard time and maybe not made it." Said Elizabeth, who backed up her affection with constant attention to Aileen throughout a dreadful series of illnesses, "We belong to each other's hearts."

In the spring of 1989, Elizabeth made another television movie, playing the boozy, drug-ridden and fading movie queen Alexandra del Lago, in an oddly tame version of Tennessee Williams's *Sweet Bird of Youth*; Mark Harmon acted her much younger lover. With her private life known to the world, this was perhaps on many counts a brave choice, but once again Elizabeth recognized a good role, and to hell with what people might say about how closely the project and the part might be seen to resemble herself and Larry Fortensky. She seemed not to be acting the role; after all, she had lived it.

Back in the time of *Cleopatra*, Elizabeth Taylor lived the picture and became the ultimate star, transferring her love from one man to another and defying the gods and the masses. Now, still the reigning star, she did not have to play at being one. She was a variant of Alexandra del Lago and had lived that character's dreary odyssey for years. Director Nicolas Roeg had only to walk her through a kind of documentary.

Around the time of her fifty-eighth birthday, in February 1990, Elizabeth felt ill, and during March she had to rest more and more. Then, in April, she entered Daniel Freeman Hospital in Marina del Rey—with a fever and sinus infection, it was reported. A week later, she was rushed to St. John's in Santa Monica, where she was registered under the pseudonym "Beth Warner," her shortened but legal name. Doctors diagnosed a particularly virulent form of bacterial pneumonia, and soon she was critically ill. Placed on a respirator and subjected to dangerous but necessary antifungal and antibiotic drugs, Elizabeth remained very near death for weeks that spring.

Those who knew her well were not surprised at this latest crisis, for Elizabeth's heavy smoking had exacerbated her long history of respiratory infections. The tabloids reported rumors that her collapse resulted not from a simple sinus infection that turned serious but from a near-lethal ingestion of drugs and alcohol. These reports were totally discredited.

In every way, the 1990 illness uncannily resembled the pneumonia episode of London in March 1961. More than a hundred reporters and photographers camped out on the lawns of St. John's, awaiting hourly bulletins to be relayed to the world. Once again, Elizabeth Taylor's apparently mortal illness demoted other world news from page-one positions. But two months later, on June 14, she was at last discharged for a long recuperation at home. Larry had been at her bedside daily at the hospital, and he was now with her permanently at Nimes Road, comforting, serving, protecting, embracing. Just so, she went with him to the bedside of his mother, who soon after died of cancer at the age of fifty-eight—exactly Elizabeth's age.

On July 26, 1991, a press announcement was released from the office of Chen Sam, Elizabeth's New York–based publicist. Elizabeth would marry Larry in October, and Michael Jackson would host the wedding at his ranch. "I never thought I'd get married again," Elizabeth said. "I was single for eleven years, which is like history-making for me!" Where, she was asked, after all these marriages, was she registered for bridal gifts? As usual, the witty riposte was instantaneous: "I'm signed up all over the world."

That summer, she appeared in her shortest but most lifelike role—in fact, she seemed to be nothing so much as herself in a commercial for the new fragrance White Diamonds, to which she also granted a license for the use of her name. Elizabeth appeared festooned with gems in the commercial, some of them hers and real, some borrowed and fake. She watched a foursome of ominous men playing poker. The youngest, best-looking among them slaps down his cards and is about to quit the game, when to the rescue comes Elizabeth, a living vision. She removes her sparkling diamond earrings and drops them on the table: "These have always brought me luck," she says and vanishes in a gauzier haze of soft focus than Metro-Goldwyn-Mayer would ever have dared. By 1994, the perfumes bearing Elizabeth's name had grossed half a billion dollars, and some of her enormous profits, like those from the sale of her wedding photos, were pledged to her own Elizabeth Taylor AIDS Foundation, which she established in 1991.

After the wedding on October 6, 1991, the Fortenskys departed for a European honeymoon, returning in mid-November, for she had promised to appear in Los Angeles at a major fund-raiser for AIDS research. As usual, she was always accompanied by a bodyguard, a personal assistant and a hairdresser. Many hundreds attended her sixtieth birthday at Disneyland in February 1992. "It's kind of astonishing that I made it!" she told Johnny Carson and the nation that February.

There was no sign of her slowing down the charity work or her promotion of expensive and lucrative fragrances. Her acting career, however, seemed finished. Except for minor excursions to studios, there was little professional activity, and this she seemed not to regret. But she did enjoy doing a voice-over on "The Simpsons" television cartoon series and a quick cameo in the feature *The Flintstones*. In the latter, Elizabeth played Pearl Slaghoople, John Goodman's comically shrewish, rhinestone-studded, prehistoric mother-in-law. "You could have married Eliot Firestone, the man who invented the wheel!" she snaps at her on-screen daughter.

In 1994, she was plump, happy and enormously wealthy. Award citations were tossed at her like rice at a wedding—the solemnities of the American Film Institute's Lifetime Achievement Award in 1993, for example, and the Jean Hersholt Humanitarian Award from the Academy of Motion Picture Arts and Sciences. She was, as never before, a hallowed Hollywood presence. And just as she used her fame to help millions she did not know, so she sped to the side of those she did—Aileen Getty and then, in the summer of 1993, Michael Jackson.

The Fortenskys flew all the way to Singapore when Jackson was on the verge of a complete breakdown following allegations that he was a child molester; that he was addicted to drugs was beyond dispute. "This is the worst thing that could happen to a man like Michael, who loves children," said Elizabeth, ever loyal. As for the drugs: "I have suffered and dealt with the same kind of medical problems now affecting my friend Michael Jackson. Because of my own experience with addiction to prescription medications . . . I [could see] for myself that Michael was in desperate need of specialized medical attention . . . I love him like a son." The following winter, she still praised the beleaguered Jackson as "the brightest star in the universe."

"Everything," she said in her seventh decade of life, "was handed to me—looks, fame, wealth, honor, love. I rarely had to fight for anything. But I've paid for that luck with disasters—the deaths of so many good friends, terrible illnesses, destructive addictions, broken marriages. All things considered, I'm damned lucky to be alive."

Elizabeth was, as she admitted, "complex, and God knows I've led a complicated life. I don't like chaos, although I sometimes create chaos."

The disorder, disarray and confusion in her life had often enough been the result not of a divided and busy existence but of a paradoxically empty one—a life for years devoid of reflection, just as she had been cheated of learning from her mistakes because from her youth she had been idolized by the world. "My life has been a whirlwind—movies, husbands, children—and I often needed guidance on how to slow it down. There were times when I couldn't take stock, when I was self-destructive and deliberately threw myself into the path of a speeding train. But I always managed to throw myself out of the way in time, including those times when I was sick."

By society's standards of success, she had done and endured and seen so much of life, had so many benefits, privileges and luxuries—and yet she was often sick at heart, anxious, a self-absorbed child. She was, in other words, the quintessence of that fantastic creature, a movie star named Elizabeth Taylor, which was her greatest and most demanding part. And she never disappointed: when the roles were not dramatic enough, her life was. "I want my tombstone to say 'She Lived.'"

This may go far toward explaining why Elizabeth Taylor has galvanized the endless fascination of millions over so many years. Despite her fame and extraordinary beauty, she has projected a recognizable humanity, strong yet vulnerable, her smile often hiding pain.

For decades, she was a kind of corporate personality, doing what millions dreamed of or feared to do, and becoming so many aspects of Woman that they were past enumerating. She had become, by the sheer variety of her life roles, a kind of totem of mass cultural desire, an exquisite girl-woman on whom everyone's fears and fantasies were projected and easily rested. There is no other way to explain her enduring, worldwide celebrity.

Scarlet woman and wearer of the royal purple, smoldering sex goddess and dying swan, raspy boozer and sensual boaster, she worked hard for decades to sustain an image she neither devised nor understood. With all the pressures and all the spurious values deriving from fame, it was perhaps inevitable that she would endure everyone's worst fear: the loss of control, the experience of almost deadly mental and physical collapse. But she had a second chance, and a third, and more.

"I'm a survivor—a living example of what people can go through and survive."

Indeed she was, for Elizabeth had sustained (besides ruptured relationships) international scandals and inconstant public attitudes, a burnt finger, an ulcerated eye, surgery for smashed spinal disks, an appendectomy, broken limbs, sprained ankles, abscesses, dysentery, every national variety of influenza, recurrent respiratory infections, near-fatal pneumonia, phlebitis, cesarean deliveries, a hysterectomy, at least one suicide attempt, drug and alcohol abuse and numerous minor infirmities. By one count, she had no fewer than seventy-three illnesses, injuries and accidents requiring hospitalization between 1947 and 1994. Michael Wilding was not speaking sarcastically when he said that she seemed allergic to good health. "During our married life something always seemed to be happening to her. It's a great shame. She's always so tired and worn out."

Again her health was major news when she had surgery for a hip replacement in 1994. During a long recuperation, she was very much a recluse in Bel-Air, with Larry in constant attendance. Finally, she emerged, wrapped in flattering layers of shimmering gold, and they appeared together at the Museum of Miniatures.

Three months later, on September 11, 1994, Sara Sothern Taylor, after suffering declining health for two years, died quietly at the Sunrise Country Club in Rancho Mirage. A few weeks earlier, she had turned ninety-eight.

The deaths of those she had loved had grieved Elizabeth— among them, those of Michael Wilding and Richard Burton, and of her friends James Dean, Montgomery Clift, Rock Hudson and Malcolm Forbes. But the passing of her mother was the last great closure to the past. Benevolently but persistently controlled by Sara from childhood through a protracted adolescence, Elizabeth had always acknowledged that her career was spearheaded by her mother's ambition, strategy and stratagems. She had often resented Sara's mastery and manipulation, and at crucial moments she had known she had to free herself from her mother's authority. But she knew, too, that without that early maternal management she would never have had anything like the spectacular success, the wealth, the fame that blighted even as it blessed. In an important way, Elizabeth was now very much on her own at last.

She had never been, in any conventional sense, a religious person, but she always clung to certain basic spiritual principles throughout her life. "I believe in God," she told a visitor to her home during a long interview, discussing recently deceased loved ones. "I'm not afraid of death—but I hope to live to about 110." To her many friends, that seemed not at all unrealistic.

"In my life, I have never, God knows, done anything by half-measures. I believe people are like rocks formed by the weather. We're formed by experience, by heartache, by grief, by mistakes, by guilt, by shame . . . I am glad that in my life I have never cut short my emotions. The most awful thing is to be numb." She paused, and her radiant, lilac-blue eyes scanned the Bel-Air cypress trees, stately and gleaming in the warm, breezeless late afternoon air.

"As for life and death, I think there is more to it all than we are aware," said Elizabeth Taylor, smiling. And with that, the interview was over.

Notes

xi ET's recitation of the lines from Gerard Manley Hopkins, quoted on the epigraph page of this book, is included in Georgina Howell, "Liz," *Vogue*, June 1991. The same essay appeared in the London Sunday *Times* magazine, Aug. 18, 1991.

Notes to Chapter One

1 For a good description of Neverland Valley Ranch, see *Life*, June 1993.
2 jack-in-the-box: Ibid.
3 They're just trying: Carla Hall, "For Liz & Larry, a Taylor-Made Wedding," *Washington Post*, Oct. 7, 1991.
   I don't know, honey: Cordell Marks, "I give my heart, says Liz Taylor," *TV Times Magazine* (London), June 12–18, 1982.
4 Elizabeth and Larry and all you guests: Penelope McMillan, "Amid Wedding Hoopla, a Town Goes Hollywood," *Los Angeles Times*, Oct. 7, 1991. See also Liz Smith's syndicated column, ibid.
   Those sons of bitches: Brad Darrach, "Living with Liz," *Life*, Feb. 1992.
   Do you want me: Quoted by Carole Bayer Sager in *Vanity Fair*, Nov. 1992.
5 Larry and I decided: "Elizabeth Taylor," *People*, Dec. 30, 1991.
   Hey, this isn't so bad: Darrach, "Living with Liz."
   pure farce: Christopher Andersen, *Michael Jackson Unauthorized* (New York: Simon & Schuster, 1994), 248.
   I never saw them: Ibid., 179.

6 Michael and I love each other: Ibid.
   We both started very young: Appearing on "The Tonight Show,"
   Feb. 21, 1992.
   an old soul: *Newsweek*, Sept. 6, 1993.
   the body of a woman: Often, e.g., *McCall's,* Jan. 1960, 128.
   We had a similar type: On "Biography—Elizabeth Taylor," Arts
   & Entertainment Network's television special, 1993.
   He's a paradox: On an Oprah Winfrey ABC-TV special on
   Michael Jackson, broadcast on Feb. 10, 1993.
   He has the quality: J. Randy Taraborrelli, *Michael Jackson: The
   Magic and the Madness* (Secaucus: Birch Lane/Carol Publishing),
   463.
6–7 On Michael Jackson's unhappy childhood, see, e.g., Taraborrelli,
   7, 12, 21, 137–38, 140, 221, 386 and 516. On a live Oprah
   Winfrey ABC-TV television special on the evening of Feb. 10,
   1993, Jackson also spoke of the physical and psychological abuse
   he endured from his father.
8 My toughest role: "Elizabeth Taylor," *Cosmopolitan*, Aug. 1961.

Notes to Chapter Two

12 I've made a million: Channing Pollock to Ward Morehouse, cited
   in Samuel L. Leiter, ed., *The Encyclopedia of the New York Stage,
   1920–1930* (Westport, Conn.: Greenwood Press, 1985), vol. 1,
   284.
   In the final scene: *The New York Times*, Oct. 24, 1922, 18.
   creditable but not startling: *The Theatre*, Dec. 1922, 420.
   a good deal of trouble: Channing Pollock, *The Harvest of My Years*
   (New York: Bobbs-Merrill, 1943), 298.
   more than duplicated: Ibid.
13 childish rubbish: Quoted in Leiter, 186.
   When I said no: Ibid.
   bitten by the Broadway bug: Hedda Hopper and James Brough,
   The Whole Truth and Nothing But (Garden City: Doubleday, 1963),
   9–10.
15 Mother had written: Sara Taylor's reminiscences are here com-
   piled from two memoirs—"Elizabeth, my Daughter," three
   monthly installments in *McCall's*, February, March and April
   1954; and "My Daughter Elizabeth," a revision of that series,
   published in *Good Housekeeping*, March and April 1989.
16 Her hair was long: "Elizabeth, my Daughter."
18 It kept her brother: Ibid.

high time: Ibid.

an old child: Ibid.; see also "My Daughter Elizabeth."

19 My earliest memory: Elizabeth Taylor, *Elizabeth Taylor* (New York: Harper & Row, 1965), 2–3—hereinafter referred to as *ET*. This book is, with some alterations and minor addenda, the transcription of a series of taped interviews with Richard Meryman of *Life* magazine, in 1963 and 1964. Large portions of her remarks were first published in *Life*, Dec. 18, 1964.

20 Never talk about: Brenda Maddox, *Who's Afraid of Elizabeth Taylor?* (New York: M. Evans, 1977), 19.

My dad and I: Helen Gurley Brown, "Girl Talk with Elizabeth the Great," *Cosmopolitan*, Sept. 1987, 242.

My brother lent: Thelma Cazalet-Keir, *The Wings* (London: The Bodley Head, 1967), 169–70.

The Cazalets thought: Quoted in the *Evening Standard*, March 26, 1963.

21 I gave up my career: "Elizabeth, my Daughter."

22 She wasn't an outstanding: Quoted in the *Evening Standard*, March 26, 1963.

23 He had to start: Helen Gurley Brown, "Girl Talk with Elizabeth," 242.

Sara Taylor did bring: An anonymous neighbor, quoted in Maddox, 7.

I don't think: "Elizabeth, my Daughter."

24 Agents came up to us: "My Daughter Elizabeth."

Notes to Chapter Three

26 I cawn't take: Frances Levison, "Elizabeth Taylor," *Life*, Feb. 21, 1949, 81.

My mother was: *ET*, 21.

27 innocent and lovely: Hopper and Brough, 9–10.

I never wanted: Quoted in Sidney Skolsky's syndicated column (e.g., the *Hollywood Citizen-News*), March 26, 1958.

She had never: Eleanor Harris, "The Elizabeth Taylor Story," *Look*, June 26, 1956, 120.

Elizabeth's mother: Hedda Hopper, in unpublished file notes in her collection at the Academy of Motion Picture Arts and Sciences, Beverly Hills.

Elizabeth always swore: Hedda Hopper, in the *Los Angeles Times*, Sept. 11, 1958.

28 teeming with life: *ET*, 14.

I want to hear: Ibid., 14–15.

29   For the details of J. Cheever Cowdin's takeover of Universal, see Thomas Schatz, *The Genius of the System* (New York: Pantheon, 1988), 234.

to assist in: The contract between Universal Pictures and Elizabeth Taylor remains in the Universal Collection at the University of Southern California, Los Angeles: Box 592, Folder 18914.

Imagine excitement: Victor Cazalet's diary entry for April 16, 1941. The verbal deal had been settled several days before; the contract, as usual, was dated later. See James, 257.

30   *I wanted to be:* "My Daughter Elizabeth."

She was painfully shy: Gloria Jean, quoted in a special magazine edition of the trade newspaper the *Hollywood Reporter*: A 75th Anniversary Salute to Universal Studios (June 1990), S-22.

and shoot rubber bands: *ET*, 7.

The kid has nothing: Quoted often—e.g., in Maddox, 24. See also Foster Hirsch, *Elizabeth Taylor* (New York: Pyramid, 1973), 23.

31   A ballerina: Aaron Latham, "National Velveeta," *Esquire*, Nov. 1977, 172.

32   At every one: Maddox, 25; similarly, J. B. Griswold, "Elizabeth Grows Up," *American Magazine*, July 1948, 106.

Now, honey: Ibid.

Here was my daughter: Ibid. 106–107.

32–33   My initial impression: Simon Banner, "Queen of the Nile," *You* magazine, *The Mail on Sunday* (London), Jan. 23, 1994, p. 20.

33   She often told me: Quoted in Jerry Vermilye and Mark Ricci, *The Films of Elizabeth Taylor* (Secaucus: The Citadel Press, 1976), 19.

They wanted to: Helen Gurley Brown, "Girl Talk with Elizabeth," 242.

35   Being in films: James Robert Parish, with Gregory W. Mank and Don E. Stanke, *The Hollywood Beauties* (New Rochelle, N.Y.: Arlington House, 1978), 305.

How come I missed: Sidney Skolsky's syndicated columns (e.g., the *New York Post*), for March 24 and 26, 1958.

Of course the child stars: Maddox, 49.

It was not a normal: Elizabeth Taylor, *Elizabeth Takes Off* (New York: Putnam's, 1987), 49; hereinafter designated *ETO*.

I had no childhood: On *Hour Magazine* television show, Aug. 21, 1987.

wasn't school: *ET*, 22.

I hated it: Richard Gehman, "Elizabeth Taylor," *Good Housekeeping*, April 1961, 183.

Poor Elizabeth: Maddox, 181.
36   overscheduled: *ETO*, 53.
     The fact is that: Ibid., 252.
37   I don't know why: "MGM Vet Lucille Ryman Carroll Recalls the Reel Adventures of Liz, Rock, Marilyn and Nancy," *People*, Nov. 2, 1987.
38–39 When I did the scene: *ET*, 163.
39   As natural and excellent: Archer Winston, in the *New York Post*, Dec. 16, 1944.
     Elizabeth Taylor emerges: Rose Pelswick, the New York *Journal-American*, Dec. 16, 1944.
     She and the picture: James Agee, in *The Nation*, Dec. 20, 1944.
     Regarding Elizabeth's campaign to keep the horse she rode in *National Velvet*, Pandro Berman's recollections have been widely documented (e.g., Maddox, 42–43). Attorney Adrian Kragen, later a law professor at the University of California at Berkeley, often reminisced about his young client's loud insistence on keeping the horse: this cited by Kirtley M. Thiesmeyer, JD, to DS, Aug. 17, 1994.
     There were from six to twelve: Eleanor Harris, "The Elizabeth Taylor Story," *Look*, June 26, 1956, 123.
40   my surrogate father: *ETO*, 25.
     Don't you dare: *ETO*, 56; more colorful variations were recounted by ET on the "David Frost Show" (Metromedia TV) in March 1972; similarly, see Charles Champlin, "Elizabeth Taylor, the Movies," *Los Angeles Times*, March 7, 1993.
41   "Loving You" was reprinted in *McCalls*, Dec. 1972, 13.
     was becoming more conscious: "My Daughter Elizabeth," 202.
     the bigger bangles: Diane Scott, "Life with Liz," *Photoplay*, Sept. 1947, 81.
42   She tried everything: "My Daughter Elizabeth," 219.
     My life was not my own: *ETO*, 53, 57
     Her life: Darryl Hickman, in the made-for-television documentary biography *Elizabeth Taylor*, Arts & Entertainment Network, 1993.
     "Elizabeth Taylor Loves Animals and Out-of-doors," *Life*, Feb. 26, 1945, 74ff.
43   Edwin Schallert, "Horses or Chipmunks—They All Love Elizabeth Taylor," *Los Angeles Times*, Jan. 28, 1945.
     no other member: Memorandum, Steve Trilling to Roy Obringer, April 1, 1946: Box 25 of the Warner Bros. Collection at the University of Southern California.

44 be subjected to: Eric Stacey, production memorandum dated April 29, 1946, found in the *Life With Father* files, Box 36B, folder #662: the Warner Bros. collection, University of Southern California.

First Aid says: Memorandum from Eric Stacey to T.C. Wright, under the heading "Elizabeth Taylor—Illnesses," dated May 27, 1946, the Warner Bros. collection.

45 For rumors of the Sara Taylor–Michael Curtiz romance, see Maddox, 56 and Alexander Walker, *Elizabeth: The Life of Elizabeth Taylor* (New York: Grove Weidenfeld, 1990), 59–60. Neither adduces any evidence, and Walker may be simply following Maddox *tout court*.

I looked on Benny Thau: Eleanor Harris, "The Elizabeth Taylor Story," *Look*, June 26, 1956, 123.

Elizabeth didn't date: Scott, "Elizabeth at Sixty," 176.

46 I think she might have carried: Kathleen Neumeyer, "Liz's 9 Lives," *Philadelphia Inquirer*, May 16, 1990, p. 4-F.

47 Miss Taylor breathes: *Variety*, Sept. 17, 1947.

grave charm and subtle authority: *New York Herald Tribune*, Sept. 20, 1947.

If my celebrity: *ETO*, 60–61.

48 Daddy is busy: ET, on the Louella Parsons radio show on KECA (ABC radio, Los Angeles), July 13, 1947: a transcript is contained in the Louella Parsons Collection at the University of Southern California, Box 5, Folder 11.

49 Please, mother: "Elizabeth, my Daughter," 51.

all tinsel and moonlight: Susan Schindehette, Karen G. Jackovich and Doris Bacon, "Still Reigning After All These Years," *People*, March 13, 1989, 87.

She wanted to know: Debbie Reynolds, with David Patrick Columbia, *Debbie: My Life* (New York: Morrow, 1988), 64.

50 I know exactly: *Seventeen*, June 1947; reprinted in *Seventeen*, February 1974.

a young woman: Archer Winsten, in the *New York Post*, Aug. 8, 1948.

a 14-carat: Irving Hoffman, in the *Hollywood Reporter*, Aug. 11, 1948, 6.

rapidly developing: Dorothy Manners in the Los Angeles *Herald-Examiner*, Sept. 4, 1948.

I had the body: Often cited—e.g., in Richard Boeth, "Elizabeth Taylor: Aftermath of a Scandal," *McCall's*, Jan. 1960, 128; James Bacon, "A Look at the Real Elizabeth Taylor," Sunday *Chicago Tri-*

bune, Nov. 9, 1958; Parsons, 253; and as early as the *Los Angeles Times*, Sept. 16, 1951. See also Sidney Skolsky's column in the *Hollywood Citizen-News* and the *New York Post*, March 26, 1958.

51 When other teenage girls: "Elizabeth, my Daughter," 37.

Notes to Chapter Four

53 My teenage vision: *ETO*, 60.
53–54 I took one look: *Time*, Aug. 22, 1949.
54 From then on: "Elizabeth, my Daughter."
We want Davis: Ann MacGregor, "Love and a Girl Named Liz," *Photoplay*, June 1949, 74.
55 Letters came in bunches: Ibid.
Elizabeth and I: *Time*, Aug. 22, 1949.
56 She has acquired: Levison, "Elizabeth Taylor," 78.
I hope not many people: *ET*, 47.
I never had: *Look*, Aug. 15, 1961, 32; Levison, "Elizabeth Taylor."
56–57 I went from childhood: ET, appearing on "Donahue," Feb. 15, 1988.
57 wildly infatuated with love: *ET*, 25. Similarly: "I guess I'm in love with love," ET to Sidney Skolsky, March 24, 1958.
58 He is expected: E.g., Earl Wilson, "Glenn Davis, Southland Grid Hero, to Wed Actress," New York *Daily News*, March 10, 1949.
Elizabeth had outgrown: "My Daughter Elizabeth."
Maybe I should have fallen: Bob Thomas, "50,000 Wails of Romance," Los Angeles *Mirror*, March 28, 1949.
I was never in love: Louella Parsons's syndicated column, in the *Los Angeles Examiner*, May 27, 1949.
Neither of us: Ruth Waterbury, *Elizabeth Taylor* (New York: Appleton-Century, 1964), 65.
59 I think she knew: Ibid., 51.
60 May I keep it? *Hollywood Citizen-News*, March 30, 1949.
She has the temperament: *Time*, Aug. 22, 1949.
That's when I knew: ET, appearing on "Donahue," Feb. 15, 1988.
The big diamond: Elsa Maxwell, "The Most Exciting Girl in Hollywood," *Photoplay*, January 1950.
61 I love her: Hedda Hopper, "Engagement Canceled for Elizabeth Taylor," *Los Angeles Times*, Sept. 19, 1949.
We went well together: *ET*, 27.
62–63 He didn't make me feel: ET, interviewed by George Stevens, Jr.,

and Susan Winslow on Oct. 18, 1982, for the documentary on George Stevens, *A Filmmaker's Journey*. The transcriptions of these interviews exist in the George Stevens Collection at the Academy of Motion Picture Arts and Sciences, Beverly Hills.

63 If she thought: Waterbury, 89, 83.

like a domineering parent: Dick Sheppard, *Elizabeth: The Life and Career of Elizabeth Taylor* (Garden City: Doubleday, 1974), 44.

64 that Monty was torn: *ETO*, 63.

a large pain: Patricia Bosworth, *Montgomery Clift* (New York: Limelight, 1992; a reprint of the original 1978 printing from Harcourt Brace Jovanovich), 184

kept in a cocoon: Liz Smith, "Elizabeth Taylor: The Endless Ordeal," *Good Housekeeping*, April 1974, 148.

my first real chance: Bosworth, 184.

At first: *A Filmmaker's Journey*.

the key to my kind of acting: Vermilye and Ricci, 90.

far beyond anything: *Variety*, Aug. 12, 1951.

shaded, tender performance: *The New York Times*, Aug. 30, 1951.

65 The trouble with me: Waterbury, p. 98.

never accepted invitations: "Elizabeth, my Daughter," 102.

66 a good student: *Life*, February 6, 1950, 44.

She made my heart hurt: Reynolds, 70.

67 I liked playing the role: *ETO*, 64.

I don't think I even: *ET*, 27.

the reason I did it: Appearing on "Donahue," Feb. 15, 1988.

Yes, because we both adore: Quoted by Sidney Skolsky in the *New York Post*, March 25, 1958.

driven by feelings: *ETO*, 64.

inexperienced and naive: Helen Gurley Brown, "Girl Talk with Elizabeth," 242.

she used more: Bosworth, 201.

68 She looked ravishing: Ibid., 177.

like the most magical: *ET*, 9.

Every time we did: Elsa Maxwell, "Honeymoon Unlimited," *Photoplay*, September 1950, 87.

68–69 I closed my eyes to any problems: *ETO*, 64.

69 He'll make a very nice: Eleanor Harris, "Elizabeth Taylor: The Men in Her Life," *Look*, July 10, 1956.

70 I didn't have one clue: *ET*, 31.

She told me: Quoted in the London *Daily Mirror*, March 1, 1988.

My first husband was: London *Evening Standard*, March 25, 1968.

disillusionment: *ET*, 29.

I fell off: Arthur Halliwell, "Men and Giddy Liz," *People* (London), July 22, 1956.

71 Can you hide me: Mervyn Le Roy and Dick Kleinser, *Mervyn Le Roy: Take One* (New York: Hawthorn, 1974), 171.
He became sullen: *ETO*, 64.
Bad things were: ET, appearing on "Donahue," Feb. 15, 1988.
really horrendous: *ET*, 31.
the marks all the way: Quoted in Maddox, 87.
so terribly: Reynolds, 164.
repeated acts: Divorce proceedings, *Patricia McClintock Hilton* v. *Conrad Nicholas Hilton, Jr.*, August 1967; cited in the *Hollywood Citizen-News*, Feb. 6, 1969.
scarred me and left me: Sheppard, 77.
She no longer confided: "My Daughter Elizabeth," 172. It is worth noting that in the original 1954 version of her story, Sara wrote, "She no longer confided in us about anything" ("Elizabeth, my Daughter," 102). The revised version is as here: Sara clearly considered herself alone the paramount repository of confidences.

72 I didn't marry a girl: Maddox, 86; similarly, on "Oprah" (February 1988), ET regretted that her fame sometimes made her an "institution" to some men and intimidated them.

73 Nick [sic] and I: Metro-Goldwyn-Mayer press release dated Dec. 17, 1950.
It's doubtful: "Elizabeth Taylor Packs Up, Goes Home to Mother," *Hollywood Citizen-News*, Dec. 7, 1950.
Nicky does like to gamble: Ibid.

74 I will file: Hedda Hopper's syndicated column, Dec. 14, 1950.
which was absolutely: *ET*, 31.
On ET's divorce, see the public record: *Elizabeth Hilton, Plaintiff* v. *Conrad N. Hilton, Jr.*, Defendant: No. D 409065, Superior Court of the State of California, In and For the County of Los Angeles, Jan. 29, 1951 (Hon. Thurmond Clarke, Judge). See also, "Elizabeth Taylor Wins Divorce on Abuse Story," *Los Angeles Times*, Jan. 30, 1951; and "A Sobbing Elizabeth Taylor Wins Divorce at 18," *New York Herald Tribune*, Jan 30, 1951.
When I married him: Leonard Mosley, "Too much too soon," *Daily Express* (London), March 23, 1958.

75 recovery was hastened: Louella O. Parsons, *Tell It to Louella* (New York: Putnam's, 1961), 253.
a mountain of flowers: Harrison Carroll, "Donen Wiring Mass of Flowers to Liz on Nineteenth Birthday," Los Angeles *Evening Herald and Express*, Feb. 26, 1951.

She clung to him: Eleanor Harris, "Elizabeth Taylor: The Men in Her Life," *Look*, July 10, 1956.

77 I am happy: To Hedda Hopper, in the Hopper Collection, Academy of Motion Picture Arts and Sciences, and in Hopper column, Dec. 14, 1950.

78 I think it is instinct: *Newsweek*, July 2, 1951.
I expected her: Harris, "Elizabeth Taylor: The Men in Her Life."
She was extremely thin: Oral History: Pandro S. Berman, interviewed by Mike Steen, on deposit at the American Film Institute, Los Angeles.
a big medieval western: *ET*, 47.

Notes to Chapter Five

81 At the sight of him: Eleanor Harris, "Elizabeth Taylor: The Men in Her Life," *Look,* July 10, 1956.
We are all thinking: "Elizabeth, my Daughter," 103.

82 The most finished: Quoted in Michael Wilding, as told to Pamela Wilcox, *Applesauce* (London: George Allen and Unwin, 1982), 22. Similarly in Herbert Wilcox, *Twenty-Five Thousand Sunsets* (London: The Bodley Head, 1967), 148.
Like all women: Ibid., 25–26.
I was nobody's idea: Ibid., 29.

83 What's she got: Ibid., 76.
He was everything: Harris, "Elizabeth Taylor: The Men in Her Life."
He represented tranquillity: *ET*, 40.

84 emotionally upset: UPI nationwide dispatch, quoting an unnamed MGM source in, e.g., "Liz Will Fly to Nicky; She's Upset over Countess [von Furstenberg]," Los Angeles *Daily News*, Oct. 13, 1951.
On the chaos at the Plaza Hotel, see Bosworth, 214, and Harris, "Elizabeth Taylor: The Men in Her Life."

85 Liz, Wilding: *Los Angeles Examiner*, Dec. 12, 1951.
I reached for: Wilding, 77.

86 I am glad: Maddox, 98.
Michael is just: Ibid.
would not have disgraced: London *Evening News*, Feb. 21, 1952, repeated in "Riot as Liz Taylor, Actor Wed: Stampede by Bobby Soxers," *Los Angeles Examiner*, Feb. 22, 1952.

88 When she takes off: London *Evening Standard*, March 25, 1968.
Her worst fault: *Ladies' Home Journal*, Feb. 1954, 149.

90 I'll never divorce Sybil: Hollis Alpert, *Burton* (New York, G. P. Putnam's, 1986), 62.

91   awesome: Quoted in Melvyn Bragg, *Richard Burton, A Life* (Boston: Little, Brown, 1988), 74–75.
All I wanted: Ibid., 57.
She was, I decided: Richard Burton, *Meeting Mrs. Jenkins* (New York, William Morrow, 1966), 5.

91–92   The exchange with ET is documented in Ibid., 9–10.

92   I didn't fancy him then: Terry O'Neill, "Here Lies Elizabeth Taylor Burton," *Ladies' Home Journal*, Feb. 1973.
We sat on a hilltop: Ted Thackrey, Jr., "Michael Wilding, Second Husband of Liz Taylor, Dies," *Los Angeles Times*, July 9, 1979.
She snatched the paper: Wilding, 112.

93   You must not rub her: Gehman, "Elizabeth Taylor."
We were best friends: ET on the "Today" show (NBC-TV), interview with Nancy Collins broadcast June 18, 1986.
She would cry on his shoulder: Wilding, 116.

94   Vivien Leigh was my heroine: Latham, "National Velveeta," 172.

95   films that never should: *ETO*, 68.

96   a nervous ailment: Associated Press wire story dated Sept. 25, 1953, e.g., "Elizabeth Taylor, in Denmark, Has Collapse," *Los Angeles Times*, Sept. 26, 1953.
It's all been: The London *Daily Sketch*, Sept. 26, 1953, and the *Los Angeles Examiner*, same date.
We are amazed at these rumors: Ibid.

97   She has a nervous heart: *Los Angeles Examiner*, Oct. 11, 1950.
If she gets a cold: David Wallace, "Elizabeth Taylor's Greatest Battle," *Ladies' Home Journal*, Sept. 1990, 226.

98   God, when I think: *ET*, 47

99   Metro wanted her: Curtis Bernhardt to Mary Kiersch, *Curtis Bernhardt* (Metuchen and London: The Directors Guild of America/The Scarecrow Press, 1986), 169–71.
when he was giving her: Stewart Granger, *Sparks Fly Upward* (New York: Putnam's, 1981), 299.
Why not be comfortable: Eleanor Harris, "The Elizabeth Taylor Story," *Look*, June 26, 1956, p. 120.
You'd better watch out: Wilding, 99.

100   I thought I'd influence: Harris, "The Elizabeth Taylor Story"; see also Richard Boeth, "Elizabeth Taylor: Aftermath of a Scandal," *McCall's*, Jan. 1960, 128.
she was always complaining: Granger, 301.

101   Details of the production of *Giant* may be found in Box 24 of the Jack L. Warner Collection at the University of Southern California, Los Angeles.

Among those considered for the role of Leslie Benedict: Jane Wyman, Jennifer Jones, Olivia de Havilland, Ava Gardner, Susan Hayward, Jean Simmons, Eleanor Parker, Maureen O'Hara, Vivien Leigh, Virginia Mayo, Rita Hayworth, Deborah Kerr, Ann Blyth, Jane Greer, Donna Reed, Katharine Hepburn, Audrey Hepburn, Anne Baxter, June Allyson, Gene Tierney, Joanne Dru, Joan Fontaine, Betsy Drake, Dorothy McGuire, Nancy Olson, Patricia Neal, Lana Turner and Jeanne Crain.

I was no longer a teenager: ET, in the Stevens/Winslow interview (as above) for the documentary film *A Filmmaker's Journey*.

102   George Stevens and Elizabeth: Ibid.

102–3 The creativity of homosexuals: ET, on the first broadcast of "Whoopi," Sept. 14, 1992; similarly on Larry King's television show, March 3, 1993.

103   who probably never met: *Vanity Fair*, Nov. 1992.
       Rock and I hit it off: *ETO*, 69.

104   Jimmy was always late: In the Stevens/Winslow interview for *A Filmmaker's Journey* (as above).
       Sometimes Jimmy and I: Many times—e.g., in the Stevens/Winslow interview, and to Larry King on TNT television, March 13, 1993.

104–5 For details of ET's illnesses, see Folder 692 of the *Giant* production memoranda (Warner/USC, as above), the entire contents of which is devoted to daily medical bulletins on her condition.

105   The details of James Dean's death have been much documented. See, e.g., Brian O'Dowd, "James Dean: The Day He Died," *Hollywood Studio Magazine*, vol. 20, no. 9 (September 1987), 5–9.
       The citations from studio memoranda are contained, as detailed above, in the "ET Illnesses" file of *Giant*.
       She's a seething mass: Harris, "The Elizabeth Taylor Story," Part 1.

106   We had a brother-sister kind: *ETO*, 69.

Notes to Chapter Six

107   I follow you around: Harris, "The Elizabeth Taylor Story," Part 3.

108   My taste buds: Ibid.
       She really became: Harris, "The Elizabeth Taylor Story," Part 1.
       I know of only: Stanley Gordon, "Elizabeth Taylor: From Tragedy . . . New Fame," *Look*, Oct. 14, 1958.
       He had offered her: Reynolds, 169.
       I was still in love: Wilding, 120.

108–9   I'm afraid in those last years: *ET*, 59.

109   You're nothing but a coward: Wilding, 121.

110   Don't ask me: Harris, "The Elizabeth Taylor Story," Part 1.

111   Details of the production of *Raintree County* are contained in Folder 7 of Production Number 1692 in the Metro-Goldwyn-Mayer collection at the University of Southern California.

112   She really was: Edward Dmytryk to DS, Aug. 29, 1994.
I had one blink: Ibid.

113   Elizabeth was afraid: Quoted in Bosworth, 300.
She really was miraculous: Dmytryk to DS.

114   Elizabeth's marriage with: Kevin McClory, quoted in Michael Todd, Jr., and Susan McCarthy Todd, *A Valuable Property* (New York: Arbor House, 1983), 310–11.
The Mocambo: Los Angeles *Mirror-News*, July 20, 1956.
Everybody knows who: Ibid., 310.

115   Dames and comedy: C. M. McCullin, "Mike Todd," *Hollywood Studio Magazine*, vol. 20, no. 9 (Sept. 1987), 16.

116   On Joan Blondell's broken arm, see Sheilah Graham, *Hollywood Revisited* (New York: St. Martin's, 1985), 184.

117   Money is only important: Charles Denton, "The Mike Todd Story—Three Great Loves Had He," Los Angeles *Herald & Express*, March 26, 1958.
When he entered: Reynolds, 168.
He was certainly: Evelyn Keyes to DS, July 14, 1994.

118   Besides actresses: Evelyn Keyes, *Scarlett O'Hara's Younger Sister: My Lively Life In and Out of Hollywood* (Secaucus: Lyle Stuart, 1977), 235.
The telephone dialogue is from Keyes to DS and Keyes, 236–37.

119   To tell the truth: Evelyn Keyes to DS, July 14, 1994.
latent intellectual: *ETO*, 70.
Drink as much as: Ibid.

119–20   I had a feeling: The quotation combines her statements found in Boeth, "Elizabeth Taylor: Aftermath of a Scandal," *ET*, 62, and *ETO*, 70–71.

120   Elizabeth, I love you: Hopper, 14.
I went from a weak man: ET, appearing on "Donahue," Feb. 15, 1988.
Much careful thought: MGM press release dated July 19, 1956, quoted in the Los Angeles newspapers (e.g., the *Mirror-News*) on July 20, 1956.

121   an ominous phone cal: Wilding, 122.

122   that she was going to marry: Todd and Todd, 313.
It isn't the Todd romance: *Time*, Sept. 17, 1956.

I love Mike: *Time*, Sept. 17, 1956.

123   I'm engaged to Mike Todd: Dmytryk to DS, Aug. 29, 1994.

It wasn't unlike: Reynolds, 169.

124   It was not until: Leonard Slater, "Mr. Edwin J. Fisher: Older & Wiser & Happier," *McCall's*, Jan. 1962, 132.

I have already had: Edwin Schallert, "Elizabeth Taylor Says She'll Reduce Film Activities If She Marries Again," *Los Angeles Times*, Oct. 26, 1956.

Details of the Taylor-Wilding divorce were widely reported— e.g., in the *Los Angeles Times*, Nov. 14, 1956, and the Beverly Hills *Citizen*, same date.

She hasn't asked me: *Los Angeles Times*, Nov. 15, 1956.

Notes to Chapter Seven

127   I love being surrounded: *ETO*, 38.

128   It seems to me: Louella O. Parsons, "Wilding Speeds Liz, Todd Plans," *Los Angeles Examiner*, Jan. 25, 1957.

Mike's the kind of guy: Waterbury, 208.

129   She doesn't want: *Look*, April 30, 1957.

I knew I wanted: *ET*, 137, 67.

130   Sure, we had: Often—e.g., Marilyn Kruse, "Has Liz Taylor Met Her Match?" Sunday *Chicago Tribune Magazine,* Nov. 10, 1957, 51.

clobbered her: Reynolds, 169–70.

131   never once come across: Leonard Mosley, "Too Much Too Soon," London *Daily Express*, March 23, 1958.

full of fireworks: Parsons, 259.

Doesn't every girl: Mason Wiley and Damien Bona, *Inside Oscar* (New York: Ballantine, 1988), 278.

I idolized Mike: Fisher, 122.

132   Elizabeth has no girl friends: Richard Gehman, "Debbie Reynolds: Her Story," *McCall's*, March 1959, 135.

Congratulations: Susan Poore, "The Secret Hollywood Won't Tell," *Inside Edition*, July 1959, 42.

Why don't you dress up: Gehman, "Debbie Reynolds: Her Story," 137.

133   It will be the twenty-fifth: "William Hickey's Photo News," London *Daily Express*, July 3, 1957.

Being Mike's wife: *Look*, Aug. 15, 1961, 32.

He was twenty-five years: *ETO*, 71.

135   I think it would be nice: Mrs. Michael Todd, as told to Joe

Hyams, "I'm Saying Good-by [*sic*] to the Movies," *This Week*, March 16, 1958.

Of course, doesn't everyone: London *Daily Mail*, Jan. 29, 1958.

136   because she's the best: *Hollywood Citizen-News*, Jan. 16, 1958.

I am finding it difficult: *Los Angeles Times*, Jan. 22, 1958.

I want to have tea: Los Angeles *Herald & Express*, Jan. 24, 1958.

Details of the Todd visit to Moscow may also be found in the Los Angeles *Herald & Express* for Jan. 27 and 28, 1958; and in the London *Daily Mail* for Jan. 27, 1958.

137   to promote: *Los Angeles Times*, Feb. 11, 1958.

I don't want: Mrs. Michael Todd, as told to Joe Hyams, "I'm Saying Good-by to the Movies."

139   Maggie was the only: Donald Spoto, *The Kindness of Strangers: The Life of Tennessee Williams* (Boston: Little, Brown, 1985), 199.

141   really intrigued: *ETO*, 74.

no technique: Ibid., 90.

You have to understand: Ibid., 91.

a beauty: Brian Moynahan, "Get Her to the Eighth on Time," the London *Independent*, Oct. 6, 1991.

Mike Todd's private plane is usually referred to, incorrectly, as *The Lucky Liz;* there was no adjective.

142   I'll wear it always: *Los Angeles Times*, Sept. 11, 1958.

Elizabeth was in shock: Reynolds, 183.

143   You're with her: Gehman, "Debbie Reynolds: Her Story," 137.

The only reason: Gordon, "Elizabeth Taylor: From Tragedy . . . New Farce," 90.

144   She was so weak: Ibid.

wonderfully kind: Hugh Corcoran to DS, Nov. 2, 1994.

well-accented: *Variety*, Aug. 13, 1958.

terrific: *The New York Times*, Sept. 19, 1958.

surprising sureness: *Time*, Sept. 15, 1958.

145   I could not sleep: *ETO*, 80–81.

146   We were cast as: Art Buchwald, "The Woes of Elizabeth and Eddie," *Los Angeles Times*, Aug. 25, 1959.

I never had that problem: Ibid.

We had lots of problems: London *News of the World*, Jan. 20, 1963.

147   My whole body: Fisher, 82–83.

148   He kissed me: Ibid., and Gehman, "Debbie Reynolds: Her Story," 137.

I fabricated a meeting: Fisher, 146.

149   Elizabeth Taylor and Eddie Fisher were: Earl Wilson, *The Show Business Nobody Knows* (Chicago: Cowles, 1971), 159.

181 I still think: *Time*, April 28, 1961, 71: the magazine substituted the word *obscenity* for *shit*.
I should've won for: ET, on the Larry King television show, March 3, 1993.
I lost to a tracheotomy: Maddox, 155.
the Academy wanted: *ETO*, 82–83.
No, . . . After all: Wiley and Bona, 330.
When the Academy forgives: Sidney Skolsky, "What Goes on at the Academy Awards," *McCall's*, May 1961, 152.

182 All those antibiotics: Eleanor Harris, "How Liz Taylor Has Changed," the *Hollywood Citizen-News*, "Family Weekly" section, June 10, 1961.
the most dramatic example: Widely reported—e.g., in "Elizabeth Taylor Tells of Fight Against Death," *Los Angeles Times* and *Los Angeles Examiner*, both for July 9, 1961.
Dying is: Ibid.; see also Maddox, 164.
The experience I had: London *Evening Standard*, March 25, 1968.

183 I'm lazy: Jack Hamilton, "Elizabeth Taylor Talks of Living Dying Acting Loving," *Look*, Aug. 15, 1964, 28.

184 to further: Widely reported in the wire services—e.g., *Los Angeles Times*, Jan. 17, 1961.

185 The new child: Sheila Weller, "The Happy New Life of Elizabeth Taylor's 'Baby,'" *McCall's*, Sept. 1982, 116.
just a little more than: Robert Deardorff, "Aftermath of an Adoption," *Redbook*, Oct. 1962, 120.

187 I awoke at five-thirty: *The New York Times*, June 9, 1963. See also the brochure, "*Cleopatra*: Making the Intimate Epic," an enclosure with the CBS/Fox LaserDisc version of the film.
She looks gorgeous: Jack Brodsky and Nathan Weiss, *The Cleopatra Papers: A Private Correspondence* (New York: Simon and Schuster, 1963), 4.

188 loved working: Rex Harrison, *A Damned Serious Business* (New York: Bantam, 1991), 182.

189 She is my child: Quoted by Wanger and Hyams, 44.
On the adoption of Maria, see "Elizabeth Taylor Talks About Being a Mother," *Ladies' Home Journal*, March 1969.
All this stuff: Tynan, "*Playboy* Interview: Richard Burton," 61.
She gives you a sense: Ibid.
He was a very poor boy: Natalie Gittelson, "Liz," *McCall's*, Sept. 1985, 135.

190 an extraordinarily beautiful: Alpert, 103.
I envied: Ibid., 102.

191   She'll be on the set: Brodsky and Weiss, 35.

Prince Charming: *ET*, 105.

I had to help: *ET*, 103; see also Alpert, 104.

191ff.   The details of the Taylor-Burton affair are, of course, documented worldwide in books, magazines and newspapers. Day-to-day specifics were anxiously documented in the Wanger diaries and in the Brodsky-Weiss correspondence, *q.v. Life* published an elegant photo-essay on Mankiewicz's intentions for the picture: "The Man Who Knows Tells the Story of a Tumultuous Epic: 'Cleopatra' Barges In," April 19, 1963.

192   in her black eyes: Bragg, 165.

argumentative and abusive: Graham Jenkins, with Barry Turner, *Richard Burton, My Brother* (New York: Harper & Row, 1988), 117.

You make me feel: Bragg, 151.

193   sitting on a volcano: Ibid.

It was hard: Wanger and Hyams, 49.

I behaved indiscreetly: Widely quoted—e.g., *Cosmopolitan*, Aug. 1961.

It's no rumor: Brodsky and Weiss, 35. To the Brodsky-Weiss correspondence and the Wanger diaries we owe the clearest understanding and proper chronology of everything surrounding the production of *Cleopatra*.

194   I'm a selfish man: Wanger and Hyams, 44.

"Jack," he told: Ibid., 52.

I fall more in love: Ibid.

At the height of it: Harrison, *A Damned Serious Business,* 180.

195   Elizabeth's suicide attempt, as described by Burton, is published in Bragg, 365–66.

Mr. Mankiewicz: Brodsky and Weiss, 62 (letter of April 14); see also Wanger and Hyams, diary entry for April 6.

The real story: Ibid.

I just got fed up: Brodsky and Weiss, 52.

The romance has changed: Wanger and Hyams, 46.

196   She was the reverse: Sally Ogle Davis, "Elizabeth Taylor, Her Way," *Ladies' Home Journal*, Nov. 1991, 268.

196–97   my home away from home: "Elizabeth Taylor and the New Cleopatra Look," *Look*, Feb. 27, 1962, 90.

197   'The more the better': Liz Smith, "Liz on Liz," *TV Guide*, June 4, 1994, 10.

furious: "My Daughter, Elizabeth," 175.

give a woman: "Elizabeth Taylor and the New Cleopatra Look."

198 When you're in a cage: *Life,* April 19, 1963.
Who do you love: Fisher, 209.
were just two actors: Sheilah Graham, 184.
Row Over Actor: The Los Angeles *Herald Examiner*, March 9, 1962, 1.
I had to get out: Fisher, 1–2.

199 Do you think: Brodsky and Weiss, 54.
those who show: On this entire matter, and for the sources of the quotations here offered, see the *Los Angeles Times* and *Variety*, both dated May 23, 1962.

200 erotic vagrancy: For the letter in *Osservatore della Domenica*, see the dispatches from United Press International and the Associated Press dated April 13, 1962, published, e.g., in the *Los Angeles Times* and *Herald Examiner*, April 12 and 13.
I watched her: Wanger and Hyams, 52.

201 a woman of force: Bosley Crowther, in *The New York Times*, June 13, 1963.

202 I need $225,000: "My Daughter: Her Life and Her Loves," 175.

Notes to Chapter Ten

203 The reflections at the beginning of this chapter owe much to ideas first expressed by the author of *America as a Civilization*, Max Lerner, in his essay, "Return of the Femme Fatale," *Ladies' Home Journal*, June 1963.

205 Will you marry Richard: Jenkins, 133.

206 I adore fighting: *Life*, Dec. 18, 1964.

207–8 a much misunderstood: Dawn Langley Simmons, *Margaret Rutherford, A Blithe Spirit* (New York: McGraw-Hill, 1983), 156.

208 Now, you shit-faced bastard: Jim Hoffman, "Liz Confesses: 'Burton's Ruining Me with Liquor!,'" *Photoplay*, April 1964, 88.
She was always: R. J. Minney, *"Puffin" Asquith* (London: Leslie Frewin, 1973), 202.
She is a director's joy: *Los Angeles Times*, Sept. 1, 1963 ("Calendar" Section), 1, 7.

209 not quietly: Thelda Victor with Muriel Davidson, "The Drama the Cameras Missed," *The Saturday Evening Post*, July 11–18, 1964.
I have always wanted: Ibid.

210 Michael never liked Hollywood: Karen von Unge to DS, Aug. 28, 1994.

211 Whatever else I do: Budd Schulberg, *Moving Pictures* (New York: Stein and Day, 1981), 130–31.

Did you see: Victor, "The Drama the Cameras Missed."

212 My children are remarkable: *Life*, Dec. 18, 1964; see also *ET*, 151.

Look at her: Ibid.

It is ridiculous: Victor, "The Drama the Cameras Missed."

My best feature: Originally, ET to Richard Meryman, in *Life*, Dec. 18, 1964; thus also later in *ET*, 170.

213 To be in his company: Jenkins, 140.

a ferocious drinker: Ava Gardner, *Ava: My Story* (New York: Bantam, 1990), 249.

I'm a Method Actor: *Life*, Dec. 20, 1963.

On the drinking bout with the press on Dec. 23, 1963, see the UPI dispatch filed by Carlos Schiebeck the following day.

214 I genuinely do not believe: *ET*, 59.

What Elizabeth wants: Earl Wilson's column in, e.g., the Los Angeles *Herald Examiner*, March 6, 1964.

There'll be someone: *Modern Screen*, May 1964.

We will wait: *Time*, Jan. 3, 1964.

On the arrival in Los Angeles, see Jack Smith in the *Los Angeles Times*, Jan. 23, 1964.

215 The queen was home: Ibid.

Richard and I love each other: Toronto *Telegram* dispatch picked up by the Associated Press, Feb. 4, 1964.

Isn't that fat: Alpert, 140.

I don't know why: Ibid., 139.

216 And they said: Bragg, 187.

Her first marriage: *Newsweek*, Oct. 5, 1964.

Richard has given me: Alpert, 142.

I rely on him: Bragg, 192.

I'm a woman who needs: Ibid.

On ET calling Burton "Dad," see Bragg, 194.

I love not being: *Life*, Dec. 18, 1964; also in *ET*, 129.

217 Backstage and out front: Stanley Elkin, "Miss Taylor and Family: An Outside View," *Esquire*, Nov. 1964, 120.

218 On the poetry reading of June 22, 1964, see *Time*, July 3, 1964, 62; the *Los Angeles Times*, June 23, 1964; *Variety*, June 24, 1964; and the Los Angeles *Herald Examiner*, June 25, 1964.

219 For the money: *Newsweek*, Dec. 21, 1964.

220 Let's have cocktails: Reynolds, 276.

The film was so bad: C. Robert Jennings, "Elizabeth Taylor, Alas!" *Los Angeles Times* magazine (*West*), May 21, 1967, 45.

221 On the Burtons' tax situation for *The Sandpiper* see, among oth-

ers, Vincente Minnelli, with Hector Arce, *I Remember It Well* (New York: Doubleday, 1974), 356–57.

not that I love: UPI wire service dispatch dated Jan. 9, 1965.

Money is more valuable: Sidney Skolsky's syndicated column—e.g., in the *Hollywood Citizen-News*, Jan. 15, 1965.

222 I had seen: Ernest Lehman to DS: his contributions to this book were made in a series of interviews on July 15 and 18, 1994.

223 I *am* George: Ibid.; see also Alpert, 169.

224 I can't go to a pub: Bragg, 201.

John Le Carré's reminiscences of the Burtons are excerpted from Bragg, 201–02.

225 I love four-letter words: *ET*, 132.

With Richard Burton: *ETO*, 87–88.

226 We both have feelings: Richard Burton, "His Liz: 'A Scheming Charmer,'" *Life*, Feb. 24, 1967.

227 I'm wonderful at playing: New York *Daily News*, May 25, 1981.

Notes to Chapter Eleven

230 taught me subtleties: Bragg, 172.

231 I am one of the few people: John McPhee, "The Man on the Billboard," *Time* (cover story), April 26, 1963.

Pure vodka: Russell Braddon, "Richard Burton to Liz: 'I Love Thee Not . . . ,'" *The Saturday Evening Post*, Dec. 3, 1966.

I had a hollow leg: Ivor Davis and Sally Ogle Davis, "Elizabeth Taylor, the Sequel," *Los Angeles* magazine, May 1987.

epic squabbles: Franco Zeffirelli, *Zeffirelli* (New York: Weidenfeld & Nicolson, 1986), 212.

232 I get a lusting: *Photoplay*, Dec. 1967.

I'm in a state of shock: Bosworth, 412.

She gave us: Zeffirelli, 217.

When she told me: Ibid.

234 Elizabeth loved her children: Noreen Taylor, "The Burtons," London *Daily Mirror*, Feb. 29, 1988.

I am just a broad: "Peter Glenville talks about the Burtons," *Vogue*, Sept. 1, 1967.

235 I drink Jack Daniel's: Noreen Taylor, "The Burtons."

Is that the famous: Widely reported—e.g., in *ETO*, 84–85; see also Liz Smith, "The $10,000,000 Jewels of Elizabeth Taylor & Jacqueline Onassis," *Ladies' Home Journal*, Dec. 1969.

236 I know I'm vulgar: Alpert, 193; see also Georgina Howell, "Liz," *Vogue*, June 1991.

screaming, drunk and abusive: Michel Ciment, *Conversations with Losey* (London and New York: Methuen, 1985), 275.

237 I have just spent: Bragg, 255.

238 They must be: Maddox, 210.

I just came out: Academy of Motion Picture Arts and Sciences: interview with ET dated Aug. 1, 1981, preserved in the George Stevens Papers, Box 2.

238–39 A Jack on the rocks: Thomas Thompson, in *Life*, Jan. 17, 1969.

239 more concerned: Fisher, 176.

It can't be alright: Bragg, 278.

sipping away: Ibid., 280.

240 stoned, unfocussed: Ibid., 287.

241 venomous malice: Ibid., 294.

When Elizabeth and Richard: Noreen Taylor, "Fighting and Boozing," London *Daily Mirror*, March 1, 1988.

We are fighting: Bragg, 316.

242 Except when we were alone: Bragg, 326–27.

243 butchered and killed: Edna O'Brien, in *Writers' News*, April 1972.

244 She was smashing: William Hall, *Raising Caine* (Englewood Cliffs, N.J.: Prentice-Hall, 1981), 166–67.

Mother's life: *Time*, May 22, 1972.

246 I made a fool of myself: Rex Reed, "Elizabeth Taylor Sees Red in 'The Blue Bird,'" *Ladies' Home Journal*, Oct. 1975.

Once I started: Bragg, 415.

247 get that woman: Edward Dmytryk to DS, Aug. 29, 1994. See also Dmytryk, 292–95.

248 I don't worry: "Elizabeth Taylor's Astonishing 'Face-lift,'" *Ladies' Home Journal*, Dec. 1973.

248–49 I told her to get out: Curtis Bill Pepper, "We Couldn't Live Without Each Other," *McCall's*, March 1974.

249 more fun: Raymond Vignale, "Liz Taylor's Private Secretary Tells All!" *Motion Picture*, Aug. 1976.

It wasn't love at first sight: London *Mail on Sunday*: "You" magazine, Oct. 21, 1990. In the transcribed interview, the magazine retained the patterns of Wynberg's accented English, here modified for clarity's sake.

I think she suddenly saw: Peter Evans, "Elizabeth Taylor," *Cosmopolitan*, Nov. 1974.

250 Make it bigger: Robert Colacello, "Liz and Andy," *Vogue*, Jan. 1974.

When Elizabeth loves you: Bragg, 417.

Our marriage has turned: Dorothy Cameron Disney, "Elizabeth

Taylor & Richard Burton: Why This Marriage Can't Be Saved," *Ladies' Home Journal*, Oct. 1973.

I've worked since childhood: Curtis Bill Pepper, "I Don't Want to Be That Much in Love Ever Again," *McCall's*, Jan. 1974.

251 I have been totally dependent: Ibid.

252 We are shooting: Henry Gris, "Liz Taylor," *Photoplay*, Dec. 1973.

I sometimes worry: Evans, "Elizabeth Talking."

Henry acquired: Ibid.

Poor Elizabeth: Ibid.

Three months from now: Ibid.

253 brooding and dramatic: Paulene Stone, with Peter Evans, *One Tear Is Enough* (London: Michael Joseph, 1975), 154.

Notes to Chapter Twelve

255 but not quite: Evans, "Elizabeth Taylor."

256 On the unpleasantness surrounding the production of *The Klansman*, see Donald Zec, *Marvin* (London: New English Library, 1979), 205–15.

My God, I can do: Dorothy Manners, "Without Waiting for Divorce, Liz Spends Day and Night with Her Lover!" *Modern Screen*, Aug. 1974.

257 The world knows Henry: Nick Longhurst, "Liz Taylor and Henry," *National Enquirer*, July 7, 1974.

259 She was indeed one of the most famous: London *Mail on Sunday*, Oct. 21, 1990.

Twenty minutes after: *People*, Sept. 15, 1975.

The rental agreement: Karen von Unge to DS, Aug. 28, 1994.

260 I don't know: Rex Reed, "Elizabeth Taylor Sees Red in 'The Blue Bird.'"

261 a disaster: Patrick McGilligan, *George Cukor: A Double Life* (New York: St. Martin's, 1991), 315.

Then for two days: *People*, Sept. 15, 1975.

We really cannot: Ibid.

My former husband: Ibid.

It was a bombshell: Henry Gris and Tony Brenna in the *National Enquirer*, Sept. 9, 1975.

I was her lover: Joyce Haber's column in the *Los Angeles Times*, Oct. 6, 1975.

262 We are stuck: Elizabeth Taylor, "Richard Again," *Ladies' Home Journal*, Feb. 1976.

Sturm has remarried Drang: Ellen Goodman in the *Boston Globe*, cited in Maddox, 233.

like a huge dream: Bragg, 433.

263 Romance with Elizabeth: *People*, March 8, 1976.
That's the Taj Mahal: *New York* magazine, April 5, 1976.

264 Actress Elizabeth Taylor's ex-boyfriend: Los Angeles *Herald-Examiner*, Feb. 16 and 17 and July 25, 1977.

265 I just laugh: Clare Crawford and Parviz Raein, "The Charming Zahedi Ponders: Can Liz Taylor Be a Diplomatic Incident?" *People*, June 14, 1976.
I love Richard Burton: Gwen Davis, "Elizabeth Taylor: My Life Is a Little . . . Complicated," *McCall's*, June 1976.

266 But I can't walk in: *Esquire*, Nov. 1977.

267 John Warnermellon: Sally Quinn, "John Warner: Rally Round the Flag," *Washington Post*, April 16, 1976.

267ff. An assessment of John Warner's career was published in *The New Republic*, Feb. 7, 1983.
My first marriage broke up: David E. Koskoff, *The Mellons* (New York: Thomas Y. Crowell, 1978), 533. See also Latham, "National Velveeta."
the horse business: Burton Hersh, *The Mellon Family: A Fortune in History* (New York: Morrow, 1978), 524.
You are such a terrific woman: Margo Howard, "The Warner Touch," *The New Republic*, Feb. 7, 1983.

268 John should have been born: *Current Biography*, Nov. 1976, 31.
He is not intellectually demanding: Howard, "The Warner Touch."
He made a serious effort: Ibid.
Being head of the U.S. Navy: Ibid.
My children suffered: Ibid.
Not everyone wants: Ibid.

269 This reminds me: Nick Thimmesch, "The Farmer (John Warner) Takes a Wife (Elizabeth Taylor)," *McCall's*, Jan. 1977.
She knows what she's up to: Dan Kristo, "Hermione Gingold," *Footlights*, June 1978.

270 I was petrified: *Los Angeles Times*, Feb. 20, 1978.
John knows what he's going to do: *Women's Wear Daily*, Nov. 5, 1976.
I lean a little: Thimmesch, "The Farmer (John Warner) Takes a Wife (Elizabeth Taylor)."

271 fully aware: *ETO*, 35.
I've never voted: *Los Angeles Times*, Feb. 20, 1978.
But if I can't: "Notes on People," *The New York Times*, Nov. 12, 1976.
I've never had an acting lesson: *Los Angeles Times*, Jan. 21, 1977.

I've always loved: E.g., Jerry Watson, "My loves, marriages and mistakes, by Liz Taylor," London *Evening News*, April 7, 1977.

272   I've never felt so much: *People*, Feb. 14, 1977.
273   We've made a deal: Ibid.
       I enjoy eating: Watson, "My Loves, Marriages and Mistakes."
274   For the first time: Adam Edwards, "Liz Taylor for the President's Wife?" *Woman's Own*, May 20, 1978.
       My husband even put on: Sandra McElwaine, "The Farmer's Wife," *Ladies' Home Journal*, Aug. 1977.
       Gee, you're large: Ibid.
       If I have to make: Graham, 185.
       We're not quitting: *People*, June 18, 1978.
275   This face has been: *Los Angeles Times*, April 3, 1978.
275–76   I'm getting kind of sick: *Hollywood Reporter*, Oct. 16, 1978.
276   I'm just so thrilled: UPI dispatch, Nov. 8, 1978.

Notes to Chapter Thirteen

277   I was losing: *ETO*, 39.
278   a domestic Siberia: Ibid., 42.
       The principal role in Elizabeth's life: Leslie Garis, "Elizabeth Taylor: She Has Conquered Everything But Broadway, and Now . . . " *The New York Times*, May 3, 1981.
279   I was the loneliest person: Vernon Scott, "Elizabeth at Sixty," *Good Housekeeping,* Feb. 1992.
       It was large and very heavy: David Lewin, "Why Liz Taylor Feels She Can Take Care of Herself," *Woman's Own*, Sept. 27, 1980.
280   In the old days: Ted Thackrey, Jr., "Michael Wilding, Second Husband of Liz Taylor, Dies," *Los Angeles Times*, July 9, 1979.
280–81   Washington is a very difficult: Helen Gurley Brown, "Girl Talk with Elizabeth the Great."
281   This town and Washington: Bruce Bibby, "Taylor Made," *Premiere*, October 1992.
       Elizabeth Taylor wore: Joan Rivers, with Richard Meryman, *Still Talking* (New York: Turtle Bay/Random House, 1991), 121, 126–27.
281–82   Congress, in my opinion: Associated Press dispatched dated Feb. 2, 1980—e.g., Los Angeles *Herald-Examiner*, Feb. 3, 1980.
282   Abe Lincoln: David S. Broder, "Draft Debate Heats Up When Warners Go at It," *Los Angeles Times*, Feb. 3, 1980. See also *New York Post*, Feb. 4, 1980.
       I am not a Republican: Latham, "National Velveeta."

Elizabeth is really stronger: Lewin, "Why Liz Feels She Can Take Care of Herself."

Well, you ought to think: *People*, March 24, 1980.

We have a very competitive: Garry Clifford, "John Warner Describes the Cozy Caucus of Two That Liz Has Made of Their Life," *People*, Oct. 20, 1980.

284 I couldn't have settled: Lewin, "Why Liz Feels She Can Take Care of Herself."

politics involves: Ibid.

Why don't you call me: *People*, April 6, 1981.

285 a robust and involving: *Washington Post*, March 20, 1981.

I think Elizabeth was good: *People*, April 6, 1981.

defensive and uncertain: *Variety*, March 4, 1981.

286 I've got you married: Ibid.

I want to give her: David Blundy, "At last—Elizabeth Taylor's Broadway Debut," London Sunday *Times* magazine, May 17, 1981.

the bronchitis: Irene Lacher, "Liz Biz," *Los Angeles Times*, April 27, 1990.

She kept growing: *Film Comment*, May–June 1986.

charm, grandeur and sex appeal: Frank Rich, in *The New York Times*, May 8, 1981.

well thought out: Brendan Gill, in *The New Yorker*, May 18, 1981.

287 random, arbitrary: Walter Kerr, "The Trouble with Miss Taylor," *The New York Times*, May 17, 1981.

underdeveloped: Jack Kroll, "Elizabeth in the Foxes' Den," *Newsweek*, May 18, 1981.

I have a sense of accomplishment: Gerald Clarke, "The Long Way to Broadway," *Time*, March 30, 1981.

My life had no meaning: Thomas Thompson, "Private Thoughts of a Former Washingtonian," *Life*, March 1982.

What a camp: Los Angeles *Herald-Examiner*, Sept. 19, 1981.

288 Drugs had become a crutch: Anne Edwards, "Elizabeth the Extraordinary," *Ladies' Home Journal*, March 1986.

288–89 hooked on Percodan: Dominick Dunne, "The Red Queen," *Vanity Fair*, Dec. 1985.

289 On the 1994 censure of those among ET's physicians who over-prescribed controlled substances, see the press for August 1994—e.g., *Time*, Aug. 22.

Elizabeth Taylor sailed into London: Nicholas de Jongh, *The Guardian*, March 12, 1982.

290 She suggests no scheming: Arthur Thirkell, London *Daily Mirror*, March 12, 1982.

She made an entrance worthy of: Jenny Rees, London *Daily Express*, March 12, 1982.

Miss Taylor is enough of an artist: John Barber, London *Daily Telegraph*, March 12, 1982.

She has moments of real power: Milton Shulman, London *Evening Standard*, March 12, 1982.

Miss Taylor looks in tiptop: Irving Wardle, London *Times*, March 12, 1982.

291   We're very much in love: New York *Daily News*, Feb. 9, 1983; see also Katherine Barrett, "Two Rare Views of Elizabeth Taylor," *Ladies' Home Journal*, May 1983.

291ff.   On the press conference and the journey to the Middle East, see David Colker, "And Liz Has a Mideast Plan, Too," Los Angeles *Herald-Examiner*, Dec. 12, 1982; and David Blundy, "Cleopatra's Hectic Peace Initiative," London Sunday *Times*, Jan. 2, 1983.

292   to try to create peace: Ibid.

I am Mother Courage: Often—e.g., Sheppard, 468; see also Rex Reed, "Elizabeth Taylor Sees Red in 'The Blue Bird,'" *Ladies' Home Journal*, Oct. 1975.

293   Regarding ET's intake of alcohol, this list of daily drinks was outlined for Larry King on his television show, March 3, 1993.

294   She's the nympho: *Los Angeles Times*, Jan. 25, 1983.

A job's a job: Ibid.

295   She can have him: Gioia DiLiberto, "For Liz and Dick . . . " *People*, July 25, 1983.

a white-tie-and-taco: Natalie Gittelson, "Liz," *McCall's*, Sept. 1985.

When Taylor should be: *Boston Globe*, April 10, 1983.

This production has: *The New York Times*, May 9, 1983.

296   I had caused my children such pain: ET, appearing on "Donahue," Feb. 15, 1988.

Notes to Chapter Fourteen

297   She was a bewildered: Phyllis Battelle, "What Liz Taylor Has Gone Through," *Ladies' Home Journal*, May 1984.

It was the first time: ET, on *Hour Magazine* television show, Aug. 21–25, 1987.

I was terrified: Battelle, "What Liz Taylor Has Gone Through."

298   Today is Friday: John Duka, "Elizabeth Taylor: Journal of a Recovery," *The New York Times*, Feb. 4, 1985.

299   Fame: Helen Gurley Brown, "Girl Talk with Elizabeth the Great."

300   I plan to be on vacation: Natalie Gittelson, "Liz," *McCall's*, Sept. 1985.

       My God, this looks: *People*, Oct. 29, 1984.

       I knew she would be devastated: London *Sunday People*, Oct. 14, 1984.

301   the best-looking man: ET to Nolan Miller, her wardrobe designer for *Hotel* and (later, among other projects) *Poker Alice*; quoted in *People*, Jan. 7, 1985.

       She has a knack: Michelle Green, "With Drugs, Booze, Flab and Another Fiancé Behind Her, Liz Lets the Good Times Roll," *People*, March 11, 1985.

       Dennis is very Brooklyn: Ibid.

302   She was absolutely wonderful: Robert Wagner, on the Arts & Entertainment Network's 1993 *Biography* special, "Elizabeth Taylor."

       Everybody on the production: Mart Crowley to DS, July 18, 1994.

303   I have to constantly pinch: "Liz Taylor Lifts a Stein," *US*, Jan. 28, 1985.

       No interviews: *People*, March 11, 1985.

       I almost made a mistake: Dominick Dunne, "The Red Queen," *Vanity Fair*, Dec. 1985.

       No matter what happens: Anne Edwards, "Elizabeth the Extraordinary."

       Never has a disease: Mary Louise Oates, "Former First Lady Ford Is AIDS Project Honoree," *Los Angeles Times*, June 28, 1985.

304   I was so angry: Helen Gurley Brown, "Girl Talk with Elizabeth the Great."

       I don't think President Bush: *Vanity Fair*, Nov. 1992.

       AIDS is not a sin: Often and widely—e.g., Long Beach *Press Telegraph*, Dec. 4, 1991.

304–5   This offends: Vernon Scott, "Elizabeth at Sixty," *Good Housekeeping*, Feb. 1992; see also *Hello!*, Aug. 1993.

305   There is an urgent need: Los Angeles *Herald-Examiner*, May 9, 1986; see also ET's appearance before the House Energy and Commerce subcommittee on health and environment, Sept. 22, 1987—documented, e.g., in the Los Angeles *Herald-Examiner*, Sept. 23, 1987.

       I don't give a shit: Ibid.

305–6   At that time: Landon Y. Jones, "Elizabeth Triumphant," *People*, Dec. 10, 1990.

306 I am here: Hearing Before the Committee on Labor and Human Resources, United States Senate, One Hundred Second Congress: Examining Methods of Providing HIV Care, Focusing on Implementation of The Ryan White AIDS Care Act. Washington, 1992: U.S. Government Printing Office.

307 It's amazing: *Hollywood Reporter*, Jan. 15, 1987 and Michael Gross, "Elizabeth Taylor's Passion, A Perfume," *The New York Times*, Jan. 15, 1987.

308 She's a little girl: Ivor Davis, "Liz—Still Lovely After All These Years," *California Living* magazine, May 17, 1987; see also Davis and Davis, "Elizabeth Taylor, the Sequel."
Filming moves: Ibid.

309 She knew he was gay: "You" magazine, London *Mail on Sunday*, Oct. 21, 1990.
I should be committed: On "Today," Feb. 1–3, 1988.
if you can fall in love: Long Beach *Press-Telegram*, Sept. 18, 1991.

310 The most beautiful creature in the world: London *Evening Standard*, March 25, 1968.
A drunk is: Duka, "Elizabeth Taylor: Journal of Recovery."
paranoid and disoriented: Susan Schindehette, Karen G. Jackovich, Doris Bacon, "Still Reigning After All These Years," *People*, March 13, 1989.
With all the drugs: "Liz Taylor," *People*, Dec. 26, 1988 and March 13, 1989.

311 I drink and do: Schindehette, et al., in *People*, March 13, 1989.

Notes to Chapter Fifteen

313 Just look at those boots: Schindehette, et al., in *People*, March 13, 1989.

314 I like the work: Ibid.
She invited me: Brad Darrach, "Living with Liz," *Life*, Feb. 1992.
You get to know: Liz Smith, "The Bride, on Eve of Her Marriage, Says, 'This Is It!'" *Los Angeles Times*, Feb. 6, 1991. See also *Life*, Feb. 1992.

315 Larry gives me: On Whoopi Goldberg's first television show, Sept. 14, 1992.

316 If it hadn't been for her: *People*, April 6, 1992.
We belong to: *Hello!*, Aug. 14, 1993.

317 I never thought: Seth Mydans, "Liz Taylor's 8th: Old Role, New Lead," *The New York Times*, Oct. 7, 1991.
I'm signed up all over the world: *People*, Sept. 30, 1991.

318 It's kind of astonishing: ET, appearing on "The Tonight Show," Feb. 21, 1992.

318–19 On the Fortenskys in Singapore with Jackson, see Charles P. Wallace and Jim Newton, "Taylor Joins Jackson in Singapore During Ordeal," *Los Angeles Times*, Aug. 29, 1993.

319 This is the worst thing: *Newsweek*, Sept. 6, 1993.

I have suffered: *Jet*, Dec. 13, 1993.

the brightest star: *Variety*, Feb. 22, 1994 and *Time*, March 7, 1994.

Everything was handed to me: Often—e.g., Shelley Levitt, "Flush Femmes," *People*, Aug. 30, 1993; see also Janet Kinesian, "Liz: Taylor-Made Reflections," *Palm Springs Life*, Dec. 1992; ET made almost identical remarks in several other published interviews that year.

complex, and God knows: Vernon Scott, "Elizabeth at Sixty," *Good Housekeeping*, Feb. 1992.

My life has been a whirlwind: Long Beach *Press Telegraph*, Dec. 4, 1991.

320 I want my tombstone to say: David Wallace, "Elizabeth Taylor's Greatest Battle," *Ladies' Home Journal*, Sept. 1990.

I'm a survivor: Often—e.g., on Carson, as above.

320–21 During our married life: Gehman, "Elizabeth Taylor."

321 I believe in God: Often—e.g., Wallace, "Elizabeth Taylor's Greatest Battle," and *People*, March 11, 1985.

In my life: Natalie Gittelson, "Liz Taylor and Brooke Shields," *McCall's*, Nov. 1981.

Bibliography

Alpert, Hollis. *Burton*. New York, Putnam's, 1986.

Andersen, Christopher. *Michael Jackson Unauthorized*. New York: Simon & Schuster, 1994.

Bosworth, Patricia. *Montgomery Clift*. New York: Limelight, 1992.

Bragg, Melvyn. *Richard Burton: A Life*. Boston: Little, Brown, 1988.

Brodsky, Jack, and Nathan Weiss. *The Cleopatra Papers: A Private Correspondence*. New York: Simon and Schuster, 1963.

Brown, David. *Let Me Entertain You*. New York: Morrow, 1992.

Burton, Richard. *Meeting Mrs. Jenkins*. New York, William Morrow, 1966.

Cazalet-Keir, Thelma. *The Wings*. London: The Bodley Head, 1967.

Ciment, Michel. *Conversations with Losey*. London and New York: Methuen, 1985.

Cohn, Art. *The Nine Lives of Mike Todd*. New York: Random House, 1958.

Cottrell, John, and Fergus Cashin. *Richard Burton—Very Close Up*. Englewood Cliffs: Prentice-Hall, 1971.

Dabney, Thomas Ewing. *The Man Who Bought the Waldorf: The Life of Conrad N. Hilton*. New York: Duell, Sloan & Pearce, 1950.

David, Lester, and Jhan Robbins. *Richard and Elizabeth*. New York: Funk and Wagnalls, 1977.

Dmytryk, Edward. *It's a Hell of a Life But Not a Bad Living*. New York: Times Books, 1978.

Ferris, Paul. *Richard Burton*. New York: Coward, McCann & Geoghegan, 1981.

Fisher, Eddie. *Eddie: My Life, My Loves*. New York: Harper & Row, 1981.

Gardner, Ava. *Ava: My Story*. New York: Bantam, 1990.

Graham, Sheilah. *Hollywood Revisited*. New York: St. Martin's, 1985.

Granger, Stewart. *Sparks Fly Upward*. New York: G. P. Putnam's, 1981.

Hall, William. *Raising Caine*. Englewood Cliffs, N.J.: Prentice-Hall, 1981.

Harrison, Rex. *A Damned Serious Business*. New York: Bantam, 1991.
———. *Rex: An Autobiography*. New York: Morrow, 1975.
Hearing Before the Committee on Labor and Human Resources, United States Senate, One Hundred Second Congress: Examining Methods of Providing HIV Care, Focusing on Implementation of The Ryan White AIDS Care Act. Washington, 1992: U.S. Govt. Printing Office.
Hersh, Burton. *The Mellon Family: A Fortune in History*. New York: Morrow, 1978.
Hirsch, Foster. *Elizabeth Taylor*. New York: Pyramid, 1973.
Hopper, Hedda, and James Brough. *The Whole Truth and Nothing But*. Garden City: Doubleday, 1963.
James, Robert Rhodes. *Victor Cazalet: A Portrait*. London: Hamish Hamilton, 1976.
Jenkins, Graham. *Richard Burton, My Brother*. New York: Harper and Row, 1988.
Junor, Penny. *Burton: The Man Behind the Myth*. New York: St. Martin's, 1985.
Keyes, Evelyn. *Scarlett O'Hara's Younger Sister: My Lively Life In and Out of Hollywood*. Secaucus: Lyle Stuart, 1977.
Kiersch, Mary. *Curtis Bernhardt*. Metuchen, N.J. and London: The Directors Guild of America/The Scarecrow Press, 1986.
Koskoff, David E. *The Mellons*. New York: Thomas Y. Crowell, 1978.
Leiter, Samuel, ed. *The Encyclopedia of the New York Stage, 1920-1930*, 2 vols. Westport, Conn: Greenwood Press, 1985.
Le Roy, Mervyn, and Dick Kleinser. *Mervyn Le Roy: Take One*. New York: Hawthorn, 1974.
Maddox, Brenda. *Who's Afraid of Elizabeth Taylor?* New York: M. Evans, 1977.
Madsen, Axel. *John Huston*. Garden City: Doubleday, 1978.
McGilligan, Patrick. *George Cukor: A Double Life*. New York: St. Martin's, 1991.
Minnelli, Vincente, with Hector Arce. *I Remember It Well*. New York: Doubleday, 1974.
Minney, R. J. *"Puffin" Asquith*. London: Leslie Frewin, 1973.
Oldroyd, Bess Riley, ed. *Between the Rivers* (3 vols.). Arkansas City, Kansas: The Home National Bank.
Parsons, Louella O. *Tell It to Louella*. New York: G. P. Putnam's, 1961.
Pollock, Channing. *The Harvest of My Years*. New York: Bobbs-Merrill, 1943.
Reynolds, Debbie, with David Patrick Columbia. *Debbie: My Life*. New York: Morrow, 1988.
Rivers, Joan, with Richard Meryman. *Still Talking*. New York: Turtle Bay/Random House, 1991.

Schatz, Thomas. *The Genius of the System*. New York: Pantheon, 1988.

Schulberg, Budd. *Moving Pictures*. New York: Stein and Day, 1981.

Sheppard, Dick. *Elizabeth: The Life and Career of Elizabeth Taylor*. Garden City: Doubleday, 1974.

Simmons, Dawn Langley. *Margaret Rutherford, A Blithe Spirit*. New York: McGraw-Hill, 1983.

Skolsky, Sidney. *Don't Get Me Wrong—I Love Hollywood*. New York: Putnam's, 1975.

Stanke, Don E. *The Hollywood Beauties.* New Rochelle, N.Y.: Arlington House, 1978.

Stone, Paulene, with Peter Evans. *One Tear Is Enough*. London: Michael Joseph, 1975.

Taraborrelli, J. Randy. *Michael Jackson: The Magic and the Madness*. Secaucus: Birch Lane/Carol Publishing, 1991.

Taylor, Elizabeth. *Elizabeth Taylor*. New York: Harper & Row, 1965.

————. *Elizabeth Takes Off*. New York: G. P. Putnam's, 1987.

————. *Nibbles and Me*. New York: Duell, Sloan & Pearce, 1946.

Todd, Michael, Jr., and Susan McCarthy Todd. *A Valuable Property: The Life Story of Michael Todd*. New York: Arbor House, 1983.

Vermilye, Jerry, and Mark Ricci. *The Films of Elizabeth Taylor*. Secaucus: The Citadel Press, 1976.

Walker, Alexander. *Elizabeth: The Life of Elizabeth Taylor.* New York: Grove Weidenfeld, 1990.

Waterbury, Ruth. *Elizabeth Taylor*. New York: Appleton-Century, 1964.

Wilding, Michael, as told to Pamela Wilcox. *Applesauce*. London: George Allen and Unwin, 1982. US/Canada title: *The Wilding Way*. New York: St. Martin's, 1982.

Wiley, Mason, and Damien Bona. *Inside Oscar*. New York: Ballantine, 1988.

Wilcox, Herbert. *Twenty-Five Thousand Sunsets*. London: The Bodley Head, 1967.

Wilson, Earl. *The Show Business Nobody Knows*. Chicago: Cowles, 1971.

Winters, Shelley. *Shelley II: The Middle of My Century*. New York: Simon & Schuster, 1989.

Zec, Donald. *Marvin*. London: New English Library, 1979.

Zeffirelli, Franco. *Zeffirelli*. New York: Weidenfeld & Nicolson, 1986.

Filmography

These abbreviations are used for personnel on each film:

P: Producer(s)
AP: Associate producer(s)
D: Director
Sc: Screenplay by
b/o: based on
DP: Director(s) of photography
Ed: Editor(s)
AD: Art director(s)/production designer(s)
S: Set designer(s)
W: Wardrobe and costumes by
M: Musical score composed by
MD: Musical director
M/L: Music/lyrics by
C: Choreographer
SE: Special effects supervisor(s)
PE: Photographic effects supervisor(s)
TA: Technical advisor

The date given after each feature-film title is that of the year in which the picture was first released for public screening.

There's One Born Every Minute (Universal; rel. 1943) P: Ken Goldsmith. D: Harold Young. Sc: Robert B. Hunt, Brenda Weisberg, b/o the novel *Man or Mouse* by Hunt. DP: John W. Boyle. Ed: Maurice Wright. AD: Jack Otterson. W: Vera West. M: H. J. Salter.

CAST

Gloria Twine	Elizabeth Taylor
Lemuel P. Twine	
Abner Twine	} Hugh Herbert
Col. Claudius Zebediah Twine	
Helen Barbara Twine	Peggy Moran
Jimmie Hanagan	Tom Brown
Minerva Twine	Catharine Doucet
Junior Twine	Carl "Alfalfa" Switzer

Lassie Come Home (MGM; rel. 1943) P: Samuel Marx. D: Fred M. Wilcox. Sc: Hugo Butler, b/o the novel by Eric Knight. DP: Leonard Smith. Ed: Ben Lewis. AD: Cedric Gibbons, Paul Groesse. S: Edwin B. Willis, Mildred Griffiths. M: Daniel Amfitheatrof. SE: Warren Newcombe. Lassie's trainer: Rudd Weatherwax.

CAST

Priscilla	Elizabeth Taylor
Joe Carraclough	Roddy McDowall
Sam Carraclough	Donald Crisp
Rowlie	Edmund Gwenn
Dolly	Dame May Whitty
Duke of Rudling	Nigel Bruce
Mrs. Carraclough	Elsa Lanchester
Lassie	Pal

Jane Eyre (Fox; rel. 1944) P: William Goetz. D: Robert Stevenson. Sc: Aldous Huxley, Robert Stevenson, John Houseman, b/o the book by Charlotte Brontë. DP: George Barnes. Ed: Walter Thompson. AD: James Basevi, Wiard B. Ihnen. S: Thomas Little, Ross Dowd. W: Rene Hubert. M: Bernard Herrmann. SE: Fred Sersen.

CAST

Helen Burns	Elizabeth Taylor
Edward Rochester	Orson Welles
Jane Eyre	Joan Fontaine
Adele Varens	Margaret O'Brien
Jane as a child	Peggy Ann Garner
Bessie	Sara Allgood
Mrs. Reed	Agnes Moorehead
Grace Poole	Ethel Griffies
Leah	Mae Marsh

White Cliffs of Dover (MGM; rel. 1944) P: Sidney Franklin. D: Clarence Brown. Sc: Claudine West, Jan Lustig, George Froeschel, b/o on the poem by Alice Duer Miller, w/ additional poetry by Robert Nathan. DP: George Folsey. Ed: Robert J. Kern, Al Jennings. AD: Cedric Gibbons, Randall Duell. S: Edwin B. Willis, Jacques Mesereau. W: Irene. M: Herbert Stothart. SE: Arnold Gillespie, Warren Newcombe. TA: Maj. Cyril Seys Ramsey-Hill.

CAST

Betsy at age 10	Elizabeth Taylor
Susan Dunn Ashwood	Irene Dunne
Sir John Ashwood	Alan Marshall
John Ashwood II as a boy	Roddy McDowall
Sam Bennett	Van Johnson
Nanny	Dame May Witty
Lady Jean Ashwood	Gladys Cooper
Colonel	C. Aubrey Smith

National Velvet (MGM; rel. 1944) P: Pandro S. Berman. D: Clarence Brown. Sc: Theodore Reeves, Helen Deutsch, b/o the novel by Enid Bagnold. DP: Leonard Smith. Ed: Robert J. Kern. AD: Cedric Gibbons, Urie McCleary. S: Edwin B. Willis, Mildred Griffiths. W: Irene. M: Herbert Stothart. SE: Warren Newcombe.

CAST

Velvet Brown	Elizabeth Taylor
Mi Taylor	Mickey Rooney
Mr. Brown	Donald Crisp
Mrs. Brown	Anne Revere
Edwina Brown	Angela Lansbury
Malvolia Brown	Juanita Quigley
Donald Brown	Jackie "Butch" Jenkins

Courage of Lassie [US Library of Congress title: *Blue Sierra*] (MGM; rel. 1946) P: Robert Sisk. D: Fred M. Wilcox. Sc: Lionel Houser. DP: Leonard Smith. Ed: Conrad Nervig. AD: Cedric Gibbons, Paul Youngblood. S: Edwin B. Willis, Paul Huldschinsky. M: Scott Bradley. Co-director of animal sequences: Basil Wrangell.

CAST

Kathie Merrick	Elizabeth Taylor
Harry McBain	Frank Morgan
Sgt. Smith	Tom Drake
Mrs. Merrick	Selena Royle

Old man	George Cleveland
Harry Davenport	Judge Payson
Bill	Lassie

Life With Father (WB; rel. 1947) P: Robert Bucker. D: Michael Curtiz. Sc: Donald Ogden Stewart b/o the play by Howard Lindsay, Russell Crouse and the book *God and My Father* by Clarence Day, Jr. DP: Peverell Marley, William V. Skall. Ed: George Amy. AD: Robert Haas. S: George James Hopkins. W: Milo Anderson. M: Max Steiner. MD: Leo F. Forbstein. SE: Ray Foster, William McGann. TA: Mrs. Clarence Day.

CAST

Mary Skinner	Elizabeth Taylor
Clarence Day	William Powell
Vinnie Day	Irene Dunne
Rev. Dr. Lloyd	Edmund Gwenn
Cora	ZaSu Pitts
Clarence Day, Jr.	James Lydon
John Day	Martin Milner

Cynthia (MGM; rel. 1947) P: Edwin H. Knopf. D: Robert Z. Leonard. Sc: Charles Kaufman, Harold Buchman b/o Viña Delmar's play *The Rich Full Life*. DP: Charles Schoenbaum. Ed: Irvine Warburton. AD: Cedric Gibbons. S: Edwin B. Willis, Paul G. Chamberlain. W: Irene. M: Bronislau Kaper. MD: Johnny Green. M/L: "Cynthia" by Johnny Green.

CAST

Cynthia Bishop	Elizabeth Taylor
Larry Bishop	George Murphy
Prof. Rosenkrantz	S. Z. Sakall
Louise Bishop	Mary Astor
Dr. Fred I. Jannings	Gene Lockhart
Carrie Jannings	Spring Byington
Ricky Latham	James Lydon

A Date with Judy (MGM; rel. 1948) P: Joe Pasternak. D: Richard Thorpe. Sc: Dorothy Cooper, Dorothy Kingsley, b/o the radio series by Aleen Leslie. DP: Robert Surtees. Ed: Harold F. Kress. AD: Cedric Gibbons, Paul Groesse. S: Edwin B. Willis, Richard A. Pefferle. W: Helen Rose. MD: George Stoll. M/L: "Judaline" by Don Raye, Gene DePaul; "It's a Most Unusual Day" by Harold Adamson, Jimmy McHugh; "I'm Strictly on the Corny Side" by Stella Unger, Alec Templeton; "I've Got a Date with Judy"/"I'm Gonna Meet My Mary" by Bill Katz, Calvin Jackson. C: Stanley Donen. SE: Warren Newcombe.

CAST

Carol Pringle	Elizabeth Taylor
Melvin R. Foster	Wallace Beery
Mrs. Foster	Selena Royle
Judy Foster	Jane Powell
Randolph Foster	Jerry Hunter
Rosita Conchellas	Carmen Miranda
Cugat	Xavier Cugat
Stephen Andrews	Robert Stack
Ogden "Oogie" Pringle	Scotty Beckett
Lucien T. Pringle	Leon Ames
Gramps	George Cleveland

Julia Misbehaves (MGM; rel. 1948) P: Everett Riskin. D: Jack Conway. Sc: William Ludwig, Harry Ruskin, Arthur Wimperis, Gina Kaus, Monckton Hoffe, b/o the novel *The Nutmeg Tree* by Margery Sharp. DP: Joseph Ruttenberg. Ed: John Dunning. AD: Cedric Gibbons, Daniel B. Cathcart. S: Edwin B. Willis, Jack D. Moore. W: Irene. M: Adolph Deutsch. M/L: "When You're Playing with Fire" by Jerry Seelen, Hal Borne. SE: Warren Newcombe.

CAST

Susan Packett	Elizabeth Taylor
Julia Packett	Greer Garson
William Sylvester Packett	Walter Pidgeon
Ritchie Lorgan	Peter Lawford
Fred Gennochio	Cesar Romero
Mrs. Packett	Lucile Watson
Mrs. Gennochio	Mary Boland
Louise	Veda Ann Borg
Colonel Willowbrook	Nigel Bruce

Little Women (MGM; rel. 1949) P & D: Mervyn LeRoy. Sc: Andrew Solt, Sarah Y. Mason, Victor Heerman, b/o the novel by Louisa May Alcott. DP: Robert Planck, Charles Schoenbaum. Ed: Ralph E. Winters. AD: Cedric Gibbons, Paul Groesse. S: Edwin B. Willis, Jack D. Moore. W: Walter Plunkett. M: Adolph Deutsch. SE: Warren Newcombe.

CAST

Amy March	Elizabeth Taylor
Jo March	June Allyson
Laurie Laurence	Peter Lawford
Beth March	Margaret O'Brien
Meg March	Janet Leigh
Professor Bhaer	Rossano Brazzi
Marmee March	Mary Astor
Aunt March	Lucile Watson

Conspirator (MGM; rel. 1950) P: Arthur Hornblow, Jr. D: Victor Saville. Sc: Sally Benson, Gerard Fairlie, b/o the novel by Humphrey Slater. DP: Freddie Young. Ed: Frank Clarke. AD: Alfred Junge. M: John Wooldridge. SE: Tom Howard.

CAST

Melinda Greyton	Elizabeth Taylor
Maj. Michael Curragh	Robert Taylor
Capt. Hugh Ladholme	Robert Flemyng
Joyce	Honor Blackman
Broaders	Thora Hird
Lord Pennistone	Wilfred Hyde-White

The Big Hangover (MGM; rel. 1950) P & D & Sc: Norman Krasna. DP: George Folsey. Ed: Frederick Y. Smith. AD: Cedric Gibbons, Paul Groesse. S: Edwin B. Willis, Henry W. Grace. Women's W: Helen Rose. M: Adolph Deutsch. SE: Warren Newcombe.

CAST

Mary Belney	Elizabeth Taylor
David Maldon	Van Johnson
John Belney	Percy Waram
Carl Bellcap	Leon Ames
Uncle Fred Mahoney	Edgar Buchanan
Charles Parkford	Gene Lockhart
Kate Mahoney	Selena Royle
Claire Bellcap	Rosemary DeCamp

Father of the Bride (MGM; rel. 1950) P: Pandro S. Berman. D: Vincente Minnelli. Sc: Francis Goodrich, Albert Hackett, b/o the novel by Edward Streeter. DP: John Alton. Ed: Ferris Webster. AD: Cedric Gibbons, Leonid Vasian. S: Edwin B. Willis, Keogh Gleason. W: Helen Rose, Walter Plunkett. M: Adolph Deutsch.

CAST

Kay Banks	Elizabeth Taylor
Stanley T. Banks	Spencer Tracy
Ellie Banks	Joan Bennett
Buckley Dunstan	Don Taylor
Doris Dunstan	Billie Burke
Herbert Dunstan	Moroni Olsen
Mr. Massoula	Leo G. Carroll
Tommy Banks	Russ Tamblyn

A Place in the Sun (Paramount; rel. 1951) P & D: George Stevens. Sc: Michael Wilson, Harry Brown, b/o the novel *An American Tragedy* by Theodore Dreiser and the stage adaptation by Patrick Kearney. DP: William C. Mellor. Ed: William Hornbeck. AD: Hans Dreier, Walter Tyler. W: Edith Head. M: Franz Waxman.

CAST

Angela Vickers	Elizabeth Taylor
George Eastman	Montgomery Clift
Alice Tripp	Shelley Winters
Hannah Eastman	Anne Revere
Earl Eastman	Keefe Brasselle
Frank Marlowe	Raymond Burr

Father's Little Dividend (MGM; rel. 1951) P: Pandro S. Berman. D: Vincente Minnelli. Sc: Albert Hackett, Frances Goodrich, Edward Streeter. DP: John Alton. Ed: Ferris Webster. AD: Cedric Gibbons, Leonid Vasian. S: Edwin Willis, Keogh Gleason. Women's W: Helen Rose. M: Albert Sendrey.

CAST

Kay Dunstan	Elizabeth Taylor
Stanley Banks	Spencer Tracy
Ellie Banks	Joan Bennett
Buckley Dunstan	Don Taylor
Doris Dunstan	Billie Burke
Herbert Dunstan	Moroni Olsen
Tommy Banks	Russ Tamblyn

Elizabeth Taylor appeared uncredited in a crowd scene in MGM's *Quo Vadis*, filmed in Rome and released in 1951.

Callaway Went Thataway (MGM; rel. 1951) P & D & Sc: Norman Panama, Melvin Frank. DP: Ray June. Ed: Cotton Warburton. AD: Cedric Gibbons, Eddie Imazu. M: Marlin Skiles.

CAST

As herself	Elizabeth Taylor
Mike Rye	Fred MacMurray
Deborah Patterson	Dorothy McGuire
"Smoky"/ "Stretch"	Howard Keel
As herself	June Allyson
As himself	Clark Gable
As himself	Dick Powell
As herself	Esther Williams

Love Is Better Than Ever (MGM; rel. 1952) P: William H. Wright. D: Stanley Donen. Sc: Ruth Brooks Flippen. DP: Harold Rosson. Ed: George Boemler. AD: Cedric Gibbons, Gabriel Scognamillo. M & MD: Lennie Hayton.

CAST

Anastacia Macaboy	Elizabeth Taylor
Jud Parker	Larry Parks
Mrs. Macaboy	Josephine Hutchinson
Mr. Macaboy	Tom Tully
Mrs. Levoy	Ann Doran
Pattie Marie Levoy	Elinor Donohue
Mrs. Kahmey	Kathleen Freeman

Ivanhoe (MGM; rel. 1952) P: Pandro S. Berman. D: Richard Thorpe. Sc: Noel Langley, b/o the novel by Sir Walter Scott. DP: Freddie A. Young. Ed: Frank Clarke. AD: Alfred Junge. W: Roger Furse. M: Miklos Rosza. SE: Tom Howard.

CAST

Rebecca	Elizabeth Taylor
Ivanhoe	Robert Taylor
De Bois-Guilbert	George Sanders
Wamba	Emlyn Williams
Rowena	Joan Fontaine
Cedric	Finlay Currie
Isaac	Felix Aylmer
Sir Hugh De Bracy	Robert Douglas

The Girl Who Had Everything (MGM; rel. 1953) P: Armand Deutsch. D: Richard Thorpe. Sc: Art Cohn, b/o the novel *A Free Soul* by Adela Rogers St. John. DP: Paul Vogel. Ed: Ben Lewis. AD: Cedric Gibbons, Randall Duell. W: Helen Rose. M: Andre Previn.

CAST

Jean Latimer	Elizabeth Taylor
Steve Latimer	William Powell
Vance Court	Gig Young
Victor Y. Ramondi	Fernando Lamas
Charles "Chico" Menlow	James Whitmore

Rhapsody (MGM; rel. 1954) P: Lawrence Weingarten. D: Charles Vidor. Sc: Michael Kanin, Fay Kanin, Ruth Goetz, Augustus Goetz, b/o the novel *Maurice Guest* by Henry Handel Richardson. DP: Robert Planck. Ed: John Dunning. AD: Cedric Gibbons, Paul Groesse. S: Edwin B. Willis, Hugh Hunt. Women's W: Helen Rose. M: Bronislau Kaper, Peter Ilich Tchaikovsky, Sergei Rachmaninoff, Franz Liszt. MD: Johnny Green. SE: A. Arnold Gillespie, Warren Newcombe, Peter Ballbusch.

CAST

Louise Durant	Elizabeth Taylor
Paul Bronte	Vittorio Gassman
James Guest	John Ericson
Nicholas Durant	Louis Calhern
Prof. Schuman	Michael Chekhov
Effie Cahill	Barbara Bates

Elephant Walk (Paramount; rel. 1954) P: Irving Asher. D: William Dieterle. Sc: John Lee Mahin, b/o the novel by Robert Standish. DP: Loyal Griggs. Ed: George Tomasini. AD: Hal Pereira, Joseph MacMillan Johnson. S: Sam Comer, Grace Gregory. W: Edith Head. M: Franz Waxman. SE: John P. Fulton, Paul Lerpae.

CAST

Ruth Wiley	Elizabeth Taylor
Dick Carver	Dana Andrews
John Wiley	Peter Finch
Appuhamy	Abraham Sofaer
Dr. Pereira	Abner Biberman
Atkinson	Noel Drayton

Beau Brummel (MGM; rel. 1954) P: Sam Zimbalist. D: Curtis Bernhardt. Sc: Karl Tunberg, b/o the play by Clyde Fitch. DP: Oswald Morris. Ed: Frank Clarke. AD: Alfred Junge. W: Elizabeth Haffenden. M: Richard Addinsell. PE: Tom Howard.

CAST

Lady Patricia	Elizabeth Taylor
Beau Brummell	Stewart Granger
Prince of Wales	Peter Ustinov
King George III	Robert Morley
Lord Edwin Mercer	James Donald
Mortimer	James Hayter
Mrs. Fitzherbert	Rosemary Harris

The Last Time I Saw Paris (MGM; rel. 1954) P: Jack Cummings. D: Richard Brooks. Sc: Julius J. Epstein, Philip G. Epstein, Richard Brooks, b/o the story "Babylon Revisited" by F. Scott Fitzgerald. DP: Joseph Ruttenberg. Ed: John Dunning. AD: Cedric Gibbons, Randall Duell. S: Edwin B. Willis, Jack D. Moore. W: Helen Rose. M: Conrad Salinger. M/L: "The Last Time I Saw Paris" by Jerome Kern, Oscar Hammerstein II. SE: A. Arnold Gillespie.

CAST

Helen Ellswirth	Elizabeth Taylor
Charles Wills	Van Johnson
James Ellswirth	Walter Pidgeon
Marion Ellswirth	Donna Reed
Lorraine Quarl	Eva Gabor
Maurice	Kurt Kasznar

Giant (WB; rel. 1956) P: George Stevens, Henry Ginsberg. D: George Stevens. Sc: Fred Guiol, Ivan Moffat, b/o the novel by Edna Ferber. DP: William C. Mellor. Ed: William Hornbeck. AD: Boris Leven, Ralph Hurst. W: Marjorie Best, Moss Mabry. M: Dimitri Tiomkin.

CAST

Leslie Linton Benedict	Elizabeth Taylor
Bick Benedict	Rock Hudson
Jett Rink	James Dean
Luz Benedict II	Carroll Baker
Vashti Snythe	Jane Withers
Uncle Bawley	Chill Wills

Luz Benedict   Mercedes McCambridge
Angel Obregon III   Sal Mineo
Jordan Benedict III   Dennis Hopper

Raintree County (MGM; rel. 1957) P: David Lewis. D: Edward Dmytryk. Sc: Millard Kaufman, b/o the novel by Ross Lockridge, Jr. DP: Robert Surtees. Ed: John Dunning. AD: William A. Horning, Urie McCleary. S: Edwin B. Willis, Hugh Hunt. W: Walter Plunkett. M: Johnny Green. M/L: "Never Till Now" and "Song of the Raintree" by Johnny Green, Paul Francis Webster.

CAST

Susanna Drake   Elizabeth Taylor
John Wickliff Shawnessy   Montgomery Clift
Nell Gaither   Eva Marie Saint
Prof. Jerusalem Stiles   Nigel Patrick
Orville "Flash" Perkins   Lee Marvin
Garwood B. Jones   Rod Taylor
Ellen Shawnessy   Agnes Moorehead
T. D. Shawnessy   Walter Abel

Cat on a Hot Tin Roof (MGM; rel. 1958) P: Lawrence Weingarten. D: Richard Brooks. Sc: Richard Brooks, James Poe, b/o the play by Tennessee Williams. DP: William Daniels. Ed: Ferris Webster. AD: William A. Horning, Urie McCleary. S: Henry Grace, Robert Priestley. ET's W: Helen Rose. SE: Lee LeBlanc.

CAST

Maggie Pollitt   Elizabeth Taylor
Brick Pollitt   Paul Newman
Big Daddy Pollitt   Burl Ives
Gooper Pollitt   Jack Carson
Big Mama Pollitt   Judith Anderson
Mae Pollitt   Madeleine Sherwood
Dr. Baugh   Larry Gates
Deacon Davis   Vaughn Taylor

Suddenly, Last Summer (Columbia; rel. 1959) P: Sam Spiegel. D: Joseph L. Mankiewicz. Sc: Gore Vidal, Tennessee Williams, b/o the short play by Tennessee Williams. DP: Jack Hildyard. Ed: William W. Hornbeck, Thomas G. Stanford. AD: Oliver Messel, William Kellner. S: Scott Slimon. W: Joan Ellacott. M: Buxton Orr, Malcolm Arnold. PE: Tom Howard.

CAST

Catherine Holly	Elizabeth Taylor
Mrs. Violet Venable	Katharine Hepburn
Dr. Cukrowicz	Montgomery Clift
Dr. Hockstader	Albert Dekker
Mrs. Holly	Mercedes McCambridge
George Holly	Gary Raymond
Miss Foxhill	Mavis Villiers

Scent of Mystery [British release title: *Holiday in Spain*] (Michael Todd, Jr.; rel. 1960) P: Michael Todd, Jr. D: Jack Cardiff. Sc: William Roos, b/o the story by Kelley Roos, w/ additional situations by Gerald Kersh. DP: John Von Kotze. Ed: James Newcom. AD: Vincent Korda. W: Charles Simminger. M: Mario Nascimbene, Jordan Ramin, Harold Adamson. TA: Ned Mann.

CAST

The Real Sally Kennedy	Elizabeth Taylor
Oliver Larker	Denholm Elliott
Smiley	Peter Lorre
The Decoy Sally	Beverly Bentley
Baron Saradin	Paul Lukas
Johnny Gin	Liam Redmond
Tommy Kennedy	Leo McKern
Fleming	Peter Arne

Butterfield 8 (MGM; rel. 1960) P: Pandro S. Berman. D: Daniel Mann. Sc: Charles Schnee, John Michael Hayes, b/o the novel by John O'Hara. DP: Joseph Ruttenberg. Ed: Ralph E. Winters. AD: George W. Davis, Urie McCleary. S: Gene Callahan, J.C. Delaney. W: Helen Rose. M: Bronislau Kaper.

CAST

Gloria Wandrous	Elizabeth Taylor
Weston Liggett	Laurence Harvey
Steve Carpenter	Eddie Fisher
Emily Liggett	Dina Merrill
Mrs. Wandrous	Mildred Dunnock
Mrs. Fanny Thurber	Betty Field
Bingham Smith	Jeffrey Lynn
Happy	Kay Medford

Cleopatra (Fox; rel. 1963) P: Walter Wanger. D: Joseph L. Mankiewicz. Sc: Joseph L. Mankiewicz, Ranald MacDougall, Sidney Buchman, b/o histories by Plutarch, Suetonius, Appian, and *The Life and Times of Cleopatra* by C. M. Franzero. DP: Leon Shamroy. Second Unit DP: Claude Renoir, Pietro Portalupi. Ed: Dorothy Spencer. AD: John De Cuir, Jack Martin Smith, Hilyard Brown, Herman Blumenthal, Elven Webb, Maurice Pelling, Boris Juraga. S: Walter M. Scott, Paul S. Fox, Ray Moyer. ET's W: Irene Sharaff. Additional W: Vittorio Nino Novarese. M: Alex North. C: Hermes Pan. PE: L. B. Abbott, Emil Kosa, Jr.

CAST

Cleopatra	Elizabeth Taylor
Mark Antony	Richard Burton
Julius Caesar	Rex Harrison
High Priestess	Pamela Brown
Flavius	George Cole
Sosigenes	Hume Cronyn
Apollodorus	Cesare Danova
Brutus	Kenneth Haigh
Octavian	Roddy McDowall
Rufio	Martin Landau
Agrippa	Andrew Keir
Germanicus	Robert Stephens

The V.I.P.s (MGM; rel. 1963) P: Anatole de Grunwald. D: Anthony Asquith. Sc: Terence Rattigan. DP: Jack Hildyard. Ed: Frank Clarke. AD: William Kellner. S: Pamela Cornell. ET's W: Hubert de Givenchy. Additional W: Felix Evans. M: Miklos Rozsa.

CAST

Frances Andros	Elizabeth Taylor
Paul Andros	Richard Burton
Marc Champselle	Louis Jourdan
Gloria Gritti	Elsa Martinelli
The Duchess	Margaret Rutherford
Miss Mead	Maggie Smith
Les Mangam	Rod Taylor
Miriam Marshall	Linda Christian
Max Buda	Orson Welles

The Sandpiper (A Filmways Picture/An MGM release; rel. 1965) P: Martin Ransohoff. D: Vincente Minnelli. SC: Dalton Trumbo, Michael Wilson, b/o a story by Martin Ransohoff, adapted by Irene and Louis Kamp. DP: Milton Krasner. Ed: David Bretherton. AD: George W. Davis, Urie McCleary. W: Irene Sharaff. M: Johnny Mandel. M/L: "The Shadow of Your Smile" by Johnny Mandel, Paul Francis Webster.

CAST

Laura Reynolds	Elizabeth Taylor
Dr. Edward Hewitt	Richard Burton
Claire Hewitt	Eva Marie Saint
Cos Erickson	Charles Bronson
Ward Hendricks	Robert Webber
Larry Brant	James Edwards

Who's Afraid of Virginia Woolf? (An Ernest Lehman Production/A WB release; rel. 1966) P: Ernest Lehman. D: Mike Nichols. Sc: Ernest Lehman, b/o the play by Edward Albee. DP: Haskell Wexler. Ed: Sam O'Steen. AD: Richard Sylbert. S: George James Hopkins. W: Irene Sharaff. M: Alex North.

CAST

Martha	Elizabeth Taylor
George	Richard Burton
Nick	George Segal
Honey	Sandy Dennis

The Taming of the Shrew (A Co-Production of Royal Films International & F.A.I. Prods./A Columbia release; rel. 1967) Executive P: Richard McWhorter. P: Richard Burton, Elizabeth Taylor, Franco Zeffirelli. D: Franco Zeffirelli. Sc: Paul Dehn, Suso Cecchi D'Amico, Franco Zeffirelli, b/o the play by William Shakespeare. DP: Oswald Morris, Luciano Trasatti. Ed: Peter Taylor, Carlo Fabianelli. AD: John De Cuir, Giuseppe Mariani, Elven Webb. S: Dario Simoni, Carlo Gervasi. W: Irene Sharaff, Danilo Donatti. M: Nino Rota. SE: Augie Lohman.

CAST

Katharina	Elizabeth Taylor
Petruchio	Richard Burton
Grumio	Cyril Cusack
Baptista	Michael Hordern
Lucentio	Michael York
Bianca	Natasha Pyne
Hortensio	Victor Spinetti
Tranio	Alfred Lynch

Doctor Faustus (An Oxford University Screen Production in Association w/ Nassau Films & Venfilms/A Columbia release; rel. 1967) P: Richard Burton, Richard McWhorter. D: Richard Burton, Nevill Coghill. SC: Nevill Coghill, b/o the play *The Tragical History of Doctor Faustus* by Christopher Marlowe. DP: Gabor Pogany. Ed: John Shirley. AD: John De Cuir, Boris Juraga. S: Dario Simoni. W: Peter Hall. M: Mario Nascimbene. C: Jacqueline Harvey.

CAST

Helen of Troy	Elizabeth Taylor
Doctor Faustus	Richard Burton
Mephistopheles	Andreas Teuber
Empress	Elizabeth O'Donovan
Emperor	Ian Marter
Beelzebub	Jeremy Eccles
Lucifer	David McIntosh

Reflections in a Golden Eye (A John Huston-Ray Stark Production/A WB-Seven Arts release; rel. 1967) P: Ray Stark. D: John Huston. Sc: Chapman Mortimer, Gladys Hill, b/o the novel by Carson McCullers. DP: Aldo Tonti. Ed: Russell Lloyd. AD: Stephen Grimes, Bruno Avesani. S: William Kiernan. W: Dorothy Jeakins. M: Toshiro Mayuzumi.

CAST

Leonora Penderton	Elizabeth Taylor
Major Weldon Penderton	Marlon Brando
Colonel Morris Langdon	Brian Keith
Alison Langdon	Julie Harris
Anacleto	Zorro David
Private Williams	Robert Forster

The Comedians (A joint effort of Maximilian Productions in Bermuda & Trianon Productions in Paris for MGM; rel. 1967) P & D: Peter Glenville. Sc: Graham Greene b/o his novel. DP: Henri Decae. Ed: Francoise Javet. AD: Francois de Lamothe. S: Robert Christides. ET's W: Tiziani of Rome. M: Laurence Rosenthal.

CAST

Martha Pineda	Elizabeth Taylor
Brown	Richard Burton
Jones	Alec Guinness
Ambassador Pineda	Peter Ustinov
Smith	Paul Ford
Mrs. Smith	Lillian Gish

Concasseur	Raymond St. Jacques
Michel	Zaeks Mokae
Petit Pierre	Roscoe Lee Browne
Henry Philipot	Georg Stanford Brown
Dr. Magiot	James Earl Jones
Marie-Therese	Cicely Tyson

Boom! (A John Heyman Production for Universal; rel. 1968) P: John Heyman, Norman Priggen. D: Joseph Losey. Sc: Tennessee Williams b/o his short story "Man Bring This Up Road" and his play *The Milk Train Doesn't Stop Here Anymore*. DP: Douglas Slocombe. Ed: Reginald Beck. AD: Richard MacDonald. ET's W: Tiziani of Rome. M: John Barry.

CAST

Flora "Sissy" Goforth	Elizabeth Taylor
Chris Flanders	Richard Burton
The Witch of Capri	Noël Coward
Blackie	Joanna Shimkus
Rudy	Michael Dunn
Dr. Lullo	Romolo Valli
Journalist	Howard Taylor

Secret Ceremony (A Universal/World Film Services Ltd/Paul M. Heller Production/A Universal release; rel. 1968) P: John Heyman, Norman Priggen. D: Joseph Losey. Sc: George Tabori, b/o the short story by Marco Denevi. DP: Gerald Fisher. Ed: Reginald Beck. AD: Richard MacDonald, John Clark. S: Jill Oxley. ET's W: Marc Bohan, Christian Dior. W: Susan Yelland. M: Richard Rodney Bennett.

CAST

Leonora	Elizabeth Taylor
Cenci	Mia Farrow
Albert	Robert Mitchum
Aunt Hilda	Pamela Brown
Aunt Hanna	Peggy Ashcroft

The Only Game in Town (A George Stevens-Fred Kohlmar Production for Fox; rel. 1970) P: Fred Kohlmar. D: George Stevens. Sc: Frank D. Gilroy b/o his Broadway play. DP: Henri Decae. Ed: John W. Holmes, William Sands, Pat Shade. AD: Herman Blumenthal, Auguste Capelier. S: Walter M. Scott, Jerry Wunderlich. W: Mia Fonssagrives, Vicki Tiel. M: Maurice Jarre.

CAST

Fran Walker	Elizabeth Taylor
Joe Grady	Warren Beatty
Thomas J. Lockwood	Charles Braswell
Tony	Hank Henry

X, Y, and Zee [British release title: *Zee & Company*] (A Zee Film & Kastner-Ladd-Kanter Production/A Columbia release; rel. 1972) Executive P: Elliott Kastner. P: Jay Kanter, Alan Ladd, Jr. D: Brian G. Hutton. Sc: Edna O'Brien. DP: Billy Williams. Ed: Jim Clark. AD: Peter Mullins. S: Arthur Taksen. W: Beatrice Dawson. M: Stanley Myers. M/L: "Going in Circles" by Ted Myers, Jaiananda; "Whirlwind"/"Coat of Many Colours" by Rick Wakeman, Dave Lambert; "Revolution"/"Granny's Got a Painted Leg"/ "Gladys' Party" by John Mayer.

CAST

Zee Blakeley	Elizabeth Taylor
Robert Blakeley	Michael Caine
Stella	Susannah York
Gladys	Margaret Leighton
Gordon	John Standing
Rita	Mary Larkin

Hammersmith Is Out (A. J. Cornelius Crean Films Inc. Production/A Cinerama release; rel. 1972) P: Alex Lucas. D: Peter Ustinov. Sc: Stanford Whitmore. DP: Richard H. Kline. Ed: David Blewitt. S: Robert Benton. ET's W: Edith Head. M: Dominic Frontiere. M/L: "For Openers"/ "Requiem"/"When Your Dreams Were Worth Remembering" by Dominic Frontiere, Sally Stevens.

CAST

Jimmie Jean Jackson	Elizabeth Taylor
Hammersmith	Richard Burton
Billy Breedlove	Beau Bridges
Doctor	Peter Ustinov
General Sam Pembroke	Leon Ames
Dr. Krodt	Leon Askin
Henry Joe	John Schuck
Guido Scatucci	George Raft

Night Watch (A Joseph E. Levine & Burt Productions Presentation/An Avco Embassy release; rel. 1973) P: Martin Poll, George W. George, Barnard

S. Straus. Sc: Tony Williamson, b/o the play by Lucille Fletcher, with additional dialogue by Evan Jones. DP: Billy Williams. Ed: John Jympson. AD: Peter Murton. S: Peter James. ET's W: Valentino. M: John Cameron. M/L: "The Night Has Many Eyes" by George Barrie, Sammy Cahn.

CAST

Ellen Wheeler	Elizabeth Taylor
John Wheeler	Laurence Harvey
Sarah Cooke	Billie Whitelaw
Appleby	Robert Lang
Tony	Tony Britton
Inspector Walker	Bill Dean
Sergeant Norris	Michael Danvers-Walker
Dolores	Rosario Serrano

Ash Wednesday (A Sagittarius Production/A Paramount release; rel. 1973) P: Dominick Dunne. D: Larry Peerce. Sc: Jean-Claude Tramont. DP: Ennio Guarnieri. Ed: Marion Rothman. AD: Philip Abramson. ET's W: Edith Head, Valentino. M: Maurice Jarre. TA: Dr. Rodolphe Troques.

CAST

Barbara Sawyer	Elizabeth Taylor
Mark Sawyer	Henry Fonda
Erich	Helmut Berger
David Carrington	Keith Baxter
Doctor Lambert	Maurice Teynac
Kate	Margaret Blye

That's Entertainment! (An MGM Picture/A United Artists release; rel. 1974) Executive P: Daniel Melnick. P & D & Sc: Jack Haley, Jr. DP: Gene Polito, Ernest Laszlo, Russell Metty, Ennio Guarnieri, Allan Green. Ed: Bud Friedgen, David E. Blewitt. Opticals: Robert Hoag, Jim Liles. Film Librarian: Mort Feinstein. M Supervision: Jesse Kaye, Henry Mancini. Sound: Hal Watkins, Aaron Rochin, Lyle Burbridge, Harry W. Tetrick, William L. McCaughey.

NARRATORS

Elizabeth Taylor
Fred Astaire
Bing Crosby
Gene Kelly
Peter Lawford
Liza Minnelli

Donald O'Connor
Debbie Reynolds
Mickey Rooney
Frank Sinatra
James Stewart

Identikit [USA: *The Driver's Seat*] (A Rizzoli Film/An Avco Embassy release; rel. 1974) P: Franco Rossellini. D: Giuseppe Patroni Griffi. Sc: Raffaele La Capria, Giuseppe Patroni Griffi, b/o the novella by Muriel Spark. DP: Vittorio Storaro. AD: Mario Ceroli. W: Gabriella Pescucci. M: Franco Mannino.

CAST

Lise	Elizabeth Taylor
Richard	Ian Bannen
Carlo	Guido Mannari
Mrs. Fiedke	Mona Washbourne
Bill	Maxence Mailfort

The Blue Bird (Fox; rel. 1976) P: Paul Maslansky. D: George Cukor. Sc: Hugh Whitemore, Alfred Hayes, Alexi Kapler, b/o the novel by Maurice Maeterlinck. DP: Freddie Young. Ed: Ernest Walter, Tatyana Shapiro, Stanford C. Allen. S: Yevgeny Starikovitch. M: Irwin Kostal, Lionel Newman.

CAST

Mother, Witch, Light, Maternal Love	Elizabeth Taylor
Night	Jane Fonda
Luxury	Ava Gardner
Cat	Cicely Tyson
Father Time	Robert Morley
Oak	Harry Andrews
Tyltyl	Todd Lookinland
Mytyl	Patsy Kensit
Grandfather	Will Geer

A Little Night Music (New World Picture; rel. 1977) P: Elliott Kastner. D: Harold Prince. Sc: Hugh Wheeler, b/o the musical play by Stephen Sondheim, Hugh Wheeler, suggested by the film "Smiles of a Summer Night" by Ingmar Bergman. AD: Arthur Ibbetson. Ed: John Jympson. AD: Laci von Ronay, Herta Pischinger, Thomas Riccabona. W: Florence Klotz. M: Stephen Sondheim. MD: Paul Gemignani. C: Patricia Birch.

CAST

Desirée Armfeldt	Elizabeth Taylor
Frederick Egerman	Len Cariou
Anne Egerman	Lesley-Anne Down
Mme. Armfeldt	Hermione Gingold
Carl-Magnus Mittelheim	Laurence Guittard
Erich Egerman	Christopher Guard
Fredericka Armfeldt	Chloe Franks
Petra	Lesley Dunlop

Winter Kills (Avco Embassy; rel. 1979) P: Fred Caruso. D & Sc: William Richert, b/o the novel by Richard Condon. DP: Vilmos Zsigmond. Ed: David Bretherton. AD: Robert Boyle, Norman Newberry. S: Arthur Seph Parker. M: Maurice Jarre.

CAST

Lola Comante	Elizabeth Taylor
Nick Kegan	Jeff Bridges
Pa Kegan	John Huston
John Ceruti	Anthony Perkins
Z. K. Dawson	Sterling Hayden
Joe Diamond	Eli Wallach
Emma Kegan	Dorothy Malone
Frank Mayo	Tomas Milian
Yvette Malone	Belinda Bauer
Gameboy Baker	Ralph Meeker

The Mirror Crack'd (EMI/Associated Film Distribution; rel. 1980) P: John Brabourne, Richard Goodwin. D: Guy Hamilton. Sc: Jonathan Hales, Barry Sandler, b/o the novel *The Mirror Crack'd from Side to Side* by Agatha Christie. DP: Christopher Challis. Ed: Richard Marden. AD: Michael Stinger, John Roberts. W: Phyllis Dalton. M: John Cameron. M/L: Irving Berlin.

CAST

Marina Gregg	Elizabeth Taylor
Miss Marple	Angela Lansbury
Inspector	Edward Fox
Mrs. Bantry	Margaret Courtenay
Heather Babcock	Maureen Bennett
Ella Zielinsky	Geraldine Chaplin
Marty N. Fenn	Tony Curtis

Jason Rudd   Rock Hudson
Lola Brewster   Kim Novak

The Flintstones (Universal, rel. 1994) P: Bruce Cohen; D: Brian Levant; Sc: Tom S. Parker, Jim Jennewein and Steven E. de Souza, b/o animated series by Hanna-Barbera Productions; DP: Dean Cundey; Ed: Kent Beyda; M: David Newman; AD: William Sandell.

CAST

Pearl Slaghoople   Elizabeth Taylor
Fred Flintstone   John Goodman
Wilma Flintstone   Elizabeth Perkins
Barney Rubble   Rick Moranis
Betty Rubble   Rosie O'Donnell
Cliff Vandercave   Kyle MacLachlan

ELIZABETH TAYLOR'S THEATER ROLES

As Regina Giddens in Lillian Hellman's *The Little Foxes*, in the USA and England in 1981 (dir. Austin Pendleton).

As Amanda Prynne in Noël Coward's *Private Lives*, in the USA only, in 1983 (dir. Milton Katselas).

ELIZABETH TAYLOR'S TELEVISION APPEARANCES

"The Lucy Show," dir. Jerry Paris (broadcast Sept. 14, 1970)
Divorce His/Divorce Hers, dir. Waris Hussein (broadcast Feb 6–7, 1973)
Victory at Entebbe, dir. Marvin J. Chomsky (broadcast Dec. 13, 1976)
Return Engagement, dir. Joseph Hardy (broadcast Nov. 17, 1978)
"General Hospital" (broadcast Nov. 10, 12, 16, 17, 19, 1981)
Between Friends, dir. Lou Antonio (broadcast Sept. 11, 1983)
Hotel, dir. Vince McEveety (broadcast Sept. 26, 1984)
Malice in Wonderland, dir. Gus Trikonis (broadcast May 12, 1985)
North and South, dir. Richard Heffron (broadcast Nov. 9, 1985)
There Must Be A Pony, dir. Joseph Sargent (broadcast Oct. 5, 1986)
Poker Alice, dir. Arthur Allan Seidelman (broadcast May 22, 1987)
Sweet Bird of Youth, dir. Nicolas Roeg (broadcast Oct. 1, 1989)

Acknowledgments

From the first day of research for this book, I was blessed with the help of many generous people.

At the Academy of Motion Picture Arts and Sciences in Beverly Hills, Sam Gill was—neither for the first time in my career nor, I suspect, the last—an invaluable source of wise assistance and prudent suggestions. With unfailing friendliness and perception, he steered me in the direction of many files I might otherwise have ignored. Also at the Academy, Sandra Archer was ready with amiable good counsel as I dug into what seemed an infinity of movie materials.

Ned Comstock, at the University of Southern California, again cleared a path for me through the thickets of complicated but crucial archives in Special Collections and in the Warner Bros. Archives. I salute his extraordinary knowledge of movie lore and his generous and friendly allotment of time on my behalf.

At the American Film Institute, Los Angeles, Alan Braun and Gladys Irvis gladly directed me and my assistants to important caches of files that clarified key occasions and events in my subject's life.

In the Billy Rose Theater Collection at the New York Public Library, Lincoln Center, the entire research and information staff was, as usual, of great assistance.

The staff of the Beverly Hills Public Library—surely one of the most fertile repositories of information in the country—again showed why California information banks are respected worldwide. This is a remarkable library, and my work was much facilitated by the splendid services and friendly staff there.

Similarly, the Research Library at the University of California at Los

Angeles is notable for the extent of its holdings and the eagerness of its personnel to facilitate difficult searches.

At the Museum of Television and Radio in New York, Jonathan Rosenthal kindly directed me to the list of important holdings relevant to Elizabeth Taylor's television appearances.

Joslyn Quinn, Special Collections Librarian at the University of Tennessee at Knoxville, guided me—thoroughly and on short notice—through the holdings in the Clarence Brown Papers.

H. W. Yorke, at the United States Military Academy Library, West Point, New York, made available critical yearbooks and documents and answered important questions of fact and tradition.

Bernard Dick, who was my college professor of Greek, is a distinguished author of many fine books on film and film culture. During my research for this book, just as years ago, he shared generously and enthusiastically, indicating facts and directing me to critical points for consideration. We met perchance while researching our respective new projects: I am grateful for renewed friendship and collegiality.

Among the many colleagues and friends who have known and worked with Elizabeth Taylor and who granted me important interviews, I have reason to be especially grateful to David Brown, Hugh Corcoran, Mart Crowley, Edward Dmytryk, Evelyn Keyes, Ernest Lehman and Karen von Unge. Many others, for their own various reasons, preferred not to be acknowledged.

Jacqueline Williams cheerfully sped all over the Virginia–Washington–Maryland area, tracking down critical materials relevant to Elizabeth Taylor's Washington years (1976 to 1981) and providing me with precious documents just when I needed them. I am grateful to my friend and colleague, that first-rate biographer Robert Lacey, for introducing me to Jacqueline.

In Los Angeles, my former assistant, Douglas Alexander, dutifully came back on board on short notice as occasional researcher and keen-eyed editor when I most needed help from afar. Likewise, the noted artist W. H. Dietrich kindly pointed me to important California contacts relative to my subject's life.

Also in Los Angeles, Rick Carl seemed somehow always to be available, providing on-the-spot access to films, television shows and ancillary materials otherwise difficult to locate. This book would be very much the poorer indeed without Rick's friendly efficiency and dependable generosity.

In London, I am fortunate to have as research assistant Erica Wagner Gilbert, a splendid critic and writer in her own right, who constantly amazes me with her sharp insights, her immediate and perceptive understanding of my subjects and her magnificent research skills. She seems to be able to find anything anywhere, and with remarkable alacrity. I am grateful for her help and her abiding friendship.

For various other acts of kindness and that support without which a writer's life and work quickly descend to chaos, I am grateful to the following friends: John Darretta, Laurence and Mary Evans, Lewis Falb, Edward Finegan, Irene Mahoney, Fred McCashland, Gerald Pinciss, Charles Rappleye and Kirtley Thiesmeyer.

Anything good in my career owes very much to the abiding wisdom and guidance of my agent and precious friend, Elaine Markson; detailing the fine points of my gratitude to her would itself require a little book. Likewise to that wondrous group at the Elaine Markson Literary Agency—Tasha Blaine, Sara DeNobrega, Elizabeth Stevens, Geri Thoma and Sally Wofford-Girand— I am indebted for constant professional cordiality and encouragement.

How fortunate I am among authors to be published by the good people at that venerable publishing house, HarperCollins:

Gladys Justin Carr, vice president and associate publisher, is a biographer's ideal editor, and I note proudly that this is the third book to appear under her banner. Always ready with the right creative counsel, Gladys is ever the most astute guide—loyal, calm, prudent and altogether a good and trusted friend. We not only work well and seriously together: we also share many hearty laughs, surely a sign of a rare and valuable collaboration.

Also at HarperCollins, Group Vice President Jack McKeown has enthusiastically supported this project from the start and has taken a direct interest in every stage of its development.

I am also grateful to Gladys Carr's editorial team for their various assistances: to Cynthia Barrett, Deirdre O'Brien and Elissa Altman, my abundant thanks. And in other departments at HarperCollins, I must note my debts to James Fox and to Brenda Segel for their vigilance and support.

In the London offices of Little, Brown—the British publisher of this book—Philippa Harrison welcomed me most enthusiastically, as did my old friend, Alan Samson. How fortunate I am to have had their important contributions, from beginning to end of this project.

Finally, a word about the name on the dedication page. Greg Dietrich, a man of many talents, worked with me occasionally from 1987 to 1993, always with boundless good cheer, a quick intelligence and admirable precision. He then joined me full-time, assuming the duties not only of research director and editorial assistant but also as a trusted collaborator who efficiently facilitates many important details of daily life and work. With gratitude and affection, therefore, *A Passion for Life* is dedicated to Greg Dietrich.

D.S.
October 12, 1994
40th anniversary of the death of Caryll Houselander

Index

husbands of, *see* Burton, Richard;
Fisher, Eddie; Fortensky, Larry;
Hilton, Conrad Nicholas, Jr.;
Todd, Mike; Warner, John William,
Jr.; Wilding, Michael
income of, 29, 31, 33, 55, 62, 77, 94,
141, 168, 171, 207, 209, 219,
237, 238, 301, 307
independence of, 60, 67, 138, 257
intuition of, 34, 49, 56, 64, 208
jewelry of, 12, 41, 54, 98, 122, 123,
127, 128, 131, 132–133, 196, 197,
224, 235–236, 241, 242, 245,
250, 256, 262, 263, 271, 279,
291, 301, 304
loneliness and isolation of, 6, 35, 36,
42, 44–47, 49–50, 53, 278–279
marital ambitions of, 48, 50
as mother, 89, 92, 94–95, 145, 211,
215, 234, 315
mothering and nurturing roles of, 7,
8, 104, 192, 315
movies as solution to life's problems
for, 35–36, 46–48, 51, 68–69, 71,
93, 119, 184, 196
near-death experiences of, 177–178,
182, 316–317
normal socializing denied to, 35, 42,
44–47, 49–50, 53
perceptions and identity of, 35–36
perfume business of, 6, 307, 317–318
perfume collecting of, 41
pregnancies and childbirths of,
87–89, 99, 100–101, 108, 125,
127, 129, 132, 133, 184–185
professionalism of, 112, 144, 169,
188, 208, 237, 269–270
public image declines of, 122,
144–145, 149, 153–155,
199–200
public image improved by, 185
reclusiveness and seclusions of, 8, 98,
143, 182, 321
shopping sprees of, 49, 57, 60, 72,
176, 234–236

shyness of, 21, 30, 35, 63, 102, 138,
266, 281
singing of, 26, 27, 28, 270
sixteenth birthday of, 50
sixtieth birthday of, 7, 318
surrogate fathers of, 17, 19, 20, 40,
45, 63, 99–100, 108, 120, 129,
138, 152, 192, 223, 242
as symbol of 1950s, 134–135
theatrical performances of, 218–219,
229, 284–287, 289–290,
294–295
TV work of, 209, 247, 274–275, 287,
301, 302, 307–308, 316, 318
U.S. citizenship renounced by, 221,
270
voice of, 3, 8, 26, 37, 42, 59, 105,
110, 164, 218, 222
wealth flaunted by, 235–236
weight gains of, 85, 108, 175, 212,
219, 223, 232, 265, 273–274, 281
weight losses of, 70, 76, 78, 109, 143,
161, 182, 187, 279, 309, 310
as woman vs. actress, 124, 137–138,
139–160, 216
Taylor, Elizabeth Mary Rosemond
(grandmother), 9, 16, 17, 22
Taylor, Francis Lenn (father), 9–10,
14–18, 27–33, 66, 201
background of, 9
as businessman, 10, 14, 22–23, 25,
48
death of, 239
marriage of, 14
in Mexico, 214
stroke of, 224
Taylor's marital problems and, 73
Taylor's relationship with, 20, 45, 59,
93, 97, 100, 120, 197, 223
on Todd, 128
Todd compared with, 133
wife's separation from, 45, 46, 48, 51,
60
Taylor, Francis Marion (grandfather), 9,
17